W9-AUZ-721

WALL STREETERS

WALL STREETERS

THE CREATORS AND CORRUPTORS OF AMERICAN FINANCE

EDWARD MORRIS

Columbia Business School

Columbia University Press
Publishers Since 1893
New York   Chichester, West Sussex

Library of Congress Cataloging-in-Publication Data
Morris, Edward L.
Wall Streeters : the creators and corruptors of American finance /
Edward L. Morris.
pages cm.
Includes bibliographical references and index.
ISBN 978-0-231-17054-3 (cloth : alk. paper) 978-0-231-54050-6 (ebook)
1. Capitalists and financiers–United States. 2. Finance–United States–History.
I. Title.

HG181.M67 2015
332.092'273–dc23

∞
Columbia University Press books are printed on permanent
and durable acid-free paper.
This book is printed on paper with recycled content.
Printed in the United States of America

c 10 9 8 7 6 5 4 3 2 1

Cover design: Noah Arlow
Cover image: Top photo: New York Stock Exchange, Jin Lee/Getty Images
Bottom photo: Curb Market, Archive Photos/Getty Images

For Peggy

CONTENTS

ACKNOWLEDGMENTS

Many at Lindenwood University played an important role in the creation of this book. The students in my January-term course—my beta site for teaching the history of modern finance through mini-biographies—were a patient audience and provided much constructive criticism. Several of my colleagues at the university, especially Ray Scupin and Peter Griffin, offered invaluable first-reader reactions to and editorial insights into the early manuscript. The staff at the library never tired of my many interlibrary requests for out-of-print books, and Carl Hubenschmidt showed a magical ability to track down obscure articles published many years ago. And I am profoundly grateful to Dean Jay Hardman and Presidents Dennis Spellmann and Jim Evans who, some fifteen years ago, helped restore my damaged psyche by opening a wonderfully fulfilling second career in academia.

The editors at Columbia University Press provided a rookie author with more support than ever expected. Bridget Flannery-McCoy combined an unrelenting cheerfulness with exacting editorial standards; she could request a full rewrite of a chapter in such a positive manner that I felt as though I had been given the opportunity of a lifetime. Her able associate, Stephen Wesley, diligently rounded up a posse of fact-checkers whose remarks gave more nuance to the book, as well as saving the author from many embarrassing inaccuracies. (I hereby absolve all those individuals from any responsibility for errors that remain.)

My most heartfelt thanks go to Peggy Morris, my smart, beautiful, and charming wife. Though a self-described recovering lawyer, she is still most judicious in her assessments. So when she read the initial draft of the first few chapters and pronounced, "This is really good!," those four words became all the propellant I needed to see the book to completion. She tolerated my writing obsession and the time it consumed with little complaint—though noting on more than one occasion that the shiny new bicycles we bought a few years ago for weekend excursions have never left the garage.

PREFACE

America has a love-hate relationship with Wall Street. We all know that "the Street" plays a vital role in the economy; it channels capital to promote new industries and create more jobs. Yet it also seems to be the headquarters for greed, inequity, and a host of other social ills. Indeed, the money changers can behave very badly in their temples.

If you don't spend your days in those temples, it can be maddeningly difficult to make sense of what goes on inside them. But it wasn't always that way. Wall Street was once a fairly straightforward place where stocks, bonds, and mutual funds were originated and sold. Now joining those plain vanilla investments are a bewildering variety of derivatives, asset-backed bonds, junk bonds, index funds, and exchange-traded funds. And while the institutions that line Wall Street were once mainly commercial banks or investment firms, trillions of dollars now flow from giant hedge funds, private equity funds, venture capital funds, and "securitizers"—based both on the Street and off.

The aim of *Wall Streeters* is to make sense of the world of high finance by telling the stories of those who shaped it—and tracing, through their biographies, the development of financial innovations, the growth of financial markets, and the causes of financial crises. As the book's subtitle suggests, the men profiled embody both the good and the bad of Wall Street, but the dichotomy is rarely all that clear. "Bad" on Wall Street is often just "good" taken to a ruinous extreme.

I've always found mini-biographies to be a great way to develop interest and learning. I remember a high school biology teacher who encouraged our class to read *The Microbe Hunters* by Paul de Kruif. That book, originally published in 1926 and still in print today, is a lively compilation of the life stories of Louis Pasteur, Robert Koch, Walter Reed, and nine other trailblazing scientists. I don't know a lot about bacteriology or immunology—but much of what I do know came from that book.

A few years later I enrolled in Economics 101 and had a similar experience. Along with a dry textbook full of charts and theory, the professor assigned Robert Heilbroner's *The Worldly Philosophers*, an account of the lives and contributions of history's great economists, from Adam Smith to John Maynard Keynes to Joseph Schumpeter. The book gave me an enduring appreciation of the dismal science of economics and the thinkers who changed the world through their ideas.

It's no great mystery why those two books made such a lasting impression. Human beings are wired to learn through stories, which is why the most effective teachers have an instinct and talent for storytelling. So shortly after I took up my second career as a professor of finance—the first career being an investment banker—I taught a short-form course that surveyed the history of modern Wall Street through brief biographies of some of its influential individuals over the last century.

Almost as enjoyable as teaching the course was the Solomon-like determination of who was in and who was out when it came to "influential." (On the first day of class I explained to my students that being influential was different from being famous. The world's best-known value investor is Warren Buffett. But Benjamin Graham, the man who literally wrote the book on value investing and who was Buffett's teacher in college, is far less famous.) The biography format worked beyond my expectations, and by the end of the course I decided to turn my lecture notes into a book.

Each of the fourteen men I selected gets a separate chapter, and their stories are told in more or less chronological order, with J. Pierpont Morgan, the dominant financier at the turn of the twentieth century, serving as the starting point and the subject of the first chapter. The remaining thirteen chapters are further divided into five parts—Reformers, Democratizers, Academics, Financial Engineers, and Empire Builders—each categorizing a different aspect of the development of Wall Street between Morgan's time and our own.

Reforms. A successful financial system requires confidence in the integrity of its markets and the staying power of its institutions—and at the beginning of the twentieth century that confidence was in short supply. Without a central bank, financial panics plagued the economy with awful regularity until a financial panic in 1907 finally spurred the formation of the Federal Reserve System. It took the combined work of an odd couple to make that happen: a cerebral, German-born investment banker and a scrappy Virginia congressman. And it took the 1929 stock market crash to finally move the U.S. Congress to enact effective financial regulation and create the Securities and Exchange Commission as part of Franklin Delano Roosevelt's New Deal legislation in the 1930s. It's unlikely that legislation would have passed absent the sensational and highly publicized congressional hearings into Wall Street practices led by a tenacious former New York prosecutor. The newly formed Federal Reserve and SEC became the two vital regulatory institutions necessary to build public confidence and promote the growth of the nation's financial institutions and markets.

Democratization. One of the important drivers of Wall Street's growth was the expansion of the securities markets to individual investors. That's in part due to the protections afforded by the SEC, but it's also due to the work of "Good Time Charlie," a colorful entrepreneur who built the world's most successful retail investment firm. Another individual—"Saint Jack"—deserves equal billing for turning the United States into "shareholder nation" through the popularization of index mutual funds and the creation of a shareholder-friendly mutual fund organization that today, with around $3 trillion under management for investors, is the world's largest.

Risk embracement. No one has tested and expanded more on the relationship between financial risk and financial return than professors in the business schools. Part III profiles three of them who, keeping one foot in academia and the other in the business world, made major differences in the practice of finance with their approaches to risk taking. The man who quantified risk and developed the field of securities analysis, for instance, ran the Graham-Newman money management firm by day and lectured in the evening at Columbia University. Around the same time, one of the legendary professors at the Harvard Business School created and managed a new and vital kind of financial intermediary called a venture capital firm. The third professor profiled is a Nobel laureate recognized for his work in creating the analytical model that spurred the derivatives market. He balanced teaching at Stanford with managing a hedge fund and demonstrated how derivatives and financial arbitrage can work to reduce investment risk—or, as in the case of his own hedge fund, grossly inflate it.

Financial engineering. Product expansion also explains much of Wall Street's recent growth. In 1949, a social activist and writer conceived of a private fund that would simultaneously invest in risky "long" and "short" positions so as to reduce risk; such funds became known as hedge funds. Twenty years later, a twenty-three-year-old Wharton graduate began taking low-rated corporate bonds under his wing and later was the major force behind their use in a wave of leveraged buyouts and corporate restructuring in the 1980s. One of his contemporaries, working at the mortgage desk at Salomon Brothers, resurrected another out-of-favor bond—one that was mortgage backed. He succeeded in devising new ways to package— "securitize"—home mortgages to make them attractive investments for institutional investors.

Deregulation. Through most of the twentieth century, U.S. commercial banks and investment banks were held in close check by their regulators— and they were not allowed to operate in each other's arena. But beginning in the 1970s, both commercial banking and investment banking were suddenly transformed and their businesses greatly enlarged by two monumental deregulatory actions—both of which were essentially forced on the authorities. In 1970, the three young principals of an upstart investment banking firm challenged the New York Stock Exchange's ban on outside ownership by making a wide distribution of shares of their common stock through an initial public offering. Over the following years, all the major investment firms went public and grew improbably large—often dangerously so—by tapping into new sources of external capital. The second challenge occurred thirty years later when a hard-charging banker forced the repeal of the Glass-Steagall Act that had prohibited the operation of commercial banking and investment banking under the same roof.

Several of the readers of the early drafts of *Wall Streeters* offered good arguments for adding individuals to the lineup or subbing out one for another. In order to keep the profiles to a manageable number, however, I stuck with the men I chose originally and, in the main, I still think I have it right. Others questioned why all of the profiles are of men, and the short answer to that question is that the world of finance in the twentieth century was almost exclusively male. When Muriel Siebert became a member of the New York Stock Exchange in 1967, the makeup of exchange members changed from 1,366 men—to 1,365 men and one woman. At that time the Exchange Luncheon Club didn't even have a ladies' room. When she rang the opening bell at the NYSE on December 28, 2007, in commemoration of the fortieth year of her membership, women were still a minority on Wall Street, yet one that was growing in number and influence. Sheila Bair, Brooksley Born, and Elizabeth Warren, for instance, had become important figures in financial regulation—though their prescient warnings did not gain enough traction to forestall the 2008 crisis. And of course Janet Yellen, the first female chair of the Federal Reserve, is likely to become a historical figure.

Another observation from early readers was that twenty or so pages per chapter are not enough to give depth to either the individual profiled or to the area of finance he influenced. That's certainly true, and I encourage readers who want more depth on the individuals profiled to consult the full-length biographies and memoirs included in the Suggestions for Further Reading section of this book. My hope is simply that *Wall Streeters* will leave you with a better understanding of the American system of finance—how it evolved and how it works today.

WALL STREETERS

Photo courtesy of the Museum of American Finance, NYC. All rights reserved.

1

J. Pierpont Morgan: 1837–1913
Jupiter

UNTERMYER: You do not think you have any power in any
   department or industry in this country, do you?
MORGAN: I do not.
UNTERMYER: Not the slightest?
MORGAN: Not the slightest.
   —J. PIERPONT MORGAN AT THE PUJO HEARINGS, 1912

It was a sultry morning in the summer of 1885 when the *Corsair* moored briefly at the Jersey City pier. Pierpont Morgan and Chauncey Depew, president of the New York Central Railroad, were already on board and waiting for the arrival of George Roberts and Frank Thomson, the president and the vice president of the Pennsylvania Railroad. Morgan had invited them onto the yacht as his guests, explaining that the venue would provide a remote, distraction-free location for negotiating an end to the destructive competition between the two railroads. But it wasn't until the trip was under way that he told his three guests the *Corsair* would continue cruising the river until a deal was reached.

Taking the executives captive was an extreme tactic but not an unusual one for Morgan. He was known for this no-exit negotiating strategy when parties became intransient but agreement necessary. This was such a case; the men all knew that irrational competition would soon destroy both companies unless they halted their rate wars and eliminated overlapping routes.

Of course, there were worse places to be held captive than aboard the luxurious *Corsair*. During America's Gilded Age an oceangoing yacht was the ultimate trapping of wealth and privilege, and Morgan's 185-foot vessel surpassed all those owned by his fellow members at the New York Yacht Club. It had a sleek black hull and could be propelled by steam or sail; its interior included a tiled fireplace and luxuriously appointed salons. First-class meals and beverages and a supply of Havana cigars were available to promote the negotiations.

The *Corsair* sailed over fifty miles up the Hudson to Garrison, then all the way back south to where the river empties into the Atlantic Ocean at Raritan Bay. Still there was no agreement. So Morgan sent the *Corsair* north again, and while the railroad men continued to talk he sat alone under an awning on the aft deck. By early evening, Roberts, Thomson, and Depew came to him with their agreement to end the rate wars and swap some of their duplicative lines. When they reached the dock and moored for the night, everyone shook hands on what would later be called the Corsair Pact.

An Anglo-American Banker

At the time of the Corsair Pact, Morgan was the senior partner of Drexel Morgan & Company, a firm that a decade later would be renamed J. P. Morgan & Company. The *Corsair* trip was an expensive midweek outing that produced no direct revenues for his firm. But he was willing to spend that time promoting a business arrangement between two competing rail-roads to preserve his reputation and that of Drexel Morgan.

Several years earlier, when he was just forty-two, he had orchestrated the largest sale of common stock in U.S. history, selling a 75 percent interest in the New York Central Railroad for the family of Commodore Cornelius Vanderbilt. The commodore had spent many years assembling the New York Central from eleven separate lines, and by the time of his death in 1877 his family owned 87 percent of the railroad's stock. But his heirs soon realized that no family members were capable of running the railroad on their behalf, so they turned to Morgan to dispose of their ownership.

Discreetly, Drexel Morgan underwrote the offering, placing much of the New York Central stock with prominent London-based firms. But in the years after the offering, the U.S. economy entered into one of its many recessions, causing the railroads to engage in ruinous competition. The New York Central lost money as a result of price wars and began curtailing necessary capital expenditures. The stock price plummeted and so did Morgan's credibility in "the City," as London's Wall Street counterpart is called.

And credibility was the very foundation upon which Morgan's banking business was built. Offering testimony many years later in a congressional hearing, he articulated his business credo:

> UNTERMYER: But what I mean is that the banking house assumes no legal responsibility for the value of the bonds, does it?
>
> MORGAN: No, sir, but it assumes something else that is still more important, and that is the moral responsibility, which has to be defended so long as you live.[1]

Morgan had much to defend, as much of his business resulted from investments by British and European interests in American enterprises—and at that time, America was an emerging market (to use today's parlance), with all of the uncertainties and risks of that market segment. Throughout the nineteenth century the economic growth of the New World created a great demand for capital from abroad, and a large portion of it was funneled through London bankers on behalf of their clients. At the same time, the country was clearly on track to join the world's largest economies—perhaps becoming the largest of any by the twentieth century. London could not afford to ignore the opportunities. Yet communication between New York and London was slow—reliable transatlantic cable was not laid until the last third of the century—and travel across the Atlantic was both slow and expensive. So the investors in Britain and the European continent looked to trusted firms like Drexel Morgan to serve as their "boots on the ground" in America to ensure that someone with both a financial and moral stake in the business was vouchsafing the merit of their investments.

Morgan took that role very seriously, but it was difficult to carry out in America's volatile and unregulated economy. There was no Securities and Exchange Commission to enforce even rudimentary disclosure about a company's business and financial condition, making due diligence a challenge. Likewise, the Interstate Commerce Commission—set up in 1887 to regulate the railroads—had very little legal authority over rates and routes until many years later. And on top of it all, the American economy of the nineteenth century was beset with one financial upheaval after another— and each was invariably followed by a depression or recession.

"Thus Ends School with Me"

Pierpont was the only living son of Juliet and Junius Morgan. Although Junius would eventually be remembered mainly as the father of America's most original and famous banker, during much of Pierpont's life the elder Morgan was an important figure in finance on both sides of the Atlantic and always a formidable and exacting influence in his son's life. The head of his own firm, J. S. Morgan & Company, Junius was a demanding father who saw his parental responsibility as a project—the project of creating an adult son with a strong character and the "right stamp." Yet the Pierpont project was a difficult one for Junius; the headstrong personality and explosive mood swings that would terrify Pierpont's partners and clients in later life were evident at an early age.

So too were a wide variety of health problems. Pierpont was troubled with disfiguring skin diseases throughout his life, with childhood skin rashes and adolescent acne followed by a disfiguring rosacea that made his nose more red and bulbous the older he became. He also suffered throughout his life from an assortment of debilitating illnesses and episodes of mental exhaustion that were treated by extended trips, usually out of the country. While in high school he lost a full school year to rheumatic fever, which (in the pattern of wealthy families of his era) was treated in part with "fresh air cures." In Pierpont's case, the cure took the form of an ocean voyage to the Azores and a stay of several months in that island chain off the coast of Portugal.

By the time he returned home to complete his high school studies, Pierpont was back in good health and managed to finish his work at the Boston English High School on schedule at age seventeen. Eager to enter the world of business, he happily reported in his diary: "Thus ends school with me."[2] But Junius had other ideas. His international business was prospering, and he moved his family to London to take advantage of a new partnership. At Junius's direction, Pierpont spent a year and a half at a boarding school in Vevey, Switzerland, followed by an equal period at the university in Gottingen, Germany. Pierpont broadened his general education at those schools, especially in math and art appreciation, but for Junius the greatest benefit was his son's better facility in French and German—putting Pierpont on a par with the multilingual partners at the great banking houses of Europe.

Though school finally came to an end for Pierpont when he was nearing twenty, his career remained under Junius's direction. In the manner of the House of Rothschild, Barings Brothers, and prestigious European banks that sent family members to other countries to act as their prince regents, Junius dispatched Pierpont to Wall Street. He was to be the family's emissary—capturing intelligence, cultivating new business, and monitoring investments. New York was now the acknowledged capital for American finance, rather than Philadelphia or Boston, and with the explosion of the country's railroad systems in the mid-1800s there were many investment opportunities. By the early twentieth century the direction of international money flows would reverse and the United States would become a lender nation, but when Pierpont arrived on Wall Street in the antebellum years of the nineteenth century, America was dependent on funding from abroad, and most of that funding was channeled through London.

Junius moved Pierpont around Wall Street like a chess piece. With his extensive financial connections he found places for his son to apprentice (all well-recommended firms where he could be valuable to both his employer and his own J. S. Morgan & Company) and to eventually enter the world of banking as a young partner of a prestigious firm. Pierpont learned the business of Wall Street, but with the railroads by far the largest consumers of new capital, he also traveled across the country to develop a firsthand understanding of that business. At a distance of three thousand miles from his father, Pierpont proved to be a remarkably able and industrious employee, albeit a querulous one not destined to spend many years of his life working for others.

The last career move in which Pierpont acted in accordance with his father's guidance—and by far the most important one—resulted in the formation of Drexel Morgan & Company. During his several years on Wall Street, Pierpont performed well beyond expectations and was outgrowing the abilities of his partners. In the same years, J. S. Morgan & Company had gained considerable standing among international financiers for its American-based investments. In 1871, Junius found an opportunity to become an even more formidable force in New World banking by partnering with the Philadelphia-based Drexel & Company. To that end, he sent Pierpont to Philadelphia to meet with Anthony Drexel, the forty-five-year-old lead partner of that firm. At the time, the Drexel firm had developed valuable European financing capabilities, not just in England but throughout the continent, through its Paris affiliate, Drexel, Harjes & Company. Following Pierpont's meeting with Drexel, a New York offshoot of Drexel & Company was formed; it was named Drexel Morgan & Company and the thirty-four-year-old Pierpont was its senior partner. The Drexel interests contributed $7 million to the venture and, since Pierpont's own financial resources were still relatively meager at the time, Junius contributed $5 million on his son's behalf.

But Pierpont had one condition before joining the newly formed Drexel Morgan partnership: a fifteen-month leave of absence to recover from recent bouts of exhaustion. Extended rest cures to recuperate from overwork would become routine for him. Saying that he could do twelve months of work in nine months—but not in twelve—he typically spent three months of the year abroad, most often on excursions to Europe and along the Nile to acquire fine art. (Much of the art he acquired is now displayed at the Morgan Library in midtown Manhattan and the Metropolitan Museum of Art.)

Upon Pierpont's return, the new firm operated at 53 Exchange Street, but a short time later constructed a six-story building—among the first in New York with elevators—with its entrance facing the corner of Broad and Wall at a diagonal. For the next century, Drexel Morgan's address, 23 Wall Street, would mark the epicenter of American banking.

Morganization

The Drexel-affiliated banks operated as an American version of Europe's elite merchant banks, but with a special charter to tame America's rapidly growing railroads to the point where they were suitable for investment. And that was not a job for the faint of heart. The railroads were far and away the most enticing place for European investors to put their money in America. But there was little regulation of that industry during the nineteenth century, and the men who organized and ran the nation's early rail lines could be an unsavory bunch, prone to misrepresenting their business and finances and making backroom deals with competitors and customers. Some wildcat entrepreneurs with not much more than a land grant raised money to fund new railroads despite a lack of experience and few realistic plans on how to operate them. Some newly organized railroads turned out to be financial schemes for bilking unwary investors with watered stock and other manipulations.

Given that state of affairs, Pierpont emerged as a vital link between European investors, with their refined sensibilities and manners, and the rough-hewn American railroaders. Pierpont had a quick and practiced financial mind, but he was also a large man with a commanding, sometimes terrifying presence. He spoke infrequently, but often explosively, and always with the certainty of someone whose word was challenged at peril. A persistent but unverified story circulated about Pierpont's throwing "Jubilee Jim" Fisk (among the most notorious of the nineteenth-century robber barons) down a flight of stairs when a railroad negotiation turned into a business brawl.

The fundamental problem of railroad investment was overbuilding and the resultant rate wars and overexpansion of trackage. In the rush to capture routes in America's vast and expanding geography, new railroads were formed with abandon—and, as a result of duplicative routes and inept management, they failed with similar abandon. Pierpont's role was often to protect the European investors' interests by reorganizing a bankrupt line in a process that became common enough to earn the term "morganization." He first gained a controlling ownership by buying up the securities of the beleaguered investors and then, through a voting trust, installed himself and trusted colleagues as directors and formed a totally new management committee to run the day-to-day business. Morganization invariably included cutting unwarranted costs—often involving questionable payments to insiders and favored third parties—and then refinancing the business with lower-cost money. That lower-cost money was usually a recognition of the bondholders' confidence in Pierpont's business acumen and integrity.

Along with resuscitating individual railroads, morganization most often involved a second step: consolidation. It was clear to Morgan that there were far too many lines for stable operations. So he took a lead role in combining competing railroads—saving them, he believed, from self-inflicted ruin. By one reckoning one-sixth of all the trackage in the United States eventually went under morganization, including nearly all of the bankrupt railroads east of the Mississippi.[3]

Nowadays, attempts to consolidate an industry are looked upon warily by the U.S. Justice Department and the Federal Trade Commission. But in Morgan's time—at least in Morgan's mind—merging railroads and their routes to create less competitive but more stable operations was a needed public service. By 1890 he could exclaim to the press about one of his morganizations: "I am thoroughly satisfied with the results accomplished. The public has not yet appreciated the magnitude of the work. Think of it—all the competitive traffic of the roads west of Chicago and St. Louis placed in the control of about thirty men! It is the most important agreement made by the railroads in a long time, and it is as strong as could be desired."[4]

In the same spirit, he extended the tenets of morganization to industries beyond the railroads—and always, he said, with the motive of reducing risk. In 1878 he and his Drexel Morgan partners led the financing of the Edison Electric Illuminating Company for Thomas Alva Edison; by 1889, and several consolidation moves later, his firm handled the initial public offering for the company—which by then had changed its name to Edison General Electric. Then in 1892—much to the dismay of Edison himself—Morgan was pivotal in combining the company with a stronger competitor, Thomson-Houston Electric, to form General Electric. The company was now large enough to control the nascent electrical industry, ensuring that there would be few price wars, patent conflicts, or duplicative facilities. While Morgan was triumphant about reducing risk in the young electrical products industry and making it large and stable enough to attract his risk-averse investors, the more entrepreneurial Thomas Edison felt otherwise. Little interested in the administration of a corporate giant, Edison sold off much of his ownership in General Electric and turned his inventive instincts toward turn-of-the-century creations, especially motion pictures.

Pierpont Morgan's crowning masterwork of morganization, however, was the formation of U.S. Steel in 1901. By the end of the nineteenth century the steel industry had eclipsed railroads as the most important U.S. industry, with massive new companies organized and capitalized to satisfy the demand for steel in new building construction, factories, bridges, and, of course, the railroads. The chain of production facilities involved in making steel was long and included ore acreage, coal mines, blast furnaces, steel mills, finishing mills, and every manner of transportation, from barges to railroad lines. Many of these facilities were partially integrated, but the goal in creating U.S. Steel was to integrate them all, consolidate them, and become both the largest operator and the lowest-cost producer in the steel business.

There were two people who together could make the envisioned U.S. Steel a reality: Andrew Carnegie and Pierpont Morgan. The Carnegie Steel Company, using the invention of the Bessemer method for mass-producing steel, had become the largest steel producer of the day. If consolidation were to succeed, Carnegie Steel needed to be involved, and the decision rested fully with the controlling shareholder—Andrew Carnegie. And only Pierpont Morgan, with his now magisterial presence among industrial moguls, would have the authority to allocate the ownership of a newly formed U.S. Steel among Carnegie and the shareholders of other companies being consolidated. And further, only he had the leadership and connections on Wall Street needed to underwrite and sell the hundreds of millions of dollars of new securities to finance the transaction.

With Carnegie and Morgan of a like mind to create the world's largest corporation, the U.S. Steel deal was put together with breathtaking speed. In January 1901, Carnegie Steel president Charles Schwab (no kin to the founder of today's investment firm of the same name) presented Morgan with a list of the logical companies for inclusion in a newly formed U.S. Steel; Morgan accepted the consolidation assignment on the spot and quickly began to negotiate the terms and arrange the financing. Within two months, Carnegie and the boards of the other targeted companies had agreed to the business plan and the allocation of ownership, and on March 3, 1901, Morgan announced the formation of the $1.4 billion U.S. Steel to the world. By the end of that month all of the shares in the new company had been spoken for in a Morgan-directed stock sale handled from the floor of the New York Stock Exchange.

In today's dollars, $1.4 billion is not a particularly large market capitalization. But in 1901 it represented approximately 7 percent of the nation's gross domestic product—equivalent to over a trillion dollars today, much more than the market capitalization of any current companies.[5] When the deal closed, Andrew Carnegie became the richest man in the world.

Jupiter

Morgan himself underwent a transformation between the formation of Drexel Morgan in 1871 and the formation of U.S. Steel in 1901—both in appearance and in reputation. The pictures of Pierpont when he was in his thirties capture a stern-looking young man with a walrus mustache, still handsome and physically fit with a full head of dark brown hair. Thirty years later his pictures show a caricature of the corpulent Gilded Age plutocrat. The walrus mustache is still there, but now sits above an intense scowl. The disfiguring rosacea is worse, and his nose is larger and more deformed. Most of his hair is gone, and what remains is white. The years of exhausting work, a hearty appetite, an aversion to any form of exercise, and at least a dozen large cigars per day had exacted their toll.

During those thirty years, however, Morgan had risen to a level of prominence and power greater than of any financier before him and any yet to follow. After the deaths of his father in 1890 and Anthony Drexel in 1893, Morgan reorganized the Drexel and Morgan entities, changing the names and ownership to his own benefit. In New York, Drexel Morgan & Company became J. P. Morgan & Company, and in Paris, Drexel, Harjes became Morgan, Harjes. J. S. Morgan in London and Drexel & Company in Philadelphia retained their names, but Pierpont appointed new managing partners for both. He was the only person with a partnership interest in all four banks—and that interest was substantial, at 35 percent in each.[6] Morgan himself became known on Wall Street as "Jupiter."

Until his death in 1913, Morgan and his partners continued to create as well as finance much of the U.S. industrial infrastructure. Yet the House of Morgan, as J. P. Morgan & Company was familiarly called, was not a bank in any traditional sense. It was more a loose confederation of a dozen or so highly capable financiers who operated from a single Wall Street address, sitting alongside one another at rolltop desks in an open, chandelier-illuminated partners' room. They continued to pursue Morgan's self-appointed mission of bringing order to the American financial system—and in the process bringing great wealth to themselves. These powerful partners achieved mythic-like stature. One Wall Street admirer went so far as to proclaim, "When the angels of God took unto themselves wives among the daughters of men, the result was Morgan partners."[7]

Morgan had planned to reduce his business activity as he grew older and to spend more time collecting art for his personal collections and for the Metropolitan Museum. But disquieting economic and social events conspired to make the later years of his life full of difficulty. Without the steadying hand of a central bank, the United States continued to suffer from financial panics, each one more virulent than the one that had preceded it. The description of Morgan's role as the country's de facto central banker to quell the panic of 1907 will follow in the next chapter. Suffice it to say here that ending the panic was an exhausting ordeal for the seventy-year-old Pierpont.

While Pierpont was cast as a hero in 1907, he soon came to be seen by many as a villain. A worldwide movement toward socialist ideologies manifested itself in the United States as a major protest against the social issues of the day, arising at least in part from the juggernaut of widespread industrialization Morgan had a hand in creating. Many viewed oppressive labor conditions, children in the workforce, and the disenfranchisement of women as the natural offspring of a capitalist economic system. And Morgan and his brother bankers came to be seen as the agents of these social ills, which an aggressively progressive brand of Democratic leadership was committed to eliminating. When Woodrow Wilson assumed a commanding lead in the polls in the 1912 presidential election, social reformers and the liberal media joined in a full-chorus castigation of Morgan, with Joseph Pulitzer's *New York World* proclaiming that he "was the last of his line. Never again will it be possible for any financier to bestride the country like a Colossus, and for one man to wield so much power for good or evil over their prosperity and general welfare, however much ability and strength and genius that man possessed."[8]

In December of that year Morgan's detractors realized their fondest wish in the form of congressional hearings on money trusts. The so-called Pujo hearings—named for Congressman Arsène Pujo, chairman of the House banking committee that convened the hearings—set the goal of investigating the concentration of economic power wielded by the large banks. And of course Pierpont, now seventy-five, was the star witness. By all accounts, the elderly banker acquitted himself well despite his bouts of defiance and his tendency toward nonsensical answers. One exchange between Morgan and the hearing's counsel Samuel Untermyer strained credulity:

UNTERMYER: You do not think you have any power in any department
    or industry in this country, do you?
MORGAN: I do not.
UNTERMYER: Not the slightest?
MORGAN: Not the slightest.
UNTERMYER: Your firm is run by you, is it not?
MORGAN: No, sir.
UNTERMYER: You are the final authority, are you not?
MORGAN: No, sir.[9]

Despite Pierpont's assertions regarding his lack of power and influence, the committee assembled compelling evidence of the interlocking directorships and business relationships that gave J. P. Morgan & Company, along with five other major banks, an outsized say in how America's business was conducted. Yet there was no evidence that the bankers' actions were conspiratorial, and the mild term "community of interests" was eventually used to describe how Wall Street chieftains exerted an unreasonable amount of control over the American economy.

But for Morgan, who fervently believed that his actions were crucial for bringing that economy under control to attract necessary capital from abroad, the hearings upset the very codes that had governed his life and business pursuits. He had acted alone throughout his long financial career without a Federal Reserve, a Securities and Exchange Commission, a Federal Trade Commission, or an antitrust unit of the Justice Department. He felt he had always performed honorably, in the best traditions of a nineteenth-century gentleman banker and with a Tory-like belief that by virtue of his class he had a fiduciary obligation to act for the greater good. Now at the end of his life and career he was faced with a hostile panel of politicians who could only scoff with disbelief when he testified about the overriding importance of character in his decisions.   During the weeks immediately following the Pujo hearings, he fell ill and lapsed into one of the states of nervous exhaustion that had plagued him since childhood. Another trip to Egypt and Europe with his family to rejuvenate his energy and boost his flagging spirits didn't work. He died a broken man at the Grand Hotel in Rome on March 31, 1913.

Part I

Reformers

There has always been a philosophical tug and pull regarding the proper amount of regulation for U.S. financial markets. At one end are the minimalists, who believe that bankers will naturally act in a responsible manner in service of their best long-term interests—what Alexis de Tocqueville called "self-interest rightly understood" in his nineteenth-century classic *Democracy in America*. The conventional wisdom of the holders of the minimalist outlook tells us that Wall Street will behave if left alone and, what's more, its ability to operate unfettered by intrusive and costly regulation will ultimately promote the greater good for Main Street.

At the other end are the realists, such as Nobel laureate Joseph Stiglitz, who hold no illusions that financiers act in accordance with their better angels but argue rather that they tend to look out for their short-term best interests with scant attention to the long-term benefits for the public weal. For that reason, according to Stiglitz and like-minded realists, self-regulation is "preposterous," and it's a national illusion that "markets are self-adjusting or that the role of government should be minimal."[1]

From the time of the publication of de Tocqueville's *Democracy in America* in 1840 through J. Pierpont Morgan's death in 1913—a time coinciding with America's emergence as a world industrial and financial power—regulatory minimalism was the state of affairs on Wall Street, and

Morgan himself treated the prospect of government regulation in a cavalier manner. When he learned in February 1902 that Teddy Roosevelt's attorney general planned to file suit to break up the Northern Securities Company, a railroad trust he had organized, Morgan called Roosevelt for a conference to discuss the matter. His suggestion for the president was simple: "If we have done anything wrong, send your man to my man and they can fix it up."[2]

Although Roosevelt was not inclined to treat the private banker as an equal and ultimately forced the breakup of the Northern Securities Company under the Sherman Antitrust Act, Morgan's presumptions were revealing. He believed that government and business could operate independently but cooperatively, and he further believed that the general public would ultimately benefit if he and other financiers of the day were unencumbered by government interference and guided largely by their own enlightened self-interest.

And while such beliefs warrant a healthy dose of skepticism, there is reason to believe that Morgan was sincere in his convictions about the efficacy of self-regulated capitalism. After all, by acting as an honest broker he attracted large pools of European money into a capital-starved American economy. The trusts he formed, those Roosevelt seemed intent on dismantling, were meant to preserve the stability of that economy by preventing "ruinous competition" in the New World's industrial sector. In the past he had certainly acted to maintain a steady economy through his outsized role in taming the U.S. business and financial cycles. Not long after his run-in with Roosevelt, he quelled the panic of 1907, just as he had played the leading role in stemming the earlier financial panics of the Gilded Age. His actions, arguably heroic, worked to the mutual benefit of the House of Morgan and the national economy.

Yet however self-enlightened Morgan's actions might have been, the panic of 1907 served as a wake-up call to Washington, and Nelson Aldrich, the Republican chairman of the Senate Finance Committee at the time, pointed out that Morgan was now an elderly man and could not be counted on to engineer a solution for the next banking crisis.[3] And what had to be done was to establish an institutional lender of last resort in the form of a central bank to provide liquidity in times of financial crisis and also to regulate the supply of money circulating in the economy and serve as the nation's chief bank examiner. The ultimate role of a central bank is to keep a country's economy stable, and as late as 1913, the year of Pierpont's death, the United States didn't have one.

Chapters 2 and 3 tell the story of how two unlikely allies, Paul Warburg and Carter Glass, combined to create an American-style central bank by effecting the passage of the Federal Reserve Act of 1913. The two men could not have been more different. Warburg, an intellectual, was a member of a prominent German banking family and had immigrated to the United States to join the powerful Wall Street firm of Kuhn, Loeb & Company; Congressman Glass was a combative, self-educated Democrat from Lynchburg, Virginia, who referred to big city bankers as "money devils." While they rarely admitted to cooperating with each other, in a two-step process they created the 1913 Federal Reserve Act and the country's first enduring central bank.

Much as the panic of 1907 ultimately served to create "the Fed" in 1913, the great stock market crash of 1929 spurred Congress to establish, in 1934, the second pillar of U.S. financial regulation: the Securities and Exchange Commission. Prior to the sweeping new securities regulation that came in as part of Franklin Roosevelt's New Deal legislation—the Glass-Steagall Act of 1933 that separated investment banking from commercial banking; the Truth in Securities Act of 1933 that mandated full disclosure in securities offerings; and the Securities Exchange Act of 1934 that created the SEC—the investment business was largely self-regulated.

Before the SEC, the New York Stock Exchange was Wall Street's self-appointed watchdog. It monitored the business practices of its members—the investment firms that conducted their business at the exchange—and it required the companies whose stock traded on the exchange to conform to a modicum of business disclosure and rules of fair practice. From all appearances and declarations, the exchange was governed by men of probity who were intent on keeping players in the stock market honest and making sure the executives of its listed companies were forthright about their business. A minimalist if there ever was one, the NYSE's president, Richard Whitney, famously declared in 1934 that "the Exchange is a perfect institution."[4]

Would that were so! Chapter 4 introduces Ferdinand Pecora, the no-nonsense realist who, during sixteen months between 1933 and 1934, directed congressional hearings into the speculative excesses on Wall Street during the Roaring Twenties. The fiery former prosecutor undermined any notion that self-regulation had been effective during those years and, through withering testimony, exposed the culpability and venality of a shocking number of men at the top of Wall Street's best-known institutions. The hearings captured front-page interest as one high-profile financier after another—from J. P. Morgan Jr. to the NYSE's own Richard Whitney—laid out sordid instances of their own self-dealing and investor abuse. Their disclosures stoked a firestorm of indignation among a public beaten down by the Great Depression, resulting in changes in the financial world far beyond anyone's expectations. As a direct outcome of Pecora's tenacity, the House of Morgan and other financial giants of the day were dismantled and, more importantly, the manner in which stocks and bonds were bought and sold underwent fundamental and constructive changes.

The two mainstays in the regulation of American financial institutions and markets have been the Federal Reserve System and the Securities and Exchange Commission. Without those two institutions, and the confidence they instill, the United States would not have become the world's financial center. And without the fortuitous emergence of Warburg, Glass, and Pecora, it is difficult to imagine how the United States would have put the necessary reforms in place to create the Fed and the SEC and thereby achieve its global financial stature.

2

Paul M. Warburg: 1868–1932
Daddy Warbucks

As to those on whom the words "Central Bank" still act
as a red rag on a bull, I ask them to study this bill carefully and without prejudice—if they can—and they will
find that even Andrew Jackson, were he alive, would not
be likely to oppose it.

—PAUL M. WARBURG

The instructions that Senator Nelson Aldrich gave his guests were painstakingly specific. They were to arrive, one at a time, on the evening of November 22, 1910, at the train station in Hoboken, New Jersey. There they would
board, as unobtrusively as possible, Aldrich's private car attached to a regularly scheduled southbound train. Once on the train and until they boarded
the island ferry at Brunswick, Georgia, they were instructed to leave their
last names behind. So Senator Aldrich would be just Nelson, and Benjamin Strong, president of Bankers Trust Company, just Ben. Abram Piatt
Andrew customarily used only his middle name, but the Harvard professor
and soon-to-be assistant secretary of the Treasury would go by Abe for the
next few days. Frank Vanderlip, vice president of National City Bank, the
largest commercial bank of its day, and Henry Davison, a senior partner
from the House of Morgan, went even further. They became, respectively,
Orville and Wilbur, claiming that at the upcoming meeting they would
always be "right." And Paul Warburg, partner of the investment banking
house of Kuhn, Loeb & Company, would be Paul.

The directions on travel attire must have been particularly awkward
for Paul. Even though it would be dark at the appointed hour, Aldrich

instructed his guests to take precautions against being identified as the prosperous financiers they were. In opera buffa fashion, they were to wear hunting outfits and assume the guise of happy-go-lucky sportsmen on holiday. But Warburg's personality was the opposite of happy-go-lucky and, unlike his fellow guests, he had never been duck hunting and didn't even own a shotgun. He was shy and bookish and, as a recent emigrant from Hamburg, Germany, still spoke with a heavily accented and awkward brand of English. He was just forty-two but had already turned bald, and that, coupled with a thick and drooping mustache, gave him a serious, somewhat sour demeanor. Purportedly, he was the inspiration for the bald-pated Daddy Warbucks character of the *Little Orphan Annie* comic strip that originated during this era.

Yet among these financially sophisticated travelers to Jekyll Island, he was by far the most knowledgeable about the subject at hand: central banking. Senator Aldrich, the Republican whip and chairman of the Senate Finance Committee, had finally decided that the time had come to gather the best minds in finance to design a central bank for the United States—and that Paul Warburg would be its chief architect.

The meetings were held in seclusion over the next two weeks at the stately and sprawling Jekyll Island Club just off the barrier reefs of Georgia. The club had been constructed for the private use of a limited roster of members, including J. P. Morgan, Cornelius Vanderbilt, and other prominent businessmen of turn-of-the-century America. Senator Aldrich was himself a wealthy man, and with his daughter's recent marriage to John Rockefeller Jr., he had little difficulty gaining access to what local Georgians called the "millionaires' club."

The club was already closed for the season, but Aldrich was able to hire a specially screened skeleton crew to take care of his Wall Street guests. Though the identities of the participants and the location of the November 1910 meetings would not be known until decades later, the deliberations during those two weeks produced the rough blueprint for the Federal Reserve Act of 1913 and the establishment of the country's first viable central banking system.

A Third Rail Issue

At the time of the Jekyll Island meeting, Senator Aldrich had served in Congress for thirty years, with all but two of those years served in the

Senate. He had risen through the ranks and, when the Republicans were in the majority, he kept a firm hand on the operations of the Finance Committee. With his long tenure in politics, he had a firsthand appreciation of the difficulties in establishing an American central bank along the lines of the Bank of England or other European central banks, and for most of that tenure he and his party were on record as opposing any such financial institution. He was sophisticated in banking matters and appreciated the potential value of a central bank, but he felt that the Old World central banking model—a privately owned, monolithic institution based in a capital city—would be unacceptable in the United States, with its disparate regional economies and a midsection deeply suspicious of concentrations of power on its East Coast.

What's more, a European-styled central bank had already been tried twice in the United States and had failed both times. Alexander Hamilton's short-lived (1791–1811) First Bank of the United States, modeled after the Bank of England, eventually ran afoul of southern agricultural interests represented forcefully by Virginians Thomas Jefferson and James Madison, who saw the country's first attempt at a central bank as being too closely aligned to northern and mercantile interests. That bank was followed five years later by the Second Bank of the United States, and it too lasted only two decades (1816–1836). The Second Bank, controlled by the prominent Philadelphia financier Nicholas Biddle, faced political firestorms when Biddle's conservative monetary policies ran counter to the interests of the westward-expanding country. In 1836 President Andrew Jackson, representing rural and populist interests, quashed the Second Bank.

But during the latter half of the nineteenth century the need for financial stability and a lender of last resort grew even more apparent after a crescendo of financial panics hit the country in 1857, 1873, and 1893. Yet paradoxically, political divisions in the United States had only deepened the antagonism toward central banking in the wake of those panics. Even Pierpont Morgan's successful, and arguably valiant, efforts to stanch the 1893 "gold panic" became controversial, as antibanking forces pointed to profits the House of Morgan reaped during the rescue. It was the widely held view that Morgan and coconspirators on Wall Street *created* the 1893 panic as a means to enrich themselves through an ensuing rescue. The central bank issue remained a political hot potato.

The political conflicts about banking were in part cultural but fundamentally sprang from differing economic interests. There were some twenty

thousand banks in the country serving small-town and agricultural interests. Farmers needed an ample supply of money to finance their activities
and, with the long lag time between planting and harvest, they viewed rising prices favorably. Bankers held just the opposite view of price inflation,
since it resulted in their loans being paid back in dollars with diminished
value. It has always been the fact in banking that inflation benefits the
debtor to the detriment of the lender.

A central bank, with its mission of preserving the value of the dollar for
international trade, was perceived to be inclined toward tight-money policies and the prevention of inflation. And that perception had the reality of
the gold standard behind it. Central banks at that time strictly adhered to
a system in which the dollar and other world currencies were pegged to a
specific weight in gold. With that system in place, expansion of the money
supply and inflation were kept in close check, much to the dismay of agrar-
ian interests.

The most vocal political opponent of central banking and its tight-
money, gold-dictated policies was William Jennings Bryan, one of Aldrich's
fellow senators and always a power to be reckoned with. He proposed a
doctrine of "bimetallism" under which the money supply would expand
according to both gold *and* silver supplies. At the 1896 Democratic convention, where he received his party's nomination for president, he punc-
tuated his easy-money proposal with two of the most memorable lines in
the history of American speeches: "You shall not press down upon the
brow of labor this crown of thorns. You shall not crucify mankind upon
a cross of gold." In the face of Bryan's great political appeal—he was the
Democratic presidential nominee in 1896, 1900, and 1908—Aldrich knew
the times were not right to propose the creation of a central bank, even
though he personally favored a central bank and tight-money discipline.
The Democrats were steadfast in their opposition, as were most of Aldrich's
fellow Republicans, although not as vociferously. Even the American Bankers Association, with its membership weighted toward the interests of the
smaller, rural banks, objected to it.

But though the odds weighed heavily against him, Aldrich, more than
seventy years following the demise of the Second Bank of the United States,
revived what had long been considered a dead cause and eventually took
the lead in the third attempt to create a new central bank for the country.
There were two events that steeled his resolve: the panic of 1907 and a
chance meeting with Paul Moritz Warburg.

A Wake-Up Call: The Panic of 1907

The collapse of banks in a panic is often described as a row of falling dominoes. However, as the 1907 panic demonstrated, it involves not just the toppling of banks of similar size, but rather the failure of those of ever-increasing size. The 1907 panic was set off by the failure of the State Savings Bank, a small bank in Butte, Montana, that became insolvent through ill-advised lending in connection with an unsuccessful attempt to corner the market in the shares of the United Copper Company. State Savings Bank's problems then spread to its New York correspondent bank, Mercantile National Bank, as that bank's depositors began making wholesale withdrawals based on rumors about its weakened financial condition resulting from its connection with State Savings. The resulting collapse of Mercantile National in turn set off additional and larger failures among New York banks, including the Knickerbocker Trust Company, the third-largest trust operation in the city.

When the even larger Trust Company of America became threatened with failure following an escalation of withdrawals by panicky depositors, Pierpont Morgan stepped in and calmly announced, "This is the place to stop the trouble, then."[1] Operating from the library of his midtown brownstone home, he acted as the de facto central bank for the nation. He assembled emergency funds and, with the help of his partners, engineered a series of confidence-inducing measures, including a fresh investment by John D. Rockefeller in National City Bank, a commitment of assistance from the U.S. Treasury Department, and an order to keep the New York Stock Exchange open. Those steps quelled the panic.

Those who found themselves nearly consumed in the vortex of the 1907 financial hurricane fully realized the consequences of operating without a central bank. But even the virulence of the panic could not overcome an inveterate national fear of central banks. In 1907, the country was still in thrall to populist sentiment and reflexive antipathy toward the Eastern banking establishment and its hard-money ways. Central banking was closely associated with the despised "money trusts" that had been the focus of suspicion at the turn of the twentieth century. A European-style uberbank with the power to create money and regulate the nation's banks remained a "third rail" issue in national politics.

Yet the United States remained the lone major economy operating without a national bank regulator and lender of last resort when the economy was operating in extremis. After the harrowing but ultimately successful resolution to the panic of 1907, and with Morgan then seventy years old, Aldrich stated what was increasingly obvious: "Something has got to be done. We may not always have Pierpont Morgan with us to meet a banking crisis."[2] As a first step toward reform, Aldrich pushed the passage of the Aldrich-Vreeland Act through Congress in May 1908, with one of its key provisions being the establishment of the National Monetary Commission to study central banking practices in other countries. In an attempt to demonstrate his commitment and objectivity toward the commission's work, the sixty-seven-year-old Aldrich announced he would retire from the Senate when his term expired two years later and devote the bulk of his last years to the issue. But well before the creation of the National Monetary Commission, Aldrich had begun his own research into European central banking policies, and that research led him to Kuhn, Loeb & Company and Paul Warburg.

A Scholarly Investment Banker

The undercurrent of anti-Semitism that pervaded the United States at the time was mirrored structurally on Wall Street, where investment banking, from top to bottom, was divided into the "Yankee" firms, with J. P. Morgan & Company clearly at the top, and Jewish firms, with Kuhn, Loeb & Company just as clearly at the top of a list that included Goldman Sachs, J. W. Seligman & Company, and Lehman Brothers. Kuhn, Loeb had risen to prominence during the late nineteenth century through its ability to organize and finance the early railroads, and its clients included the Union Pacific Railroad and the Pennsylvania Railroad, competing with J. P. Morgan's Northern Pacific and New York Central. Using their considerable brainpower and links to European capital sources, the two firms continued to compete for industrial preeminence in the next century. If J. P. Morgan claimed General Electric and Standard Oil of New Jersey as exclusive clients, Kuhn, Loeb held Westinghouse and Royal Dutch Petroleum just as securely.

In December 1907, Aldrich had called on Kuhn, Loeb's eminent managing partner, Jacob Schiff, to inquire about practices of the Reichsbank, Germany's central bank. During the visit, Schiff summoned junior partner Warburg to provide Aldrich with more informed answers. Warburg was born in Hamburg into a prominent banking family that controlled M. M.

Warburg & Company, an important European banking firm that traced its lineage back to the Renaissance. As a young man, Warburg worked in banking and foreign trade in London and Paris and traveled widely in the Far East before returning to Hamburg and a partnership in M. M. Warburg. During his travels and apprenticeships he had gained firsthand knowledge of European-style central banking, and long before he had any thought of immigrating to America, he had already become an outspoken advocate for a U.S. central bank.

Warburg's eventual move to the United States, and the important role he would play in the cause of its monetary reform, came about as a result of a "dynastic" marriage between him and Nina Loeb, a daughter of Kuhn, Loeb founder Solomon Loeb. Though not observant Jews, Warburg and his family mixed and married primarily—and carefully—with the best of New York's Jewish society.

At the time, Kuhn, Loeb was the only investment banking firm that rivaled the power and influence of the House of Morgan, and the marriage served to further Kuhn, Loeb's financial prominence by strengthening the bonds between two great banking families. M. M. Warburg and Kuhn, Loeb worked jointly in a multitude of cross-Atlantic financings, with Paul maintaining a partnership in each firm, and he and Nina dividing their time about equally between New York and Hamburg.

But that arrangement proved unsatisfactory to Nina, an accomplished musician who missed a yearlong continuity with New York's cultural venues. So in 1902 the couple moved permanently to New York. Their permanent residence there led to a more settled family life and a greater focus in Paul's professional life. Though he was a shy intellectual who hardly conformed to the image of the robber barons and rapacious financiers of the era, he quickly became a prominent U.S. banker by virtue of his keen intellect and served on the boards of a diverse roster of major companies, including Wells Fargo & Company, Western Union, and the Baltimore & Ohio Railroad.

But if banking was his occupation, central banking was his preoccupation. Upon taking up residence in the United States—he would not get around to trading his German citizenship and becoming a naturalized American until 1911—he grew ever more mystified as to why the United States had no central bank. America would soon be the largest economy in the world, but it still had no institution in place to provide liquidity and orderliness to the financial markets to avoid the increasingly frequent and increasingly damaging panics. With his working familiarity with the

Reichsbank, the Bank of England, and the Banque de France, it was incomprehensible to him that the task of preventing future crises would be left to the House of Morgan or, in its absence, to some other unknown and unchartered private-sector financial institution. It was as if the city of New York, at the beginning of the twentieth century, had rejected a professional fire department in favor of volunteer firefighters.

A Voice in the Wilderness Is Finally Heard

Prior to his 1907 introduction to Aldrich at the Kuhn, Loeb offices, Warburg had sounded warnings about the rising danger of letting an economy move forward without ongoing adjustment mechanisms or, more perilously, without any reliable contingency measures in the event of serious, panic-inducing disruptions to the financial system. In 1906, in a speech before the New York Chamber of Commerce, he was particularly forceful (and prescient) about the danger of a coming financial catastrophe: "I do not like to play the role of Cassandra, but mark what I say. If this condition of affairs is not changed, and changed soon, we will get a panic in this country compared to which those which have preceded it will look like child's play."[3] And in early 1907, before the panic in the fall of that year would bear out his concern, he wrote an article for the *New York Times*, "Defects and Needs of Our Banking System," that crystallized his seminal thoughts on an American version of a central bank.[4] Although he was steeped in the ways of privately owned European central banks located in capital cities, he did not believe that a U.S. central bank necessarily had to conform to their structures and policies. But still, "some sort of organization" was necessary to provide liquidity and emergency lending. In the article he wrote:

> Nearly every country of the world claiming a modern financial organization has some kind of central bank, ready at all times to rediscount the legitimate paper of the general banks. Not only have England, France and Germany adopted such a system, but all minor European States as well—and even reactionary Russia—have gradually accepted it. In fact, Japan without such an organization could not have weathered the storm through which she has recently passed, and could not have achieved the commercial success which she now enjoys.[5]

The *Times* article, however, stirred little interest, even among the big city, Republican-leaning bankers. The tepid response was probably no surprise to Warburg, since the *Times* article was actually an expanded version of a proposal that went nowhere on Wall Street. He had drafted a confidential memorandum on a central bank for his Kuhn, Loeb partners shortly after his arrival in the United States, and they in turn circulated it to other New York bankers for review. The memorandum found its way to James Stillman, president of the National City Bank of New York, who made a special trip to Kuhn, Loeb to confront the firm's young partner about his controversial proposal. "Warburg," he asked, "don't you think the City Bank has done pretty well?"

"Yes, Mr. Stillman, extraordinarily well," the ever-polite Warburg replied.

"Then why not leave things alone?"

With uncharacteristic brashness, Warburg responded, "Your bank is so big and so powerful, Mr. Stillman, that, when the next panic comes, you will wish your responsibilities were smaller."[6]

A few years later, in the midst of the panic of 1907, a more open-minded Stillman once again visited Warburg at Kuhn, Loeb, asking to review the memorandum he had earlier dismissed. "Warburg," he said, "where is your paper?"

"Too late now, Mr. Stillman. What has to be done cannot be done in a hurry. If reform is to be secured, it will take years of education work to bring it about."[7]

The panic of 1907 did not take down Stillman's National City Bank, in part because John D. Rockefeller made an emergency $10 million injection into the institution in a highly publicized demonstration of confidence. But many other banks and trust companies fell, and scores of New York Stock Exchange investment firms were on the brink of failure. This panic served to finally awaken a broader public interest in the financial reform long championed by Warburg. The *New York Times*, at the height of the panic, asked him to write a follow-up piece to expand on his financial blueprint, and on November 12, 1907, he published "A Plan for a Modified Central Bank."[8] Warburg's prior writings and his occasional speeches drew only mild interest before the panic, but now, after his ideas about the fragility of the financial infrastructure had become painfully confirmed, they attracted widespread interest. In particular, Warburg's article caught the attention of Senator Aldrich, the person most able to act on his recommendations.

Shaping the Aldrich Plan

Warburg, a prolific writer who many years later would produce a two-volume history of the creation of the Federal Reserve System, was energized by Aldrich's December 1907 visit. He followed up with a flurry of letters to the senator on bank reform modeled on the practices of the European central banks, especially the Reichsbank. Warburg did not elect to accompany Aldrich and the other members of the National Monetary Commission on their fact-finding visits to the central banks of Europe—presumably he knew enough about the banks from his earlier direct experience at M. M. Warburg—but while they were abroad he crystallized his thoughts in a monograph titled "The Discount System in Europe." In what would be called today a "white paper," Warburg laid out the problems of the current inflexible U.S. monetary structure and suggested an alternate, European-like mechanism that would allow the money supply to expand and contract according to the needs of the economy.[9]

His paper identified a major contributing cause of instability in the U.S. banking system: the requirement under the provisions of the National Banking Acts of 1863 and 1864 that U.S. banks with a national charter issue banknotes backed by U.S. government bonds. That requirement reduced the threat of inflation, since it tied money creation to a fixed and measurable base. But it also carried with it the new problems associated with a fixed, or "inelastic," currency. Because the reserves backing banknotes were required to be invested in U.S. government bonds, the money supply was unintentionally fixed and could not be increased or decreased in a way that would accommodate the needs of the economy. Because there was no apparent connection between the level of economic activity and the supply of bonds, banks were often forced to retrench at exactly the wrong time in the business cycle. During periods of heavy lending—before the harvest or holiday seasons, for instance, or during robust business expansion—there was limited monetary flexibility to handle the swelling need for lendable funds, and tying money supply to government bonds outstanding inevitably retarded economic growth, because government bonds tend to be retired in an expanding economy, thus reducing the currency supply just when an increase would be required to support business expansion.

Warburg's paper suggested a European solution, under which a central bank is charged with establishing a "window" to which commercial banks may go to sell—"rediscount"—the loans they had earlier made but which now remained frozen on their balance sheets for lack of a resale alternative. By freeing up those illiquid bank assets, the European central banks created additional sources of funds for lending and adjusted the money supply to the level needed to sustain business activity. At the same time, they were able to prevent artificially high or low levels of interest rates.

The companion problem to the fixed money supply was the difficulty in the United States of summoning up a lender of last resort to quell budding financial panics. There was no effective means of marshaling the reserves that banks were required to hold under the provisions of the National Banking Acts toward a common cause of providing emergency liquidity to stem financial panics. In fact, as evident from the experience of the prior panics, rather than sharing, the banks held on even more tightly to their reserves. That practice served the purposes of the reserve bank doing the hoarding but worsened the overall state of liquidity. Eventually this caused the entire financial system to seize up.

It was just that kind of seizure that propelled the panic of 1907. Absent a central bank during that crisis, Pierpont Morgan cobbled together a virtual central bank by gathering funds from the major New York banks and prevailing upon the U.S. Treasury to make an offsetting emergency deposit in those banks. The Treasury funds were authorized by then president Teddy Roosevelt, who did so, no doubt, based largely on the long-standing reputation of the seventy-year-old Morgan. But the spectacle of the federal government providing public funds to privately owned banks to prevent a financial disaster made the need for central control vivid. Rather than facing financial crises on an ad hoc basis, there clearly needed to be a system for centralizing the reserve funds that the individual member commercial banks had on hand to make additional funds available from a common pool. Without a central bank to play that role, the U.S. economy would continue to careen from one financial crisis to another, relieved only by patchwork and improvised relief efforts.

Aldrich's Road to Damascus

But Aldrich's recognition of the need for a central bank did not mean he was sold on Warburg's proposal, which argued that commercial loans, rather than Treasury bonds, should back the currency. And after his travels to Europe in 1908, he was not sure about the wisdom of a single powerful bank in the mode of the Bank of England, the Reichsbank, or the Banque de France in a country with the geographical expanse of the United States. That concern was heightened by the serious reservation about a single bank held by George Reynolds, who was president of the American Bankers Association and a key member of the National Monetary Commission. And then there was the overweening concern: the European central banks were privately owned and independently operated, a feature that proved to be the undoing of both the First and Second Banks of the United States. At a time of growing distrust of corporate trusts and robber barons, a central bank with little or no government oversight seemed politically doomed.

The point at which Aldrich came around to Warburg's way of thinking—his conversion on the road to Damascus, as Aldrich himself would describe it—appeared to have come about after a talk Warburg gave at New York's Metropolitan Club. That talk, in the fall of 1908, was arranged by Aldrich and was in the form of an address to the members of the National Monetary Commission after their recent fact-finding trip to Europe. By this time, the usually reserved and publicity-shy Warburg had become a high-profile proponent of European-style currency management. He did not hold a rigid view that a new U.S. central bank should operate entirely free of government involvement, only that it should have a mechanism similar to that found in the European central banks—one that would allow for sensible adjustments of the money supply to promote the economy and, most crucially, to halt the worsening financial crises that had plagued the country since the mid-nineteenth century. That was the message he delivered at the Metropolitan Club.

At the conclusion of the Metropolitan Club address, Aldrich took Warburg aside and commented, "Mr. Warburg, I like your ideas. I have only one fault to find with them. You are too timid about them."[10] That the once-recalcitrant Aldrich was won over by his ideas "came like a thunder bolt from a clear sky" to Warburg, and from that point on he became the leading, if unofficial, advisor to Aldrich and the commission.

Warburg soon realized, to his surprise, that one of his roles would be to cool down the recently converted Aldrich. "Whereas before I had doubted whether the Senator could ever be persuaded to consider any central reserve plan," he said, "I now found it my part to dissuade him from going too far in that direction. Accordingly, I explained to the Senator why any attempt to establish a full-fledged central bank, in the European sense, appeared to me to be inadvisable."[11] Now, in a reversal of roles, Warburg found it necessary to caution Aldrich about much of the country's "deep-seated prejudices and suspicions" about a central bank and, at least for cosmetic purposes, suggested calling it a reserve bank instead of a central bank. More substantively, he attempted to sow the seeds for the new organization being jointly managed by the government and private interests, as opposed to the purely private enterprise model that prevailed in Europe. To further appease regional interests, he suggested that any new central bank have a network of regional branches with which it would share operating control and policy making.

The Jekyll Island retreat followed the pivotal Metropolitan Club meeting, and members of the "hunting party" that Aldrich had assembled proved up to the task of distilling the broad findings of the National Monetary Commission and organizing them into a piece of legislation that would fit the peculiarities of the U.S. financial structure and political realities of the day. As a result of the consensus that had emerged from the Metropolitan Club, the Jekyll Island participants were in agreement about the big issues and, in a little over a week's time, they produced a comprehensive document that would be called the Aldrich Plan and presented to Congress. As National City Bank vice president and Jekyll Island participant Frank Vanderlip stated:

> Of course we knew that what we simply had to have was a more elastic currency through a bank that would hold the reserves of all banks. But there were many other questions that needed to be answered. If it was to be a central bank, how was it to be owned: by the banks, by the government, or jointly? Should there be a number of institutions or only one? Should the rate of interest be the same for the whole nation? In what open market operations should the bank be engaged?[12]

By the time the conferees had boarded Aldrich's private car for the return trip from Georgia, they had confronted all of the issues—including those that were largely political. The final version of the Aldrich Plan conceived of a central bank innocuously named the National Reserve Association and, rather than operating out of a single New York headquarters, the association would consist of a string of fifteen banks throughout the United States. Moreover, the Jekyll Island meeting served to soften those who objected to any form of political control of the association, and a consensus emerged that the government should be represented in both governance and regulatory matters.

The association would, as Warburg had originally conceived, rediscount commercial paper offered to it by a bank member in order to produce increased elasticity of the money supply. And it would serve as a fiscal agent for the U.S. Treasury in gathering reserves of these member banks in the event a lender of last resort was needed. On January 19, 1912, a little more than a year following the Jekyll Island meeting, the National Monetary Commission presented its final report on its two-year-long study, with the Aldrich Plan as its spine.

Road Show

The construction of the Aldrich Plan turned out to be largely a collaborative effort, though the other Jekyll Island participants were quick to label Warburg as a "first among equals" in the highly successful conference. But Warburg immediately realized that the next phase would require political skills far different from the financial acumen of the Jekyll Island conferees. So, given his reserved personality—to say nothing of the prospect of returning full-time to his lucrative partnership at Kuhn, Loeb—one would have expected him to let the politicians carry the plan to a legislative conclusion. But as a self-proclaimed "fanatic" on bank reform, he had a personal stake in legislative success and explained his rationale for his continuing role as an advocate: "From the conclusion of the Jekyll Island conference until the final passage of the Reserve Act, the generalship was in the hands of political leaders, while the role of bank reformers was to aid the movement by educational campaigns and, at the same time, to do their utmost to prevent fundamental parts of the nonpolitical plan from being disfigured by concessions of political expediency."[13]

Rather than backing away from the sales side of the job after he had established the intellectual framework for reform, the cerebral Warburg moved right into the fray. Assuming an out-of-character role as a reformer and political activist, he headed a forty-five-state organization with the unwieldy name of the National Citizens' League for the Promotion of a Sound Banking System. The league barnstormed across the country delivering the message of bank reform, with Warburg often giving lectures and distributing pamphlets to business leaders and any interested citizenry on the importance and urgency of reform. The name Paul Warburg and the concept of sound banking principles became joined—so much so that by 1912, Teddy Roosevelt, who ran unsuccessfully that year for president under the banner of the Bull Moose Party, proclaimed that Warburg would be the ideal person to run a new central bank. "Why not give Mr. Warburg the job? He would be the financial boss, and I would be the political boss, and we could run the country together."[14]

But with Warburg's heightened public profile came exposure to the rough-and-tumble politics of America in the early twentieth century. William Jennings Bryan, with his strident brand of populism, had rallied much of the nation against the powerful Eastern banking interests and vilified the sound money principles that Warburg had long stood for. At the same time, practitioners of an uglier variety of populism used ad hominem arguments to counter Warburg's views on banking. In a country whose interior was heavily populated with fundamental Protestants, the views of an Eastern Jew were often suspect. Likewise, Warburg's very recent change of citizenship from Germany to the United States was seen as too late and too politically motivated. Often, the criticism of Warburg was blatantly anti-Semitic and hostile. In a four-word summary of his objections to Warburg's later nomination to the first Federal Reserve Board, Democratic Congressman Joe Eagle of Texas proclaimed simply that Warburg was "a Jew, a German, a banker and an alien."[15] At other times the attacks on Warburg were more subtle and humorous, such as the Daddy Warbucks attribution.

Apparent Defeat

It would be a stretch to blame the tough sledding the Aldrich Plan ultimately faced in Congress on Warburg's prominence in its conception. After all, he was only one member of the lineup of Eastern bankers that angry populists of the age held in low esteem as an elite group of financial swindlers. As the 1912 presidential campaign took shape, the Aldrich Plan came under nearly universal disapproval. The Democratic candidate and ultimate victor, Woodrow Wilson, ran on a platform that could not have been clearer: "The Democratic Party is opposed to the Aldrich Plan or a central bank."[16] And Roosevelt, despite his earlier glowing opinion of Warburg's work, withdrew the support of his Bull Moose Party; he cited a belated concern that the Aldrich Plan would place the country's currency and credit system in private hands, not subject to effective public control. Even Republican candidate Howard Taft, in his unsuccessful run as the incumbent, failed to endorse the plan named after his fellow party member and longtime head of the Senate Finance Committee.

So despite additional changes made to the legislation proposed by Aldrich, including the major concession that would allow for the presidential appointment of the directors of the proposed National Reserve Association rather than their election by banking interests, the legislation was doomed to failure. It appeared to Warburg and other supporters of bank reform that their efforts had all been for naught. With Wilson's convincing win in the 1912 election and the Democrats regaining control of Congress, the reformers feared that the United States, soon to become the world's largest economy, would continue to operate for the indefinite future without a central bank—and, in the face of the inevitable next round of financial panics, without a lender of last resort.

But they were wrong. Even before Wilson had been inaugurated, a new and unlikely champion of a U.S. central bank would emerge in the form of Carter Glass, a Democratic congressman from Lynchburg, Virginia, and an apostle of William Jennings Bryan.

3

Carter Glass: 1858–1946
Unreconstructed Rebel

I don't know anything about banking, but I guess I can learn.

—CARTER GLASS

It was a snowy December 26, 1912, when Carter Glass traveled from Virginia to Princeton, New Jersey, to meet with President-elect Woodrow Wilson. Glass was an energetic young Democratic congressman from Lynchburg, Virginia, and during his four-year tenure on the House Banking and Currency Committee he had been an outspoken opponent of establishing a central bank in the United States. His maiden speech in Congress, in fact, was a denunciation of the Aldrich-Vreeland Act that provided for the National Monetary Commission—the congressional task force set up to simply *study* the question of central banking for the United States.

Yet the purpose of his visit was to present Wilson with a central bank alternative to the Republican-proposed Aldrich Bill, which called for a national reserve along the lines of that formulated by Paul Warburg. Glass and his fellow Democrats were muted in their opposition to the Aldrich Bill throughout 1912, probably anticipating that they would regain control of Congress and the White House later that year. And though opposition to the Aldrich Bill—and for that matter opposition to central banking in any form at all—had been a universally approved plank in the Democrats' platform, the issue of a central bank rarely rose to any meaningful level of debate during the just-completed presidential election. But Glass, now chairman of the House Banking and Currency Committee, recognized that the country's banking system was in need of urgent reform. On November 7, just two days after the election, Glass sent Wilson a letter requesting a meeting on "the entire subject of a reorganization of the banking and currency system" that stated, "While we did not think it would be prudent to complicate the Presidential contest by taking any definitive action at the last session of Congress, the committee has not been idle and we have gone into much work of detail and have, indeed, formulated, tentatively, a substitute for what is known as the Aldrich bill."[1]

In their admiring 1939 biography of Glass, authors Rixey Smith and Norman Beasley grandly describe the brief December meeting between Wilson and Glass as "an historic day in America, and the world. Within two hours a great federal reserve system, under which the entire economic life of a nation will soon be permanently organized, will here be born."[2] So according to this telling, the framework of what would soon become the Federal Reserve System was not conceived on Georgia's Jekyll Island in 1910, but two years later at Woodrow Wilson's home in Princeton, and accordingly the "father" of the Federal Reserve was Carter Glass rather than Paul Warburg.

The Unreconstructed Rebel

In 1902, the year Paul Warburg moved to New York from Germany to become a partner of Kuhn, Loeb & Company, Carter Glass moved to Washington to begin his first term as a congressman. Warburg was a well-educated but self-effacing gentleman from a prominent European banking family; Glass, the fifth of twelve children, was from a family of scrappers and duelers. He came of age during the South's hardscrabble years of Reconstruction, and was just old enough to recall the turmoil of the Civil War and how the "blue-coated devils" overran and occupied his native Virginia. A lifelong bantam weight—he stood five feet, four inches tall and weighed just over one hundred pounds throughout adulthood— he was always spoiling for a fight and reveled in an underdog status.

Yet Glass was no country rube. His formal education ended at age thirteen, but he developed impressive intellectual abilities under the tutelage of his father, who owned and managed the *Lynchburg Daily Republican*. As a young man, Glass worked for the paper as a printer's apprentice, then later became a reporter and eventually the paper's publisher. He undertook his own version of a great books self-study program, with a personal reading list that included the works of Plato, Edmund Burke, and Shakespeare. His interest in the last somehow developed into an obsession with the notion, which had currency at the time, that the plays attributed to Shakespeare had actually been written by Sir Francis Bacon. That opinion (which seemed to grow more rigid as Glass aged) was peppered through his own writing, and he referenced it, perhaps unwisely, in conjunction with his barely concealed claim to the fatherhood of the Federal Reserve.

Through the editorials of the *Lynchburg Daily Republican* and other newspapers he later published, Glass championed Democratic Party causes. He entered politics at a young age, becoming clerk of the Lynchburg City Council at twenty-three, and shortly thereafter the representative of his Lynchburg region in the Virginia state legislature. As a product of the Old South, Glass was an unrepentant states' rights advocate, and while in the Virginia congress sponsored bills, repugnant by today's more enlightened standards, that blatantly disenfranchised African Americans. Much later, Franklin Roosevelt nicknamed him "the Unreconstructed Rebel" for clinging to Confederate mores and socially conservative politics.

Up Against the Money Devils

A pivotal point in the development of his political outlook, including his antipathy toward the Eastern banking establishment, occurred at the 1896 Democratic National Convention in Chicago where, as a Virginia delegate, he was enthralled by William Jennings Bryan and his immortal "Cross of Gold" speech. Glass was elected to Congress in 1902, and he thrived in his role as a Bryan-inspired financial populist—especially after being appointed to the chairmanship of a House banking subcommittee and then, in 1912, becoming chairman of the committee itself. He openly referred to Eastern bankers as "money devils" and relished playing a self-proclaimed David up against the banking Goliaths. He was prone to speaking and writing of himself in deprecating, third-person descriptions—"The banking subcommittee, with a mere country editor for its chairman was not taken seriously" and "He had no special qualifications for the committee's work beyond the information absorbed in these years of discussion and a reasonable amount of common sense acquired as a practical printer."[3]

Despite his later outspokenness on matters of finance, Glass initially had little interest in the committee. As a junior congressman he coveted a chair on the Foreign Affairs Committee, but the House leadership denied him that role, offering membership on the Banking and Currency

Committee as a consolation. Glass was not enthusiastic about the alternative but, resigned to that or no assignment at all, replied, "I don't know anything about banking, but I guess I can learn."[4]

The serendipitous appointment of Glass to the House banking committee was a fortunate quirk of history. He is best remembered as one of the two sponsors of the Glass-Steagall Act of 1933, a major and long-enduring part of Franklin Roosevelt's New Deal initiatives that separated investment banking from commercial banking. He is less known today for his indispensable and unlikely role in establishing the nation's central bank though passage of the Federal Reserve Act of 1913.

As with his position on the banking committee, he took on the Federal Reserve task much by accident. In 1912, Louisiana Congressman Arsène Pujo had convened a congressional committee to look into the concentration of financial power in the United States. It was a time of widespread distrust of big business and Wall Street, and Pujo was intent on investigating the so-called money trusts of the day. He subpoenaed J. P. Morgan and other leading bankers and industrialists to testify in open hearings as to the workings and financing of their business. Glass, as part of the inquiry and by now a recognized speaker on banking topics, was appointed to head a subcommittee to look into the "scheme" for a central bank as set forth by the Republicans in the Aldrich Plan.

Although the Pujo deliberations did not unveil the sinister plotting and underhanded financial dealing many had anticipated, they did reveal an extraordinary level of control of American industry by banks and stoked the public's growing unease with capitalism and its financiers. For example, the calculations of the committee's staff revealed that Morgan and his partners held seventy-two directorships at forty-seven industrial companies. Similarly, officers of Wall Street's largest bank, First National Bank, held seats on the boards of eighty-nine companies, in many cases sitting alongside Morgan partners. All in all, the eighteen largest financial institutions in the country controlled capital resources that totaled an amount equivalent to two-thirds of its gross national product.[5] And the revelations of concentrated wealth played into the hand of the Democratic Party's powerful populist wing, already vocal in its dislike and distrust of J. P. Morgan and East Coast bankers in general. At the party's 1912 convention, the ever-fiery William Jennings Bryan introduced a sweeping resolution that would have barred the selection of any presidential candidate "who is the representative or under any obligation to J. Pierpont Morgan, Thomas F. Ryan, August Belmont, or any other member of the privilege-hunting and favor-seeking class."[6]

In 1912, it was not common knowledge that Nelson Aldrich had, just two years earlier, convened a meeting on Jekyll Island among the vilified leaders of Wall Street—several of whom were brought to testify before the largely hostile Pujo committee—to formulate a U.S. central bank. That revelation could have provided the Democrats with powerful ammunition during the hearings, but in the end it probably would not have mattered. Aldrich's connections to Morgan, Rockefeller, and the other titans of the day were well known, and the central bank initiatives taken during President William Howard Taft's one-term administration were already doomed when Woodrow Wilson trounced him in his 1912 bid for re-election. The Democrats captured control of both the White House and Congress, and that party could not have been any clearer in its opposition to central banking.

Wilson's nomination at the Democrats' stormy summer convention had been cemented only after William Jennings Bryan released his delegates to Wilson. As a result, the party platform that emerged from that convention contained a plank brokered by the Bryan forces—whom Warburg would characterize as "a powerful wing wedded to the wildest monetary and banking doctrines"[7]—with an unambiguous statement that the Democratic Party was opposed to central banking in general and in particular to the Aldrich Plan or a U.S. central bank.

An Unlikely Ally

The Aldrich Bill, which looked so promising when it had been introduced in the Senate in January 1912, had become a dead issue upon Wilson's victory. At the beginning of the year, Republican Warburg was convinced that the idea of a central bank had already "triumphed." But by the end of 1912, he viewed the prospect of pushing legislation through Congress to be an impossible task due to the "ignorance, prejudice, vagaries, and conceit within the ranks of the Democratic party."[8] Yet it was precisely at that point that Glass—who in Warburg's mind embodied all of these negative attributes of his party—began to exhibit both his newfound expertise in central banking and his long-standing political acumen.

The "mere country editor" with populist bona fides became the chairman of the House banking subcommittee at a crucial time in the nation's financial history. In his work for the Pujo commission, the self-educated Glass had taken the opportunity to learn about central banking on his own, and he soon realized that the issue needed immediate attention. The panic of 1907 and its near toppling of the country's primitive financial structure were not yet a distant memory, and Glass understood the continuing peril the country faced in operating without a central bank. What he called the "Siamese twins of disorder," an inelastic currency and a fractionated reserve system, were still powerful destabilizers of the U.S. economy, and he knew that it was just a matter of time before the next financial panic surfaced. Glass understood that without a well-designed currency-management system that could adjust to normal seasonal cycles and recurring business cycles, liquidity would once again become a problem for banks and their customers. And if the lack of liquidity led to bank failures, there was still no lender of last resort to prevent new financial panics, no institution that could stave off the next chain reaction of ever-larger failures that would cripple the economy. Glass realized the country needed a central bank to avert the next financial crisis—he just could not call it that.

Determined to avert a financial panic during the new Democratic administration, Glass acted with an unrelenting urgency. He brought the monumental and complex Federal Reserve Act of 1913 to completion in exactly one year's time, from his initial meeting with Wilson the day after Christmas in 1912 until its final passage by the House and Senate on December 23, 1913. Glass received assistance from able committee members and staff, but any tracing of the bill's progress shows Glass pulling the laboring oar. The Senate version of the House bill was sponsored by Robert L. Owen of Oklahoma, the first chairman of the newly established Senate Committee on Banking and Currency, but after winding through debate and conferences, it wound up differing little from the House version Glass had authored. The resulting Federal Reserve Act (initially the Owen-Glass Bank and Currency Act) was essentially a Glass production with only minimal reconciliation.

Winning Over the Populists

The speed with which the act was passed was certainly due in part to the strong Democratic mandate after the 1912 election, in which Wilson captured forty of the then forty-eight states, and the Democrats secured large pluralities in both the House and Senate. The challenges Glass faced, however, were driven less by the Republicans than by opposition from within his own party.

Not surprisingly, the most formidable opposition came from Bryan with his Andrew Jackson–like opposition to any form of central banking. Now elevated from senator to secretary of state in Wilson's administration, Bryan focused much of his vehemence about Glass's bill to a proposal to remove the U.S. government bond backing from the currency in favor of Federal Reserve notes backed by the banks. For Bryan, this went directly against a conviction he had held for some twenty years based on his fear of control by bankers with their reverence for hard money and the gold standard. Backing down on that issue for him and his followers was tantamount to a metaphorical crucifixion on a cross of gold.

At the same time, the continuance of government bond backing was totally unpalatable to Glass, since that ill-advised policy, initiated some fifty years earlier through the 1864 National Banking Act, was at the very heart of the currency problem. In a 1927 memoir he wrote:

> The national currency was inelastic because it was based on the bonded indebtedness of the United States. For half a century we banked on the absurd theory that the country always needed a volume of currency equal to the nation's bonded indebtedness and at no time ever required less, whereas we frequently did not need as much as was outstanding and quite often required more than it was possible to obtain. So, when more was needed than could be gotten, stringencies resulting in panics would be precipitated. When currency was redundant, it was sent by interior banks to the great money centers to be loaned on call for stock and commodity gambling.[9]

Glass and Bryan remained at loggerheads over the issue, and when Owen, heading the Senate's legislative efforts, sided with Bryan, the matter of the U.S. backing of the currency wound up on President Wilson's desk. For Glass, the issue showed a profound lack of understanding about the security of the proposed Federal Reserve note, and he pled earnestly with the president to withhold his support of formal government backing. Glass recalls the argument he presented to Wilson:

> The liability of the individual member bank, with the double liability of its stockholders; the considerable gold cover with the 100 percent commercial secondary reserve; the liability of the regional banks, individually and jointly, as well as the double liability of the member banks; the banking instinct behind every discount and every

rediscount transaction; the right of the regional bank to reject business and, finally, the power of the Federal Reserve Board to withhold
notes. The suggested government obligation is so remote it could
never be discerned.[10]

Wilson listened attentively to Glass's argument and concurred with his rea-
soning but, in a nod to Bryan's intransigence on the issue, suggested that the
congressman "surrender the shadow but save the substance" by preserving
the full faith and credit government guaranty without tying the level of
currency to outstanding bonded indebtedness.[11] Glass was not happy but
agreed to go along with the "innocuous camouflage." The inclusion of the
U.S. government's backing to the bill assuaged Bryan sufficiently to gain his
support of the act.

On the crucially important matter of the Federal Reserve's governance,
however, the populists held sway and Wilson remained firmly in their camp.
Those who conceived the original framework of the Aldrich Plan on Jekyll
Island would probably have preferred a central bank based on a European
model, one with a single bank located in New York City and governed by an
independent board representing the private sector. But bowing to political
realities, the Aldrich Bill they presented to Congress in 1911 envisioned a
system of fifteen national reserve banks across the country, with a central
board that included a mix of government appointees and bank and business representatives. The Glass-originated bill was similar to the Aldrich
Bill, in that it called for regionally headquartered federal reserve banks,
but the composition of the controlling board would tilt toward government appointees, with bankers given only minority representation. Glass
felt strongly that a board composed *entirely* of government officials and
appointees would subject the Federal Reserve to undue political influence
and convinced Wilson's new secretary of the Treasury, William McAdoo, as
to the wisdom of a balance between business and government appointees.

But even a minority representation from business was too much for
Secretary of State Bryan, and Wilson was eventually brought in again as
a tiebreaker to make the final decision on the composition of the Federal
Reserve's board. In a meeting convened to win over Wilson's support on
the issue, Glass summoned prominent members from the American Bankers Association to visit with Wilson in the White House for the purpose of
reinforcing Glass's arguments. Each had his say, with an approving Glass
looking on. But at the end of their presentations, Wilson, after a thoughtful
delay, asked: "Will one of you gentlemen tell me in what civilized country

on the earth there are important government boards of control on which private interests are represented?"[12] There being no effective rejoinder from the bankers, the progressive arm of the Democratic Party carried the day, and the Federal Reserve wound up with a board composed entirely of presidential appointees—and with its headquarters in Washington, D.C.

Governor Warburg's Brief Tenure

Among Wilson's nominees for the founding seven-member board was none other than Paul Warburg. In a letter dated April 30, 1914, Wilson—no doubt mindful of the financial consequences of Warburg's altruism in giving up a lucrative Kuhn, Loeb partnership for the low-paying governorship of the Fed—stated in closing, "I feel that your counsel would be invaluable to the board and I sincerely hope that you may see your way to making the sacrifices necessary to accept." Warburg accepted the appointment the next day, writing, "Whether any personal sacrifices are involved or not, it is a rare privilege." The financial sacrifice was substantial: during the four years of his service as a governor he would be earning only $12,000 annually, a competitive salary for the position, but a pittance in comparison to the half-million yearly income he was walking away from as a private banker.[13]

What Warburg may not have realized at the time, however, was that his sacrifices would not be just monetary but would include giving up the treasured privacy of his personal and professional life. While the other six nominees sailed through the Senate confirmation hearings, Warburg was subjected to cross-examination in a manner reminiscent of the Pujo hearings a few years earlier. The senators seemed more eager to reopen the subject of Kuhn, Loeb's control of the money trusts than to examine Warburg's central banking credentials or his views on economic and monetary policy. Faced with this pointed hostility, and no doubt harboring second thoughts about his extraordinary financial sacrifice, he asked the president to withdraw his nomination. But in a commendable show of Wilson's commitment to establishing a competent and politically independent board, the president convinced the Republican banker to continue through the confirmation process. In August 1914, Warburg was named as a founding board member.

Wilson's confidence in Warburg was well placed. Just as Warburg had emerged as the intellectual force that fashioned the framework for the central bank four years earlier, he now became the obvious board member to prepare the Federal Reserve for its newfound responsibilities. To do so, he wrote and pushed through Congress a multitude of amendments to the Federal Reserve Act—most of which were opposed by Carter Glass, territorial about the bill and loath to see it modified—that better positioned the bank to deal with the convertibility and mobility of gold. Though the amendments were mind-numbingly technical, they would make it possible for the Federal Reserve to become the de facto central bank for the Allied countries in the looming Great War. For his accomplishments, Wilson further recognized Warburg in August of 1916 by naming him as the Federal Reserve's first vice chairman. Indeed, he likely would have named Warburg chairman, had the Federal Reserve Act not required at the time that the current secretary of the Treasury serve in that role.

Warburg's prominence, though, was short-lived. In one of the ironies of history, Warburg—who had capably structured the Federal Reserve for effective wartime finance—became for many a popular villain. Outlandish rumors swirled about his being in the service of Kaiser Wilhelm and acting as a double agent to enfeeble the nation's financial ability to wage war. His still-pronounced German accent, coupled with the fact that his brother Max was assisting in financing the Central Powers' war efforts through the Hamburg-based M. M. Warburg, fueled the rumors and gave them credence. That the Federal Reserve had become the fiscal agent for the sale of Liberty Bonds to finance America's war efforts only made these accusations more pernicious.

The whispering campaign grew with such persistence that Warburg offered to withdraw his name from Wilson's list of nominees when his term expired in August 1918. In a long and sad letter, Warburg wrote to Wilson: "Certain persons have started an agitation to the effect that a naturalized citizen of German birth, having a near relative prominent in German public life, should not be permitted to hold a position of great trust in the service of the United States." Warburg clearly hoped Wilson would stand on principle and nominate him for another four-year term, writing, "If for reasons of your own, you should decide not to re-nominate me it is likely to be construed by many as an acceptance by you of a point of view which I am certain you would not wish to sanction."[14]

Much to Warburg's dismay, however, it was not until the last possible minute that he finally got a letter in response from the president. In it, Wilson praised the vice chairman for his "indispensable counsel in these first formative years of the new system," but went on to say, "I read between the lines of your generous offer that you will yourself feel more at ease if you are free to serve in other ways."[15] To Warburg the praise was too faint and the letter much too late in coming and, moreover, totally disingenuous.

A Question of Paternity

Warburg left Washington in a despondent frame of mind and returned to New York. He did not return to Kuhn, Loeb, but assumed—or reassumed— directorships of a score of prominent businesses of the day, including the First National Bank of Boston, the Union Pacific Railroad, the B&O Railroad, and the Western Union Telegraph Company. In 1921, he founded the International Acceptance Bank in New York, merging it later with the Bank of Manhattan, and in a renewed commitment to the public weal, founded the Council on Foreign Relations and other philanthropies.

The gentlemanly Warburg would have likely lived out the rest of his life comfortable in the knowledge that he had made significant, if not widely appreciated, contributions to his adopted country through his early work in the creation of the Federal Reserve System. But for Carter Glass, it had long been of utmost political importance that the Glass Bill remained differentiated from the Aldrich Bill, and Glass took great pains to stress that his bill was more than just a repackaged version of the Aldrich Bill. In order to make that differentiation clear, it was necessary—at least in Glass's mind—to clarify who the legitimate "father" of the Federal Reserve was. The only two contenders for that title, of course, were Warburg and Glass.

With his 1927 memoir, *An Adventure in Constructive Finance*, Glass laid out a highly charged argument for himself—or, alternatively, in a polite demurral for Woodrow Wilson, who signed the Federal Reserve Act into law—as the rightful father of the Federal Reserve. He begins the book by stating, "It's not especially important to have it precisely determined who was the author of what is known as the Federal Reserve Act."[16] But then throughout the first three chapters he offers arguments refuting any ascription of the credit to the drafters of the Aldrich Bill.

Warburg could give a grudging recognition to Carter Glass's need to distance himself from Nelson Aldrich and other Republicans in order to gain the vote of William Jennings Bryan and key Democrats. But *Adventure* went far beyond what was politically necessary for Glass, and its publication seemed to shake any complacency Warburg may have felt about the allocation of credit for the founding and early successes of the Federal Reserve. Particularly galling to Warburg was Glass's rhapsodic and self-aggrandizing critique of the value of the Federal Reserve in connection with the financing of World War I:

> I agree with the considered judgment of those eminent bankers of this and other lands who have said that the World War could not have been financed but for the Federal Reserve Act. The real value of this one achievement of Wilson's administration might be fairly appraised by simply leaving to the human contemplation what further slaughter and destruction would have ensued or what would be our situation today had we lost the war with the Central European Powers![17]

Warburg's rebuttal to Glass's slapdash and hyperbolic *Adventure* followed three years later in the form of a massive and scholarly retort: *The Federal Reserve System: Its Origin and Growth.* The two-volume tome, with each volume exceeding eight hundred pages, was written between 1927 and 1930, much of it during extended breaks in Pasadena, California, while Warburg was serving in New York as chairman of the Bank of Manhattan. And there is little doubt what motivated his writing it: "Miss Clio, the Muse of History," Warburg wrote, "is a stubborn lady, entirely devoid of a sense of humor, and once she has made up her mind, it is exasperatingly difficult to alter her verdict. It is inadvisable, therefore, to delay too long the correction of inaccuracies, particularly in cases where silence might fairly be construed as assent."[18]

Warburg's *Federal Reserve System* seeks to set the record straight on developments before and after passage of the Federal Reserve Act. Taking straight-on Glass's assertion that the act was a one-year, Democratic creation, Warburg begins his book by making a more expansionary case, stating at the outset: "In order to be accorded its proper place, the reserve system must be looked upon as a national monument, like the old cathedrals of Europe, which were the work of many generations and of many masters, and are treasured as symbols of national achievement." He then traces the origins of the Federal Reserve to the seminal November 1910 Jekyll Island meeting at which the Aldrich Plan was hatched, but calls it "merely a several days' conference among a small group of men." (Despite the passage of twenty years, Warburg apparently felt bound to a blood brothers' oath not to reveal the colorful and clandestine circumstances surrounding the meeting or the names and stature of the men in attendance.) He then, in a methodical style much like an extended lawyer's brief, takes the reader through the Aldrich Bill, then its successors—the Glass Bill and the Owen-Glass Bill—and finally the resultant Federal Reserve Act of 1913. Through two chapters and 228 annotated pages, Warburg provides a side-by-side comparison of the Aldrich Bill with the Federal Reserve Act.

It's doubtful that many readers, then or since, have taken the time to study Warburg's section-by-section analysis, but even a cursory review shows that—Glass's protestations notwithstanding—the bills are remarkably similar. The National Reserve Association of the Aldrich Bill becomes the Federal Reserve System; the number and location of cities with reserve banks changes slightly; and many other nonsubstantive differences are identified. But one comes away from the review convinced that Congressman Glass was able to create distinctions without differences for the simple expedient of convincing his like-minded colleagues that they would not be voting for a repackaged version of the Republican-drafted Aldrich Plan.

Glass's reticence in attributing any contribution from Warburg's and Aldrich's efforts shows up amusingly in his use of terminology. While Glass was wont to equate the Aldrich Plan with central banking, he refused to utter the dreaded term "central bank" in connection with the Federal Reserve System created in his legislation. In a footnote to his *Adventure* memoir, he painstakingly explains that "wherever the term 'central bank' occurs in this narrative it means a 'central bank of banks' dealing only with the member bank of a system and not a central bank in the European sense, transacting business with the public."[19] But in his book, Warburg recounts a telling conversation with Glass during which Glass expresses frustration that the Federal Reserve Board is not able to exert more power over the regional banks.

> "But Mr. Glass," Warburg said, "the Board has no power in the premises to force the banks and, moreover, would not that make it a *central* bank?"
>
> "Oh, hell," Glass answered, "it *is* a central bank."[20]

Warburg passed away in 1932 at age 63, shortly after the publication of his book. Glass long outlived Warburg and devoted his considerable energy and combative personality to public service, much of it in the cause of reforming the financial establishment. In 1919, Wilson named him secretary of Treasury, just in time to oversee the National Prohibition ("Volstead") Act that Congress had passed over Wilson's veto that year. During his brief tenure at Treasury, Glass also advocated for financial assistance for the recently defeated Central Powers and, with his proprietary interest in the Federal Reserve, was a tireless critic of speculative lending and pushed for tighter lending regulation.

But Glass's preferred venue was Congress—he would decline an offer many years later from Franklin Roosevelt to serve again as Treasury secretary—where he could more effectively engage his reformist impulses. So upon the death in 1919 of Virginia's senior senator, Thomas S. Martin, Glass left his Treasury position after less than a year's service to fill the vacated Senate seat, a seat he would occupy until his own death in 1948.

Glass reappears prominently in the next chapter as a seasoned, if still scrappy, senator. He was often at swords' points with Franklin Roosevelt, but played a prominent role in the shaping of key financial reforms and regulation put in place by the New Deal's president. He remains best known today for the Glass-Steagall Act of 1933 that stayed on the books until its controversial repeal in 1999. But his pushing through Congress the long-needed legislation for a central banking system for the United States—albeit in a testy, unacknowledged, and odd-couple fashion with Paul Warburg—remains his most meaningful contribution to American finance.

The Fed's First Hundred Years

The Federal Reserve System—"the Fed," as it came to be called—was born in controversy and has remained there ever since. On the eve of the passage of the 1913 act, Charles Lindbergh Sr., a Minnesota congressman and father of the famed aviator, proclaimed that giving monetary powers to the government perpetrated "the worst legislative crime of the ages." As late as 1998, a harshly critical book about the Federal Reserve titled *The Creature from Jekyll Island* dredged up nearly a century of allegedly nefarious actions orchestrated by a cabal of financiers. And in 2010, a book called simply *End the Fed* was published by the well-known Libertarian presidential candidate Ron Paul.

The more temperate and reasoned criticism of the Fed over its first century, however, relates to its "mission creep." As conceived by both Glass and Warburg, the institution's purposes were important but narrow in scope: to provide for currency elasticity and to forestall financial panics. Though there is a close connection between price levels and the amount of currency circulating in the economy, in its early days the Fed's mission did not include controlling the level of inflation. The gold standard under which the country operated was assumed to control prices, at least over the long run. Likewise, even though the original Federal Reserve Act provided the mechanism for open-market operations—the Fed's main instrument for effecting monetary policy in modern times—the central bank in its early years had largely confined its business to the passive buying and selling of "real bills"—the IOUs that commercial banks created in their business lending.

The reviews of its early years of operations are mixed. During the first years of the Fed's existence, as both Warburg and Glass were proud to point out, it played a crucial role in financing the war efforts of the Allies. In the succeeding decades, however, it made colossal blunders. In the years leading up to the 1929 stock market crash, its policies were far too accommodating and stoked the fires of financial speculation. And then, during the ensuing Great Depression, it made the opposite error by restricting the availability of money just when the economy needed it most. The Fed's tight-money policy during the Great Depression may have simply been a consequence of an underappreciation of the power of monetary policy. Or it could have been a reflection of the well-known views of Andrew Mellon, Herbert Hoover's secretary of the Treasury—and, under the law at the time, chairman of the Fed's board of governors—that the economy would best be served by a hands-off approach that would eventually clear out the "rot" he believed had infested the country's economy. But Mellon's dictate to "liquidate labor, liquidate stocks, liquidate the farmers, liquidate real estate" resulted in a commensurate contraction of the money supply that Nobel Prize winner Milton Friedman would term the "Great Contraction of 1929–1933." That action served to prolong the economic pain of the Depression.

Over most of the mid-twentieth century the management of the economy was a bifurcated effort, with monetary policy the primary responsibility of the Federal Reserve and price stability the main indicator of its success. Fiscal policy, by contrast, was handled by the elected officials of the U.S. Congress and the president, using the instruments of government spending and taxation to promote full employment. In the landmark Employment Act of 1946, fiscal policy was viewed as the primary driver of the economy, and the president, through a newly formed Council of Economic Advisers, was required to prepare a yearly economic report from the president that spelled out employment goals and policies, along with the fiscal measures that would be undertaken to implement the policies and achieve the goals. The Federal Reserve and monetary policy were in decidedly supporting roles.

As "monetarists"—in particular Friedman and others at the University of Chicago—gained influence in their demonstration of the potency of monetary policy on the economy, the importance of the Fed's activities grew commensurately. In 1978, Congress passed the Humphrey-Hawkins Full Employment Act, in which the Fed's mission was vastly expanded beyond controlling inflation and, despite the protests of monetarists and Keynesian economists alike, it was charged with promoting full employment—and, for good measure, growth in gross domestic product and balanced trade and government budgets. As part of the Humphrey-Hawkins Act, the Fed's governors were required to deliver a semiannual monetary policy report outlining its success in achieving these laudable, but most often contradictory, goals. In time, the chairs of the Federal Reserve, with their vastly expanded mandate, became, alongside the president, the most important spokespersons on the economy. Paul Volcker, Alan Greenspan, Ben Bernanke, and Janet Yellen became household names.

And during the twenty-first century, the Fed's mission grew to encompass goals and responsibilities far beyond the imaginations of Warburg and Glass. Until the 2008 financial catastrophes, the Fed had limited its open-market buying and selling almost entirely to Treasury securities—the rock-solid bills, notes, and bonds of the U.S. government—and conducted monetary policy largely through the country's commercial banks. But in the midst of the crisis, the Fed, relying on a once-obscure section of the Federal Reserve Act of 1932 that allowed expanded lending to entities other than commercial banks in "unusual and exigent circumstances," made emergency loans to investment banks, including Goldman Sachs, Morgan Stanley, and Merrill Lynch. And it turned out that those loans were just for starters, with the Fed's lending eventually extended to American subsidiaries of foreign banks, including Britain's Barclays Bank, Switzerland's UBS, Japan's Mizuho Securities, and France's BNP Paribas. Industrial concerns as far-ranging as General Electric, General Motors, and Harley-Davidson received bailout funding.

During the so-called Great Recession, the Fed's unconventional central banking activities were expanded to include "quantitative easing," a program of asset purchases to stimulate the economy in a time of low interest rates. The assets the Fed bought continued to migrate far beyond U.S. Treasuries and grew to unprecedented amounts. Glass and Warburg would no doubt have been stunned by the thought that the modest collection of twelve federal banks they created a century ago would today be the repositories for a multi-trillion-dollar portfolio of government, corporate, and mortgage-backed securities.

The Fed's expansion also extended to its regulatory role. The Federal Reserve Act of 1913 gave the Fed a bank examination function, but mainly in coordination with other government agencies. At the time, virtually all of the country's tens of thousands of banks were one-office, one-business "unit bank" institutions. If they were national banks, they were supervised by the U.S. comptroller of the currency; if state banks, by state agencies. But that changed as the banking industry consolidated and diversified through holding companies. Through legislative action during the latter half of the twentieth century, the Federal Reserve was given the primary role in approving and regulating holding companies. As holding companies became the dominant structure for banking, the Fed became the super-regulator of banks.

The development of the other superregulator of the financial system, the Securities and Exchange Commission, is the subject of the next chapter. Glass had an important role in shaping the SEC and other New Deal securities legislation, but the driving force was a former prosecutor named Ferdinand Pecora. In many ways, Pecora and Glass were alike: lifelong Democrats, combative players, born reformers, and self-promoters—and those shared characteristics may explain why, as the following pages detail, they rarely saw eye to eye.

4

Ferdinand Pecora: 1882–1971
Hellhound of Wall Street

Those old Wall Street boys are putting up an awful fight
to keep the government from putting a cop on their
corner.

—WILL ROGERS, 1934

On October 24, 1929, the inevitable end of the stock market frenzy arrived.
Despite the price collapse that day—which later came to be called Black
Thursday—there remained widespread confidence that the market would
soon right itself. To that end, a group of the big names on Wall Street met
at J. P. Morgan & Company, across the street from the New York Stock
Exchange, to devise a plan. Those with long memories recalled how J. Pierpont Morgan had called together a similar group of bankers in the middle
of the panic of 1907 and mapped the steps to save a U.S. financial system
that seemed headed for total collapse. So when the media reported on the
coterie of top bankers entering the front door of the "House on the Corner"
at 23 Wall Street, the mood of most investors turned from despair to at least
a cautionary hope.

In its cover story on the meeting, *Time* magazine profiled Morgan partner Thomas Lamont, who was leading the ad hoc rescue group. In the lofty
prose that once characterized the magazine, the article described Lamont
as, "a cosmopolite, who knows, understands, and likes the thousands of
people of all nations with whom he does business. When nations gather
together, as at Versailles in 1919 and at Paris in 1929, Mr. Lamont is summoned to speak for US finance." To add financial substance to the personal
abilities of Lamont and his colleagues, *Time* declared, "Behind the group

of bankers that met day after day at No. 23 Wall Street there glittered the world's greatest single pool of liquid wealth."[1]

The bankers referred to were indeed an august group, made up of the heads of the country's largest banks, including Charles Mitchell of National City Bank, Albert Wiggin of Chase National Bank, Steward Prosser of Bankers Trust, and William Potter of Guaranty Trust. To demonstrate the depth of the pool, the magazine estimated the combined assets of their banks to be $10 billion. The implicit message was that these men and their institutions had the wherewithal and commitment to nip any stock market panic in the bud.

By the conclusion of their brief Black Thursday meeting, the banker entourage had jointly pledged to support the price of common stocks trading on the New York Stock Exchange. The funds—later estimated to be $240 million—were entrusted to NYSE president Richard Whitney. Whitney went from post to post on the trading floor in the afternoon of Black Thursday and bid for stocks, sometimes at prices in excess of the offer price, in order to demonstrate confidence from the top. At the end of the day the Dow Jones Industrial Average, after having fallen by 11 percent in the morning, closed that afternoon just slightly below its opening level. Lamont famously understated the market turmoil of Black Thursday by saying, "There has been a little distress selling on the Stock Exchange." *Time*, in a vastly premature conclusion, said "Thus did Confidence win its subtle race against Panic."

The banker group continued to meet during subsequent days, but acted with fading commitment and bravado. On October 28 and 29, soon dubbed Black Monday and Black Tuesday, the stock market came under even greater pressure, with the Dow falling another 25 percent. On Tuesday, the single-day volume of shares traded reached 16.4 million, a record level that would not be exceeded until 1969.

There would be no more staged buying programs. Instead, the NYSE governors, along with Whitney, Lamont, and other members of the initial rescue team, met out of sight in the exchange's basement, where the strategy discussion changed from offense to defense. No one had any appetite for making additional confidence-building investments in the stock market, and now it was a question of whether the stock exchange, under an unprecedented barrage of sell orders, should shut down. In a token display of confidence, the NYSE remained open for business, but its trading hours were shortened, and a few day long "holidays" were observed for clerks to get ahead of the paperwork created by panic selling.

As difficult as it might have been to fathom, the damage to the stock market was far from over. After the initial precipitous drop during the fall of 1929, during which stock prices were nearly cut in half, the markets continued a relentless slow motion decline during the next three years. By 1932, stocks had declined by more than 80 percent from their 1929 levels. And as bad as things were on Wall Street, they became even worse on Main Street. Beginning in 1930, bank runs began to plague the nation's agricultural heartland and before long spread east and west to larger cities. Unable to meet the cash demands of panicky depositors, nearly eleven thousand banks shut their doors and never opened them again.

During this period, the still-young Federal Reserve did exactly the opposite of what Paul Warburg and Carter Glass had intended it to do. Rather than halting an incipient panic by acting as a lender of last resort, the central bank made things worse by letting the money supply contract by 30 percent and standing by while half the country's banks failed. With few banks able or willing to lend, the economy nosedived and unemployment increased from around 3 percent just before the stock market crash to more than 25 percent in the 1930s. Irresponsible financial management—both in the private sector and in government, both in the equity markets and the debt markets—had taken an ugly and long-lasting toll on the American people.

Despite the difficulties the country faced, Whitney and the other figures of the high finance establishment were still considered, in the first few years after the crisis, to be responsible businessmen who had little effective control over unsavory stock market participants—organizers of hit-and-run investment pools, proprietors of the infamous "bucket shops" of the day, and high-pressure stock promoters who preyed on unsophisticated investors. Those "operators," viewed by the American public with a peculiar mix of admiration (for their outlaw ways) and disdain (for their disregard of ethics), ran stocks up or down on rumors or outright lies and then reaped the trading gains while the unsuspecting investors were left holding the bag. They were thought to be at the opposite end of the Wall Street spectrum from the private banker and his ilk, who were still perceived as responsible and law abiding, though no more able to control the actions of the bad guys on Wall Street than to control the continuing and sickening slide of stock prices.

But in 1933, all this changed. A series of hearings first launched by Herbert Hoover in 1932 to investigate the U.S. securities markets in the aftermath of the crash were given new vigor after the election of

Franklin Roosevelt and upon the appointment of a new lead counsel for the hearings—Ferdinand Pecora, a reform-minded, former prosecutor from New York with no illusions about bankers and brokers. By the conclusion of the so-called Pecora hearings, many of the same revered bankers who met at the House of Morgan in October 1929 found themselves the subject of a 1933 *Time* story, "Wealth on Trial," with a far different tone from previous issues. As a result of Pecora's "trial" and later investigations, National City Bank's president, Charles Mitchell, would be indicted for tax evasion; Chase Bank's president, Albert Wiggin, would lose his position and reputation with disclosures about his insider trading; NYSE president, Richard Whitney, would be sent to the Ossining New York State prison ("Sing Sing") for embezzlement; and the once mighty and revered House of Morgan would be dismantled. But beyond the misfortunes of Wall Street's titans, the Pecora commission would provide the impetus for groundbreaking legislation to change the balance of power between Washington and Wall Street and establish a regulatory framework designed to give ordinary investors a better shot at success.

The Right Man for the Job

In April 1932, Senator Peter Norbeck convened hearings before the Senate Banking and Currency Committee to investigate the causes of the 1929 crash.[2] The hearings came after pressure from President Herbert Hoover, near the conclusion of his first and only term. The embattled president had met privately with directors of New York Stock Exchange earlier in 1932 in an unsuccessful effort to enlist their voluntary support in reining in the bear raiders whom he held responsible for the relentless fall of stock prices throughout his presidency. During the four years of his administration, the Dow had fallen from a high of $381 in 1929 to a low of $41 in 1932, and Hoover steadfastly believed that the cause-and-effect relationship ran from stock prices to the condition of the overall economy—rather than the counter, and more generally held view, that stocks reflect the consensus opinion of the country's economic future. So refusing to acknowledge that a falling stock market presaged deepening economic woes to come, Hoover held on to the view that short sellers—market speculators who sell stocks they do not own in the hope that they can "cover" their sales in the future by buying at a lower price and pocketing the difference—were to blame. He believed they were flooding the markets with their sell orders and driving down stock prices to artificially low levels for their own profit, but at the expense of the broader economy. Although Hoover had long believed that regulation of stock exchanges was unconstitutional, he pressed Norbeck and his Senate banking committee to launch a formal inquiry into short selling, bear raids, and other perceived market abuses.

It was with only lukewarm enthusiasm, however, that the committee complied with Hoover's request and began the task of interviewing stock exchange officials, brokerage executives, and other market participants to uncover manipulation and other instances of wrongdoing. The stock market crash was now three years distant, and Wall Street reform was not the foremost issue for the average citizen. Even before the crash, fewer than 2 percent of adult Americans owned stock. Yet in 1932, a quarter of those adults were unemployed and another significant number had lost their life's savings in a bank failure or crop failure, and there seemed to be no end in sight to a deepening social and economic malaise. Newspapers barely covered the hearings. The topical image of the day was no longer the floor of the stock exchange, but rather soup kitchens, lines around busted banks, and dust bowls in the heartland.

Carter Glass, now the ranking member of the Senate Finance Committee with a term as secretary of the Treasury under Woodrow Wilson behind him, had little interest in the hearings and little confidence they would go anywhere. And when they got under way in early 1932, with NYSE president Whitney as the committee's first witness, Glass's skepticism seemed well-justified. Whitney, supremely arrogant yet highly knowledgeable about the workings of the stock market, easily deflected Norbeck's questions. Republican Norbeck, a former well-driller whose primary accomplishment during his time in Washington was the erection of the Mount Rushmore monument in his home state of South Dakota, admitted that he was a neophyte in financial matters and not the ideal person to lead an investigation into the ways of Wall Street. At one point during Norbeck's tepid questioning of Whitney, a weary Senator Glass offered, "Mr. Whitney, I am beginning to wonder what we are here for."[3]

Part of the reason the hearings fizzled later in 1932 was the realization in Congress that the political landscape would undergo radical change following Franklin Roosevelt's increasingly certain landslide victory during that year's presidential campaign. During the course of the campaign Roosevelt talked of reform of the financial establishment and the need for greatly broadened disclosures in connection with the sale of securities. Assessing the new political climate with a Democratic White House and Congress, Norbeck—a self-described "prairie Republican" and one of the few from his party who was reelected in the 1932 election—began to search for a more forceful lead counsel for his investigative committee, one who would be better suited to Roosevelt's reform-minded agenda. But after several of Norbeck's early choices for the position proved unsuitable or turned him down, and with time running out in the lame duck period between changes in the administration, he reconciled himself to finding someone who would merely summarize the 1932 hearings rather than continue them in 1933. In what became the most consequential decision of his political career, Norbeck called Ferdinand Pecora to gauge his interest in a few months' work directing the banking committee's closing work and summarizing its proceedings.

When Pecora picked up the phone at his Riverside Drive apartment in upper Manhattan on January 22, 1933, he was caught unaware by Senator Norbeck's proposition that he serve as the new chief counsel to wrap up the hearings. Pecora, a former assistant district attorney for the State of New York, knew vaguely about the hearings, which had begun with some fanfare nearly a year earlier. But in the intervening months, news of their deliberations had faded from the headlines; when Norbeck called, Pecora was not even aware the hearings were still under way. Nonetheless, he immediately told the senator he was interested.

Pecora, a longtime Tammany Hall Democrat, was an odd candidate for the job. As a prosecutor for New York, his experience in the world of finance was limited to bringing to justice the owners of bucket shops— essentially, fly-by-night bookie operations that handled bets based on the prices of stocks and commodities. His reputation as a hardworking lawyer with a high success rate in the courtroom was well deserved, but his knowledge of finance was limited and, unlike his predecessors in the position, he had never been associated with any of the Wall Street firms that conducted a sophisticated business or securities practice. Yet to Norbeck, Pecora's immediate and high level of interest in the job quickly overcame his apparent lack of directly relevant experience. Within days of the senator's call, Pecora was on a train from New York to Washington and in Norbeck's Capitol Hill office to accept the appointment.

Personal considerations no doubt played a role in Pecora's interest in the job. His failed attempt in 1930 to secure the Democratic nomination for district attorney cut short his prosecutorial career and precipitated a move into private practice. Yet he liked the limelight of politics and relished the prospect of seeking another office. The public exposure he would enjoy from the Senate hearings could only help toward that end. So he jumped at the opportunity, even though he would have to move temporarily to Washington, D.C., and the committee counsel position paid just $255 per month—about half of his compensation at the law firm where he was working. Even though closing down the Hoover-initiated hearings was not a task that was expected to survive long after Roosevelt's inauguration in March, the job could enhance Pecora's future prospects. All in all, Pecora felt that the upside of the position justified the cut in pay and some time away from his family.

But Pecora greatly underestimated how long he would be gone. In the course of wrapping up the banking committee's work, he discovered the Senate had provided for a broader inquiry than he—and apparently Norbeck—had assumed. Rather than being confined to short selling and other market manipulations, the committee enjoyed a far-reaching mandate to investigate the sale of new securities. Norbeck, whose prairie Republicanism put him at the progressive end of his party's pole, welcomed Pecora's revelation, and by February the committee, rather than terminating its work, was back in session and focusing on the origination and sale of new securities issues.

After Franklin Roosevelt was sworn in as president a few months later, the breadth of Pecora's work expanded. In his inaugural address Roosevelt lambasted the bankers, charging that "the money changers have fled from their high seats in the temple of our civilization" and promising to "restore that temple to the ancient truths." And to move more tangibly on the promise of his address, he urged Duncan Fletcher, the Democratic successor to Norbeck as the chairman of the Senate Banking and Currency Committee, to expand the committee's mandate to "include all ramifications of bad banking so that the government will be able to guard against their continuance and prevent their return."[4]

Fletcher and his committee widened their investigative scope to include financial and operating information about the banking witnesses they called to Washington for testimony. But Wall Street lawyers advised their banking clients to rebuff Fletcher's subpoena for such information, alleging that the committee did not have the requisite authority. Fletcher retaliated by obtaining enabling legislation from Congress to allow his committee "to make a thorough and complete investigation of the operation by any person, firm, co-partnership, company association, corporation, or other entity in the business of banking, financing, and extending credit."[5]

So the battle had begun—and would clearly require a much longer time commitment than Pecora had first envisioned. Yet it would be a battle that he relished. Pecora's tenacious personality and modest background proved to be ideal for the David and Goliath contest—here was a child immigrant from Sicily with a rags-to-riches story, taking on the titans of Wall Street. Pecora was short in stature and weighed just 140 pounds; he grew up in a coldwater flat and had a milk route in the morning and a paper route in the evening; he was the valedictorian of his public high school; and he received a law degree through part-time study while working as a clerk at a law firm—coincidentally just down the street from the House of Morgan. He had a resumé that played well at any time, but especially well with a Depression-era population looking for someone to punish for their misery. Wall Street titans may not have been the actual perpetrators of economic misfortune, but they were easy targets.

Business journalist John Brooks characterized the pompadoured Pecora as "three-quarters righteous tribune of the people, one-quarter demagogic inquisitor," and that makeup seemed an ideal combination for the task at hand.[6] In his interrogation of the lords of Wall Street, he tended to stir up populist ire against them for practices that were often not illegal or even unethical but easy for the public to understand and likely to breed the greatest amount of resentment. His manner of roiling of the waters, a technique he had honed well as a rough-and-tumble prosecutor, gave him a cloak of authority when he dealt with more complex and technical issues that were beyond the full comprehension of legislators and the public alike. Playing into Pecora's hand, the bankers, always flanked by lawyers from New York's most powerful firms, showed nothing but disdain for the cigar-chewing counselor. For the aristocrats of finance it became a wholly unfathomable experience, with merciless interrogations and sensational revelations dutifully reported each morning in the tabloids. But in later years, Pecora would be able to state without undue hyperbole that "never before in the history of the United States had so much wealth and power been required to render a public accounting."[7]

A Different View of the House of Morgan

A public accounting could not have been a more unwelcome experience for J. P. ("Jack") Morgan Jr., the controlling partner of the House of Morgan at the time of the Pecora hearings. Twenty years earlier, in 1912, the elder

J. P. Morgan had undergone a similar grilling during congressional hearings conducted by the Pujo committee in connection with the so-called money trusts of the day. Jack's father performed awkwardly and often unconvincingly, but nothing of great negative import came out of the hearings with respect to him or his business. Yet the experience was clearly traumatic for the seventy-five-year-old Morgan, and his family would forever link his death in 1913 to the toll the hearings took on him. Jack, a retiring and even more private individual than his father, could not have been looking forward to sitting across from Ferdinand Pecora.

Of course, he wouldn't have much of a choice. With the expanded scope of the hearings, Pecora was given much broader subpoena powers and his targets were no longer able to avoid testifying or handing over the requested bank documents. Stonewalling upon advice of counsel was not an option, and Morgan would have no alternative to directly answering Pecora's questions. And more important than the expanded powers were the energy and personality of the new lead counsel. Pecora was a tireless investigator. He worked twelve- to eighteen-hour days, directing the hearings by day and reviewing boxes of evidence by night, often dropping off to sleep beside the discovery documents with a partially smoked cigar at his side. He led the hearings with a large measure of confidence in himself and in the cause he was championing, and he was only too eager to take on the most hallowed name on Wall Street: J. P. Morgan and Company.

With a full-scale assault on the House of Morgan now the evident plan, the firm geared up for a vigorous defense. A retinue of Morgan partners and lawyers took up extended lodging in a suite of rooms occupying five floors of Washington's Carlton Hotel, where every evening they prepared for the next day's confrontation with Pecora and his committee members. The chauffeur-driven Morgan partners arrived in high style each morning for the hearings. This daily event drew a substantial crowd of aggressive onlookers at the steps of Capitol Hill, who—if they had passes or could elbow their way past the guards—stayed to view the proceedings firsthand in the chandeliered Senate Caucus Room. If not, they would have to settle for reading about them on the front page of the next day's newspapers.

The publicity and hubbub surrounding the meetings did not sit well with Senate banking committee member Glass. When he had engineered the passage of the Federal Reserve Act twenty years earlier, the hearings on that act were staid affairs; he, unlike Pecora, made no attempt to turn them into staged public spectacles. His concern with the current hearing's media frenzy was especially acute with respect to the interrogation of the Morgan partners, some of whom Glass had worked with closely during his brief tenure as secretary of the Treasury. Glass, like most other establishment leaders inside or outside government, held the House of Morgan in high esteem and felt that its partners were being dragged before an inquisition and vilified with little factual justification. He was the sponsor of pending banking legislation—including what would soon become the landmark Glass-Steagall Act—and worried that Pecora's grandstanding in the Caucus Room, especially when Wall Street's most respected leaders were testifying, could backfire and kill the bill. Glass preferred closed-door sessions with members of Congress and their staffs, and he was particularly critical of Pecora's decision to drag Jack Morgan into the fray as the star witness. Putting distance between himself and his fellow committee members with respect to the character of the proceedings, the outspoken Glass remarked, "We're having a circus here and the only things lacking are peanuts and colored lemonade."[8]

This comment was picked up by the press and only served to stoke the theatrics of the Senate hearings. An enterprising press agent for Ringling Brothers Circus seized upon Glass's remark and brought Lyla Graf, Ringling's circus midget, into the hearings during a break. After proclaiming that "the smallest lady in the world wants to meet the richest man in the world," the agent coaxed her to sit without invitation on Jack Morgan's lap.

Morgan handled the surprise advance with grandfatherly aplomb and engaged her in polite conversation.

> MORGAN: Why, I've got a grandson bigger than you.
> GRAF: But I'm older.
> MORGAN: How old are you?
> GRAF: Twenty.
> PRESS AGENT: No, she's thirty-two.
> GRAF: I'm only twenty.
> MORGAN: Well, you certainly don't look it. Where do you live?
> GRAF: In a tent, sir.[9]

The disparity between Morgan, the big-bodied plutocrat of Wall Street, and Graf, the diminutive tent dweller, provided a bizarre but vivid image. Chairman Fletcher appealed to the press to omit pictures or a description of the Graf incident in their news accounts, but none of the newspapers covering the hearing—with the exception of the *New York Times*—could resist. The incident was a political cartoonist's dream; the *Baltimore Sun* carried a depiction of a small Uncle Sam sitting in Morgan's lap with the title "Midget Gets a Thrill." The stunt humanized Morgan to an extent, but it also had the effect of promoting the hearings to an even broader audience. "I told you so," was Glass's terse response.

More substantial than the Graf incident was the media bombshell caused by the revelation that none of J. P. Morgan's twenty partners had paid income taxes in the Depression years of 1931 and 1932. Making matters worse from a public relations standpoint, Jack Morgan could not recall the years in which he had actually paid taxes. (It turned out that he had not paid taxes in 1930 either.) A practiced interrogator, Pecora moved on to another issue after establishing the nonpayments, letting the revelation play out in the headlines before Morgan's attorneys could show that, due to off-setting losses in prior years, the partners had no actual tax liabilities. There was no illegality and, except to those holding the view that the wealthy are duty-bound to make voluntary payments to the government, no ethical lapse. But by the time the Morgan lawyers regrouped and presented their complicated accounting explanation, the public relations damage was done.

However, the most sensational revelation of the Morgan testimony had to do with the firm's preferential treatment of certain high-ranking customers. This issue again was not strictly illegal at the time but certainly smacked of impropriety and elitism. The firm, acting in its role as an underwriter of common stocks, would purchase shares for its own account from the issuing company and then, much like a wholesaler, resell them to other investment firms for distribution. In some instances, a "when-issued" market developed between the time the firm purchased the shares from the company and the time the actual public distribution occurred, with buying and selling in that market reflecting the expected future price of the stock. In the stock market of the Roaring Twenties, that time delay often created a considerable gap between the price that an underwriter like Morgan paid and the when-issued market value, with the difference representing pure profit. The House of Morgan, holding itself somewhat above the plebian marketing function, did not have its own sales organization and did not deal with the public at large. But the Morgan bankers felt little compunction about sharing an underwriting windfall with a preferred list of the firm's friends.

In the instance of Alleghany Corporation, a railroad holding company, the Pecora panel determined that, in January 1929, the House of Morgan sold 575,000 shares to a list of 175 fortunate individuals at $20 per share when the same stock was then selling in the when-issued market at prices between \$33 and \$37 per share. There were no strings attached to the transactions, so the recipients of Morgan's commercial largesse were free to immediately sell the stock and realize a profit of around \$15 per share. With an average purchase of over 3,000 shares, profit realized from each Morgan bequest was close to \$50,000—a very large sum of money in 1929.

Similar instances of Morgan's disposing of securities at cut-rate levels involved the distribution of Johns Manville and Standard Brands. While testifying before the committee about those transactions, Morgan partner George Whitney (brother to NYSE president Richard Whitney) did his best to rationalize the practice by emphasizing that the individuals on his firm's preferred list were those who were sophisticated in business and could afford to take the risk of owning common stock. Pecora, with his characteristically acerbic wit, commented, "Many there were who would gladly have helped them share in that appalling peril."[10] It was plainly evident that membership on one of Morgan's preferred lists was less about an individual's willingness and ability to bear risk and more about the potential to return the favor in some way to the House of Morgan. In his memoirs, Pecora artfully referred to the presumed reciprocity as "the silken bonds of gratitude in which it skillfully enmeshed the chosen ranks of preferred lists."[11]

Beneficiaries of the stock allocation included a dazzling array of leading citizens, including government officials (among them former president Calvin Coolidge; the former and current secretaries of the Treasury, William McAdoo and William Woodin; and a former secretary of war, Newton Baker); chief executive officers of major corporations, most of whom were Morgan's banking clients (including Owen Young of General Electric, Myron Taylor of U.S. Steel, Walter Teagle of Standard Oil, and Walter Gifford of AT&T); the heads of business and political organizations (including the heads of the Republican National Committee and the Democratic National Committee, Charles Hilles and John Raskob, respectively); prominent lawyers (including Silas Strawn, former head of the American Bar Association; Albert Milbank of Milbank, Tweed; and John Davis of Davis, Polk and Wardwell); fellow financiers (including Charles Mitchell of National City Bank; Charles Baker of First National Bank; and Albert Wiggin of Chase National); and a collection of American icons of the day (including aviator Charles Lindbergh and war hero John Pershing).[12]

Whitney and his partners only dug themselves in deeper as they replied to dogged questions from Pecora about the firm's motives in bestowing its financial gifts. Pecora's after-hours diligence uncovered a number of pieces of correspondence from recipients who, grateful for Morgan's benevolence, made the mistake of memorializing their gratitude in writing. Morgan partner William Ewing wrote to William Woodin, who at the time of the stock distribution was president of American Car and Foundry Company and at the time of the hearings was secretary of war, explaining that, "There are no strings tied to this stock, and you can sell it whenever you wish. We just want you to know that we were thinking of you." In another transaction that made it clear that the bequests were a bit shady, a Morgan partner told lawyer Albert Milbank, "It probably is unnecessary for me to add that I hope you will not make any mention of this operation." And the recipients of the stock also left a paper trail that belied the Morgan defense that there was no intended quid pro quo, with Democratic Party leader Raskob returning his cleared check with a note to Whitney stating, "I appreciate deeply the many courtesies shown me by you and your partners, and sincerely hope the future holds opportunities for me to reciprocate."[13]

The disclosure of the preferred lists elevated Pecora to national celebrity as he reduced the reputations of much of the American power establishment. Some legal historians point to other Morgan actions brought to light by Pecora that were even more cynical but were underreported given their complexity and the difficulty of capturing them in headlines or succinct talking points. The formation of the utility holding company, United Corporation, for example, seems to have served no ostensible business purpose beyond producing outsized profits for the Morgan partners—and another list of favored insiders. J. P. Morgan & Company, trading on its then-impeccable reputation, was able to bring together a far-flung group of gas and electric utilities to produce a combined entity that had a value far beyond the sum of its parts. Moreover, the new United Corporation had a capital structure that included a set of options for Morgan and its preferred list of investors that favored them with the lion's share of any appreciation in the common stock price of the company—to the distinct disadvantage of United's public shareholders. It is estimated that for a $10 million cash investment at the time of United's creation in 1929, the Morgan investors reaped a profit of over $19 million by 1933 and, based on the options they held, a potential profit of $80 million. By contrast, the shares owned by the public shareholders would have suffered a potential diminution in value of approximately 25 percent.[14]

When the fiery Pecora challenged George Whitney on the "public purpose" of the United Corporation deal, the best the witness could come up with was that it was an opportunity for investors to diversify their holdings of public utility stocks. But in reality, as Pecora would demonstrate with his relentless probing, the complex corporate creation served to the detriment of the public shareholders and was little more than an artifice to add to the wealth of the Morgan group at the expense of the public investors.

Despite the continued protests of the Morgan partners to the contrary, the Pecora hearings revealed the 1933 version of the House of Morgan to be as venal as any of its Wall Street brethren and contributed to the breakup of the mighty powerhouse at 23 Wall Street. At the time the hearings commenced, Carter Glass's Banking Act of 1933—known more commonly later as the Glass-Steagall Act—remained stalled in the Senate. After just three days of Pecora's interrogation of the Morgan partners, however, the Senate passed the bill with a voice vote; the House quickly followed suit, and the president signed the bill into law as one of the first pieces of his New Deal legislation. The bill contained a number of important banking initiatives, including federal insurance of bank deposits, but for the House of Morgan the devastating provision of the bill was the requirement for Wall Street firms, including private banks such as the House of Morgan, to choose between commercial banking and investment banking. Some of the large commercial banks, seeing the handwriting on the wall, had earlier discarded their investment affiliates, and most of the major investment houses, such as Kuhn, Loeb, had only a limited deposit business or other commercial banking trappings and therefore were little affected. But for the House of Morgan, the integration of both forms of banking for its prestigious client list was an integral aspect of its business operation.

In arguing against the Glass-Steagall Act when it was proposed, Jack Morgan had spoken not so much about the dismantling of his firm, but on a predicted crippling effect on the economy:

> The question has been raised whether a private banker should be permitted to accept deposits. If we, for instance, should be deprived of the right to receive deposits which clients wish to leave with us, we should very probably have to disband a large part of our organization, and thus should be less able to enter in the future that important service in the supply of capital for the development of the country which we have rendered in the past.[15]

But as Pecora noted in his memoirs, "no disaster befell" when J. P. Morgan & Company restricted itself to purely banking and deposit functions and formed a new firm, Morgan Stanley & Company, to carry on its investment business.[16] And no disaster befell for the next sixty-six years, between the time of the passage of the Glass-Steagall Act and its ultimate repeal in 1999, when latter-day bankers, using arguments similar to those presented decades earlier by Jack Morgan, convinced Congress that the provisions of the 1933 act were harmful to the U.S. financial system and the overall economy.

Sunshine Charlie's Moral Hazards

The testimony by the Morgan partners before the Pecora commission made the best news copy, and the boost it gave to the Glass-Steagall Act's passage was clearly of lasting importance. But dramatic testimony by other Wall Street chieftains, both before and after the main act appearance of the Morgan financiers, served to lay the groundwork for even broader and farther-reaching securities legislation, including the Securities Act of 1933—the so-called Truth in Securities Act—and the Securities Exchange Act of 1934. And no testimony was more consequential to the creation of these two acts than that of Charles Mitchell, chairman of the board of National City Bank.

Mitchell was one of the first major witnesses before the commission, and when he entered room 304 of the Senate office building—the hearings were later moved to the larger Senate Caucus Room—he was entirely self-possessed. As described by Pecora, "Mitchell was an impressive figure, forceful, self-confident, and persuasive. He was then about fifty-six years old, a self-made man in the American tradition, raised to the financial heights by his innate capacity."[17] Indeed, "Sunshine Charlie" Mitchell had climbed his way from his modest roots in Chelsea, Massachusetts, to become president of National City Bank, which alternated from year to year with Chase National Bank as the largest bank in the country.

His path to success at National City Bank, however, was not as a traditional commercial banker but rather as an entrepreneur at the affiliated National City Company, a corporate entity formed by the bank to skirt state laws that banned banks from engaging in stock trading and other securities-related businesses. When Mitchell joined National City Company in 1916, it was just an inconsequential, four-person operation, but under his guidance it grew rapidly, and by 1929 it was the nation's largest investment company, with nineteen hundred employees working in sixty-nine offices in fifty-eight cities. By virtue of his success, he was named president of the parent bank in 1921, and for the dozen years leading up to the Pecora hearings, Sunshine Charlie's was the public face of National City Bank.

At the outset of the hearings he seemed to harbor few concerns about his ability to handle any questions the senators or their counsel might pose to him about the bank. He came into the proceedings with a reputation for riding roughshod over bank regulators and other functionaries of the government. When, for instance, the Federal Reserve tried to tamp down stock market speculation in 1929 by limiting the amount of margin borrowing available to purchase stock, Mitchell—himself a member of the Fed's board of governors—instructed National City Bank's lenders to go counter to the central bank's wishes by increasing National City's supply of "broker loans." Despite Senator Glass's move to force Mitchell's resignation from the Fed's board for that action, Mitchell's reckless disregard for prudent policy went without consequence, and arguably added to the dimension and devastation of the subsequent crash. Following the collapse of the stock market and the economy, Glass openly opined that Mitchell "more than forty others is responsible for the present situation."[18]

Yet if Mitchell had any second thoughts about his role in the nation's financial debacle, it wasn't apparent by his demeanor at the start of the questioning. He seemed blinded by an unrelenting high opinion of himself, oblivious to the public's increasingly jaundiced view of Wall Street and to the general uneasiness caused by the "bank holidays," which had ordinary citizens fearing for the safety of their bank deposits. The general public was mistrustful of "banksters." And while Mitchell approached the hearings cavalierly, Pecora had spent days and nights preparing for them by combing through the last several years of minute books of both National City Bank and National City Company. Pecora came into the hearings knowing that he had armed himself with enough damning information to level the unsuspecting banker.

Beyond being well trained in conducting the painstaking, behind-the-scenes work of legal discovery, Pecora—a successful prosecutor—was experienced in how to bring drama to the courtroom. In particular, he knew the value of painting an unattractive personal portrait of the accused early on in the proceedings. So on the first day of questioning, he established Mitchell's bona fides as a powerful banker who earned over $3.5 million during the three-year period between 1927 and 1929—while the average U.S. worker in pre-Depression 1929 earned around $3,000 per year and the senators questioning Mitchell just $9,000. Perhaps the public could have stomached that as an unavoidable by-product of a free-market economy, but the crowning indignity was the disclosure, forced by Pecora, that Mitchell had engineered an odious "wash sale" of stock. Mitchell, in the tax year ending 1929, entered into a sham transaction with his wife under which he sold her $2.8 million of National City stock and shortly thereafter bought it back at the same price, for the sole purpose of recording a tax loss through the arrangement. The declaration of that "loss" on his income tax filings resulted in a reduction of taxes paid to the U.S. government of over $500,000.

Pecora's beginning the first day of the hearings with the disclosure of Mitchell's multimillion dollar tax maneuver was akin to a boxer landing a near knockout punch in the first round, leaving his opponent reeling for the remainder of the fight. Mitchell then faced ten days of unrelenting questioning by Pecora—so severely damaging that, just three days into his testimony, Mitchell resigned his position as president of National City Bank, and by day ten, was the subject of a criminal inquiry into tax evasion. At the end of his testimony, *Time* ran an article titled "The Damnation of Mitchell,"[19] and before the year was out Mitchell was indicted by a federal grand jury for tax fraud.

After establishing Mitchell's venality, Pecora structured the two weeks of his testimony as a kind of morality play to establish the need for corrective legislation to prevent future abuse of naive investors by greedy bankers. Through his questioning of Mitchell, Pecora brought to light a system of perverse incentives—a "moral hazard" in today's terminology—by which the National City Bank's board of directors fostered large bonuses for top management at the expense of the bank's shareholders and, especially, its customers.

At the heart of the bonus system was a "management fund," established for the president and vice presidents of National City Company to provide them with a 20 percent share of the company's operating profits after the shareholders had received an 8 percent return on the equity they had invested in the business. So after the shareholders received that 8 percent return—a return in line with what an investor might expect from holding the common stock of a typical, conservatively run bank—the management team's formula bonus kicked in, with the top executives pocketing one dollar for every additional five dollars the bank brought to the bottom line. This participation in the "superprofits" of National City resulted in a level of yearly compensation far above the $25,000 to $50,000 range that was typically paid to the top management of major commercial banks. In Mitchell's case, he received, $1,056,000 in salary and bonuses in 1927 and $1,366,000 in 1928. In 1929, a year the bank lost money, he still received a total compensation of $1,108,000, with no "clawbacks" or other arrangements requiring him to repay the bank or its shareholders.[20]

The bank's one-sided compensation arrangement for its top executives led to predictable behavior. As Pecora summarized, "It needs no psychologist to see how, under such an arrangement, the officers must have been under the most alluring temptation to produce, in some fashion, those superprofits from which alone their own gains flowed. And bear in mind that there was no possible risk of loss of their own money to deter them."[21] With little to lose and everything to gain by subjecting the bank and its customers to rapid expansion and risky business practices, Mitchell and his well-incentivized lieutenants geared up the National City Bank's investment affiliate for all-out growth.

The other moral hazard that surfaced in parallel with a no-risk compensation scheme was a growing clientele of unsophisticated investors who would absorb, in many cases tragically, the downside of the risks to which National City Company had exposed them. Many of these investors were entering the securities markets for the first time, initiated through the purchase of government-guaranteed Liberty Bonds and then moving on to the more speculative investments that emerged during the economic boom of the 1920s. At that time, no organization was more aggressive in leading this newfound group of investors into these investments than National City Company and its "customers' men," whose mission was to expand the lure of quick riches to a growing American middle class.

One technique Mitchell favored for motivating the bank's salesmen was to take them atop a skyscraper and emphasize an expansive view of the potential market for customers. "There are six million people with incomes that aggregate thousands of millions of dollars," he would proclaim. "They are just waiting for someone to come and tell them what to do with their savings. Take a good look, eat a good lunch, and then go down and tell them."[22]

Of course, providing financial advice is not inherently bad, as long as the advice is given with the best interests of the client in mind. The problem with Mitchell's top floor marching orders was that much of this rapidly created sales force was untutored in the basics of responsible investing. Like Mitchell, they usually came from sales backgrounds outside the financial services sectors. As Pecora would later describe National City Company,

> The atmosphere, one notes, was precisely like that of any nonbanking large scale organization. There was not even a hint of recognition that, after all, these were not tangible goods such as automobiles or aluminum ware or Fuller brushes that were being sold, but securities, the

true value of which the public was in no position to judge, and which it purchased largely on faith in the integrity and presumed conservatism of the National City Bank.[23]

So with salespeople who see themselves as commission generators rather than investment counselors, and with a compensation structure that produced short-term commissions at the expense of well-conceived, long-term advice, the emphasis was on volume rather than quality. Many of the purchasers of National City's products were naive and unsophisticated, and perhaps just as many knew better but were consumed by their own greed. But whatever their state of mind, much of what the investors purchased from the bank turned out to be disastrously inappropriate or fraudulent.

At the root of the National City Company's inevitable problems—certainly for its customers, but eventually for its shareholders and the management of National City Bank—was its unchecked growth. In its early years, the company was content to serve as a retailer for the securities created by J. P. Morgan & Company, Kuhn, Loeb & Company, and the other reputable wholesalers of the time. But with a growing and aggressive battalion of customers' men under its employ, National City simply ran out of merchandise and chose to "manufacture," using Mitchell's term, its own products to satisfy the rising demands of its sales force and the investing public. By 1929, National City Company was selling more securities than were originated in that year by J. P. Morgan and Kuhn, Loeb combined.[24] Indeed, over the course of the ten years preceding the Senate hearings, National City Company manufactured or participated in securities offerings aggregating over $20 billion.

Unfortunately for its customers, National City's newly manufactured products were of a decidedly lower quality than the securities originated by the established investment banking firms and were sold with much higher than typical commissions. The portfolios of the bank's unwary customers were increasingly filled with second-rate securities, earlier rejected as too risky by other Wall Street underwriters. But the bank's sales force, ravenous for yet more high-commission products to sell, was largely unaware that they were selling picked-over merchandise.

In a further effort to keep the pipeline full, Mitchell and his investment bankers literally scoured the world for new products and found Latin America to be a bountiful source for securities offerings. During his questioning of Mitchell about those deals, Pecora zeroed in on the bonds that National City sponsored for the states of Brazil and Peru and for corporations such as the Lautaro Nitrate Company of Chile and the Cuban Dominican Sugar Company. The bank's customers knew little about those countries and enterprises and relied on the institution's underwriters to vouch for the creditworthiness of the issuers. But the information Pecora found in the bank's files about those entities often differed markedly from that contained in the bare-bones offering circulars the bankers prepared for prospective customers. It was never disclosed to the hapless investors, for instance, that Peru had recently defaulted on its prior debts. Or that the proceeds of the Cuban Dominican common stock they purchased would be used to bail out National City Bank from the bad loans it had made to that company. Or that the very future of Lautaro Nitrate's business was imperiled by the looming prospect of synthetically manufactured nitrogen.

Toward the end of his two-week questioning of Mitchell in 1933, Pecora asked his witness about proper disclosure:

> PECORA: Yes; but isn't the National City Company the largest investment company selling securities to the public?
> MITCHELL: I should think probably; but I would not want to make any boast about that, Mr. Pecora.
> PECORA: It would not have been unbecoming for the National City Company to have taken the lead in bringing about a change in custom with regard to putting out fuller information to the public?
> MITCHELL: We are doing it every day. We are issuing to the public today more complete information regarding the condition of the companies that we finance than we ever have in our history, and we are trying to go a very long way. We are trying to blaze a trail with respect to that.
> PECORA: When did you commence to blaze that trail?
> MITCHELL: I should say a year and a half ago. We have learned much. We have all made mistakes, and a man that cannot profit by it certainly is not very worthy. We are trying to blaze the way for investment finance into a higher ground than it has been.[25]

After Pecora had demonstrated that Mitchell and his National City bankers had been performing far below the high ethical levels expected of securities underwriters, he next established their involvement with an activity that was totally devoid of ethical standards: running investment pools. Pecora showed little mercy toward Mitchell or the other once-mighty financiers who found themselves unlucky enough to be sitting across from him at the hearing, but he was especially unmerciful when it came to the subject of investment pools, perhaps the most egregious form of market manipulation carried out in the frenetic stock markets of the 1920s.

Investment pools were created when financiers entered into secret arrangements through a "pool manager" to coordinate their purchase of stocks in well-known companies that had a "'story." After their purchase, they colluded to pump up the value of these selected stocks by planting rumors and bogus news accounts and providing stockbrokers with out-sized incentives to tout those stocks to the public. When the stocks' prices reached some level judged unsustainable by the pool manager, the insiders quietly bailed out, leaving smaller or less informed investors holding the bag. If those chump investors had purchased their stock on margin, they likely owed large sums of money in addition to holding the deflated stock.

After some definitional sparring between Pecora and Mitchell—the lat-ter preferring that pools be referred to more benignly as "joint accounts" or "syndicates"—it was demonstrated that National City Bank was an active lender to pool operators. What's more, the bank itself became the subject of a large and seemingly successful pool. With the aggressive Charlie Mitchell at the helm of the fast-growing bank, pool operators had an ideal "story stock." But the truly surprising revelation was that the bank's own invest-ment affiliate, National City Company, was the moving force behind the pool formed to manipulate the bank's own stock.

Mitchell had demonstrated some signs of cautious action against these activities; in January 1928, he'd gone so far as to have the stock of National City Bank removed from trading on the New York Stock Exchange due to detected manipulation. At the time, the stock was selling for $785 per share, already ten times its book value. From then on, National City Com-pany became the main trader in the stock, and its stockbrokers became its chief promoters. By the following January the stock had climbed to $1,450, and by spring of 1929 it reached $2,925—or $585 after a subsequent 5–1 stock split—only to fall to $21 per share, postsplit, in the Depression's after-math.[26] Pecora, with his tenacious all-day and all-night discovery work into the National City Bank stock pool, pieced together how the management of the investment affiliate generated enormous commission revenues and profits by orchestrating the pool's activities between several parties: its own brokers (who received "premium" commissions for sale of the bank's stock), market makers in the bank's stock at dozens of other brokerage firms, the "specialist" in the stock, and Dominick & Dominick, a well-known Wall Street firm at the time and the nominal pool operator.

In the same manner that Pecora eventually elicited an under-oath recanting from Mitchell of the misleading and inadequate disclosures to investors, he eventually coaxed his exhausted witness to a much-belated admission of the error of his ways with respect to manipulative pool operations:

> MITCHELL: If you ask me on the back-look I think finding ourselves often in what would be termed stock market operations, is unfortunate, and I would not do it again. As a matter of fact, I would rather look to the time when we would be completely out of that sort of thing. I do not believe that it is a thing that we should be doing, Mr. Pecora.
>
> PECORA: When did you first reach that conclusion?
>
> MITCHELL: Oh, at the same time that many of us began to feel the headache from that which had gone before.
>
> PECORA: Well, the headaches of some people have been so extensive they have forgotten when they commenced.
>
> MITCHELL: That is right.
>
> PECORA: What was the date when you reached the conclusion?
>
> MITCHELL: Oh, I should say in recent months, Mr. Pecora.[27]

A Board Chairman Profits from His Shareholders' Losses

No stranger to prosecutorial hyperbole, Pecora would avow in *Wall Street Under Oath*, his 1939 account of the hearings, that with respect to Mitchell, "Greed and irresponsible banking could go no further." And in a later chapter on Albert Wiggin, chairman of Chase National Bank, he was again unequivocal, stating that "in the entire investigation, it is doubtful if there was another instance of a corporate executive who so thoroughly and successfully used his official and fiduciary position for private profit."[28] Determining which of the two chairmen engaged in the greater amount of financial impropriety would be a close call, but there was certainly a case for Wiggin after his testimony before the Pecora panel.

Following National City Bank's lead, Wiggin had Chase National create an investment affiliate called Chase Securities Corporation. It conducted a much smaller business than that of National City Company but was not above manipulating the stock of its own parent bank to benefit market opportunists and insiders through investment pools. During the four years between 1927 and 1931, Chase Securities sponsored eight separate pools in the stock of Chase National. Some of the pools were consecutive, and some were overlapping, but all of its members were the primary beneficiaries of the increase in the price of the common stock of the bank from $115 to $283 between 1927 and 1929—just as the hapless investors who were not members of the pool were its victims as the stock fell. By the time Wiggin testified before Pecora in 1933, the stock was trading at less than $18 per share.

Like Mitchell, Wiggin objected to referring to the organized manipulation of stocks for the benefit of insiders as pool operations. He preferred the less stigmatized term "trading account."

> PECORA: Then if this account had been formed by a number of participants that would comply with your definition of a pool, you still would not call it a pool, even if it were a pool?
> WIGGIN: I would not like to call it a pool, no, sir.
> PECORA: What is there offensive about the term "pool," Mr. Wiggin, that causes you to shy away from it?
> WIGGIN: Just the reputation of the word.[29]

It turned out that Wiggin was even more sensitive to the terminology used in connection with short selling. During the course of Pecora's investigation, it was revealed that Wiggin and other corporate entities under his control had, while he was serving as the bank's president, profited to the tune of over $10 million through undisclosed short sales of common stock—with the stock being that of Chase National itself.

In July 1929, Wiggin, as the chief executive of the bank, could no doubt sense the impending financial calamity and the inevitable negative impact it would have on Chase. On that basis, he sold approximately 42,000 shares of the bank's stock short through one of his personal companies, with the objective of reaping a profit when he repurchased the Chase shares at a lower price to cover his short position. The speculation paid off handsomely, and it did not appear to bother Wiggin that his action was in direct contradiction to his job as the bank's steward. He was under hire to increase the value of the stock but had established a reward for himself for doing just the opposite.

Unlike Mitchell's tax evasion scheme, there was nothing strictly illegal at the time about Wiggin's short sale, but it set a new high-water mark for business impropriety. In his testimony, however, Wiggin would not budge from his position that a short sale actually was beneficial, since it provided "buying power." (When a short sale is covered, it creates a buying demand from the short sellers who need to purchase the shares in the market for return to the owners from whom they borrowed the shares in the first place.)

> PECORA: Then this short position commenced about a month before the more or less famous market crash of October 26, 1929.
>
> WIGGIN: It began; yes.
>
> PECORA: I suppose you made them because you read the financial skies and concluded that the trend was going to be downward in the value of the Chase Bank stock.
>
> WIGGIN: I do not think I was wise enough for that.
>
> PECORA: Do you think, Mr. Wiggin, it is a sound and ethical policy for a national bank to make loans to individuals among its officers or directors, either individually or through the medium of private corporations, to engage in market activities in connection with the stock of the bank itself?
>
> PECORA: I think so, as long as the loans are properly secured. I think it is highly desirable that the officers of the bank should be interested in the stock of the bank.[30]

Wiggin's testimony, depending on one's viewpoint, is either a cynical attempt to defend the indefensible or an illustration of how far self-delusion can be stretched by a desperate witness. But reaping more than $10 million in profit—of which $4 million was realized between September 19, 1929, and December 11, 1929—based on privileged information about one's own organization violates anyone's idea of responsible stewardship. In his memoir, Pecora gave Mitchell some grudging praise, noting that he lost a great deal of money through his personal investment in National City Bank and "went down with his ship in the hour of crisis." Wiggin, by contrast, used the troubles of his own institution to enrich himself, even to the point of selling shares into the investment pools Chase Securities had promoted. Even more egregious, he borrowed money from Chase National to "cover" the short positions he had established on his own bank.

Yet when Wiggin engineered his lucrative short sale in 1929, and indeed when he was testifying about it in 1933, he had done nothing illegal. Nevertheless, in a show of contrition, Wiggin later renounced the $100,000 per year payments the board of the Chase National Bank had bestowed upon him. But he never made a voluntary return of any of the $10 million short sale gain he had provided for himself and his affiliated "investors."

Another Look at Whitney's Perfect Institution

When Pecora accepted the opportunity to lead the Senate hearings in Washington in early 1933, he expected to be back home in New York after a few months. But the breadth and extent of the financial wrongdoing he had unearthed, along with the unexpected public attention, led to an extension of the hearings through the following May. By the time the hearings had wrapped up in 1934—and due in no small part to the revelations resulting from them—Congress had passed the landmark Glass-Steagall Act of 1933 to reform and restructure much of the nation's financial system and the Securities Act of 1933 to provide investors with full disclosure before they purchased new issues of stocks and bonds. But what the hearings also made evident was that market reform and regulation were necessary not just at the time securities were brought to the market but also after they began trading in the "secondary" market.

At the time, the New York Stock Exchange was the main location for secondary trading in stocks, and the responsibility for ensuring that trading was fair and orderly was left to the self-regulatory apparatus of the exchange and its member firms. But after more than a year of increasingly damaging revelations about pools and other market manipulations on Wall Street, the Pecora commission brought into question the assumption that the NYSE and the other stock exchanges of the day were capable of watching over their own activities. So in 1934, Pecora decided it was time for a second appearance at the hearings of Richard Whitney, the president of the exchange.

To say that Whitney resisted his reappearance is a vast understatement. When he had testified before the Senate Banking and Currency Committee as its first witness over a year earlier, during the pre-Pecora days, he had dazzled the panel of senators with his defense of the exchange's actions during the crash and its status as a self-governing entity. An urbane and confident witness, he welcomed and easily dispatched the softball questions lobbed his way.

But in 1934, it was clear that his return appearance would be very different, and he threw up every legal barrier he could to prevent an encore. When Pecora sent one of his aides to present a questionnaire to Whitney on the NYSE's business, Whitney responded furiously—and famously—"You gentlemen are making a great mistake. The Exchange is a perfect institution."[31] He was steadfast in his assertion that the exchange was capable of handling any necessary reform from within, and he backed up his resolve by mustering the NYSE's member investment firms spread across the country to gather political support toward blocking governmental regulation of their business. Their efforts led Will Rogers, in a typically trenchant observation, to remark, "Those old Wall Street boys are putting up an awful fight to keep the government from putting a cop on their corner."[32]

Putting a cop on the corner, though, is exactly what Pecora would accomplish, and it started with Whitney finally being brought before the commission for a second time. Little remained of his self-confident and condescending demeanor. He began as a grudging witness, unbending in his answers and his certitude about the ability and willingness of the NYSE to police its own affairs without the U.S. government's interference. Pecora was unconvinced, and through Whitney's testimony he created a record of the exchange's ineffectiveness in preventing or halting blatant stock market manipulation, including the infamous stock pools that were carried out on the floor of the stock exchange.

The success of a pool depended in large part on the trading acumen of the pool manager, who was often an NYSE "specialist"—the person who, ironically, is charged with maintaining the orderliness in the stock's trading on the exchange. In running a pool, the specialist would "take a stock in hand" and, acting through matched trades and other manipulations with conspiring investors in the pool, push the stock to price levels that had little to do with market reality. It was usually clear that a pool operation was under way when a stock's price became untethered from reality—but the fact that the stock was in play often had the perverse effect of drawing more speculators into the pool. Most outsiders—those who were not affiliated with the operator—probably knew the music would stop at some point and that if they were slow to react, they could be left with a substantial loss when the stock price suddenly returned to more reasonable levels. What they probably didn't know, however, was that the pool was under the "supervision" of one of the NYSE specialists.

One such NYSE specialist, Michael Meehan, was behind some of the largest and most notorious pools of the day. He was the specialist for Radio Corporation of America, one of the glamour stocks of the 1920s, and the organizer of two successful pools in "Radio"—successful, at least, to the pool's secret investor group who backed Meehan. But in his testimony,

Whitney consistently downplayed the importance of pool operations on the exchange (though some 105 pools involving NYSE-listed stocks were ultimately identified) and steadfastly denied that the exchange had any responsibility to curtail the manipulation that invariably enriched the privileged pool members at the expense of the public at large.

> PECORA: Is it easily possible for a group operating through the medium of a pool to exercise temporarily, at least, or for the purposes of the operation, a control of the market prices?
>
> WHITNEY: I will answer yes, sir; on the conditions . . .
>
> PECORA: The market price of a given security?
>
> WHITNEY: As long as the stock and their money hold out, yes.
>
> PECORA: Yes. And to that extent, those persons are able to exercise a control, are they not?
>
> WHITNEY: By bidding and offering, yes.
>
> PECORA: By bidding and offering. Now, what steps, if any, does the Exchange take to prevent that kind of control?
>
> WHITNEY: I do not know of any, Mr. Pecora.[33]

In his examination of Whitney, Pecora wasn't looking for a smoking gun, such as the House of Morgan's "preferred lists" that turned up in the prior year's hearings, but rather wanted to establish a record of the need for government oversight of the securities markets. To do that, he demonstrated repeatedly throughout his questioning of Whitney that the exchange's self-regulatory efforts weren't protecting the investor. In addition to the lack of strictures on market making, Whitney would ultimately admit that the NYSE and other exchanges offered little in the way of trading oversight and corporate disclosure for investors. While the recently passed Securities Act of 1933 called for full disclosure of all "material" information affecting the securities and issuers of newly offered stocks and bonds, at the time of issue, the exchange did next to nothing to ensure the provision of full and complete information on a continuing basis thereafter.

Throughout his testimony, Whitney avowed that his exchange was run by individuals of impeccable integrity and that the information provided by its listed companies was full and accurate, and he expressed dismay that Pecora made the presumption of dishonesty rather than honesty. In the verbal dueling between the two, the courtroom-hardened Pecora got to the heart of the philosophical argument with respect to regulation in his question to Whitney: "In other words, you would rather discover the dishonesty after it has come to light or after its evil effects have been manifested, than prevent the dishonesty beforehand?" Whitney's response boiled down to an Alice-in-Wonderland statement that since no such incidents of dishonesty came to the attention of the NYSE, it must not exist.

Yet dishonesty and its evil effects had come to light by the bushelful throughout the protracted hearings, and by the time they finally wound down in May 1934, it was starkly evident to Congress that a largely self-regulated Wall Street was not up to the task of providing investor protections in the secondary market. In the following month, Congress passed a piece of companion legislation to the Securities Act of 1933—the Securities Exchange Act of 1934—to bring regulation to the NYSE and other exchanges and to protect investors from a host of fraudulent market activities. Rather than specifying a long list of such fraudulent secondary activities in the 1934 act, however, Congress provided for the establishment of the Securities and Exchange Commission to draft rules on securities trading—and to serve as the cop on the corner for Wall Street.

Unsurprisingly, the new commission quickly drafted what were initially known as "anti-Wiggin rules," requiring that all corporate insiders provide regular information on their trading activities. Although Whitney did not believe it necessary, the rules of the 1934 act also required that companies with publicly traded securities provide full business and financial disclosures on both a regular and as-needed basis through the SEC. And, of course, antimanipulation rules were set forth to outlaw the activities that were the modus operandi of the investment pools that Whitney would never concede were operated at his perfect institution.

Pecora and His Foils in Later Years

Since he had such a direct hand in the creation of the SEC, Pecora would have liked to have been its first chairman. As he had observed when the 1934 act was passed, the legislation would only be as good as the commissioners the president appointed—and Pecora certainly had a high opinion of himself. But Franklin Roosevelt had a very different kind of person in mind and, much to the consternation of Pecora, appointed the SEC commissioners with the tacit understanding that they would choose Joseph Kennedy as the SEC's first chairman. Kennedy, father to future president John F. Kennedy, had enlarged his fortune by participating in the very pools whose cynical and manipulative practices Pecora had so effectively exposed. Enraged, but acting the good soldier, Pecora agreed to serve as one of Kennedy's commissioners, but resigned after just six months to become a member of the Supreme Court of New York.

Roosevelt probably made a good choice with Kennedy. Pecora, who was wont to refer to all of Wall Street as a "glorified gambling casino" and who was dubbed the "hellhound of Wall Street" by the bankers, was unlikely to promote the kind of cooperative alliances with the financial community that would be necessary for a smooth transition into a newly regulated Wall Street. By contrast, Kennedy knew the ways of the financial world from an insider's viewpoint—Roosevelt later commented on his Kennedy appointment by stating, "Set a thief to catch a thief"—and bankers and brokers could feel that, however controversial his appointment might appear, at least he was one of them.

As for Pecora's main foils, they took highly divergent paths following the hearings. The House of Morgan partners did just fine. Despite Jack Morgan's predictions about the resulting damage to the financial system that would follow the separation of investment banking from commercial banking, the ability of businesses to raise money in the capital market was little impaired. Nor were the finances impaired of those partners who had to choose between J. P. Morgan & Company and Morgan Stanley & Company as their continued place of business.

With the fortune he amassed during the early years of the Depression, much of it from insider trading in the stock of Chase National, Albert Wiggin became a noted art collector and benefactor to museums. Wiggin's counterpart, Charlie Mitchell, underwent an admirable and successful rehabilitation. Following the low point of his career (marked perhaps by the 1933 "Damnation of Mitchell" article in *Time*) he endured a criminal trial in which he was ultimately acquitted of tax evasion. During his legal ordeals, he accumulated a mountain of debts and civil tax liabilities that he could have extinguished through personal bankruptcy; instead, he took the more noble approach of selling his home and other real estate interests to make good on the full amount of his liabilities. He then started over in the securities industry and eventually became chairman of Blyth & Company, a well-respected investment banking firm.

Richard Whitney, however, experienced a decidedly different form of rehabilitation. It turned out that he had another persona, far different from that of the rational president of the New York Stock Exchange—he was also a compulsive and very unsuccessful market plunger. Behind his ostensible wealth, financial probity, and social pedigree, he was addicted to imprudent stock speculation and failed at one venture after another. In order to stanch his losses and meet his margin calls, Whitney began borrowing from any willing lender, including his brother, Morgan partner George Whitney. When willing lenders were fully tapped out, he resorted to embezzlement from his yacht club and, later, from the New York Stock Exchange itself. His misadventures landed him a ten-year sentence in the state prison.

As for Pecora, he remained an effective public servant but never again realized the fleeting fame he had achieved between January 1933 and June 1934 as the lead counsel for the Senate Committee on Banking and Currency. After a fourteen-year term on the bench of the New York Supreme Court, he attempted to win the mayoralty of New York City and had the backing of both the Democratic and Liberal parties, but came in second in a three-way race. After his loss he resigned himself to a professional life in a private law practice out of the limelight he so reveled in. Yet it would be difficult to identify anyone who had accomplished more in a year and a half than Italian immigrant Pecora. The sweeping New Deal securities legislation he was so central in creating fostered a much more level playing field for investors in their dealings with Wall Street. And with respect to the bankers and brokers, it is no stretch to state that he saved them from themselves.

Part II
Democratizers

Before World War I, participation by ordinary individuals in the securities markets was close to nonexistent. When J. P. Morgan & Company and the other major banks of the turn of the century raised capital through stock and bond issues, they turned to institutional investors such as insurance companies, trust companies, and a small core of very wealthy families that were, in effect, institutions. The great majority of secondary trading in those issues on the stock exchanges was between the same institutional investors or, more often, between the traders doing business on the exchange floors. There was no "retail" market for stocks and bonds of any note.

That would begin to change, however, with the sale of Liberty Bonds to a wide swath of Americans as part of the financing of World War I. Liberty Bonds were the initial capital market investment for the great majority of their buyers, and just when the government began paying off its debt at war's end, the country was entering the prosperity of the 1920s. The new industries and fast-growing companies emerging during that time provided an enticement for some investors to recycle the proceeds of Liberty Bond repayments into the stocks and bonds of new enterprises. But the experience of many, perhaps most, of those investors did not end well. If they did not become the victims of pool operators or the shoddy investment merchandise manufactured by the likes of Sunshine Charlie Mitchell at National City Bank, their investments lost much of their value following the stock market crash of 1929.

The good news about the plight of the early retail investors, however, is that there weren't many of them. There was a great deal of public interest in the ever-ascending stock market during the Roaring Twenties, but for the overwhelming majority of Americans the market was just something watched from afar. Unlike today, when over half of U.S. adults have a direct personal stake in the stock market, in 1929, at the height of the speculative frenzy, little more than 1 percent of the U.S. population was "playing the market." For the great majority of Liberty Bond holders, their patriotism did not extend to a reinvestment in American enterprise.

And it stayed that way for some time. The Great Depression and the austerity of World War II washed out any significant interest by Main Street in Wall Street—and vice versa. But the postwar prosperity and the expansion of a middle class with discretionary income led to a reawakening of interest in the securities markets from a new and much larger contingent of retail investors. Much of that renewed interest arose from the growing and more widely spread affluence in the mid-twentieth century, but some of it surely came from the investors' sense that they now had a better than fighting chance to do reasonably well by virtue of the New Deal securities legislation and the greater transparency and fair practice it promoted. With the creation of the Securities and Exchange Commission and the tough legal requirements for full disclosure in the sale of stocks and bonds, President Franklin Roosevelt could proclaim with some justification that the markets were now characterized by both caveat emptor *and* caveat vendor.

There is unlikely to ever be a truly level playing field for the Wall Street professional and the retail investor, but the investment firms that prosper long term when dealing with individuals are those that proclaim and actually practice fair dealing with their customers. And the firm that pioneered the customer-friendly model first and most successfully was the post–World War II version of Merrill Lynch. Chapter 5 describes how that firm, founded and led by the visionary Charles Merrill, adopted unheard of practices to gain the confidence of investors. Research reports were prepared for Merrill Lynch's customers, who were encouraged to "investigate, *then* invest" rather than speculate based on market tips, and its brokers—now called "account executives"—were salaried, usually college graduates, and all products of Merrill Lynch's comprehensive training program.

Merrill Lynch would later stray far from its core mission of serving the retail customer, but the firm and its many imitators were a significant reason for the surge in participation by small investors in the stock market. By 1970, at the end of the Soaring Sixties, over three-quarters of the trading volume on the New York Stock Exchange was accounted for by the retail segment of investors, and the number of U.S. households owning stock increased more than tenfold from that of the Roaring Twenties. This unprecedented movement to everyman capitalism was accompanied by a cultural shift in the American public's view of business and finance, and when *Time* magazine compiled its list of the one hundred most influential individuals of the twentieth century, Charles Merrill was included and properly credited for creating a "shareholder nation."

Despite his insistence on providing small investors a fair shake in the market, Merrill had a blind spot regarding mutual funds. He remained adamant throughout his lifetime that retail investors were better off assembling their own portfolios of securities under the guidance of his firm's account executives, and throughout his tenure as chairman of the board of Merrill Lynch between 1940 and 1956, he forbade the sale of mutual funds. That policy remained in force for many succeeding years, but a growing number of investors began opting for mutual funds as a safer and more sensible way to participate in the securities markets. The migration of small investors to mutual funds was especially notable during the tough investment environment of the 1970s and early 1980s, when those investors with battered securities portfolios increasingly ceded the job of investing to mutual fund professionals.

That common sense shift in investment strategy to mutual funds—few individuals have the time or inclination to construct a do-it-yourself stock portfolio—was bolstered by another major change: the abandonment by many corporations of "defined benefit" pension plans for their employees. Those corporations, as sponsors of such plans, used to guarantee pension payments upon employee retirement and took responsibility for funding and managing the plans' investments. Today, however, most company employees are on their own when it comes to retirement planning and fend for themselves through "defined contribution" plans, mainly the now-familiar 401(k) plans. Most individuals typically (and rationally) use common stock–based mutual funds—or the close substitute, exchange-traded funds—as the investment of choice for the equity portion of their 401(k) plans. As a result of the shift to defined contribution retirement plans, more than 50 percent of today's American households have a direct interest in the stock market, and that interest is mainly in the form of mutual funds and exchange-traded funds.

Mutual funds or ETFs are the right choice for most individuals for the diversification and professional management they provide. Furthermore, investing in the stock market, nerve-racking though it may be, is still considered the best way to fund a decent retirement or to realize other long-term financial goals. But from their inception, there had been a major drawback to mutual funds, namely the exceedingly high fees mutual fund companies routinely charged their investors. The combination of high commissions to purchase or sell a fund—the so-called front-end and back-end loads—along with stiff management fees, cut deeply into the investment returns the mutual funds' owners ultimately realized, making it more difficult to accumulate a sufficient nest egg over time.

Chapter 6 describes how John Bogle came to the rescue of the mutual fund investor. Based on the assertion in his senior thesis at Princeton University in 1951 that mutual fund managers provide no better performance than the overall results of the stock market—and buttressed by later academic studies and his own experience as a mutual fund executive that confirmed his assertion—Bogle launched the world's first index mutual fund for retail investors. At first derided as "Bogle's folly," his low-cost, indexed mutual funds—very low cost since minimal management is required—simply mimic the results of the Standard & Poor's 500 Index and other well-known market indexes. As a result, the users of those funds, whether for a 401(k) plan retirement or otherwise, have an economical means to capture the well-established benefits of equity investing. Due to "Saint Jack's" creation, investors on Main Street are very close to being on the same plane with Wall Street.

5

Charles E. Merrill: 1885–1956
The People's Capitalist

With a fervent belief in the small investor as the foundation of the stock market, "Good Time Charlie" made
America the shareholder nation.
                                        —TIME, 1998

Throughout the early part of the twentieth century, individual investors in
the securities markets were of two distinct—and opposite—types. At one end
of the pole were very wealthy and conservative investors who were usually
advised by one of the large banks. Their investments were made for the long
term and were chosen among secure bonds and, less frequently, the common
stocks of well-established rail or industrial corporations whose dividend-
paying ability was never in question. At the other end were the speculators—
often fancying themselves as operators—who purchased securities for
short-term gains, basing their decisions on tips and often participating in
pools and other price manipulation schemes. Some of the speculators were
professional traders associated with a stock exchange or one of its member
firms; others were amateurs who sporadically took a flyer on a highly touted
stock—usually with an unhappy conclusion. The only thing these two investment types had in common was geography. They both tended to live in New
York and other big cities. Middle-class citizens in America's heartland tended
to place their savings with insurance companies or, more often, with commercial banks or savings banks. Main Street had not yet met Wall Street.

That started to change with the advent of Liberty Bonds. Undertaken
by the U.S. government to finance the country's military efforts in World
War I, the celebrity-led, patriotism-themed campaigns to sell the bonds

covered every state in the nation and eventually raised $17 billion—the majority purchased in small-bond denominations by some eleven million citizens. When the war bonds came due, a small but nevertheless substantial minority of Liberty Bond purchasers reinvested the funds in other bonds or, less often, in the stock market. The Liberty Bonds became the gateway investment for a new middle-class investor and fostered a nascent retail securities market.

Two financiers seized the opportunity that the maturing Liberty Bonds presented: Charles ("Sunshine Charlie") Mitchell, whom we met in the last chapter, and the more laudable Charles ("Good Time Charlie") Merrill, whom we meet in this one. As their nicknames suggest, both were outgoing and optimistic by nature, and the early growth of their organizations— Mitchell's National City Bank and Merrill's Merrill Lynch—was due in no small part to their considerable abilities as salesmen. They were the promoters of "everyman capitalism," the new and uniquely American phenomenon of ordinary investors making direct investments in the stock and bond markets.

The Difference Between Good Time Charlie and Sunshine Charlie

On the surface, Mitchell and Merrill had much in common. Unlike the aristocratic financial chiefs in charge of most of the major financial institutions of their day, neither Mitchell nor Merrill came from wealth or from banking families; they were born in solidly middle-class homes, Mitchell in Chelsea, Massachusetts, and Merrill in Glen Cove Springs, Florida. Both attended Amherst College, and both started their careers in other fields before ending up on Wall Street. Most crucially, both men recognized that the Liberty Bond sales would have lasting effects on how people saved their money—and would potentially expand the customer base and profits for their respective financial institutions.

Despite the outward similarities of Mitchell and Merrill, the advice their institutions offered could not have been more different. In their pursuit of outsized profits for the bank and bonuses for themselves, Mitchell and his far-flung sales force looked upon the new crop of Liberty Bond-primed investors as sheep to be shorn. When the investor demand that National City had created exceeded the issues that originated from the leading investment banks, the bank began to promote risky securities that the reputable investment bankers wouldn't touch. And when the feverish bidding for existing stocks in the secondary market sent the stock market to irrational levels in the late 1920s, Mitchell chose not to heed the calls for restraint. On the contrary, he stoked the speculative fires by using his board position at the Federal Reserve to promote ample liquidity for the banks to make margin loans to investors to facilitate their stock purchases.

The advice coming from Merrill Lynch was far different.[1] In 1928, while the markets were growing ever more frothy with the influx of new money from less than sophisticated investors, Charles Merrill was sending all-hands notices directly to the firm's customers, urging special caution in their stock market investments and especially with respect to the use of margin account debt in financing them. "We do not urge that you sell securities indiscriminately," one letter said, "but we do advise, in no uncertain terms, that you lighten your obligations, or better still, pay them off entirely."[2] Evidently, many heeded his advice. Shortly before the onset of the Great Crash, Merrill could report with satisfaction that the firm's customers had greatly reduced their use of margin debt, and it is highly likely that they did better than most investors when the market crashed and then went into its long slide throughout the ensuing Great Depression.

The difference in the approaches to their customers—exploitive in the case of Mitchell's National City Bank, responsible in the case of Merrill Lynch—would ultimately shape the directions of both institutions and the enduring legacies of the two men. As a result of Merrill's policies and business philosophies, the average investor was finally offered the opportunity to participate in the securities markets with a reasonable prospect of success. With "account executives"—a term Merrill borrowed from the advertising business—carefully screened before hiring and then subjected to a comprehensive training program, Merrill Lynch transformed the image of the stockbroker from that of a fast-buck hustler to a professional. And the firm's service to small investors was greatly enhanced by the production of professional research to aid them in determining the merits of securities. The retail securities business evolved from one fueled by tips and speculation to one in which investors were able to intelligently "investigate, *then* invest." With vastly different business visions, Merrill Lynch prospered and National City Bank eventually disbanded its once large investment unit.

The retail segment of the capital markets, and in particular one that was fair and legitimate, is rightly associated with the rise and growth of Merrill Lynch. And Charles Merrill, with his forceful personality and commitment to the success of the individual investor, was the undisputed driver of this transformation. His story can be told through the three successive and distinct business ventures and business personas that he took on during his professional life: a scrappy investment banker who founded the original version of Merrill Lynch; a behind-the-scenes controlling shareholder who was responsible for much of the development and success of Safeway Stores; and finally and most enduringly, the visionary and chief executive of the second version of Merrill Lynch, one of America's iconic businesses.

Act One: Investment Banker for the Retail Trade

Following an undistinguished academic career that began at Amherst and ended without a degree at the University of Michigan, Merrill leveraged his personal contacts and engaging personality into an entry-level job in 1909 with the firm of George H. Burr & Company. At that time, financial services businesses were not easy to categorize, and many provided a mix of unregulated financial services. Burr & Company was primarily a "factor," meaning that it advanced money to retailers and other businesses that sold their wares on credit. Factors removed the collection uncertainties of credit-issuing retailers by buying the accounts receivable they created. Many of Burr & Company's clients were chain stores that routinely extended credit to their customers—but in doing so often suffered a liquidity squeeze while they waited for those customers to pay their bills. Burr & Company and other factoring firms removed the retailers' liquidity problems by buying their accounts receivable at a discount and then made money when the accounts were settled at full price.

Factoring was Burr & Company's primary business and served as Charles Merrill's introduction to the business of retailing. But not long after Merrill arrived at the firm, George Burr assigned to him the job of assisting the firm's clients in raising longer term capital through the stock and bond markets. Burr & Company was not alone in expanding from short-term financing into the securities business; Goldman Sachs and Lehman Brothers, for instance, had their nineteenth-century origins as buyers and sellers of the IOUs that merchants used to finance inventories and receivables. When those firms developed into more broadly focused investment banking houses, many of their initial clients were retailers with whom they had long-standing relationships, including R. H. Macy's, Gimbel Brothers, F. W. Woolworth, and Sears, Roebuck.

Burr & Company, likewise, focused on its major retail clients in its push into the securities market. Young Merrill, faced with doing an investment banker's job within a factoring business, found that he excelled at his new position, and it ultimately served as the nexus for the two elements that would shape his career and the eventual creation of Merrill Lynch: investment banking and retailing. While at Burr & Company, he negotiated and sold a major securities offering for S. S. Kresge, which at the time was a fast-growing chain of variety—"five and dime"—stores. And though Burr & Company would remain an inconsequential player among Wall Street underwriters, the Kresge deal gave Merrill personal visibility on Wall Street; by the summer of 1913 he had taken a job at Eastman Dillon & Company, a substantial and prestigious investment banking firm.

That relationship, however, was contentious and short-lived. Eastman Dillon, like other established firms, was interested in financing railroads and "industrials" and found little it liked about the emerging chain store business. Merrill felt differently and on his own had built a book of business in the emerging retail industry. Yet the new corporate clients Merrill brought in were shunned by the Eastman Dillon partners, and he soon realized that he was doomed to go nowhere at the tradition-bound firm. Following arguments with Eastman Dillon's managing partner over the firm's refusal to handle a financing proposal he had prepared for up-and-coming chain store operator McCrory Stores, Merrill resigned in frustration. Shortly thereafter, at age twenty-nine, he launched Charles Merrill & Company, with one assistant and his longtime secretary as his first two employees.

Before long, the company became Merrill Lynch & Company with the addition of Edmund Lynch, Merrill's friend and business associate, to the young investment banking partnership. Lynch, a former salesman of soda fountain equipment, brought little in the way of securities experience. But he was careful and methodical, and therefore an ideal complement for Merrill, who tended to be more intuitive and to jump at opportunities without full study. Lynch was comfortable with the operational aspects of Merrill Lynch, while the affable Merrill preferred functioning as the firm's chief rainmaker, scouring the United States for new investment banking deals and clients. Theirs would become a long-lived and fortuitous combination.

The early version of Merrill Lynch was never in the same league as premier Wall Street firms such as Kidder Peabody, Dillon Read; Goldman Sachs; or Lehman Brothers, and was nowhere near J. P. Morgan or Kuhn,

Loeb. But Charles Merrill was one of the few investment bankers of the time who understood the developing chain store business and could envision nationwide retail organizations, and as a result Merrill Lynch wound up as the provider of initial capital for the likes of S. S. Kresge, McCrory Stores, J. C. Penney, Western Auto, Walgreen Drugs, and—most importantly for Charles Merrill's second career—Safeway Stores.

In the first version of Merrill Lynch, however, the firm acted not just as a traditional underwriter and wholesaler but also as an investor. While other investment bankers purchased a company's securities with the intention of immediately distributing them to outside investors, Merrill Lynch and its partners, like today's private equity firms, typically took personal investment positions in the stocks of their clients and negotiated attractive stock purchase options as part of the firm's underwriting compensation. With the advent of comprehensive securities legislation in the 1930s, it became more difficult for investment firms to act as both principal and agent in new issues, but the formula worked well for Merrill Lynch at the time. By virtue of smart investing—and the ebullient stock market of the 1920s—Charles Merrill, Ed Lynch, and their junior partners had become very wealthy men, amassing a portfolio of stocks, bonds, and cash estimated at between $50 to $100 million.[3]

Through one of the best calls in the history of business, these men were able to retain much of their fortunes by unwinding their investment banking business just before the ravages to the stock market and the Great Depression set in. The partners of Merrill Lynch—as a result of extreme pressure from managing partner Charles Merrill—liquidated much of their common stock holdings in the final years of the Roaring Twenties. Between 1928 and 1930, when Charles Merrill was urging the firm's customers to lighten their exposure to the stock market, he was following his own advice with respect to the entire firm. With his gloomy—but correct—view in 1928 that the stock market was due for a fall, he not only sold much of the firm's stock holdings, he also transferred Merrill Lynch's six retail brokerage offices to another firm and quietly disbanded the firm's investment banking unit.

His decision to undertake a major liquidation was not universally popular with his partners, most of whom were more upbeat about the market than he—and also reluctant to face the tax consequences that would result from realizing gains as they turned their stock positions into cash. But Merrill, by force of personality as much as by the terms of the Merrill Lynch partnership agreement, had the ultimate say in the firm's business. And what he was saying in 1928 and 1929 was that the party would soon be over and it was time to sell. After getting nowhere with polite cajoling, Merrill put his foot down and, in a letter to junior partner Sumner Cobb, he commanded that the firm's portfolio of stockholdings, totaling near $50 million, be sold immediately, saying, "Nobody seems to give a damn and I don't like it one little bit. You and Ed know my feelings, and you must let me decide when enough is enough."[4] Merrill went so far as to use the power of attorney he held over Lynch's affairs to rearrange his vacationing partner's *personal* holdings of stock.

Of course, Sumner Cobb, Edmund Lynch, and the other partners would ultimately be immensely grateful that their leader exerted a heavy hand in the firm's well-timed liquidation. They wound up among a minority of Wall Street partners who entered the Depression years of the 1930s flush with cash and able to repurchase stocks at a fraction of the inflated values at which they were selling a few years earlier.

Act Two: Grocer

Following the winding down of its business, Merrill Lynch had shrunk to a one-office holding company, with Charlie Merrill and Ed Lynch serving as the two remaining partners and devoting most of their time to the oversight of a handful of large investments in selected companies, including a controlling interest in California-based Safeway Stores. But the two partners eventually took divergent paths. Ed Lynch maintained his business interests in the newly emerging motion picture industry, but most of his vast wealth and energies were directed toward country clubs and a life of hedonism. Sadly, his life of leisure was cut short by an untimely death in 1938 at age fifty-two while on an Atlantic Ocean voyage.

Throughout the Depression years, while Wall Street was in the doldrums, Merrill focused his interests on Safeway Stores. Upon the division of the firm's investments among the partners, he wound up with an ownership position in the securities of Safeway that was sufficient to wield operating control of the Oakland, California–based food chain. He was never a full-time executive of the company and had no official title, but with transcontinental flight just becoming a practical travel option, he spent as much time in Oakland guiding the development of Safeway's business as he did in his office in New York.

His time on the West Coast was much more satisfying than tending to his remaining business interests in New York. With the stock market mired in a long bear market, revenues from both the brokerage and the investment banking businesses had dried up. Between 1929 and 1938, brokerage commissions at U.S. investment firms fell by roughly 80 percent. And the investment banking business wasn't much better. Despite some pickup in the underwriting of stocks and bonds in the mid-1930s, another setback in the economy in 1937 put the new-issue market and investment banking side of the business on the skids once more. At the same time, E. A. Pierce & Company—the forty-office retailer that had assumed Merrill Lynch's retail business—hovered close to insolvency and survived the trading drought of the 1930s only through the lifeline of a $5 million investment from Charles Merrill, Ed Lynch, and other of their partners.

Safeway Stores, though clearly affected by the ravages of the Depression, presented a much less grim picture. Investors might stop trading securities, but families still had to eat. With over three thousand stores in 1930— the second largest U.S. grocery chain behind A&P at the time—Safeway enjoyed the scale and buying power to outperform, and in many cases to simply outlast, its smaller rivals. Moreover, the chain was in the forefront of a new model of grocery store, one that reduced labor costs by replacing clerks with customer self-service and eliminated traditional services such as delivery and credit sales in exchange for lower food costs.

Merrill delivered value to Safeway far beyond that expected of an outside investor. Using the deal-making skills he had honed on Wall Street, he attracted top managers to Safeway by designing compensation packages that tied their performance to ownership of the company's stock. He also negotiated a host of strategic acquisitions that expanded the chain's geographic reach and put his Wall Street experience to good use in effectively tapping the financial markets to support the company's growth.

But just as surely as Merrill's Wall Street acumen helped develop Safeway during the Great Depression—and continued to build his fortune in the process—the lessons he learned about running a high-volume, low-profit margin business sparked the seminal ideas for the second version of Merrill Lynch and the third act of Charles Merrill.

Act Three: Wall Street Retailer

While Merrill's attention was on Safeway, E. A. Pierce & Company languished. The firm stayed true to its goal of becoming the nation's premier retail broker. And as a result of its absorption of the six Merrill Lynch offices in 1930 and the acquisition of other smaller retail chains, E. A. Pierce had grown to be the country's largest stockbrokerage by the end of the decade. But in reality, the firm was just limping along and few of its forty offices were operating profitably.

At the time E. A. Pierce's partnership agreement was near its legal expiration in early 1940, liquidation looked like a sensible, and perhaps the best, alternative. As a result of continuing losses, the firm's capital was nearly depleted, and there was little relief in sight. With the seemingly endless economic malaise overhanging the country, securities trading slowed to a trickle on the New York Stock Exchange, and more individual investors were closing accounts than were opening them. Yet it was in that year, with E. A. Pierce and the rest of the securities industry on their last legs, that fifty-four-year-old Merrill decided to return to Wall Street full-time and take over as managing partner of the firm.

This time, however, he envisioned a Merrill Lynch far different from the firm that had gone dormant in the 1930s. The new firm would be recapitalized and reinvigorated with a business philosophy and operating style far different from the informally managed partnership model that characterized the investment banking world. He planned to transplant the organizational structure of a large corporate organization to Wall Street and to that end needed to make E. A. Pierce, already a sizable securities retailer, even bigger. He merged the E. A. Pierce organization with another large brokerage firm of the day, Fenner & Beane, to form Merrill Lynch, Pierce, Fenner & Beane. And with that, Charles Merrill became the majority owner of what was by far the country's largest retail sales force.

In its second life, Merrill Lynch emerged as a one-line business: securities retailing. Whereas the original Merrill Lynch made its money primarily from investment banking and investing in corporate clients, in its 1940 reincarnation the firm ceded the moribund corporate finance side of the business to the established investment banking houses and concentrated on the small investor. Investment banking made Merrill a very wealthy man, but from now on he would dedicate much of his fortune to a radically new business plan that had the individual investor as its sole focus.

Merrill was confident that he could duplicate Safeway's success at Merrill Lynch with a similar customer-focused business mission that entailed "bringing Wall Street to Main Street." His idea went counter to orthodox thinking in a business that saw quick profits and big deals as the path to riches—and in which "buyer beware" was the watchword for customers. Besides, the numbers of the retail sector of the investment business were going the wrong way.

Based on statistics compiled by the New York Stock Exchange, the number of U.S. households with active brokerage accounts continued to shrink and, at around one million in 1940, was substantially lower than it had been ten years earlier.[5] But despite the gloom that had prevailed over the investment business, Merrill, with the benefit of a decade of firsthand retail experience in the everyman business of food retailing, was sure that by regaining the trust of small investors Merrill Lynch would eventually succeed.

In addition to his high self-regard for his abilities and vision, Merrill, unlike the vast majority of his Wall Street contemporaries, believed that the regulatory changes of the New Deal were highly supportive of his retail-focused plan. For one thing, the Glass-Steagall Act of 1933, which separated the securities business from the commercial banking business, forced National City Bank, Chase National, and other commercial banks to disband their securities affiliates; now the business of the retail investor belonged solely to investment firms. Equally important, the fairness requirements of the securities legislation of 1933 and 1934 provided for a heightened transparency and truthfulness in the sale of securities to all investors. The new regulations were not going to immediately bring back the many ordinary investors who had been victimized by the manipulations of investment pools and insider information schemes of the 1920s, but at least the groundwork had been laid for an operating philosophy based on trust rather than suspicion. With the federal government's new set of rules and regulations, individual investors had the comfort of tough legal enforcement to back up the legitimacy of their transactions in the markets. Indeed, from the standpoint of the new Merrill Lynch, the securities legislation was a vital component of a marketing plan that would be based on restoring and maintaining customer confidence and a business model in which "know your customer" was a crucial requirement for success.

Merrill took the opportunity of an April 1940 branch manager meeting at New York's Waldorf Astoria Hotel to set forth his vision for the newly established Merrill Lynch. Merrill opened his speech by saying, "Although I am supposed to be an investment banker, I think I am really and truly a grocery man at heart. I have been in the chain store business, you know, ever since 1912."[6] Over the next two days, he and his partners laid out the particulars of a revolutionary new retail business plan that would blossom into one of the most successful American enterprises of the twentieth century.

The overarching theme of the branch manager conference was customer trust and a necessary reinvention of the sales function to earn it.

In order to make all investors feel welcome to do business with the firm, the so-called odd-lot investors—those who traded stocks in fewer than the standard 100-share round-lot denominations and were generally unprofitable and shunned by Wall Street brokers—were no longer discouraged from doing business at Merrill Lynch. From now on, Merrill Lynch would absorb those losses willingly as a front-end cost to nurture an investor loyalty that would prove profitable as the customers became more substantial investors in the future.

The treatment of the firm's customers, actual and prospective, switched from solicitation to consultation. Rather than using the typical hard-sell approach, with the customer being lured into a trade based on a stockbroker's feel for the market—or, even worse, tips—the assembled branch managers were instructed to bring the customer further into the decision making process, abiding by Merrill's long-used maxim to "investigate, *then* invest." That simple piece of advice became omnipresent in Merrill Lynch sales materials, and it was backed up by a research department, separate from the sales organization, that assisted customers at no charge in their investment investigations.

Much more often than before, the newly named account executive would be recruited from the ranks of college graduates, whose diplomas evidenced brain power and who were not beholden to the conventional thinking of the old-timers in the securities business. Since courses in securities analysis were not offered as part of a college curriculum at that point, Merrill Lynch developed supplemental training programs, and all prospective account executives were required to spend their first six months at the firm's New York headquarters learning the basics of the business. That, too, was a radical and expensive policy, but Merrill viewed it as a necessary investment for the quality firm he wanted to build. There was always the risk that the young and well-trained brokers would be hired away by a rival firm, but the practice continued with apparent success for many years.

But Merrill did not stop with the upgrade in the quality of the firm's account executives. He also radically changed the way they were compensated. Merrill was an early user of market research, and a study he commissioned found that brokerage firm customers were highly suspicious of the motives of stockbrokers. That led to a new compensation scheme in which the account executive's pay at Merrill Lynch was switched from the industry standard commission-per-trade basis to a yearly salary plus bonus. The main purpose of the change was to prevent commission churning, a practice in which brokers encouraged frequent and unnecessary adjustments in their clients' portfolios solely to generate commissions from the buying and selling of the securities. Providing fixed salaries lessened that temptation and reassured customers that recommended securities transactions were in their best long-term interest—rather than in the best short-term interests of the salesperson.

The determination of the account executive's pay package was made by the branch manager, whose role also underwent drastic change. Rather than being a commissioned producer with side administrative responsibilities for managing the branch office, he—or very rarely she—was now a full-time manager whose job was to run the branch for maximum productivity, including supervising and recruiting the highest-quality sales and administrative employees. The branch manager was also charged with acting as the firm's official representative in the geographic region served by his or her branch.

To alert the country and potential customers to these extensive structural changes, Charles Merrill again broke with the status quo and undertook a major advertising campaign. Merrill was a longtime proponent of advertising and had used well-targeted ads to attract investment banking business as far back as his days at Burr & Company—a time when the old-line investment banks were disdainful of as much as a sign on the door. Even at mid-century, advertising in the securities business was not widespread and still somewhat suspect. The New York Stock Exchange, employing that mind-set, imposed limits on the scope of advertising it allowed its member firms to employ.

Whatever those NYSE limits might have been, Merrill Lynch may have tested them with its large and conspicuously placed print ads. The firm put its full-page, education-oriented ads in the nation's major newspapers, the first being a six-thousand-word attempt to explain the securities markets on a single broadsheet. It was titled "What Everybody Ought to Know About This Stock and Bond Business" and read more like an academic primer than a punchy sales piece. But the ad became famous and ran through most of the 1940s, prompting about three million requests for reprints. It was a masterstroke that served to associate Merrill Lynch with serious and responsible investing. The ads caught the attention of the emerging middle-class investor in the post–World War II years—and a high percentage naturally gravitated to Merrill Lynch when it was time to consider the purchase of stocks and bonds.

Charles Merrill was the acknowledged mastermind behind the revolutionary new Merrill Lynch—now dubbed "We the People" and "The

Thundering Herd" by a still-leery Wall Street—and the firm became one of the most successful businesses and recognized brands on the globe. Sadly, a debilitating heart attack in 1944 limited Merrill's direct involvement in the firm to just a few years. After that time, until his death in 1956 just a few days shy of his seventy-first birthday, he rarely visited the New York headquarters or any of the branches. He remained the firm's chairman of the board and its major shareholder, but his hands-on management days ended with the onset of his illness.

The business he conceived, however, continued to thrive during his lifetime, and Merrill Lynch accounted for an ever-growing percentage of the trading volume on the New York Stock Exchange. And that volume itself was increasing at a fair clip in the 1940s. After a short fall-off in stock trading in 1941 and 1942 with the onset of World War II, business picked up in the later war years and, with the end of the conflict and the government no longer sopping up investment dollars to support the war effort, new stock and bond issues once again boomed. By the war's end in 1945, more than twelve hundred companies had their stock listed on the New York Stock Exchange.

Merrill Lynch prospered as well with wartime growth. In its first full year in business, 1941, the firm realized revenues of $8.6 million and a partnership profit of approximately half a million dollars; in 1945 the revenues had more than tripled to $28.1 million and pretax profits climbed to $8.8 million; and at the time of Merrill's death in 1956, revenues and pretax profits were around $70 million and $16 million, respectively.[7]

The firm accomplished that remarkable growth and profitability by staying true to its retail investor orientation, generally eschewing business with institutional customers such as insurance companies and pension funds, and limiting its investment banking business to selling new issues originated by other firms. By the mid-1950s the firm had over one hundred retail offices and four thousand employees, both measures roughly double the levels at the time of the firm's 1940 makeover. By the time of Merrill's death in 1956 his firm was serving nearly half a million investors and remaining by a wide margin the nation's largest broker.[8]

It was no surprise that Merrill Lynch's success attracted the notice of some of Wall Street's older firms, who transformed themselves into "wire houses"—investment firms with national branch systems connected at the time through telephone or telegraph lines. E. F. Hutton, Bache, PaineWebber, and Dean Witter began to more actively solicit retail investors across the country, while scores of regional firms headquartered in all the major cities served the small investor through their own branch networks. Data on the total number of retail customers the wire houses actually served in their early years is difficult to come by, but by any reasonable measure it was a good business to be in during the mid-twentieth century.

One such measure of the vibrancy of the retail business is the growth in the number of individuals owning common stock. As Merrill was winding up the business of the first version of Merrill Lynch in 1928, media accounts made it appear that "everybody" was buying and selling stocks. Stories abounded about stock tips passed to and from alert barbers, chauffeurs, and shoe shiners. But the actual figures show that the stock market was mainly a spectator sport at that time for the vast majority of Americans. Around 1.5 million people actually owned any shares of common stock in 1929, a little more than 1 percent of the country's population of roughly 120 million.[9] So it is unlikely that more than 1.5 percent of the adult population were stockholders. In 1952, however, when the Brookings Institution conducted the first "scientific" study of stock ownership, it found that the number of U.S. citizens owning common stock had grown to 6.5 million, with 1.3 million of those stockholders purchasing their first shares in the three years prior to the study. When the study was duplicated in 1956, the results showed even stronger growth, with an additional 2.1 million shareholders, pushing the total number to 8.6 million.[10] Looking at the numbers in a different way, near the height of the speculative fervor of the 1920s, maybe one out of seventy adult Americans owned stock; in the year of Merrill's death in 1956, that ratio became one out of twelve. By the end of the long-run bull market that extended from the mid-1950s until 1969, the New York Stock Exchange reported that approximately 30 million adult Americans owned stock, representing one of every four adults.[11]

While Merrill and the firm he created prospered, they also rescued the reputation of the investment business from its sordid state. The creation of a fair and legitimate retail segment of the capital markets was a singularly American phenomenon, and today, with roughly half of U.S. adults now investing directly or indirectly in securities, the United States remains an outlier as far as the percent of individual participation in the market. Merrill Lynch played no small part in this development, and Charles Merrill's biographer, Edwin J. Perkins, puts him in the pantheon of the world's most influential men of finance:

> As result of his achievements, Merrill's influence equaled the impact of all previous American financiers, including his only legitimate

rival, J. P. Morgan. In democratizing the stock market, Merrill created an enterprise that gave middle-class households access to a far wider range of investment opportunities. He truly brought Wall Street to Main Street.[12]

Though there are no reliable measures of the level of investment success Merrill Lynch's half-million retail customers actually enjoyed, the progressive and even-handed manner in which they were treated no doubt led to their prosperity as well. Charles Merrill's personal life had its share of imbroglios; with his flashy lifestyle and succession of trophy wives and extramarital affairs, "Good Time Charlie" was a fixture in the New York gossip columns. But with respect to his firm's customers, he can fairly be described as having done well by doing good.

Merrill Lynch After Charles Merrill

The Merrill name has always remained at the lead of whatever string of names would identify it over the years, but no Merrill heirs have had any significant participation in the business affairs of the firm since Charles Merrill's death. His older son, Charles Jr., has spent his life in education, founding and serving as headmaster of a private school in Boston; a younger son, James, was a novelist and poet. Both sons, while independently wealthy as a result of their father's success, showed no interest in a career in the investment business and, because he was somewhat dictatorial and difficult in his domestic life, they kept a distance from him.

A strong business lineage was carried forward, however, by Robert Magowan, husband of Charles Merrill's third child, Doris. Neither Doris nor Robert showed any apparent scarring from Merrill's strong personality or scandalous personal life, and Robert played an important role in the development of Merrill Lynch during the 1940s and early 1950s. He also gravitated to Charles Merrill's earlier business love, Safeway Stores, and Magowan and later his son served as able CEOs of the grocery chain through the second half of the twentieth century.

Merrill Lynch prospered through the 1950s and 1960s, remaining the country's largest and most successful retail brokerage operation by adhering to the tenets of its founder. To a large extent, Merrill's vision was preserved through a promote-from-within strategy, and the top management of Merrill Lynch was populated mainly with those who learned the "Merrill

Lynch way" by starting out as account executive trainees and working their way up from the ranks. A high-profile example of that path to the top was Donald Regan, who, despite his Harvard College degree and experience as a decorated lieutenant colonel in the Marines during World War II, started at the bottom as one such trainee in 1946. By 1971, he had become Merrill Lynch's CEO, a position he held for ten years before moving to Washington to serve as President Ronald Reagan's secretary of the Treasury and later his chief of staff.

When Regan took the reins of Merrill Lynch in 1971, the firm was not considerably different from the highly successful retail-oriented business that Charles Merrill had presided over a few decades earlier. But the scale of its business had changed, with the number of branch offices and account executives growing exponentially as Merrill Lynch became the main beneficiary of the widening participation by an expanding American middle class in the stock market. Arguably, Merrill Lynch was not just the fortunate participant in the growth of the retail investment business but, as a result of its relentless advertising and financial education programs and through its refreshingly responsible approach to customer service, was itself one of the reasons for that growth.

Whatever its larger role in the securities industry, through the 1960s Merrill Lynch had prospered by remaining true to its single-minded mission of providing high-quality retail brokerage services. But in the 1970s, under the guidance of Regan, the soul of the firm began to change with two new and interrelated strategies: raising large amounts of capital and diversifying its operations beyond a retail focus. First, the company converted from a partnership to a corporation and later launched an initial public offering, becoming the second investment firm to go public and the first member firm to have its own shares listed on the New York Stock Exchange.

Regan had earlier bemoaned the difficulties of managing a partnership and the near impossibility of raising growth capital in that format. In his memoirs he wrote, "I can recall myself the day when Merrill Lynch had 117 partners. That made for a huge and unwieldy kind of organization, and whenever there was a need for additional capital the managing partner would go around to each of the partners and ask for additional capital contributions in order to finance Merrill Lynch's growing business."[13] Public ownership, in Regan's view, served as a solution to both the management and capital impediments of a partnership form of organization. By dint of its 1971 initial public offering, Merrill gained access to large amounts of external capital and became the largest investment firm in the world—no longer just in terms of employees but also in terms of its balance sheet.

With capital no longer a constraint, Merrill Lynch, over the less than glorious remainder of its history, widened its mission far beyond retail brokerage and launched a diversification strategy aimed at expanding Merrill Lynch into a "financial supermarket." During the Regan years of the 1970s, Merrill Lynch entered the insurance business by buying the Family Life Insurance Company, and then, with a string of real estate–related acquisitions, it became a major presence in real estate brokerage, relocation services, and mortgage finance.

In addition to acquisitions, the firm also pursued an internal diversification program, making major pushes into institutional sales, trading, and investment banking. The aim of the investment banking initiative was to garner underwriting business by convincing corporate CFOs that Merrill Lynch's vast retail *and* institutional sales capabilities would enhance the success of new public offerings. It was a sales pitch that worked well and put the firm among the top underwriters of new issues.

However, the Merrill Lynch name still did not have the cachet of the more prestigious, relationship-based securities originators such as Goldman Sachs, Morgan Stanley, or First Boston. Merrill Lynch was typically brought in as a comanager of a deal, forgoing the greater prestige and higher fees of the "book running" managing underwriter. In an attempt to remedy that situation, Regan engineered the acquisition in 1977 of White, Weld & Company, an old-line investment banking house. Merrill Lynch was only marginally successful in retaining the more talented members of that white-shoe firm, but the acquisition did set in motion a program to recruit and develop its own high-quality investment bankers.

In the 1980s, under the direction of a new chief executive, William Shreyer, the firm shed its real estate–related businesses and launched a major international initiative and doubled down on its investment banking and trading operations. That strategy was generally successful but had its share of ups and downs. Presaging the Wall Street–wide excesses that led to the 2008 financial crisis, in 1987 Merrill Lynch lost a Wall Street record $377 million in one day on ill-conceived mortgage banking trades. And then, in 1994, it entered into a $437 million settlement with Orange County, California, in connection with derivative trades gone bad. It became a byword on Wall Street that "whenever there was a calamity, Merrill Lynch was there." But despite the missteps, by the beginning of the twenty-first century Merrill Lynch had become a powerful global securities firm. It sat atop the rankings of investment bankers in terms of new underwritings and established a major presence in wealth management. The firm earned handsome returns on its shareholders' investment and the price of its stock soared to an all-time high by the beginning of 2001.

Unfortunately, things changed later in that year when Stan O'Neal was appointed president and soon thereafter CEO. In what ultimately resulted in the end of Merrill Lynch's independence, the firm grew prone to taking big risks. Unlike Charles Merrill, who sized up Wall Street's risks during the 1920s and went directly counter to most other firms, O'Neal and his new management team had a follower mind-set. Like many of the other major Wall Street firms, Merrill Lynch loaded up its balance sheet with the exotic mortgage-backed securities that would shortly become "toxic assets." Soon after its marriage of convenience with Bank of America, those assets ultimately required the bank to take an extra $20 billion from the Troubled Asset Relief Program to handle its Merrill Lynch–related problems as part of the U.S. government's 2008 Wall Street bailout.

Charles Merrill would not have been happy to see what happened to his creation. Under the direction of the empire-building management that followed him, the last several decades saw a transformation of Merrill Lynch from a dominant retail brokerage business into an unwieldy and unfocused financial conglomerate. The new version of the firm now occupies a backseat in the "big city, bright lights" businesses of investment banking and trading, while its retail operation, having long abandoned customer confidence-building initiatives such as a salaried sales staff, is just another financial services provider under the umbrella of Bank of America. Its account executives, who at one time set the industry standard, are no better or worse in the public's eye than the rest of the salespeople in the investment business.

In the end, the plight of Merrill Lynch confirms the Bogle rule, set forth by John Bogle, who is the subject of this book's next chapter: "When an institution goes down, one condition may always be found: It forgot where it came from."[14]

© Bogle Financial Markets Research Center

6

John C. Bogle: 1929–
Saint Jack

The honest steward who charges least, wins most. But not for himself; for those investors who entrust their assets to his care. It is not all that complicated.

—JOHN C. BOGLE

Savvy stock market investors put their focus on costs. They can't control the ups and downs of the market, but short-term price movements aren't of great concern for investors who are in it for the long haul. They have faith that the age-old upward trajectory of market prices will continue and that their patience will ultimately be rewarded with attractive investment returns.

Costs are a different story. They are killers when it comes to long-term results. Commissions, advisory fees, management fees, administrative costs, and taxes all add up, year in and year out, to undermine investment success. But unlike the stock market, they are *very* controllable, and the tight-fisted investor who keeps them in check will inevitably do well.

For most of the twentieth century, however, investing in the stock market was an unavoidably expensive proposition. Charles Merrill was the great friend of the small investor, yet Merrill Lynch—like Wall Street in general—was a costly place for the retail investor to do business. That state of affairs changed dramatically for the better due to two events that took place on May 1, 1975.

The Mayday Revolutions

One of the May 1, 1975 events was the abandonment by the New York Stock Exchange of its fixed-commission schedule. Since the exchange's founding in 1792, the NYSE had forbidden the investment firms that traded on its floor from charging their customers a commission below its published rate schedule. But after many years of protests from investors, primarily from the large institutional investors, the Securities and Exchange Commission finally ordered an end to the practice—busting the cartel-like system that had set artificially high rates for almost two centuries.

The securities industry predicted that Mayday, as it became known among brokers, would mark the demise of its business by removing the crutch of dictated rates. And while hundreds of weak firms eventually failed or merged as commissions plummeted in a newly free market, a vibrant new kind of discount broker soon emerged to take up the slack. With now-familiar names such as Schwab, Scottrade, and TD Ameritrade, these discount brokers moved in quickly to become a new sector in the securities industry. Many had electronic trading platforms and promoted cut-rate costs for the small investor. The retail investor, in fact, was the primary beneficiary of the Mayday dictate from the Securities and Exchange Commission—institutional investors had already figured out how to avoid fixed fees through "soft-dollar" arrangements and operating in the "third market"—as the average commission cost per share of stock traded fell dramatically, from 80 cents per share before Mayday to around 4 cents per share in recent years.

The other Mayday event, one that would ultimately prove equally momentous for individual investors, was the founding of the Vanguard Group by John "Jack" Bogle. While the elimination of the NYSE's fixed-commission schedule made headline news, Bogle's new company went unnoticed. The mutual fund business had reached a level of maturity and acceptance, and there were already 389 mutual funds available in the market. But the mutual fund the Vanguard Group would shortly launch would have a radically different approach than the 389 funds that had preceded it: it would not try to beat the market, just to match it.

The claim to fame for the typical mutual fund in 1975 was "superior performance," measured by the investment return it provided to the fund's shareholders as compared to some benchmark return, such as the Standard & Poor's 500 Index. Today, this type of mutual fund is referred to as "actively managed," and these funds search for success by hiring the best and brightest available research analysts, portfolio managers, and traders in an attempt to outperform the market. The costs of this talent—all borne by the funds' investors—are necessarily steep.

Bogle's new approach was shockingly different. Based on his well-supported view that few, if any, fund managers are able to consistently beat the market, the goal of his new fund was to merely *match* market performance rather than try to exceed it. The strategy is simplicity itself, since it is just a duplication of the S&P 500's investment results. That task requires no expensive investment talent, just a computer and a competent programmer, and is now referred to as "passive management." Passive management has built-in economies of scale, with the fixed costs, moderate as they are, spread across more shareholders as the fund grows. Cost control, not stock-picking prowess, is the key to success of an index fund.

Immediately after the First Index Investment Trust was rolled out in 1976, it became the subject of widespread derision. There was something un-American about a fund that aspired to be just average, and the dean of mutual funds at the time—Edwin Johnson III, head of the Fidelity Fund—said aloud what most competitors likely thought: "I can't believe that the great mass of investors are going to be satisfied with an ultimate goal of just achieving average returns on their funds."[1] The index fund was referred to as "Bogle's folly," and not given much chance of success. But the idea had been germinating in Bogle's mind since he was a college student twenty-five years earlier at Princeton University. He continued to believe the idea had merit and forged ahead with his low-cost idea despite skepticism from the mutual fund establishment.

Madly in Love with Mutual Funds

It was not a foregone conclusion that Bogle would ever go to college, much less Princeton. When he was born in May 1929, his family was prosperous. But things soon changed, beginning with the stock market crash later that year, which wiped out much of the family's wealth. The ensuing Depression deepened their problems. The family spiraled toward poverty, moving often, and always into progressively less desirable housing. Young Jack and his two brothers worked throughout their school years to keep the family afloat, and he held jobs ranging from paperboy to bowling alley pinsetter. With the benefit of scholarships and financial assistance from an uncle, however, all three boys were able to attend boarding school at the prestigious Blair Academy in northwestern New Jersey.

But college was a different story, and only Jack—by far the best student among his siblings—could be spared from the need to support the struggling family. So his brothers stayed home and Jack went to Princeton, helped by a scholarship and part-time work waiting tables in the university's Commons. Determined to justify his good fortune, he worked hard at Princeton and did well, including the receipt of an A+ grade on a senior thesis titled *The Economic Role of the Investment Company*. Bogle chose the thesis topic somewhat by chance after reading a 1949 *Fortune* magazine article on the emerging mutual fund business that he came upon in Princeton's Firestone Library. But during his thesis research, Bogle "fell madly in love" with the mutual fund industry—an industry to which he would devote his long career and that he would eventually transform.[2]

A mutual fund is a basket of a large and diverse group of securities—sometimes bonds, sometimes stocks, and sometimes a combination of the two. By purchasing a fund, investors hope to achieve the kind of diversification and expertise that they could not achieve on their own. Mutual funds, however, were not often the investment of choice when Bogle entered that industry in 1951, right out of school. Charles Merrill, for one, was a lifelong skeptic about the value of mutual funds and did not allow Merrill Lynch's account executives to sell them during his 1940 to 1956 tenure atop the nation's largest retail brokerage firm. Merrill was sincere and conscientious about treating the retail investor fairly, yet he felt that his well-selected and well-trained account executives, aided by quality investment research, could tailor a securities portfolio to the unique requirements of the firm's customers.

But over time, the virtues of mutual fund investing prevailed, as the expanding middle class found the stock market to be an enticing place for savings and mutual funds to be a sensible investment vehicle. Investors came to realize that while an individual and his advisor can, in theory, construct a portfolio with the same amount of diversification as a mutual fund, it's hard to do in practice—and isn't very likely to happen. Also in theory, individuals, with the aid of good research, can pick stocks and bonds as ably as a mutual fund's professional managers—but that's even less likely to happen, and individual investors, on the whole, are not successful stock pickers.

And as institutional investors gained prominence in the stock market in the latter part of the twentieth century, the challenge to the retail investor choosing to go it alone only grew more formidable. In an interview with *Institutional Investor*, the legendary institutional money manager and market commentator, Charles Ellis, offered a graphic view of the retail investor's plight:

> Retail investors make certain characteristic mistakes repetitively. Today over 80 percent of the transactions are done by institutional investors. Now, these people are different. Smart, competitive, tough, they work all day, every day—weekends and nights—getting ready in advance to be on the other side of each and every one of your transactions. So when the retail investor says, "I intend to beat the market," the market he is talking about is not some neutered beast; it's the sum of all the smartest, toughest minds in this business. When you come to market to sell, the only buyers you'll find are the ones who are thrilled that you just came into the cross hairs on their sniper scopes.[3]

Aside from anecdotal evidence such as that offered above, there is also, thanks to the fast-growing field of behavioral economics, ample evidence that individuals acting alone make poor investors. University of California finance professors Brad Barber and Terry Odean painstakingly tracked the trades of ten thousand retail investors over a six-year period between 1991 and 1997, looking for instances in which one stock was sold and shortly thereafter another was bought in its place. The investors, as a whole, realized returns that were spectacularly bad, approximately 3.3 percent lower per year than if they had simply held on to their original investments.[4]

Yet the arguments for holding common stocks still remain compelling. Over any sufficiently long period, common stocks provide investors with highly attractive returns, and those investors with the patience and stomach to ride out the inevitable ups and downs of the markets are generously rewarded. So despite the cynical aphorism in the investment business that mutual funds are "sold not bought," a professionally managed mutual fund is a good choice for retail investors. Buying a fund is the logical if-you-can't-beat-them-join-them investment strategy. Nowadays, buoyed by the advent of 401(k) plans, about half of all Americans own common stocks. Some 401(k) participants own stocks directly, but the preponderance own stocks indirectly through mutual funds. And Jack Bogle has been along for the entire ride.

Whiz Kid Years

A mutual fund–based strategy of common stock investing eventually caught fire with Americans in the latter half of the twentieth century, but when Bogle joined Philadelphia-based Wellington Fund in 1951—his first job after college and one that he got based on the strength of his senior thesis—the amount of savings of U.S. households dedicated to mutual funds was tiny. Families were more inclined to put their investment money into life insurance programs, savings deposits at the bank, or U.S. savings bonds. The total amount of savings in those three savings programs was $178 billion; by contrast, just $3 billion of savings were invested in mutual funds.[5]

It didn't take long for Bogle, ambitious and talented, to become the heir apparent to the Wellington Fund's founder, Walter Morgan, and Bogle's close relationship with Morgan gave him much influence regarding the direction of the firm. By 1958, when he was just twenty-nine, he convinced Morgan to establish a new all-equity fund, later to be called the Windsor Fund. The Wellington Fund, like most of the substantial mutual funds at that time, was "balanced," meaning that it invested in both stocks and bonds. The idea of creating a family of funds under one management company, each with a separate set of investment policies such as the common stock-focused Windsor Fund, is common today, but was novel in the 1950s.

The Windsor Fund enjoyed early success, but it remained dwarfed by the Wellington Fund, and Bogle wanted to do more. He wouldn't have to wait long. In 1965, Morgan gave his protégé the title of executive vice president and the authority to increase the diversity and vitality of the Wellington Fund management organization as a whole. As Bogle relates it, his promotion came with a broad mandate to transform Wellington by fixing its problems, including "(1) an overreliance on a single, highly conservative balanced (stock and bond) fund; (2) the lack of an aggressive equity fund during the "go-go" era of the Sixties stock market; (3) a paucity of investment management talent at the firm; and (4) a complete dependence on the mutual fund business."[6]

It wasn't long before Bogle came up with what looked to be a brilliant and comprehensive solution: a 1967 merger with one of the "hot" fund management teams of the day, Thorndike, Doran, Paine & Lewis. The firm of young and ambitious investment managers looked to have the energy and market expertise needed to reenergize the tradition-bound Wellington firm. He would later call the move impetuous and stupid but at the time it appeared to be a coup in the mutual fund industry, and Bogle was anointed president and chief executive of the combined company. During the next several years, he and the management talent that came with the merger put an aggressive expansion program in place for the Wellington Management Company. The number of Wellington-managed funds increased from two to ten, including funds whose investment policies were based on rapid growth (Ivest Fund), emerging industries (Explorer Fund), technology (Technivest Fund), and with an investment philosophy that would become anathema to Bogle in later years, a fund structured to capture short-term price trends and turn over its portfolio rapidly (Trustees' Equity Fund).

While the stock market cooperated, Bogle and the Wellington Management Company enjoyed good fortune, and the merger with Thorndike, Doran, Paine & Lewis seemed well conceived. But with the severe falloff in stock prices in the mid-1970s—the major indexes fell around 50 percent—things came apart. His high-flying investment strategies and the addition of new and aggressive equity funds to the Wellington family of funds produced performance that was even worse than that of the market overall. As would be expected, Wellington's funds suffered massive withdrawals by their unhappy shareholders. Since the reinvention of Wellington through rapid growth and fund diversification was Bogle's initiative, he was rightfully assigned the blame, and the Wellington board of directors, in January 1974, fired him as their president and chief executive.

On the very next day, however, Bogle met with the collective boards of the funds that were *managed* by Wellington Management. Like other mutual fund management companies, Wellington was paid an annual fee by the funds to select investments, market the funds, and handle administrative tasks. By law, each of the individual funds has a governance structure separate from that of the management company—their own board of directors—but in reality the boards of those funds are typically handpicked by the management company, and they are generally ineffectual. Bogle reengineered that arrangement by appealing to the boards themselves and bypassing the management company.

In an adroit feat of boardroom maneuvering, Bogle, after meeting with the boards of the individual funds, negotiated an arrangement with Wellington that shifted the control over day-to-day administration to a new company owned by the funds' shareholders—and managed by him. Under the arrangement, Wellington continued to run the vital investment management and marketing activities, with Bogle's new company handling the routine tasks of bookkeeping and reporting. His ingenuity in reshaping the management structure helped him keep his job and cement his leadership position—and it eventually led to the creation of a shareholder-friendly, mutually owned corporate structure unique in the mutual fund industry.[7] A great admirer of Admiral Horatio Nelson, Bogle renamed his reconstructed mutual fund enterprise the Vanguard Group, after the HMS *Vanguard*, one of the flagships Nelson sailed throughout many of the sea battles of the Napoleonic Wars.

Proscriptions and Prescriptions

The dramatic change in Bogle's professional life must have led to some soul-searching. While still in his thirties he had become the hard-charging chief executive of Wellington; at age forty-five he was fired. Yet he was still just at midcareer and had a new mutual fund vehicle to start over with. What directions would he take? Surprisingly, he reached back to the ideas he advanced in his 1951 Princeton thesis, and those ideas shaped the mission of the Vanguard Group. He called the ideas "proscriptions and prescriptions." In a mixture of boasting and self-deprecation he said:

> Today it's easy for me to make two diametrically opposed statements about those proscriptions and prescriptions: (1) They represent the mindless prattle of an idealistic, immature college student, unwise in the ways of the world; and (2) they represent a carefully thought out philosophy and a remarkably prescient design for the firm I would found twenty-three years later.[8]

The strongest *pre*scription the twenty-one-year-old Bogle made in his thesis was on the matter of responsible governance—"the prime responsibility of mutual funds must always be to their shareholders"—arguing that their overarching goal was to "serve those shareholders in the most efficient, honest, and economical way possible." While the strongest *pro*scription was to avoid promising the investor that mutual funds could outperform the overall market—"mutual funds should make no claim of superiority over the market averages."[9]

Both his prescription and proscription, in fact, turned out to be remarkably prescient and would serve as the two guiding principles of the Vanguard funds into the twenty-first century. They were also given strong undergirding in 1962 with the SEC's publication of the *Study of Mutual Funds*, conducted by professors at the Wharton School of the University of Pennsylvania.

The Wharton study covered the years 1952 through 1958 and, coincidentally, was commissioned by the SEC to address Bogle's two areas of concern: governance that was not often in line with the best interests of the mutual fund's shareholders and misrepresentation about investment performance. The study pointed out that the board of directors of a mutual fund was, in theory, beholden to the shareholders and was charged with selecting the most effective management company to handle the distribution (sales and marketing of new shares), investment advisory (management of the portfolio), and fund administration. The way it worked in practice, however, was that the management company itself organized the fund and then handpicked compliant directors to do the fund's bidding. Despite the appearance of independence, the management company often ran the fund according to its own best interests rather than those of the shareholders. So it was hardly a surprise that the study found virtually no instances of a mutual fund board dislodging a management company that was ready and willing to continue as the fund's advisor.[10]

In a position of effective control of a mutual fund, a management company enjoyed an unfettered ability to charge yearly management fees of its choosing rather than fees that came about as a result of good faith negotiation with an independent board. The Wharton study found that the investment management fees charged to mutual funds run for the benefit of *retail* investors were a multiple of the fees management companies charged their *institutional* investor clients through arm's-length negotiations. In addition to the yearly fees for running the funds' portfolios, the management companies could also determine the commissions required to be paid by the funds' shareholders when they bought or sold shares in the funds—the so-called front-end and back-end loads. The study found that the loads paid were generally in the neighborhood of 8.5 percent on the front end. But the handful of no-load funds in existence at the time—those funds charging no commissions to buy or sell mutual fund shares—performed as well as the funds with a load. Contrary to the expected outcome in commerce, investors were not getting what they paid for.

Bogle, invoking the idealism of his senior thesis from many years earlier—"fund managers must treat their shareholders in the most efficient, honest, and economical way possible"—converted the newly organized and mutualized Vanguard Fund into a no-load fund in 1977. He abided by the precept of treating the fund's shareholders as owners—for the simple reason that they *are* the owners. He likened the act of charging the industry standard 8.5 percent fee to starting 8.5 yards back in a 100-yard race. Put another way, if investors are buying only $91.50 of underlying securities for a $100 investment, it's hardly possible for them to realize competitive returns—and they are certainly not being treated in the manner owners deserved to be treated. For that reason, Vanguard operated without the mutual fund industry's customary sales load.

Reducing the other major cost borne by fund shareholders, the annual fee the fund paid the management company to supervise the investments, was a more complicated decision. Obviously, someone had to perform those vital functions. Professional management and portfolio diversification was the sine qua non of a mutual fund, and under the mutual structure that he had engineered for Vanguard, Bogle was able to monitor and control expenses by bringing the investment advisory functions in house.

Rather than paying a highly padded fee to an affiliated management company that in reality controls the fund management, Vanguard's *funds* dictate the terms to the management companies they employ. Under the Vanguard approach, the shareholders pay the actual costs associated with their funds rather than the costs plus a markup. As a result, they often wind up paying a management fee that is as much as a full percentage point lower. Despite its shareholder-friendly mission, the SEC initially and inexplicably declined approval of the mutualized structure of the Vanguard Group. But after four years of appeal, the commission gave its unanimous approval in 1981, stating, "The Vanguard plan actually furthers the Investment Act of 1940 objectives, and promotes a healthy and viable complex in which each fund can better prosper."[11]

Cost control became the new byword of Vanguard, and Bogle, in trumpeting the success of his mutual fund enterprises, cited this as a major explanation for superior returns to shareholders. Each year he would point to the funds' overall expense ratio, calculated by taking the funds' total costs and dividing them into the assets under management. The biggest chunk of fund expenses is almost always attributable to managing the portfolio, but a not inconsequential amount of expenses are incurred in connection with record keeping, custodial services, taxes, legal expenses, and accounting and auditing. In any case, the cost-conscious Bogle could point to a constant decline in the Vanguard expense ratio over the years, reaching just 0.35 percent in 1996, the year he relinquished his CEO title.[12]

While costs measured in one-hundredths of a percentage point may seem miniscule, they add up and punish the investment returns of the shareholder. By Bogle's estimate, the combination of management fees, sales charges, marketing costs, brokerage commissions, and operating expenses amounts to an annual cost of more than 2.5 percent for the typical mutual fund.[13] If one accepts that 2.5 percent number as reflective of a mutual fund that charges front-end loads and pays nonnegotiated fees to outside management companies, and then compares that number to a Vanguard 0.35 percent all-in cost, the results are striking.

Consider a stock fund in which the underlying annual return for the investments in the portfolio is 8 percent per year. After expenses, the shareholder of the typical mutual fund would net just a 5.5 percent return, whereas the Vanguard shareholder's net return would be 7.65 percent. In terms of the effect on capital accumulation, that means that over a ten-year period, the investor who makes a $10,000 investment in the first year and realizes the 5.5 percent annual return would see his or her money grow to $17,081; if he or she invests as a Vanguard shareholder, the investment would be worth $20,899. If the investor is saving for the longer term, perhaps retirement in thirty years, the results are even more dramatic due to the power of compounded interest. The typical fund investor would have accumulated $49,840, compared with the Vanguard investor's $91,290.[14] Based on such examples, Bogle summed up much of his investment philosophy with this advice: "Don't let the miracle of long-term compounding of returns be overwhelmed by the tyranny of long-term compounding of costs."[15]

But more is involved in comparing one fund's expense ratios with another. For one thing, the decline in the Vanguard average cost ratio reflected the changing nature of the funds being managed under the Vanguard umbrella. In 1974, stock funds and balanced funds (those containing both stocks and bonds) accounted for 97 percent of the assets managed; by 1990, that had dropped to only 35 percent, with the remainder accounted for by bond funds and money market funds that required far less investment management.

The major reason for the Vanguard's tiny fee structure, however, is more fundamental—and monumental. The overwhelming reason for the reduction in costs was the move that Bogle and his Vanguard Group began in 1975 toward index-based investing. Such funds require no high-powered and high-priced investment analysts and portfolio managers, but rather just a market technician and a computer program to structure a fund to exactly mimic the results of an index, most often the S&P 500. The costs of running this kind of fund are next to nothing. In reality it is a simple concept, yet this low-cost, passive management approach would ultimately change the face of mutual fund investing and result in Vanguard's becoming the world's largest mutual fund organization.

The Case for Indexing

The argument for index fund investing harkens back yet again to Bogle's Princeton thesis and its assertion that fund managers should "make no claim to superiority over the market averages." The twenty-one-year-old Bogle recognized, perhaps intuitively, that investing, whether through mutual funds or otherwise, was essentially a zero-sum game. With hundreds of thousands of participants in the stock market, all of them scrutinizing publicly available information to maximize their investment returns, the burden of proof would seem to be on any individual or fund management claiming superior knowledge or instincts.

Sophisticated investors have long known that beating the market is a fool's errand. As a well-read young student who was infatuated by the market, Bogle may have gained early wisdom from the seasoned stock market traders of the day. It's likely he had read *Reminiscences of a Stock Operator*, Edwin Lefevre's thinly fictionalized 1923 biography of Jesse Livermore, the most famous stock speculator of the early twentieth century. In that book, Lefevre has his subject assert,

> I have been in the speculative game ever since I was fourteen. It is all I have ever done. I think I know what I am talking about. And the conclusion that I have reached after nearly thirty years of constant trading, both on a shoestring and with millions of dollars in back of me, is this: A man may beat a stock or a group at a certain time, but no man living can beat the stock market! It's like the track. A man may beat a horse race, but he cannot beat horse racing. If I knew how to make these statements stronger or more emphatic I certainly would. It does not make any difference what anybody says to the contrary. I know I am right in saying these are incontrovertible statements.[16]

But prior to the 1962 Wharton study, there was little hard evidence to challenge the allegations coming from the newly emerging mutual fund industry that professionally managed funds would produce investment returns in excess of the market overall. Mutual fund organizations and salespeople made uncorroborated claims that their highly trained and experienced securities analysts and portfolio managers, through active management, were market champions. Going beyond the legitimate claim that mutual funds were a sensible alternative for people unfamiliar with the financial markets, sponsors often claimed that their funds could actually outperform those markets. The Wharton study of mutual funds provided a rigorous test of those claims.

Since there was no broad index of the stock market during the 1952–1958 time frame of the study (the Standard & Poor's 500 Index debuted in 1957), the Wharton researchers compared a mutual fund's performance with a randomly selected portfolio of stocks made up of the same asset class as the fund. In a nutshell, the study found no significant difference between the performance of the funds studied and the randomly selected portfolio of stocks, and in fact, the funds studied usually performed worse than the randomly chosen portfolio after taking into account the fees and expenses of running the portfolio.

The study drew widespread popular and political notice, with the finding regarding the actual success of actively managed funds garnering the most attention. In 1967, U.S. Senator Thomas McIntyre constructed stock portfolios by throwing darts at the stock listings in the newspaper and found that they were as profitable as those produced by the professional market analysts. Burton Malkiel, a Princeton professor and author of the best-selling *A Random Walk Down Wall Street*, took the comparison further, opining that "a blindfolded chimpanzee throwing darts at *The Wall Street Journal* can select a portfolio that can do just as well as the experts."[17] The *Wall Street Journal* itself got into the act itself by sponsoring a dartboard contest in which professional investors were invited to compete with selections chosen by merely throwing darts at its stock listings. (After one hundred separate contests, the "pros" won sixty-one times and the "monkeys" thirty-nine times, resulting in the *Wall Street Journal* proclaiming victory for securities analysis. But the academics, including Malkiel, countered that the *Journal* used incorrect methodologies in the dartboard contest, absent which the professionals would have done no better than the dart throwers.)

Since the time the Wharton study came out, more than fifty years ago, its methodologies have been challenged, but its conclusions have been confirmed and reconfirmed—the results are always the same. Of the thousands of mutual funds available to investors—and today there are more mutual funds than there are publicly traded stocks—precious few have been identified that *consistently* beat the Standard & Poor's 500 Index or other appropriate yardsticks. When adjusted for risk or investment goals, they perform no better than a similarly adjusted index. Most tellingly, the amount of fees charged to their investors has no correlation with the funds' results.

In investment and finance textbooks, the reason professionals do no better than randomly made investments is ascribed to the "efficient market hypothesis." And the EMH is based on what is pretty obvious: all market movements occur with new information, and no single individual has a crystal ball that can predict when that new information will occur or what it will be. With millions of investors seeking profitable information on which to trade, and ready to pounce in an instant, the results of the Wharton study and its successor studies are not surprising.

Though Bogle would never fully embrace the notions of the EMH, he offered it up as a worthy challenge for anyone professing to outperform the market: "I know of no serious academic, professional money manager, trained security analyst, or intelligent individual investor who would disagree with the thrust of the EMH: The stock market itself is a demanding taskmaster. It sets a high hurdle that few investors can leap."[18] And there is little question that Bogle was greatly influenced by work of the theory's prominent advocates. He was inspired by Professor Malkiel's *Random Walk Down Wall Street* and also by institutional investor Charles Ellis's 1975 article "Loser's Game" in the *Financial Analysts Journal*, which made the case that investors did not—and could not—outperform the market.[19] But his primary inspiration came from Nobel laureate Paul Samuelson's open call for a retail-oriented index mutual fund. In a 1974 article titled "Challenge to Judgment" in the *Journal of Portfolio Management*, Samuelson threw down the gauntlet by challenging anyone to "produce brute evidence" that an active investing strategy can be superior to a passive index strategy. He further suggested that "some large foundation set up an in-house portfolio that tracked the S&P 500—if only for the purpose of setting up a naïve model against which a mutual fund's in-house gun-slingers can measure their prowess . . . The American Economic Association might contemplate setting up for its members a no-load, no-management-fee, virtually no-transaction-turnover fund."[20]

Bogle viewed Samuelson's challenge as the opportunity of a lifetime—his chance to put into reality the ideas he had first conceived at Princeton a quarter of a century earlier. Ever his own man, he diligently performed his own confirming work "by hand" on the comparative results of equity mutual funds and a stock index. He analyzed thirty years' worth of average investment returns from mutual funds and then compared their results to the S&P 500, and found that the index enjoyed a 1.6 percent per year *advantage* in investment returns—and, of course, that advantage sprang from the fact that the index returns are not burdened by significant management fees.[21]

To distinguish his framework from the EMH, which was then derided on Wall Street, Bogle came up with his own principle: the CMH, or cost matters hypothesis. If the cost of running a fund could be reduced by using an index-based passive management approach rather than employing highly paid managers, the fund's costs could be dramatically lowered with the aim of providing its shareholders with much higher investment returns. He would declare that "we don't need to accept the EMH to be index believers . . . not only is the CMH all that is needed to explain why indexing must and does work, but it in fact enables us to quantify with some precision *how well* it works. *Whether or not the markets are efficient, the explanatory power of the CMH holds*" (Bogle's emphasis).[22]

His custom-made analyses of stock market history and his formulation of the CMH formed the cornerstones of his successful argument to the Vanguard board for the creation of an index fund. And so in August 1976, Vanguard created a fund designed to exactly duplicate the Standard & Poor's index of 500 stocks: the First Index Investment Trust.

It was also at that time that Vanguard began its transition from a minor affiliate of Wellington to a powerful and independent mutual fund company. As described earlier, Wellington ceded only the administrative functions of fund management to Vanguard, keeping the investment management and marketing for itself. But with a no-load commission structure, the First Index Investment Trust, later renamed the Vanguard 500 Index Fund, was sold directly rather than through the brokers that Wellington controlled, so there was no significant marketing required. By the same token, with a fund that aims only to duplicate the S&P 500, there is no real investment management. Thus, the Vanguard 500 Index Fund—and the succeeding Vanguard funds—could now operate independently from Wellington. Bogle later stated that the emergence of a separate, shareholder-controlled Vanguard Group from beneath the Wellington umbrella, "was one of the great acts of disingenuous opportunism defined by the mind of man."[23]

The Vanguard Flywheel

Like many revolutionary ideas, the index fund movement was at first dismissed as a ludicrous and unmarketable idea—"the pursuit of mediocrity"— and its debut was anything but propitious. There were, however, some high-level supporters. Both Malkiel and Ellis sat on the First Index Investment Trust's board and became investors, and Malkiel later credited the

Vanguard's index funds for providing for the education of his six children and fifteen grandchildren.

And there was also interest in the idea within certain institutional firms. David Booth and Rex Sinquefield, both MBA graduates of the University of Chicago, where much of the groundwork for the efficient market hypothesis was laid, used an indexing strategy beginning in the 1970s for their institutional clients. Booth worked at Wells Fargo Bank and Sinquefield worked at the American National Bank of Chicago. In 1981 they teamed up to form the highly successful Dimensional Fund Advisors, providing indexing strategies for institutional clients and financial advisors.

But even with its impressive supporters, it was difficult in 1976 to find a Wall Street firm willing to handle the initial stock offering for an endeavor that aimed to be average. Dean Witter & Company ultimately agreed to take on the project, but it could only sell $11 million of the targeted $150 million offering. And that tepid reception was followed by Vanguard's lackluster growth through the remainder of the 1970s. The mainstay of its mutual fund family, the Wellington balanced fund, was redeeming more shares than it was selling and the First Index fund was not catching fire with the investing public. Total assets under management for the fund family remained essentially flat during the period at approximately $2 billion, and they were only at that level because of the growth of new money market funds and bond funds.

Eventually, of course, index funds would attain remarkable success, conforming to a flywheel type of growth that Jim Collins described in his best-selling *Good to Great*. In that book he explains how "great" companies often begin slowly but surely and eventually gain great momentum, "Pushing with great effort, you get the flywheel to inch forward, moving almost imperceptibly at first. You keep pushing and get the flywheel to complete one entire turn. You keep pushing, and the flywheel begins to move a bit faster. Then at some point—breakthrough! You're pushing no harder than during the first rotation, but the flywheel goes faster and faster."[24]

During the start-up years of the late 1970s, with his Vanguard organization employing as few as 28 employees and the assets under management at the funds hovering at something less than $2 billion, Bogle would often invoke his message of confidence: eventually the fund will catch on as customers begin to understand that the low-cost approach best serves their long-term needs. But the First Index fund, with its controversial and decidedly unexciting passive, index-based investment strategy, continued to be a tough sell.

By 1980, however, the flywheel finally began to turn, and Vanguard's assets under management increased to $3 billion. That achievement was cause for celebration, and Bogle began his custom of gathering all of the "crew members," Vanguard's term for its employees, and delivering a congratulatory speech. The first, in September 1980, was titled "A Time to Dance," and like the forty-two similar speeches that would follow during Bogle's reign, it was laced with literary allusions and closed by exhorting the crew to aim for even higher goals. In the first speech, he chose a verse from poet Robinson Jeffers: "Lend me the stone strength of the past and I will lend you the wings of the future."[25]

During his speeches, some of the more jaded crew members likely rolled their eyes at the drama and importance Bogle attributed to the firm's accomplishments, especially as he quoted the likes of Shakespeare, Rudyard Kipling, the Bible (mainly Ecclesiastes), and, of course, Lord Nelson. And the omnipresent nautical theme was everywhere—the company cafeteria was referred to as the Galley, and the fitness center and company store were called Ship Shape and the Chandlery, respectively. When Vanguard reached the size that supported its own campus, each of the various buildings carried the name of one of Nelson's ships—*Victory, Zealous*, and so forth.

Bogle's approach may have been cornball, but it succeeded. Vanguard's assets reached the $4 billion milestone in the following year, commemorated by his September 1981 speech, "Growth Has Its Season," which featured Marcus Aurelius's comments about the river of passing events. Then, in August 1982, less than a year later, he and the crew members celebrated passing the monumental $5 billion asset level with a speech that was titled "The More Glorious the Triumph" and drew upon both Thomas Paine and the ever-quotable Lord Nelson for inspiration. The flywheel was in motion now, and passing subsequent billion-dollar levels was occurring too frequently to justify a special event or speech. By 1985, Vanguard would top $16 billion; by 1990, $55 billion; and by 1995, Bogle's last year as chief executive, $180 billion.

A large part of Vanguard's extraordinary growth is rightfully attributed to Jack Bogle's vision and leadership, but the mutual fund industry itself was the beneficiary of several very favorable trends during the 1980s and 1990s. The long bull market in stocks that began in 1982 had the effect of rekindling investor interest in equity investing, and of course the asset value of the underlying stock funds increased along with the rising market values. At the same time, the prices of bonds increased substantially with the rapid fall in interest rates. From the double-digit levels of the late 1970s and early 1980s—some bonds carried rates of over 20 percent to attract willing investors during that time—interest rates quickly fell back to a more normal range of between 5 and 7 percent, and bond prices soared.

And most important of all, the Revenue Act of 1978 that provided for the creation of employer-sponsored 401(k) plans beginning in 1980 caused a sea change in how pension plans were created and funded. Where defined-benefit plans had once been standard, the defined-contribution approach took their place, and individuals became increasingly responsible for funding their own retirement—and making their own investment choices. For that reason, the percentage of U.S. households owning common stock, either directly or through self-directed pension plans, grew to well over 50 percent in 2000. And increasingly, the vehicle of choice for making those stock (and bond) investments was the mutual fund.

Over the same time span, Vanguard was increasing its market share of the mutual fund business in each and every year.[26] The gospel of index investing had spread beyond its early champions in the academic community and within a few institutional advisory firms, and Vanguard was the beneficiary of this increased interest in passive management. And at the same time, indexing at Vanguard was developing well beyond just tracking the S&P 500 stock index. In 1986 Vanguard introduced the first bond market fund, and later in that decade it introduced the Total Stock Market Index Fund to match the broader Wilshire 5000 Index. (The S&P 500 includes the largest 500 U.S. stocks by market capitalization; the Wilshire 5000 Index includes the next 4,500 largest.) The Small-Cap Index Fund was created based on the widely followed Russell 2000 Index of smaller publicly traded companies.

The index fund proliferation at Vanguard only increased in the 1990s. As a result of Bogle's persistent goading, Standard & Poor's developed separate indexes for growth stocks and value stocks, and Vanguard quickly developed the two new funds designed to track them. In 1992, an international equity index fund was launched, followed in 1994 by an emerging market index. By 1995 Vanguard was managing a family of eighty-two funds, and of the twenty-nine funds added in the 1990s, twenty-five were index funds.

Years of Setbacks, 1996 to 2000

The momentum of the Vanguard enterprise carried through the remainder of the 1990s and into the twenty-first century, but beginning in late 1995

Bogle suffered a succession of serious health problems and professional disappointments. He had lived throughout his life with heart arrhythmia, experiencing a major heart attack at age thirty-one, followed by a succession of additional attacks requiring extended hospital stays.

It appeared that, like Charles Merrill, Bogle would be required to retire prematurely from the business world. Although the installation of a pacemaker in 1967—he was one of the early beneficiaries of that procedure—and the use of various heart medications worked marginally well, by October 1995 his heart had deteriorated to such an extent that his cardiac physician delivered the news to Bogle that he was threatened by "a catastrophic cardiac arrest—a guillotine about to drop."[27]

To the congenitally optimistic Bogle, however, that was good news—and his optimism was warranted. With the right side of his heart no longer pumping, he became eligible for a heart transplant, his last-ditch hope for survival. He soon found himself in an in-residence cardiac unit at Philadelphia's Hahnemann Hospital, where he was kept alive by intravenously administered liquids and, along with several other patients in need of a heart transplant, awaited a new heart. The medical profession honors a no-favoritism policy in the awarding of a transplant—Bogle described the process as being "as democratic as a traffic jam"—but his turn finally came in February 1996 after a four-month wait.

During the ordeal of waiting, he continued to work on business. The Vanguard family of funds by that time numbered eighty-five, and he wrote the annual letter to shareholders for each one. But at this point his role at Vanguard had become, if not ceremonial, greatly reduced since his 1995 decision to turn over the CEO position to longtime Vanguard employee John Brennan. Bogle remained chairman of the board and had managed the transition of operating control to Brennan by the book, making him president in 1992 and conferring the chief executive and chairman titles officially as of January 1996. He acknowledged his own age—sixty-seven years old when he stepped down—as well as his faltering heart, and said all of the right things about Brennan's capabilities and his "confidence that my vision had been firmly established and that we had built an organization fully capable of carrying on our mission."[28]

It is not uncommon for founders of a business to have difficulty letting someone else take full control of the reins, but in Bogle's case a better than expected recovery from his health problems made the transition even tougher. When he entered Hahnemann Hospital in 1995 he was desperately ill, and it was not at all certain he would receive his transplant in time or, if he did, would regain his energy. But after a short recovery period, Bogle was back in fighting form. He began damning Brennan with faint praise and resented those instances when Brennan was given credit for Vanguard's solid performance in the latter half of the 1990s.

By all accounts, Brennan was a highly competent CEO and particularly skilled in moving the company into Internet applications, an area in which Vanguard had lagged behind some of its competitors. But Bogle bristled when the later successes at Vanguard were trumpeted in the media without giving due notice to his own influence, and he gave voice in the press to what he thought was second billing—or worse, no billing at all—regarding his past and ongoing contributions to the company's success. Brennan, not a self-aggrandizer by nature, refused to comment on Bogle's public statements regarding Vanguard's management, but the board took the steps it believed were needed to remove the disruptive founder, who now carried the title of "senior chairman." It took action in 1999 by asking for Bogle's resignation when he reached the mandatory retirement age of seventy. Bogle maintains that it had always been an understanding of the board that the policy would not apply to him as the founder, and other Vanguard directors had been allowed to remain on the board past the age of seventy. But for whatever reason, the board—probably in the spirit of removing the distraction of further feuds and giving a vote of confidence to Brennan—voted to require Bogle's resignation.

The news of his involuntary resignation spread rapidly among Vanguard shareholders, stirring a massive protest to the board's decision. In retreat, the board members reconsidered, but Bogle turned down their offer for reinstatement on the board. As with his earlier 1974 firing as CEO of Wellington Management, however, he ultimately landed on his feet, finding a position that was a perfect match for his talents, experience, and time of life. His new title was founder of Vanguard and president of a newly established Bogle Financial Markets Research Center.

Happy Endings

For well over a decade Bogle has continued to write and deliver speeches to an expanding audience. While his early efforts borrowed from a wide spectrum of intellectual thought, they were primarily inspirational in purpose and had a fairly narrow focus on Vanguard and on reforming the mutual fund business. Today at the Bogle Center, he and his small think tank staff continue to focus their efforts on reform, but the scope has expanded well beyond Vanguard and mutual funds to issues such as shareholder rights, corporate governance, entrepreneurship, and most especially, personal and business ethics. He also serves as a Vanguard ambassador, visiting the company's far-flung offices, and with his latest moniker of Saint Jack, makes an appearance at the reunions of the "Bogleheads," a fan club of investors who have benefited emotionally from his homey inspirational messages, as well as financially from his creation of an indexing strategy for investing.

Meanwhile, the Vanguard flywheel has continued to turn faster and without apparent limits. Under the direction of its third CEO, veteran Vanguard employee Bill McNabb, Vanguard was managing over $3 trillion in assets by 2014—some 35 years after Bogle and his crew celebrated the addition of the companies first *billion* dollars of growth. And those crew members now total around 14,000, up from the original 28 on hand for that celebration. At the time of this writing, Vanguard had 74 index funds under management, including the Total Stock Market Index Fund, which, with $370 billion under management in 2014, was the largest in the industry. Perhaps most significantly for the company's shareholders—Bogleheads or no—the expense ratio has continued to decline and now sits at an average 0.19 percent, so investors are paying just 19 cents for every $100 dollars under Vanguard management.

His "cost matters hypothesis" continues to overarch his thinking, and in 2009, in a lecture on business ethics at Columbia University, Bogle estimated the effect of Vanguard's low-cost structure for its shareholders. He pointed out that his fund's expense ratio of 0.20 was a full 1.1 percent below the 1.3 percent for the average mutual fund. Applying that difference to the $1 trillion under management at Vanguard at the time resulted in savings of $11 billion to its shareholders. He used that example to underscore the benefits of a mutual fund that was structured to serve just one master: the fund's shareholder. He told his audience that he was probably naive in naming his low-cost fund Vanguard, since the word connotes being the leader of a new trend, saying "under our at-cost structure, all of the profits go to the fund shareholders, not to the managers, resolving the transcendent conflict of interest of the mutual fund industry. In any event, the leader, as it were, has yet to find its first follower."[29] (Many imitator index funds have been formed—including several within the Fidelity Funds family—but there are no known funds that fully employ Vanguard's investor-friendly mutual structure.)

Bogle has not had to rely on himself to sing the praises of low-cost, index investing. In 1999 *Fortune* pronounced him to be one of the four most influential investment figures of the twentieth century, and in 2010 William Baldwin, longtime writer of *Forbes*, took the occasion of his last letter as editor of the magazine to issue an apology (of sorts) for the magazine's hypercritical commentary on Bogle and Vanguard. "It's a bit late in coming," Baldwin wrote, "but I'd like to officially retract a story *Forbes* published in May 1975 that pooh-poohed the creation of Vanguard Group by John C. Bogle." After chronicling the success of Vanguard, Williams writes, "Bogle, 81, is retired from management but is as vociferous as ever an evangelist for cost-cutting. I think he has done more good for investors than any other financier of the past century."[30]

And in a 2005 speech before the Boston Security Analysts Society, the ninety-year-old Paul Samuelson, Bogle's inspiration and one of the foremost economists of the century, went even further: "I rank this Bogle invention along with the invention of the wheel, wine and cheese, the alphabet, and Gutenberg printing: a mutual fund that never made Bogle rich but elevated the long-term returns of the mutual-fund owners. Something new under the sun."[31]

Part III
Academics

In the early years of the twentieth century, there was little connection between Wall Street and academia. Most of the prominent financiers had not bothered with higher education at all, and those who did—like Pierpont Morgan and Paul Warburg—received a classical education at a university and then followed that up with an apprenticeship at a bank, where they picked up practical knowledge on the job. During the course of that century, however, university-affiliated business schools grew in number and prominence, especially as their focus expanded from vocational undergraduate programs to respectable graduate schools at leading universities.

As the schools gained acceptance in the business world, many of their star professors led dual professional lives, splitting their time between the academy and industry, sometimes with profound effects. In particular, the field of finance has been inalterably shaped by three men whose careers encompassed both the classroom and the real world: Georges Doriot of Harvard, who formed and managed the first venture capital firm; Benjamin Graham of Columbia, who wrote the book on security analysis; and Myron Scholes, who variously taught at the University of Chicago, the Massachusetts Institute of Technology, and Stanford, and laid much of the foundation for the growth of the derivatives markets.

Doriot, Graham, and Scholes made their marks during successive eras and in very different areas of finance, yet they shared common experiences. All three were immigrants to the United States at an early age, and each was a remarkably precocious student and later a success in business. Yet each suffered remarkable setbacks during his professional life.

Doriot's setback came near the end of his career as a venture capitalist. That career had started in 1946, when a group of Boston businessmen approached him about managing a newly formed "industrial development company"—the term "venture capital" was not yet in use. At that point, he was already a long-tenured professor at the Harvard Business School. He accepted the challenge of running the American Research and Development Corporation and, over a twenty-seven-year stretch, built the company into a highly successful enterprise and, more lastingly, established the pattern for and feasibility of professional venture capital investing. Through highly selective investments in new technologies, coupled with some luck in funding the enormously successful Digital Equipment Company, the mustachioed Frenchman validated the concept of institutionally backed venture capital investing through dedicated pools of capital.

Unfortunately, General Doriot—he rose to brigadier general during World War II and proudly retained the title in civilian life—suffered from an inability to delegate or attract successor talent. And for someone who quickly recognized and acted on technical innovation, he was stubborn in his refusal to adopt the limited partnership format that had become for his competitors the logical and successful form of organization for venture investing. So even though American Research had much to do with establishing Boston as an incubator for new, high-tech enterprises, and everything to do with creating the venture capital industry, the company was ingloriously sold to a conglomerate and soon liquidated.

Where Doriot's problems came late in his career, Graham's came early. After his graduation from Columbia as salutatorian, he declined the university's offer to stay on and teach—he had his choice between mathematics, English, or philosophy—electing instead to travel downtown to make his way in the investment business. He did extraordinarily well on Wall Street and was still in his early thirties in 1926 when he founded Graham-Newman, the money management firm he would run for the next thirty years.

During the waning years of the Roaring Twenties his investment acumen had become widely recognized and, after managing Graham-Newman during business hours, he returned to Columbia in the evenings to deliver a well-attended lecture series on his investing strategies. He was riding high, pleasing the Graham-Newman clients during the day and inspiring his students at night. But the 1929 stock market crash and the long-lasting depression that followed had a disastrous effect on Graham-Newman, with the accounts Graham was managing on his investors' behalf plummeting in the 1930s to just a fraction of their pre-crash values.

By 1934, however, he had distilled the Columbia lectures and his Wall Street experience, hard knocks and all, into the seven-hundred-page *Security Analysis*, the first rigorous approach to determining the value of stocks and bonds. The book, cowritten with Columbia University professor David Dodd, transformed stock selection from a hit-or-miss, tip-based activity into a methodical and rational process. The book's risk-wary, quantitative approach remains in wide use today, and *The Intelligent Investor*, a more accessible book he wrote in 1949 to encapsulate his ideas for a wider audience, is still in print. His former Columbia student, Warren Buffett, called *The Intelligent Investor* "by far the best book ever written on investing."

In Scholes's case, his most spectacular success and failure occurred simultaneously. He won the Nobel Prize for Economics in 1997, and the next year lost most of his wealth following the collapse of Long-Term Capital Management, the multibillion-dollar hedge fund he had cofounded a few years earlier. Both events were impacted by the development of the derivative securities in which Professor Scholes had played a major role. Professional investors recognize his name from the Black-Scholes option pricing model for which he, along with Robert Merton from MIT, received the Nobel award. He rejected any notion that the informal title "Father of Derivatives" was appropriate for him or his research colleagues, but it was the methodology he developed jointly with Merton and Fischer Black that became key in pricing and understanding derivatives.

Judiciously used, derivatives reduce business and investment risk. But when used for speculation they can also be, as Warren Buffett famously described them, "weapons of mass financial destruction." It was Scholes's conceit—if Doriot's fatal flaw was stubbornness, Scholes's may have been hubris—to operate as though his models were infallible. But when events in 1997 and 1998, especially in Asia and Russia, caused financial turmoil not anticipated by the models, Long-Term Capital Management lost $4.5 billion, wiping out the investors' equity and requiring a Federal Reserve–led bailout of its debt holders to forestall a financial panic.

By the twenty-first century the connection between the universities and the real world of finance was well established. In some financial sectors an MBA is considered a license to practice, and the business schools do a commendable job of supplying bright and well-prepared graduates to work on Wall Street. Less well known, perhaps, is the direct role faculty members often play through consulting and sometimes managing financial institutions. The work of the academics profiled in the next three chapters shows how important that role can be.

7

Georges F. Doriot: 1899–1987
Dream Builder

I am building men and companies.

—GEORGES DORIOT

Failure didn't come naturally to General Georges Doriot. By 1957 (at age fifty-seven), he had long enjoyed renown as an inspirational teacher at the Harvard Business School and as a highly valued consultant and director for countless companies. The French-born Doriot was also in the final stages of founding INSEAD, which would soon become Europe's premier business school. He had also seen success in the military, receiving the Distinguished Service Medal in 1946 for his efforts in World War II as a brigadier general. But now he was faced with the possibility of failure. His signature creation—the American Research and Development Corporation—was flailing, and in a move full of significance and foreboding for Doriot, the Massachusetts Institute of Technology decided to sell its ownership in the company.

Eleven years earlier, with high hopes for success, Doriot and MIT president Karl Compton had organized a group of prominent Boston businessmen to form ARDC as the world's first institutionally funded and professionally managed venture capital fund. The rationale was compelling: MIT and other Boston-area universities produced an abundance of new technologies and commercially feasible products, but many didn't make it to the marketplace due to a lack of financial sponsorship. ARDC's role, as Doriot and Compton saw it, was to act as a gatekeeper to the marketplace by screening and funding developments that had commercial promise.

With the highly regarded General Doriot directing the day-to-day operations and with a ready source of risk capital after a public sale of its stock, ARDC looked to be an ideal vehicle to spur Boston's post–World War II economy and enrich its own investors. Compton put MIT's imprimatur on the idea in 1947 by directing the institution to become one of the founding investors of the new company.

But when Compton died in 1954, the institution's principal contact became Horace Ford, who served as treasurer of both MIT and ARDC. Ford had an insider's look at Doriot's operation and didn't like what he saw. Some of ARDC's early investments did reasonably well and were liquidated for a profit, but most turned in middling financial results or faded away into bankruptcy. The few-dozen portfolio companies that remained were producing aggregate cash flow that was barely sufficient to meet the day-to-day expenses of running ARDC, and there was little left over for the investors. And the telltale indicator of ARDC's success, the performance of its stock, was distressing. The shares of the company rarely moved above their 1946 initial public offering price of $25 and had sold for as little as $16. The considerable risk that shareholders had assumed by purchasing shares in a venture capital company justified a major financial return on their investment. But after the first ten years, MIT and ARDC's other investors would have done better by keeping their money under their mattresses. It seemed clear to Ford that ARDC was a losing proposition, and in 1957 he directed MIT to dispose of its holdings and not consider any future funding of the company. It was a dark day for Doriot when MIT threw in the towel.

But Doriot's distress would not last long. In the same year that MIT divested its ownership, ARDC made a $70,000 investment in Digital Equipment Company, a small enterprise formed by two MIT-trained engineers that would finally validate the wisdom of venture capital investing— and make it painfully clear that MIT had sold its stock at precisely the wrong time.

Wunderkind Years

Doriot's many successes during his long career—the eventual flowering of ARDC would become his last and most important—were a product of a no-nonsense outlook on life that valued accomplishment above all else. He could not countenance wasted time, and that included sleeping.

He regularly woke in the early morning after only a few hours in bed and worked through the rest of the night at his desk—a desk with a stopwatch atop it so he could better control and measure the amount of time he devoted to his various tasks. He was a man of little frivolity and the caricature of the fussy and demanding martinet in the classroom. Pencil thin and standing at five foot ten, he is portrayed in the few available pictures of him as someone exceedingly formal and unbending in bearing, appearance, and habits. He wore a dark-colored suit every day—and required his MBA students to do likewise; "sport coats are for college kids," he would caution them—with a neatly folded handkerchief protruding from his breast pocket and often with the Legion of Honor ribbon in his lapel. His shirts were white, with cuffs and stickpins in the collar. His pipe was a constant companion through adulthood (he died of lung cancer at eighty-seven), and over the years his triangular mustache remained unchanged, save for its eventual transition to grey.

Doriot's drive and no-nonsense personality were likely shaped by the swings of fortune his family experienced in his early years in France. He was born in pre–World War I Paris and spent his childhood in a strict and financially comfortable Lutheran household. His father was a prominent automobile engineer who played a key role in the development of the first Peugeot, and business and manufacturing were imprinted on young Georges during frequent visits to the auto factories of the early twentieth century. During most of the war years he studied science and technology at a Paris lycée, interrupting his studies in 1917 to enlist in the French army at age seventeen. By that time the tide was turning in favor of the Allies, and he escaped direct combat, but based on his technical proficiency and leadership, the teenage Doriot was awarded an officer's rank in an artillery vehicle unit.

The war was not so kind to Doriot's father. The automobile manufacturing plants his father had a role in shaping had been converted to war-related production, and there was little prospect of a return to their original business any time soon in the badly war-torn French economy. His father made an abortive attempt to start an automotive venture on his own, but it failed for lack of financial backing, and the family's modest fortune dwindled to almost nothing. Doriot, who returned to the lycée and received a baccalaureate degree in science in 1920, found France's professional prospects similarly bleak. Upon his father's advice, twenty-one-year-old Doriot left for America with the plan to study engineering at the Massachusetts Institute of Technology and, after a few years, perhaps return to France.

His biographer, Spencer Ante, describes Doriot's transition to the United States as follows:

> He left France with two important items. In one pocket, he kept a letter of introduction to a gentleman named A. Lawrence Lowell and in his other pocket Georges carried a small French coin, a symbol of his father's fortune, which had been destroyed by the war. The letter, which would radically change the course of Georges's life, represented the bright light of the future; the coin embodied the dark weight of Doriot's recent past.[1]

It must have been some letter that he carried with him. Although Doriot had allegedly never heard of Harvard University, much less its president Lawrence Lowell, he matriculated at the Harvard Business School rather than MIT shortly after his first meeting with President Lowell. Reflecting the nature of U.S. business at the time, manufacturing management was a major part of the MBA curriculum, and that line of education appealed to him more than the heavily technical curriculum available at MIT. The notion of graduate study in business was still a fairly new idea, with the Harvard Business School becoming the first to offer an MBA degree in 1908. With few credentialed scholars of business subjects available—there was little in the way of academic research in business disciplines at the time and few quality doctoral programs until 1922, when Harvard launched its own doctorate of business administration—the school relied on experienced businessmen, as much as academics, to teach its courses. Although Doriot didn't have the requisite undergraduate degree, he was granted admission to the business school as a "special student," much as he had become an officer of the French army at a very young age through a battlefield commission.

Like most of his classmates, he stayed at Harvard for just the first year of core curriculum studies, entering the workforce directly and forgoing the second year and a degree. Rather than returning to France, which was still reeling from the aftershocks of the war, Doriot took a job on Wall Street with an affiliate of Kuhn, Loeb & Company, the same firm that Paul Warburg had joined about twenty years earlier and the only real rival to J. P. Morgan & Company at the time. Unlike Warburg, however, Doriot was not related to anyone at Kuhn, Loeb, and the firm did not have a history of taking in non-family, much less non-Jewish, partners.

The ambitious Doriot would not likely stay long with a firm in which the top spots looked unattainable. But during his four years at Kuhn, Loeb,

Doriot gained a window into the world of high finance—an experience that would serve him well in later years, providing invaluable insights and contacts he would need at ARDC. Although he lacked investment banking experience, he worked extremely hard and distinguished himself in the eyes of the Kuhn, Loeb partners. For example, when those partners organized a new company to pioneer innovative industrial processes, they chose Doriot as one of the company's seven initial directors. He was just twenty-four at the time but clearly steeped in the ways of developing technologies and precociously competent in business analysis.

Doriot, however, seemed driven more by accomplishment that was measured by end products, whether in successful people that he nourished or organizations he created, than by the personal riches he could create for himself on Wall Street. When Harvard Business School dean Wallace Donham contacted him in 1925 to return to Harvard as an assistant dean, he quickly accepted the position. At the time, an assistant deanship was an administrative job rather than a faculty position, but Doriot, with his knowledge of manufacturing, was soon catapulted into the classroom to teach a course entitled Factory Problems and the Taylor System.[2] And so began a teaching career in which Doriot taught hundreds of manufacturing classes during his long run at the Harvard Business School. He was brilliant in the classroom, with his courses generally oversubscribed. In 1929, shortly after his thirtieth birthday, he received a promotion to full professor, the highest rank available in academe, with the accompanying title of "professor of industrial management."

Doriot's brilliance shone outside the gates of Harvard as well. His reputation for insight into business problems spread throughout the business community, and he became a highly sought out consultant and board member, first for Boston-area companies and later for businesses throughout the United States. During the challenging years of the Great Depression, he sat on the board of around twenty companies, in some cases assuming the chairmanship, and acted as a consultant or advisor for countless more. He was also an active writer; during his Kuhn, Loeb days he published articles in the *New Republic* on the repatriation of war debt, and in later years he continued to publish other articles, most also dealing with global economic matters.

Through his thirties, Doriot kept up a frenetic pace of teaching, travel, writing, and consulting. All of his off-campus commitments took him away from the business school—and away from his wife, the ever-patient Edna, a Harvard research assistant whom he married in 1930—but with his workaholic ways and devotion to his students, there was no apparent ill effect on his teaching effectiveness. In fact, with the Harvard Business School having adopted its still highly vaunted case method as its primary form of instruction in 1924, Doriot's extensive real-world experience only enhanced his courses. But in 1946 Doriot was presented with an opportunity that not only changed his life but that eventually transformed the landscape of much of American business.

ARDC: Before Digital Equipment Company

In the years just before World War II, several groups of prominent New Englanders—industrialists, financiers, and educators—saw the imminent decline of textile and garment businesses in their region and began making plans to develop replacement industries. One of the key actors in this effort was Ralph Flanders, an industrialist and inventor who later became the president of the Federal Reserve Bank of Boston. The case he made for nurturing new industries still resonates in the twenty-first century: "We cannot depend safely for an indefinite time on the expansion of our big industries alone. We need new strength, energy and ability from below. We need to marry some small part of our enormous fiduciary resources to the new ideas which are seeking support."[3]

Two especially energetic groups soon sprang up to address the matter, the New England Council and Enterprise Associates, and they both recognized the opportunity and the problem. The researchers at local universities, particularly at MIT, were prolific in coming up with ideas and products with substantial commercial viability. The difficulty in developing them further always seemed to be a lack of financial resources. Joining forces, the two groups reached a consensus that a pool of "development capital" for investment would be crucial for turning university research into commercial enterprise. They began work on structuring a fund dedicated to providing risk capital for new businesses that were addressing fast-growing new markets and emerging technologies. It was to be the first large-scale, institutionally backed foray into what would later become known as venture capital investing.

At the time plans for a capital fund were becoming final, however, the United States entered World War II, and everyone's focus, including Doriot's, shifted to the war effort. Doriot's reputation had spread to Washington, and he was summoned to the White House shortly before the war began to meet with Franklin Roosevelt. President Roosevelt proposed that Doriot join the armed services and assist in developing the nation's readiness for what looked to be an inevitable conflict with Nazi Germany. Doriot readily agreed to the president's proposal and entered the U.S. Army as a lieutenant colonel—after, that is, he gave up his French citizenship and became a naturalized citizen of the United States.

During the war, Doriot coordinated the work of scientists at the Pentagon with the Quartermaster Corps in the field, honing management skills that would later prove highly useful as a venture capitalist. Prior to his release from the army in 1946, he had risen to the rank of brigadier general and was awarded the Distinguished Service Medal, the highest recognition available in the armed services for a noncombatant. For the remainder of his life as a civilian, the outwardly modest but stiffly formal Doriot let it be known that "General" was his preferred form of address.

Developments in the wake of the war had only bolstered the case for the professionally managed venture capital fund the New England boosters had championed. The GI Bill, by underwriting the cost of college and postgraduate education for veterans, greatly expanded the skilled labor force necessary for running technology-based businesses. World War II had also brought about new and lasting partnerships between the U.S. government and research universities. Before the war, the estimated $40 million dedicated to basic scientific research was largely funded and conducted by private industry; the government was just a bit player. That changed with the need for defense-related research and development during the war, and the government began contracting with universities and foundations to perform the needed work. The Office of Scientific Research and Development alone entered into some $90 million in research contracts with universities in 1943.[4] And as World War II transitioned into the Cold War and space programs, the level of scientific research contracted to universities only grew. In simple R&D terms, venture capital firms generally provide money for the *development* phase of a product, so the increase in the university *research* budgets only spurs the need for such firms.

What's more, with the economy readjusting from artificially high wartime spending and capital investment, there was an immediate need for a fund dedicated to venture capital funding. The time was right for Ralph Flanders and the organizers of the proposed venture fund to revisit their prewar plan. As expected, they selected Doriot as their obvious and unanimous choice to run the business. Doriot agreed to head the budding company with two stipulations: that he be allowed to keep his academic rank and position at Harvard (with a greatly reduced teaching load) and that Flanders would hold the chief executive title until Doriot was formally released from the U.S. Army in December 1946. After Doriot agreed to take the job, a board of directors was formed, along with an advisory board of MIT scientists. On June 6, 1946, American Research and Development Corporation began operations. It was the world's first professionally managed venture capital fund and, like virtually all that would follow, it was to be funded by sophisticated institutional investors.

At least that was the plan. Clearly Doriot would provide the professional management, but institutional investors, trained to operate with the risk-avoidance dictate of the "prudent man rule," balked at an investment in ARDC. The fund-raising efforts were further imperiled by Wall Street underwriters who considered ARDC to be more of a social experiment than a profit-seeking entity. In the end, two second-tier investment houses agreed to sponsor ARDC's initial public offering in late 1946, but only on a "best-efforts" basis at $25 per share. The two firms would attempt to sell the 200,000 shares offered, but if they couldn't spark enough investor interest for the entire $5 million deal, they weren't willing to backstop any shortfall with their own funds. At the offering's conclusion, only $3.5 million was raised, and of that amount, just $1.8 million came from the targeted institutional investors.[5] The remainder represented shares purchased by individuals, primarily ARDC directors and their friends and family.

Despite its disappointing initial public offering, the small staff at ARDC went to work. By the end of 1946, ARDC made its first investment: a $150,000 loan, convertible into common stock, to Circo Products, a Cleveland-based company that made low-tech equipment for the automobile industry. The next two investments were in companies founded by MIT scientists and were far more high-tech: a $200,000 investment in High Voltage Engineering Corporation (X-ray equipment) and a $150,000 investment in Tracerlab (radioactive isotopes).

Unmoved by the business or social connections of entrepreneurs looking for money, Doriot followed an egalitarian strategy of giving every proposal that reached ARDC a good look, no matter who was behind it. He and his small staff reviewed hundreds of business plans, but selected just a handful to invest in. The deserving few that ARDC funded, however, were the beneficiaries of much more than capital. Though Doriot and his lieutenants avoided any direct, day-to-day management of their portfolio companies, they were more than willing to tap into their vast network of contacts to help find customers and specialized advisors. They also lent wise and sympathetic ears to the entrepreneurs who ran the businesses. As the president of a successful ARDC company put it, "This is a lonely job and there aren't many people I can talk to about the problems. I got plenty of psychic income from Doriot—and that was very important."[6]

Yet Doriot received little such psychic income from the investors in ARDC. During their first decade running the company, Doriot and his associates climbed the learning curve of venture investing, creating and figuring out the business at the same time. After their exhaustive analysis and due diligence efforts on several hundreds of businesses, by the mid-1950s they had invested in just a few dozen companies. Those portfolio companies held great promise, but with ARDC's decision to focus on "early-stage" businesses, tangible results would be a long time coming. For Wall Street investors (then as now), immediate profits tend to count more than future profits, and ARDC had little to show for its first several years in business. In the face of a rapidly ascending stock market during the late 1940s and early 1950s, the stock of ARDC was at best "flat," and more typically trading well below its IPO price of $25. ARDC and its founder were more often derided by the investment community than praised.

Doriot once shot back, complaining:

> Too many bankers and counselors have forgotten the history of the early years of our industrial giants of today. The first fifteen years of companies and of human beings are very much alike—hope, measles, failures, mumps, reorganizations, scarlet fever, executive troubles, whooping cough, etc. are parts of one's daily life. Hopes, disillusions, hard work, are all necessary, particularly during the first ten or fifteen years before a stable and healthy body or corporation can begin to exist.[7]

The early and mid-1950s were challenging for Doriot, and he must have experienced a cognitive dissonance between the two worlds in which he lived. At Harvard he was "Le Grand General," presiding over his classroom with authority and enjoying the adulation of students for his intellectual prowess and professional accomplishments. From the perspective of Wall Street, however, he produced little but disappointment and—perhaps for the first time in his professional life—began doubting himself. He bemoaned the fact that he was no longer able to find attractive investment opportunities and in 1954 wrote in his personal diary, "We do not know of any interesting projects. We do not know where to find interesting projects."[8] In that year his number-two person left the company, and Karl Compton, MIT's president and a consistent cheerleader for ARDC, passed away.

But despite any doubts Doriot harbored, he remained a staunch defender of the business. When MIT cast a vote of no confidence by divesting its ownership in ARDC, Doriot attempted to downplay the broader implications of MIT's stock sale by ascribing the decision wholly to the school's treasurer, Horace Ford, whom he dismissed as "weak and uninteresting" and never a believer in ARDC in the first place.[9] Those who still did believe in ARDC, however, would soon see their faith rewarded.

ARDC: After Digital Equipment Company

The second ten years in ARDC's history were in stark contrast to the first ten, finally proving the ultimate wisdom of patient investing and the viability of the venture capital business—and making the investors in the company's stock very happy. The turning point came in 1958, when a number of ARDC's long-term holdings started to catch fire, including two of the three investments the company made shortly after opening its doors in late 1946: High Voltage Engineering and Tracer Lab. But the real transformation of ARDC's fortunes came with its investment in a start-up operation called Digital Equipment Company.

In 1957, ARDC purchased a 70 percent equity position in DEC for $70,000, leaving the remaining 30 percent for the company's two MIT-trained founders, Ken Olsen and Harlan Anderson. At the time of the investment, DEC was just a fledgling three-man venture, operating from the corner of an abandoned woolen mill. Its focus was on building small-sized computers for scientific and medical applications—soon to be called minicomputers, since they were dwarfed in size by IBM's hulking mainframes.

Unlike the great majority of new ventures, DEC produced positive earnings from its first day in business. And with the DEC investment showing immediate promise, ARDC began to regain investor confidence. By 1958, the stock was consistently trading above its $25 initial offering price, and in 1959 it had climbed to $40 per share. With the stock at that level, Doriot launched another best-efforts sale of ARDC stock, raising $4 million through the issuance of 100,000 new shares. The proceeds from the offering enabled Doriot to solve his chronic problem of an inadequate level of investable funds. Through the first years of its existence, ARDC had to rely on dividends from portfolio companies or an occasional sale of one of the fund's holdings to supply additional operating capital; funds available for new investments never climbed much above a million dollars. Following the offering, ARDC enjoyed a cash position of roughly $5 million, much of which Doriot and his staff, after their methodical due diligence and highly selective approach to investing, deployed into the new technologies of the 1960s. The increased magnitude of ARDC's business also earned the company a 1961 listing on the New York Stock Exchange, and by that time the stock was trading above $60 per share. At the time of the NYSE listing, ARDC, after its prolonged and often barren gestation period, had finally attained critical mass, with investments in thirty-seven companies having a combined value of over $30 million.

ARDC's success, however late and painful in coming, helped pave the way for an emerging venture capital industry that would operate beyond the confines of Boston. In 1958, the California-based Draper, Gaither & Anderson venture fund was organized and served as the forerunner of the Silicon Valley investment partnerships that eventually dominated the business.[10] Also in 1958, a much larger competitive threat to ARDC arose following legislation by the U.S. Congress that created the Small Business Investment Company (SBIC) program with the charter to invest in new and emerging companies—and with the benefit of a host of special tax incentives, loan subsidies, and a $250 million initial appropriation of funds. In 1967, before the end of the first ten years of their existence, the several hundred newly formed SBICs passed the $1 billion mark in investments.

In 1967, despite the advent of new privately and publicly backed venture funds, ARDC was far and away the most prominent and successful player in the business. That year *Fortune* magazine published a major story on ARDC, "General Doriot's Dream Factory," in which it tabulated that the net-asset value of the company's forty-five companies at the time of the article had grown to $160 million. The article painted a deservedly sympathetic portrait of Doriot and profiled many of the companies ARDC had nurtured and grown. But the takeaway piece of information from the article was that, of the $160 million of value cited, fully $125 million, or 78 percent, was attributable to its $70,000 investment ten years earlier in minicomputer manufacturer Digital Equipment Company.[11]

DEC itself had gone public in 1966 at an IPO price of $22 per share, and within a year its stock price had soared to $70 per share. Doriot's decision ten years earlier to back DEC resulted in an 1,800-fold increase in that inspired investment. ARDC's spectacular return on its DEC investment captured the attention and imagination of the business world, and DEC served as an early example of how a "disruptive technology" can quickly turn an industry on its head—and create unheard of wealth for its backers. Prior to DEC, computers were mainframe monsters that required a separate room with raised floors to channel the vast cabling and special air conditioning to control the heat they generated. DEC, with its computers the size of a file cabinet, was a direct challenge to the business of the then-dominant IBM. The company ushered in the second generation of computing and changed the world of technology.

DEC also changed the way investment bankers and commercial bankers viewed their role. In 1967, the major Wall Street firms more or less limited their clientele to Fortune 500 companies with a demonstrated history of paying dividends on their common stock and a near certain ability to make interest and principal payments on their bonds. When Lehman Brothers, then one of the largest and most prestigious investment firms, was considering underwriting DEC's IPO, its partners were less than enthusiastic. The deal was assigned to a junior Lehman investment banker who would later remark, "I was a young associate and no one at Lehman had the slightest interest in doing an offering. No one knew what a minicomputer was. There was a prejudice that IBM was the only company that would ever do good. It was a throwaway and it was thrown at me."[12]

Before long, however, all of Wall Street's investment banks aggressively sought alliances with venture capital firms in the hope of handling breakthrough initial offerings. DEC's success encouraged more adventuresome behavior on the commercial banking side as well; Morgan Guaranty Trust, as the banking offshoot of the House of Morgan was known at the time, virtually insured the success of the DEC deal by committing to purchase 20 percent of the shares the Lehman-led underwriting group had to sell. That represented a sea change in investment philosophy from the days when an earlier generation of Morgan partners felt it necessary to combine three separate businesses to form IBM into a corporation that was large and safe enough to finance.

The remarkable success of DEC and its IPO also served as a confirmation of an investing model that was subsequently adopted by all successful venture capital firms. A key component of the model is the common sense–dictated practice of diversification. A venture capital firm is similar to a mutual fund, with holdings in a sufficient number of companies so that the poor performance of some of those holdings is offset by the superior performance of others. With a venture capital fund, the portfolio companies are mostly privately held and their securities are essentially illiquid; they also produce a range of investment gains and losses that is exceedingly wide. With DEC, ARDC finally had the kind of outlier success that can make venture capital so lucrative.

As Digital Equipment continued to lead the migration of computer users away from their mainframes to its desk-sized minicomputers, the value of the stock of both Digital Equipment and ARDC grew rapidly and in tandem, with one being the proxy for the other in the minds of many investors. One could make the point that ARDC was responsible for DEC's success through both its investment and the mentoring given to chief executive and founder Ken Olsen; the counterpoint is that the entrepreneurial Olsen, through his spectacularly successful Digital Equipment, created the success and viability of both ARDC and modern venture capital investing.

Whatever the case, it's indisputable that DEC was by far ARDC's best investment, illustrating the importance to venture capitalists of landing the occasional whale in an ocean of small fish. The annualized investment return that ARDC generated over its twenty-five-year life was 15.4 percent, a rate four to six percentage points higher than one would have realized during the same period by investing in a blue-chip stock portfolio such as the thirty stocks making up the Dow Jones Industrial Average. That would seem to be a fair premium for the risk inherent in venture investing. However, absent ARDC's investment in DEC, the annualized twenty-five-year return would have been more than cut in half, to just 7.4 percent.[13] That return would have been only slightly higher than that provided by a low-risk, investment-grade corporate bond—not nearly enough to stir the imagination of a venture capital investor.

Yet the fact remains that ARDC, after its very slow start, managed to produce those outsized returns for its investors. Throughout the go-go years, as the latter half of the 1960s would become known, ARDC was the first and brightest shining star of the venture capital business. But that enormous success also revealed flaws in the way the fund was structured— and flaws in the way Doriot managed it.

ARDC in Decline

After DEC's public offering, Doriot and a handful of his longtime staff members became very wealthy based on their early purchase of founders' shares of DEC common stock. But most of the other key players at ARDC did not share in the financial success, including several who had become upper-level managers of the fund. John Shane, an ARDC vice president recruited during the glory years of the 1960s, lamented, "It didn't matter when it was dimes and nickels, but when it was $20 million per person we were somewhat disappointed."[14]

Nor was there much wealth created for the venture capitalists at ARDC when other holdings ripened to financial success. Another vice president, Charles Waite, would later remark that after portfolio company Optical Scanning went public, "The CEO's net worth went from 0 to $10 million and I got a $2,000 raise, and so that was what eventually led to my leaving the firm."[15] Shane soon followed Waite out the door. The biggest loss to ARDC, however, was the resignation of William Elfers, a fifteen-year veteran of the company and Doriot's heir apparent. Elfers left to form Greylock Capital, a new venture firm organized in a partnership format that would allow for a more inclusive sharing of the wealth among its partners. Greylock, better able to recruit talent, would eventually overtake ARDC and become Boston's premier venture firm.

The crux of the compensation problem was Doriot's decision to set up ARDC as a mutual fund under the provisions of the Investment Company Act of 1940 and with accompanying supervision by the SEC. In the early years, Doriot was successful in negotiating important regulatory exemptions for ARDC, including how much stock it could own of a single business. That became key, since the 1940 act specified that a fund cannot hold more than 5 percent of the stock of any company, and ARDC almost always owned a greater percentage interest in its portfolio companies—most notably its 70 percent initial position in DEC. Doriot made little progress, however, in arguing for the issuance of stock options to his management team from the companies in which ARDC invested. Avoidance of a conflict of interest in the management of a fund is at the bedrock of the 1940 act, and it makes perfect sense in maintaining objectivity in the management of a typical mutual fund. But it is unworkable for a venture capital fund, where success—and financial reward—depend on a symbiotic relationship between the managers of the fund and the managers of the companies in which it invests.

Given the enormity of the problem caused by an inadequate compensation arrangement at ARDC, Doriot showed a perplexing lack of imagination in solving it. Conceivably, ARDC could have been taken private and freed from the inhibiting strictures of the 1940 act. Or more simply, it could have created affiliated new limited partnership funds along the lines of those successfully pioneered by the West Coast firm of Draper, Gaither & Anderson and followed by William Elfers at Greylock. A limited partnership turned out to be the perfect format for a venture fund. It was highly conducive to raising money from institutional investors who wanted to share in the investment returns but not assist the general partners in the management or share in their personal liabilities. And it was free from the constrictive SEC regulation that had long plagued ARDC. Indeed, when Elfers bolted from ARDC, he formed Greylock as a partnership and, based on the reputation he had established at ARDC, quickly raised $5 million from an A-list of wealthy families.

In the end, Doriot's inaction on the matter seemed to be the result of personality rather than structural impediments. In the 1967 *Fortune* article, the author quotes Doriot as describing his job as "building men and companies," with financial rewards only a by-product. "If a man is good and loyal and does not achieve a so-called good rate of return, I will stay with him." And using his own modest lifestyle as a model, he worried that his "good and loyal" men would fall victim to wealth that was attained too quickly, with their professional drive stalled when they could "start buying twenty-cylinder Cadillacs, fifty-room mansions, go skiing in summer, and swimming in winter."[16]

His overarching goal of creating the innovators and companies that would change the world—as opposed to the more worldly goals of producing an attractive investment return for ARDC's shareholders and wealth for ARDC's managers—was noble. Yet it often manifested itself in a somewhat patronizing manner, in which he referred to ARDC's companies as his children (a weighty comparison, given that Doriot and his wife made an apparent decision not to have children, believing they could not adequately support them on a professor's pay during the Great Depression). In the *Fortune* interview he told the article's author that, "We have our hearts in our companies, we are really doctors of childhood diseases here. When bankers or brokers tell me I should sell an ailing company, I ask them, 'Would you sell a child running a temperature of 104?'"

His views were those of a caring if condescending professor and an ascetic man nearing seventy. In addition, he likely had an overblown estimate of his influence on the men and companies he believed he was building. Peter Brooke, one of Doriot's former students at Harvard and later a leading figure in the expansion of venture capital investing internationally, would remark:

> A lot of mystique was created by the founder of the industry, Georges Doriot, who deserves every bit of the credit for inventing modern venture capital but who was also a bit of a showman. Doriot and his staff were very serious about all the good things they were doing for their portfolio companies. ARDC's office was like a movie set, filled with earnest young men convinced that they were determining the future of American business.[17]

As the accelerating defections of his top talent vividly showed, however, it was unrealistic to think that all of these "earnest young men" would subscribe to Doriot's altruistic view of the world. By 1970, the tangible financial rewards available to talented associates and young partners at other venture firms was growing only more apparent, and Doriot had a crisis of leadership on his hands.

Compounding the problems was another of Doriot's management foibles: an unwillingness to delegate. With his inflexible personality and his proprietary view of his creations and ideas, he had little confidence that anyone else could deliver on his vision. During the course of his forced retirement from Harvard, which was in line with the policies of the institution at the time, he simply cancelled Manufacturing, the popular business school course he had created and long taught. In his eyes, no other professor could present it with sufficient effectiveness.

With ARDC he had more control over his succession—and decided there wouldn't be one. His board members, taking their governance responsibilities seriously, set up a planning group called the Committee on 70, corresponding roughly to both the year 1970 and Doriot's age. But Doriot did not see any need to step down and continually dodged the issue. He took a passive-aggressive approach to the process, determining that all the candidates the board proposed as his successor had one or another fatal flaw. In 1972, with nothing to show for the work of the Committee on 70, Doriot and his board essentially finessed the succession issue by seeking a merger partner. In early 1972, the board accepted a $400 million offer from Textron, one of the major conglomerates of the day.

With the keenness of hindsight, it's hardly a surprise that the Textron arrangement failed. The compensation issue that had bedeviled ARDC only grew worse within a constrictive corporate structure and, after a brief time away from the controls, Doriot again became chairman of the company, now a subsidiary of Textron. With Doriot in his midseventies and just a skeleton management staff remaining, new investment activity dwindled to a trickle. By 1976, ARDC had atrophied to a dormant holding company, and Textron took the course of least resistance by liquidating its portfolio in as orderly and profitable a manner as possible during the lackluster economy of the mid-1970s.

The Private Equity Offspring

Self-inflicted personnel and structural problems led to an unfortunate ending for ARDC, but Doriot's legacy remains large and the broader impact of his "dream factory" has been monumental, transforming the way new businesses and industries are developed and funded. In addition, in the 1970s and 1980s the venture capital industry produced a new offspring: the professionally managed and institutionally funded private equity firm.

In some ways private equity and venture capital are alike. They are both invariably structured as limited partnerships, and the general partners that run the show are highly selective in their search for investments. Their managers also add value beyond the initial capital infusion, providing invaluable advice and contacts, recruiting qualified and effective directors to the board, and guiding the company's top management through a "liquidity event" when it is time to exit the investment by going public or selling the business.

Likewise, both types of operations seek high returns through high risk. Yet there is one essential difference: venture capital is about taking *business* risk and private equity is about taking *financial* risk. Doriot's ARDC and latter-day venture capital firms invest in young companies with less than fully tested products and business models with the goal of creating revenues and profitable growth in entirely new markets. DEC remains the prototype of a company funded by venture capitalists.

Private equity is a much different story, with its success depending on well-executed and well-timed financial engineering, usually in some variation of a leveraged buyout, or LBO. Leverage, in the parlance of finance, is the use of debt; in an LBO, the underlying business of the company being invested in remains largely unchanged, but its balance sheet—and often its management team—is totally revamped.

As far as capturing the imagination of the financial world, the counterpart of the DEC story is that of Gibson Greeting Cards. In 1982, former secretary of the Treasury William Simon, through his company Wesray Capital Corporation, purchased all the common stock of Gibson Greeting, then the third-largest greeting card business in the United States, for a total of $80 million. Only $1 million of that purchase price was said to have been contributed through Wesray-supplied equity, with the balance of the funding coming from various forms of debt obligations. The leverage-to-equity ratio of the Gibson Greeting deal was roughly 80:1—highly leveraged by any standard.

Just sixteen months later, Gibson Greeting went public, with the proceeds of the offering being used mainly to pay off the debt that had been incurred for the purchase. After the IPO, the value of the shares of common stock that Wesray bought for $1 million grew to $44 million. Simon and his partners enjoyed an investment return previously unheard of—on the scale of DEC but realized much more quickly.

Following the success of the Gibson Greeting deal, many more LBO investment firms were formed, and the few that had already existed at the time, Kohlberg Kravis Roberts being the most notable, were able to substantially increase their access to institutional funding. At the same time, with the advent of plentiful debt funding through junk bonds, LBOs grew in size as well as in number.

Some of the existing venture funds, tempted by the highly publicized returns from LBOs, branched into the turf of private equity. But today venture firms rarely support both the traditional and private equity approaches to the venture capital business. The skills required are very different; the former entails evaluating new business growth opportunities, while the latter requires evaluating the opportunities through recapitalizing a balance sheet and rejuvenating a management team. Venture capital firms and private equity firms, though each large in number and scale, tend to go their separate ways.

A Proven Format

The successor firms to ARDC, both those operating in traditional venture capital and in private equity, were given a boost by favorable policy changes coming from the U.S. government during the late 1970s. In 1978 the U.S. Congress reduced the maximum tax rate on capital gains from investments to 28 percent from 49 percent, an obvious benefit to a business whose primary mission is to produce such capital gains. Then, in 1978, the Labor Department clarified the "prudent man" rule, opening the field of venture capital investing to pension funds. Following the latter development, private and public pension funds have consistently accounted for much of the money channeled to venture capital partnerships.

According to the National Venture Capital Association's 2013 yearbook, there are now more than 1,200 active traditional venture capital funds, and the amount they currently have under management approaches $200 billion.[18] Boston remains a major center for venture funding, but California, and in particular the Silicon Valley region, has long eclipsed New England as far as venture capital investing. The technology-driven entrepreneurs drawing their inspiration from success stories like those of MIT's Ken Olsen still have a major presence in the technology-equipped buildings along the Route 128 ring around Boston, but that is all dwarfed by similar activity on or around Sand Hill Road near Stanford University.

Perhaps as remarkable as dollar and geographic growth is the basically unchanged modus operandi that Doriot pioneered at ARDC. Intense due diligence and extreme selectivity—ARDC investigated several thousand investment candidates from which it selected just a hundred or so over its thirty-year history—is the enduring practice in all successful venture funds. And the longer-term record shows that even with that careful approach, the results of venture investing tend to conform to that of its pioneer, and most venture-financed companies in the aggregate produce just mediocre returns on investment given the high degree of risk the partners assume. Yet just one standout performer in a fund, a counterpart of DEC, such as Apple, Oracle, Genentech, Starbucks, Amazon, FedEx, Facebook, or Google, keeps money flowing to venture funds.

As might be expected, that flow is highly erratic and fluctuates from year to year depending on recent successes and the availability of exit strategies for funds looking to liquidate their holdings. In periods in which there is ebullience in the market for IPOs and high equity prices—the dotcom frenzy of the late 1990s being an example of a particularly receptive market—money tends to flow to venture capital funds without limits. In those times, overcapacity becomes the concern, with too much money chasing too few quality deals. During periods of market pessimism and a drought of exit possibilities, the opposite problem occurs, and deals that should receive funding go begging.

Yet despite its notorious cyclicality, the venture capital business, using the format that Doriot invented many decades earlier, sows the seeds of innovation that propel the economy. In 1946, when Ralph Flanders, president of the Boston Fed, threw his support toward the creation of ARDC, he put his finger precisely on the broader benefits of venture capital investing:

> The continued maintenance of prosperity and the continued increase in the general standard of living depend in a large measure in finding financial support for that comparatively small percentage of new ideas and developments, which give promise of expanded production and employment, and an increased standard of living for the American people.[19]

Flanders and the other backers of ARDC would have been happy to know that in the twenty-first century more than $20 billion flow into new companies each year from venture funds. And while that represents just about one-tenth of 1 percent of U.S. banking transactions, its impact is disproportionately profound. According to Tom Perkins, founder of the prominent Silicon Valley firm Kleiner Perkins Caufield & Byers and a former president of the National Venture Capital Association, venture capital investment from professionally managed venture funds has been leveraged over time into some twelve million private-sector U.S. jobs, which is roughly 11 percent of all such jobs in the American economy.[20]

Though Charles Merrill and Georges Doriot were contemporaries, they operated in very different spheres of the financial markets; it is not likely that they ever met. Yet both men made their impact by broadening the focus of American finance to the benefit of its smaller actors. Merrill gave retail investors, for the first time, a fair and even-handed approach to expanding their wealth by investing in securities. Doriot performed a similar task by creating a way for new businesses with promise to tap the capital markets. He gave each and every budding entrepreneur an audience—and for many he provided the means to build their dreams.

8

Benjamin Graham: 1894–1976
Dean of Wall Street

I should say, Senator, that I am something of an academic man myself. . . . They made me a professor because I am a practical operator.

—BENJAMIN GRAHAM

On an early spring afternoon in 1911, sixteen-year-old Benjamin Graham took the West Side subway from Fulton Street in downtown Manhattan all the way uptown to 116th Street, then walked a few blocks to the home of Frederick Keppel, dean of Columbia College. Graham was self-conscious about his grimy work clothes and hands still dirty from working all day in a machine shop. But after work was the only time he could get away, and so Dean Keppel accommodated him by suggesting an early evening meeting at Keppel's house. The year before, Graham had been devastated when Columbia turned him down for a scholarship, and he had no idea why the dean was so interested in seeing him now.

Meeting in his study, in the glow of fresh embers from the fireplace, Keppel explained the reason he asked Graham to visit. "You know, we're frightfully embarrassed about you in the registrar's office. The fact is, Grossbaum, you won a scholarship here last year but we didn't give it to you."

Graham—his family changed their name from Grossbaum to Graham during the wave of anti-German sentiment brought about by World War I—was perplexed. Precocious and intellectually ambitious, he'd had his heart set on entering Columbia College at age fifteen. He was a math prodigy but also a devotee of the classics of literature. Growing up he lived in the worlds of the *Iliad* and the *Odyssey* and devoted one of his preteen summers to learning French so he could read authors in the original. When he was interviewed for the Pulitzer Scholarship the year before and was asked about the most meaningful book he ever read, he responded enthusiastically that is was all the volumes of Edward Gibbon's *Decline and Fall of the Roman Empire*—he said that he personally identified with Septimius Severus and other Roman heroes. The rejection that had followed this interview was a profound blow to the young intellectual's ego. But suddenly, that rejection seemed to be undergoing a reversal, and Graham was at a loss. "How . . . how did that happen?"

"You have a brother or a cousin, Louis Grossbaum, who has been here for three years on a Pulitzer Scholarship," Keppel replied. "When we awarded yours the registrar's office got the names mixed up. They couldn't give a scholarship to a boy who already had one, so they gave yours to the next fellow in line."

The error had been even more costly than Graham first understood. As the dean explained, he hadn't been awarded the Pulitzer Scholarship but had actually won the more comprehensive full-tuition Columbia Alumni Scholarship, given to the student with the highest entrance examination score. Keppel said that Columbia would set the matter straight by awarding him the Alumni Scholarship for the coming fall.

"But I've lost a whole year," Graham said.

"True, true, and we're genuinely sorry about our mistake," Keppel responded, "but you would have been much too young to get the most out of college if you had started a year ago. This machine-shop training of yours is the best thing for you. You'll have much more savoir faire and maturity than the other boys of your age."[1]

For Graham, of course, the work at the machine shop wasn't done simply to develop savoir faire. His failure to receive a scholarship had left him with no choice but to abandon his Columbia ambitions; after a rapid decline in family fortunes, he simply had no means to afford a college education. When he was one year old, the Grossbaums—father, mother, and three sons—moved to New York from London to expand the family's china and bric-a-brac business, and Graham remembered an upper-middle-class early childhood, with "Mademoiselle," his French governess, supervising play in Central Park and "Cook" preparing the family meals. But his privileged life ended abruptly when his father succumbed to pancreatic cancer at age thirty-five and, shortly after, the family business folded under the inept management of Graham's uncle Maurice. His mother was forced to turn their home into a boardinghouse, and the family shuffled between living there and living at Uncle Maurice's flat, where Graham and his brothers shared bedrooms and one bathroom with his cousins.

Growing up, Graham held dozens of successive jobs to shore up his family's precarious financial situation, beginning with delivery of the *Saturday Evening Post* and including his current job at the Fulton Street machine shop. Before starting his most recent job, he attempted to salvage his college hopes and briefly attended the City College of New York, an institution with free tuition. But in what he acknowledged as "pure, unadulterated snobbishness," he was profoundly dejected by the quality of his classmates and dropped out of CCNY in favor of pursuing a blue-collar career.

His ultimate decision to start at Columbia the following fall did not mark an end to his working days. Though Columbia's tuition was handled by the alumni scholarship, Graham still had to finance his living expenses with a string of part-time jobs, including tutoring the children of army officers, ushering at a vaudeville house, cashiering at a movie theater near the Bowery, and operating a punch-card machine for an express delivery company. But even with the burden of balancing work and studies, Graham finished Columbia's four-year program in two-and-a-half years, more than making up the year he had lost because of the registrar's clerical error. He was elected to Phi Beta Kappa and, by virtue of attaining the second-best grades among his classmates, served as the class salutatorian.

Nevertheless, he found little personal joy in college, reflecting ruefully that "I had always dreamed of college life as the halcyon period of youth, a wonderful combination of education, friendship, romance, athletics, and all-around fun. Alas! Looking back at my own college career, I recall no such happy interlude."[2] His comments reflect a lifelong regret about his inability to cultivate friends, develop personal relationships, and think beyond his own ambitions. In another reconsideration of his college years he said, "At Columbia, a group of such friends did me the honor of inviting me to join the leading Jewish fraternity—Zeta Beta Tau. I declined, saying I could afford neither the time nor the money involved. I should have made the time and borrowed the money."[3]

Graham may not have been enchanted by Columbia, but Columbia was enchanted with him. In the month preceding his graduation in the spring of 1914, he was offered teaching positions in the departments of mathematics, philosophy, and English. But Dean Keppel, who continued as Graham's trusted advisor throughout his brief stay at Columbia, counseled him to delay accepting a life in academia and to enter the business world instead. Shortly afterward Keppel introduced him to Samuel

Newburger, a partner in the Wall Street firm of Newburger, Henderson & Loeb. Graham, who had dropped the sole economics course he had enrolled in, hardly knew the difference between a stock and a bond. But with his personal and family financial conditions still shaky, Wall Street looked promising, and he took the job Newburger offered. Starting at $12 per week he delivered securities to and from the firm's headquarters on Broadway, with the prospect of becoming a bond salesman after he learned the business from the ground up. Few would have guessed, least of all Graham, that he would someday return to Columbia with the informal title of "Dean of Wall Street."

Mr. Market and Intrinsic Value

By the time Graham retired from Wall Street in 1956, investing in common stocks had become a respectable endeavor, and that respectability was due in some important measure to Graham's methodical and commonsense approach to what would become known as value investing. But upon his arrival at the Newburger firm in 1914, putting common stocks in a portfolio was not considered to be a legitimate form of investing but rather a speculation that had appeal only to the naive and greedy—and to the market operators who stood ready to take advantage of such naiveté and greed. As a result, well-recommended young men looking to enter the respectable sector of high finance often began their career as bond salesmen. Like Graham, they rarely had any familiarity with the bond market when they entered the business. Nick Carraway, F. Scott Fitzgerald's narrator in *The Great Gatsby*, may have been typical, saying, "I graduated from New Haven in 1915 and decided to learn the bond business. Everybody I knew was in the bond business, so I supposed it could support one more single man."[4]

But unlike Nick Carraway, Graham had little of the self-assurance and few of the social contacts needed to deal comfortably with the old-money bond buyers who managed the trust and insurance companies where the bonds were placed. He recounted that after some time on the job, "I had brought in absolutely no bond sale commissions to offset my $12 per week emolument."[5] But he did develop a keen understanding of how bonds were structured, and in his early days at Newburger, Henderson & Loeb he diligently read—practically memorized—Lawrence Chamberlain's *The Principles of Bond Investment*, the definitive textbook on the subject. Yet his book knowledge produced no revenue for the Newburger firm, and he found himself eyeing a job as a "statistician" with a rival firm, where he could put his analytical and writing skills to work by preparing reports for use by the sales force—and enjoy a raise to $18 per week.

When he announced his planned resignation to Samuel Newburger, however, the managing partner was incensed that another firm had violated Wall Street protocol by stealing a valued employee. Graham protested, "But I'm not cut out for a bond salesman; I'm sure I'd do better at statistical work." Newburger, not wanting to lose his bright young employee, replied, "That's fine. It's time we had a statistical department here. You can be it."[6] Graham stayed, even though his initial raise for doing so was only to $15. Over the succeeding nine years at Newburger, Henderson & Loeb, with most of that time coinciding with his twenties, Graham rose rapidly through the firm's ranks, and by 1923 he was a full partner with an unusual arrangement under which he had no liability for any of the firm's risks but was nevertheless entitled to 2.5 percent of its profits.

Graham's success might reasonably be ascribed to his development of a single revolutionary concept in the field of securities analysis: intrinsic value. Heretofore, common stocks were often bought and sold based primarily on the prospects for movements in their price, with little thought given to what the underlying business of the company was worth—or even what its business was about. With the full-disclosure requirements of securities laws still decades away, common stockholders received precious little information about publicly traded companies after they had purchased shares of stock in an initial offering. Absent that information, investors— in reality, speculators—attempted to time their stock purchases by divining the length and breadth of market moves. The players in the infamous stock pools that would reach their disastrous zenith later in the 1920s based their decisions on tips, rumors, inside information, and a gut sense of price "momentum."

But throughout the craziness of the Roaring Twenties, Graham was designing and implementing a much more rational and profitable method of investing in the stock market, one based on digging up enough information on a business to ascertain its fundamental value and then comparing that value to the price at which the security was trading in the market. His commonsense procedure created easy decision rules. If, based on analysis, it is possible to determine that the underlying or intrinsic value of a stock is $20, but at the same time you find that it is selling in the market at $18, the stock is presumably worthy of purchase. Graham was fond of putting the disparity between calculated intrinsic value and market price into a

Mr. Market metaphor. Sounding like a character out of a children's book about the stock market, Graham describes Mr. Market as your obliging partner

> who every day tells you what he thinks your interest is worth and furthermore offers either to buy you out or to sell you an additional interest on that basis. Sometimes his idea of value appears plausible and justified by business developments and prospects as you know them. Often, on the other hand, Mr. Market lets his enthusiasm or his fears run away with him, and the value he proposes seems to you a little short of silly.[7]

So, if Mr. Market stands willing to sell you shares of common stock for $18 that you calculate to be worth $20 each, should you buy them? By Graham's investment approach, not necessarily. He imposes a second condition that is central to his decision making: an adequate margin of safety; that is, a difference that is large enough to absorb any miscalculations made in estimating the intrinsic value or just some amount of bad luck that might be encountered. So an $18 price may not be low enough—but that, of course, raises the question of how large the cushion needs to be. Graham devoted significant thought to this question, and a quick example involving his first major success at Newburger, Henderson & Loeb is illustrative.

In a stock pick that Graham would credit with being "the real beginning of my career as a distinctive type of Wall Street operator,"[8] he carefully calculated the value of the several holdings of the Guggenheim Exploration Company that would shortly be available to the company's shareholders upon the earlier announced intention to dismantle the holding company and distribute shares of the individual businesses to the stockholders. At the completion of his analysis he was certain that the sum of the Guggenheim parts was greater than the whole, meaning that the price for which Mr. Market was willing to sell the whole company was less than the value the shareholders would receive a few months later upon liquidation. By Graham's calculations, the total value of Guggenheim's interests, mainly its holdings of copper mining companies throughout the West, equated to a per-share stock price of $76.23. Yet the price of Guggenheim's own shares on the New York Stock Exchange was just $68.88. So in Graham's parlance, Mr. Market was willing to sell those shares at a price that discounted their value by $7.35, or nearly 10 percent.[9] It was a discovery that the youthful

Graham would describe in hyperbolic terms: "Here was I, a stout Cortez-Balboa, discovering a new Pacific with my eagle eye. Imagine!"[10]

Cortez-Balboa or not, that discovery was just the first of many "arbitrage" opportunities that Graham would unearth. Putting a successful arbitrage in place was fairly simple. In the case of the Guggenheim transaction, for instance, it required the simultaneous purchase of shares of Guggenheim and the short sale of the appropriate number of shares in companies that Guggenheim owned, including shares in such companies as Kennecott Copper, Chino Copper, and American Smelting. But was the margin of safety sufficient to protect against the risks? There was always a possibility that the Guggenheim shareholders would not approve the proposed transaction or some legal problem would delay or scuttle the whole plan. Also, the sale of the separate holdings would be a short sale, and all sorts of problems could crop up in that connection.

But as Graham would recount, the 10 percent cushion was all that was needed in this case: "The dissolution plan went through without a hitch; the profit was realized exactly as calculated; and everyone was happy, not least myself."[11] Besides making his mark at Newburger, Henderson & Loeb, he also made a great deal of money for himself. He had earlier negotiated a new arrangement whereby he would be allocated a 20 percent share of the firm's profit on the transactions he engineered—a profit in the Guggenheim case that totaled $7.35 for each of the "fair number" of shares the firm purchased. Whatever his personal profit from the transaction, it was sufficient to establish his value to Newburger, Henderson & Loeb, and his weekly salary more than tripled to $50 week. His profit was also sufficient to buy his first car and announce his engagement to Hazel Mazur, the first of his three wives.[12]

Unlocking Value

By 1923, Graham was not just serving as Newburger, Henderson & Loeb's "lead statistician," but also running much of the firm's operations and systems business, handling its over-the-counter business, and, despite a self-professed ineptitude at selling, bringing in a respectable number of new customers. But as was probably inevitable for someone with his intellect and drive, Graham soon outgrew the confines of a traditional Wall Street firm. So after nearly a decade with the Newburger firm, he left to open his own money management company, where he could focus on his well-developed competence in securities analysis and enjoy hefty performance fees from his clients. After going it alone for a few years, he formed an agreeable partnership with Jerome Newman, one that would last for thirty years. Newman handled the administrative aspects of what would become the Graham-Newman Corporation and, between the two of them, they raised the initial several hundred thousand dollars from investors eager to tap into Graham's recognized money management abilities.

Many of the new firm's early successes followed the pattern of the Guggenheim Exploration transaction, with Graham-Newman making money for its clients and, of course, for the firm's two partners by ferreting out profitable arbitrage and other special situations. Through his financial detective work, for instance, Graham determined that the market was placing a value on the chemical company E. I. du Pont de Nemours that was no more than the value of its holdings in General Motors stock. That meant that the chemical business effectively had no recognized value—Mr. Market was willing to sell all of DuPont at a stock price that reflected only its ownership in General Motors. To take advantage of that anomaly, Graham put in trades to purchase DuPont common stock and at the same time sell short seven times as many shares of General Motors. His firm benefited handsomely when the rest of the market woke up to the obvious mispricing of the DuPont stock. At the conclusion of the transaction, Graham no doubt understated the profitability of the transaction for the Graham-Newman partners and investors by remarking matter-of-factly that "in due course a goodly spread appeared in our favor, and I undid the operation at the projected profit."[13]

Likewise, he discovered by searching through public records at the Interstate Commerce Commission that the pipeline companies spun off from the Standard Oil Company under the provisions of a 1911 antitrust action owned an enormous amount of investment-grade railroad bonds— and that the value of those bonds alone exceeded the market value of the publicly traded common stocks of the pipeline companies that held the bonds. Graham made large investments in the Northern Pipeline Company, and by 1928 Graham-Newman was its second-largest shareholder, behind only the Rockefeller Foundation. Taking an activist approach to investment that would not fully bloom on Wall Street for years to come, Graham led a series of shareholder actions and lawsuits against Northern Pipeline to coerce its recalcitrant management to put the shareholders' interest in front of their own by distributing the bonds to the owners of the Northern Pipeline common stock. It took years, but Graham eventually prevailed in having the bonds turned over to the company's shareholders. Between that distribution and an increase in the price of Northern Pipeline's stock, Graham and his firm more than doubled the value of what became one of Graham-Newman's major investments.[14]

Although most of the investments undertaken by Graham-Newman over the decades were not strictly arbitrage-related like Guggenheim, DuPont, and Northern Pipeline, most were, in one way or another, special situations in which securities could be purchased at less than their liquidation value. Those special situations were discovered through Graham's painstakingly thorough screening of investment opportunities, in which he looked for companies whose intrinsic value had gone unrecognized by Mr. Market and that offered a substantial margin of safety to mitigate risk. In his methodical style, Graham categorized special situations into six separate classes: class A: standard arbitrages, based on a reorganization, recapitalization, or merger plan; class B: cash payments, in recapitalizations or mergers; class C: cash payments on sale or liquidation; class D: litigated matters; class E: public utility breakups; and, as a catch-all category, class F: miscellaneous special situations.[15]

A Signature Investment

The most "special" of Graham's special situations would be an investment in a business that could, if necessary, be liquidated at any time at a profit but which also had the potential for unexpected—"speculative" in Graham's way of looking at things—upside benefits in the future. Fitting this description perfectly, especially the upside benefits part, was Graham-Newman's 1948 purchase of a half-interest in the Government Employees Insurance Company. This became, by far, the firm's most successful investment.

Known more commonly as GEICO, and nowadays often associated with its green, Cockney gecko mascot, the company at the time of the investment was a twelve-year-old automobile insurance operation that sold its policies directly to government employees through the mail. It enjoyed reduced costs through bypassing agents and selling its insurance products to a set of policyholders who had fewer than average accidents. A low-cost, low-risk business like GEICO was made to order for Graham. When GEICO's founder was willing to sell his half-ownership at the very reasonable price of $720,000, Graham jumped at the opportunity, even though that amount represented about one-quarter of Graham-Newman's assets under management at the time.[16]

Due to provisions of the Investment Company Act of 1940, it was not permissible for investment managers to own more than 10 percent of any company, so the GEICO shares were distributed to the Graham-Newman investors. By the time Graham-Newman shut down its business in 1956, the value of the GEICO shares had risen over elevenfold, from $51 to $614. For the investors who held on to those shares, the value of the GEICO holdings at their peak would reach a 1972 high of $16,823 per share.[17]

Graham's GEICO investment illustrates another aspect of his investment approach that is even more fundamental than his Mr. Market and margin of safety maxims, namely his assertion that "investment is most intelligent when most businesslike."[18] When he bought the controlling position in GEICO, he was buying a business for the long haul, a totally different mind-set than that used by most investors, who buy or sell a *stock* if and when it hits some near-term price target.

Throughout his investing and writing careers, Graham felt the need to clarify, over and over again, the importance of approaching investment as a business proposition. At its core, his admonition to think like a businessperson is a plea to fully understand the fundamentals and risks of the business one is considering investing in. Further, if the investment conclusion is based on facts and solid judgment, Graham encouraged investors to trust their knowledge and experience and make investment decisions independent of the opinions of others—especially the opinions of those who have commission or other incentives.

When the market wouldn't conform to his rational approach to investing, he could, like a frustrated schoolteacher, slip into a scold, as he did in a *Forbes* article he wrote at the nadir of the stock market in the early 1930s. Stockholders, he wrote,

> have forgotten that they are *owners of a business* and not merely owners of a quotation on the stock ticker. It is time, and high time, that the millions of American shareholders turned their eyes from the daily market reports long enough to give some attention to the enterprises themselves of which they are the proprietors, and which exist for their benefit and at their pleasure.[19]

The tone of the 1932 article no doubt reflected Graham's frustration with Mr. Market's inability to assign a correct value to common stocks, many of which were selling far below their liquidating value. But it also underscores a crucial requirement of successful value investing—the recognition of irrational pricing by *other* investors coupled with a willingness to think like businesspeople and correct their mistakes by buying or selling at the "right" prices. During the 1930s, however, Mr. Market was stubbornly refusing to adhere to rational business behavior. What Graham was experiencing was an apt confirmation of the remark attributed to John Maynard Keynes that "markets can remain irrational a lot longer than you and I can remain solvent." He scaled back his stock market investments, but in the irrational 1930s the joint account he was managing fell in value from $2.5 million in 1929 to around $750,000 at the time of his *Forbes* article.[20]

The GEICO investment also illustrates another of Graham's short but profound principles of value investing: *If a common stock is a good investment it is also a good speculation.* That statement, first attributed to him in a pamphlet he wrote for Newburger, Henderson & Loeb's customers, called "Lessons for Investors," would serve as the lynchpin of much that he would later say and write about successful investing.[21] In the case of the GEICO investment, the $51 price per share paid in 1948 could be easily tested by the many financial yardsticks Graham applied—working capital, reserves, stability of cash flow, and so forth—to justify its *current* value without regard to any improvements or growth in its operations that might unfold in the *future*. GEICO's future prospects *might* brighten later, but the $51 price didn't include any need for that to happen—and, as usual with his investments, the price had a built-in margin of safety in the event things somehow worsened.

In poker terms, Graham didn't bet on the come; he played the hand he was dealt and never assumed cards that would come his way later would improve that hand. Walter Schloss, a prominent investor who happened to be in the Graham-Newman office at the time the GEICO investment was made, recalls Graham saying "Walter, if this purchase doesn't work out, we can always liquidate it and get our money back."[22]

So why is a good investment like GEICO at $51 in 1948 also a good speculation for future years? In a word, because any upside benefits are free. If good things happened to GEICO's business beyond 1948—which they certainly did—the investor enjoys the eventual upside without paying for it up front. Graham believed that investors, like all mortals, are incapable of divining the future and therefore should not pay up for long-term prospects. As Graham put it, "An investment operation is one which, upon thorough analysis promises safety of principal and an adequate return. Operations not meeting these requirements are speculative."[23] Yet if a sound investment happens to also provide outsized returns, so much the better, and in a portfolio made up of solid investments, some, like GEICO, will go on to become bonanzas—"all this and heaven too," as Graham would characterize such an investment.[24]

What the Record Shows

Graham was the ultimate empiricist. The success of an investment depended on the return that it produced; a money manager's acumen was judged by the numbers and nothing but. Without the success of GEICO included, however, the long-term record of Graham-Newman is good but not sensational. In a 1977 monograph prepared by Irving Kahn and Robert Milne, both editors at the time of the *Financial Analysts Journal*, the authors attempted to compare the results of Graham's investment partnerships over time and found that—again, without GEICO, it should be emphasized—the results for investors, after Graham and Newman's fees were taken into consideration, were not significantly different from those realized by investing in the Standard & Poor's 500 Index or the Dow Jones Industrial Average. John Bogle's first index fund was still many years away, but investors would have done about as well investing in that kind of low-cost mutual fund as they did with Graham-Newman. For eleven-and-a-half years—from January 31, 1945, when public information about Graham-Newman's investments became available through the *Moody's Manual of Banks and Finance Companies*, until the firm's dissolution in 1956—Graham-Newman experienced an annual rate of return of 15.5 percent. By comparison, the S&P 500 had a return of 18.3 percent.[25]

But during that time, the GEICO investment, to comply with Securities and Exchange Commission investment advisor requirements, had been distributed to the Graham-Newman partners. If it is assumed that the investors who received the GEICO stock held on to it until 1956, the record of Graham-Newman partners would have been much better. Kahn and Milne calculate that 100 shares of Graham-Newman would have appreciated in value from $11,413 on January 31, 1948, to $70,413 on August 20, 1956, the date of the firm's liquidation. The same amount invested in the S&P 500 would have grown to only $30,968.[26] Kahn and Milne also point out that on a risk-adjusted basis, a Graham-Newman stock portfolio would have been less risky than the S&P 500.

The authors—one of whom, Kahn, was an assistant to Graham at Columbia University—attempt to portray Graham's value-based investment style as producing an alluring combination of low risk and superior return. Yet when looking at the record, with and without GEICO, it's an inescapable conclusion that some measure of the Benjamin Graham lore is based on his being lucky in addition to being very smart and diligent. Graham, always straightforward if not self-effacing about his investment record, would reflect in 1973 that "ironically enough, the aggregate profits accruing from the GEICO investment decision far exceeded the sum of all the others realized through twenty years of wide-ranging operation in the partners' specialized fields, involving much investigation, endless pondering, and countless individual decisions."[27]

Supporting the irony, Graham notes that the GEICO investment broke many of his own rules. It was indeed purchased at an initial price that was below what it could presumably be liquidated for, but other parts of the Graham-Newman rule book were summarily disregarded, including the rule of never investing more than 5 percent of the fund in any one security; the GEICO investment was closer to 25 percent. And later, when the price of GEICO's common stock soared past any reasonable estimate of its liquidation value, Graham still hung on to the investment, embracing the price momentum philosophy of a growth investor. Graham's response to these contradictions? "There are several different ways to make money in Wall Street."[28]

Something of an Academic

So while Graham was clearly a talented money manager, this alone cannot account for the legendary status he has achieved. At Graham-Newman's high point, the firm was managing no more than $20 million, not a major amount even in the 1950s, and its record, if GEICO is stripped away, was at best average. So if he had simply run Graham-Newman as a successful but low-profile operation using his profitable investment rules and standards, his name might be little remembered. But he was at heart more of an academic than an operator, and his widely aired ideas on investments and investing changed the way Wall Street worked. It was Graham's intellectual contribution of rationalizing the basis for buying and selling securities that gave him such high standing in the investment world.

In his 1955 testimony before Senator James W. Fulbright, chairman of the Committee on Banking and Currency of the U.S. Senate, the "Dean of Wall Street" made his focus clear:

> GRAHAM: I should say, Senator, that I am something of an academic man myself.
>
> FULBRIGHT: I did not know that.
>
> GRAHAM: I have the title of adjunct professor of finance at Columbia University, and I give a course in the evaluation of common stocks.
>
> FULBRIGHT: I saw you on television in an Ed Morrow show, but I did not understand that you were a professor. I thought they had brought you in as a practical operator to tell them how it was done. I misunderstood.
>
> GRAHAM: They made me a professor because I am a practical operator.[29]

Indeed, throughout his long career as a "practical operator," Graham's academic side was always evident. During his early days at Newburger, Henderson & Loeb, he gravitated toward writing rather than selling, preparing analytical write-ups for the firm's sales force and customers, and as his investment philosophy began to take shape, he wrote pamphlets for nonprofessionals, called "Lessons for Investors." For the investment community, he prepared several articles for a leading publication of the time called the *Magazine of Wall Street*, with the first article, "Bargains in Bonds," hinting at his opportunistic investment approach. His later articles in the same magazine developed analytical frameworks far beyond anything that had been used in the past, prompting the editor of the magazine to confide to Graham: "Ben, neither I nor anyone else around here can make head or tail of your formulas. It looks as if you've done the whole thing with mirrors. But I've enough confidence in you to publish the article anyway."[30]

After dozens of articles for the *Magazine of Wall Street*—with occasional pieces prepared for more theoretical publications such as the *American Mathematical Monthly*—Graham began thinking of writing a textbook to put in one place the ideas he had formulated and successfully practiced over the years. In 1927, just a year after he had formed his partnership with Jerome Newman, he approached Columbia University with the idea of giving a series of evening lectures, collectively called Security Analysis, on both bond and common stock investing in order to test and refine his approaches in front of interested Wall Street professionals. The university was receptive, and Graham began to teach his course to a large and growing audience, always assisted by the young Columbia faculty member, David Dodd, who faithfully compiled notes from each of the lectures with an eye toward organizing them later into a book. Because of the breakthroughs in the field of investment selection covered by the lectures and because of the heightened interest in the stock market in the 1920s, Graham's courses soon were vastly oversubscribed, with standing room only availability in Columbia's lecture halls.

It was seven years before the Security Analysis lecture course became a comprehensive textbook by the same name—and Graham was grateful that the book took so long to produce. He needed the input from his students to better shape the book to their needs, but even more important, he wanted to incorporate the lessons from the horrendous damage of the extended stock market collapse of the 1930s. For Graham that damage was experienced firsthand, as the accounts he was managing on his investors' behalf plummeted in value from $2.5 million in 1929 to less than a third of that amount by 1933.[31] In his words, he was able to "pour into *Security Analysis* wisdom acquired at the cost of much suffering."[32] (Recognizing that this suffering was felt more tangibly by his investors than by himself, Graham entered into an agreement with those investors to reduce his management compensation at the beginning of 1934 until the investors were made whole—which happened by the end of 1935.[33])

Security Analysis became his magnum opus and was eventually published in 1934—a seven-hundred-page doorstop of a book coauthored with Dodd. In the first paragraph of the book's preface, the authors set the tone, stating that it is "not addressed to the complete novice" and that the book's emphasis is on "distinguishing the investment from the speculative approach." Then, in fifty-two comprehensive, detailed, and well-written chapters, the authors describe the various financial instruments for investment and set forth an analytical framework for determining their value. Nothing like *Security Analysis* had ever been written and, for the adherents of the value approach to investing, nothing has been written like it since. The best known of the large number of value investors today is Warren Buffett, one of the world's two or three richest individuals. In the foreword to the sixth edition of *Security Analysis* in 2009, Buffett proclaims that the book, and later his personal association with Graham and Dodd while he was a student at Columbia in 1950 and 1951, provided the road map for his own investing and that "there's been no reason to look for another."[34] As though other endorsements are needed, Barton Biggs, a noted hedge fund investor and the developer of Morgan Stanley's research department, recalls that when he was first considering a career in securities research, his father gave him a copy of *Security Analysis* and instructed him to read it from cover to cover. After he did so and returned the dog-eared, underlined book, his father gave him a new one, saying, "Do it again."[35]

Thankfully for nonprofessional investors—those who consider themselves closer to the "complete novices" referred to by Graham and Dodd than to Warren Buffett—there is another road map. Fifteen years after the publication of the first edition of *Security Analysis* (subsequent editions of the book would follow in 1940, 1951, 1962, 1988, and 2009), Graham wrote a book for the lay investor called *The Intelligent Investor*. That book, subtitled *A Book of Practical Counsel*, narrows the investment focus primarily to common stocks, and the "intelligent investor" who picks up the book need only be capable of understanding the basic measures of investment value for those stocks (dividend yields, price-to-book ratios, price-to-earnings ratios, and the like). But in yet another ringing endorsement, Buffett states in a revised edition of *The Intelligent Investor* that when he read the book for the first time in early 1950 as a scrawny nineteen-year-old—he claims to have read every book in the Omaha Public Library on investing by the time he was eleven—he was certain it was the best book on investing ever written. Though he presumably graduated to the next level by studying *Security Analysis* at Columbia, he avers that he still holds that opinion about the merits of *The Intelligent Investor*.[36]

Gone Are the Good Old Days

In 1956, less than ten years after the publication of *The Intelligent Investor*, the sixty-two-year-old Graham decided to dissolve the Graham-Newman Corporation and distribute the fund's securities to its investors. His decision was marked by a yearning to leave the marketplace and devote himself more fully to a stimulating life of the mind. "We were no longer very challenged after 1950," he wrote, "and the things that presented themselves were typically repetitions of old problems which I found no special interest in solving."[37] So he parted without tears from the day-to-day money management business and New York City, and moved to Beverly Hills where he had time to fulfill his far-ranging intellectual interests, including teaching at the University of California–Los Angeles and translating novels.

But among his reasons for shutting down Graham-Newman must have also been the changes in the financial markets that made the mission of his firm increasingly difficult to accomplish. In annual reports to his investors he had set forth a twofold investment strategy:

1. To purchase securities at prices less than their intrinsic value as determined by careful analysis with particular emphasis on the purchase of securities at less than their liquidation value.
2. To engage in arbitrage and hedging operations.

From his early days at Newburger, Henderson & Loeb, he had invested in accordance with those two guidelines. As the years passed, however, developments in the securities markets had conspired against him. With respect to arbitrage and hedging, the number of players was growing, and it was increasingly difficult to find profitable transactions. Investment houses and other specialty Wall Street enterprises were setting up trading operations to locate money-making arbitrage situations, and while Wall Street might still offer acres of diamonds for the taking, there were now many more investors searching for those diamonds.

Making matters tougher—if fairer for investors generally—the passage of New Deal–era securities legislation made corporate information more current, accessible, and nonproprietary. It was no longer necessary to travel to Washington, D.C., as Graham had, to search through the bowels of the Interstate Commerce Commission for information about the bond holdings of the Northern Pipeline Company. Initially, Graham was skeptical about the value of the New Deal's securities legislation, maintaining that the SEC's disclosure requirements did not assure the soundness of securities and pointing to the questionable character of many of the stock offerings coming after the Securities Act of 1933. In *The Intelligent Investor*, written sixteen years later, he acknowledged that "the SEC has virtually revolutionized the conduct of investment banking and brokerage and has significantly affected the conduct of corporate affairs in relation to stockholders."[38] He held fast to his belief that the basics of successful investing remained intact and based on the cold, hard facts. But it is undeniable that, under the disclosure requirements of the far-ranging securities acts of the 1930s, those facts became available for all to see with far less effort—and over time the opportunities to benefit from mispriced securities became less frequent.

As for purchasing securities at less than their intrinsic value, the new securities reporting requirements were also making that task less arduous for analysts. With companies required to regularly prepare and disclose audited financial statements, the job of screening for investment opportunities that Mr. Market was undervaluing became far simpler. And to some extent, Graham, with his penchant for spreading the gospel of value investing, was acting as his own worst enemy. His well-attended lectures at Columbia University and his frequent articles on how to locate undervalued securities had the effect of creating more imitators—and fewer unique opportunities for Graham-Newman.

An even greater hindrance to finding sufficient opportunities that fit the bill for a Graham-approved investment was the long-term bull market that began in the post–World War II years and continued through the late 1960s. That market boom produced a great deal of new wealth for investors but at the same time frustrated Graham in his search for common stocks that had the defensive attributes and margin of safety he required in stock selection. The reason for the increased level of stock prices was, in his mind, obvious: the willingness of investors to use speculation about a business's long-term prospects in determining the price they were willing to pay for a security. He believed long-term speculation was foolhardy and inevitably based on overly optimistic assumptions as to the rate and duration of earnings growth.

Graham regularly and vociferously decried the overvaluation of the stock market in talks in the 1950s, writing articles that bore titles such as "The New Speculation in Common Stocks" and "Stock Market Warning: Danger Ahead." In the end, however, it must have appeared that speculation on Wall Street was not going to go away any time soon, and finding bargains in the market with Graham-Newman's criteria would be a near impossibility. He lamented, "We can look back nostalgically to the good old days when we paid only for the present and could get the future for nothing. Shaking our head sadly we mutter, 'Those days are gone forever.'"[39] So, having long since created a fortune, he folded his long-running money management firm and headed to the warmer climes of California and, later, to Aix-en-Provence in France.

A Far-Ranging Intellectual

Graham was a man of monumental drive and accomplishment. By virtue of writing the original and revised versions of *Security Analysis* and *The*

Intelligent Investor, teaching courses at Columbia, providing testimony as an expert witness, and writing for professional publications such as the *Financial Analysts Journal* (signing his articles with the pseudonym "the Cogitator") and popular publications such as *Forbes* and *Barrons*, Graham accomplished as much or more than a full-time and very successful professor. All the while, of course, he was holding down his "day job" at Graham-Newman, one that would consume the full attention and energy of more ordinary individuals.

Still, he had many ambitions that extended beyond Wall Street—and for the most part he would remain unsatisfied in fulfilling them. He had long been an aspiring playwright, and in 1934 he wrote and produced a Broadway show called *Baby Pompadour*, a play that revolved around a big-time journalist and his loopy chorus-girl mistress. It closed after a few days when critics panned it. Another ultimately frustrated ambition was making a mark in public service. During the Great Depression, deflation was a major impediment to economic recovery, and he believed he had devised a commodity-based plan to stabilize the nation's currency. His plan was encapsulated in a much-belabored book titled *Storage and Stability* that was published in 1937. After initial excitement about the plan being adopted by the U.S. government when Franklin Roosevelt's advisor recommended it, that venture, like *Baby Pompadour*, also came to naught when the president ultimately rejected Graham's ideas.

In any balanced analysis, Graham's professional setbacks were few and, in the context of his many achievements, largely inconsequential. The personal side of his life, at least by his telling, was a different story. In *Memoirs*, Graham repeatedly bemoaned his inability to make personal connections. He was a selfless teacher and mentor and a faithful and honest steward of the money entrusted to his care as a money manager; he was not an observant Jew, but taught a children's worship class in his synagogue; and Warren Buffett—who bestowed a grand compliment on his mentor by naming his first child Thomas Graham Buffett—said that Graham embodied "an absolutely open-ended, no-scores-kept generosity of ideas, time, and spirit . . . if encouragement or counsel was needed, Ben was there."[40]

But Graham, by contrast, thought that his first wife, Helen Mazur, probably got it right when she sized him up as being "humane, but not human," and a sense of estrangement nagged at him for the duration of his life. His regret for not joining a college fraternity served as just one of the examples he enumerated of his emotional coldness; he confessed that he could be everybody's friend but never one's bosom buddy. "Something within me rebels at the idea of exclusiveness or monopoly in human relations. This makes me, if not a bad friend, at least an impossible crony—and, I must add, a fundamentally unsatisfactory lover."[41]

His history of three unsuccessful marriages—to Carol Wade and Estelle Messing, after Helen Mazur—and a little-disguised string of dalliances would lend credence to that self-professed rebellion against much exclusiveness in the area of human relationships. As Buffett recounts, "It was all open and everything that Ben liked women. And women liked him. He wasn't physically attractive—he looked like Edward G. Robinson—but he had style."[42] In the latter part of his life, however, he formed what appeared to be a long-term, satisfying, and monogamous relationship with a French citizen, Marie Louise "Marlou" Amingues, and, for some twenty years, they divided their time between California and France.

The twenty-year relationship with Amingues roughly corresponded to his time away from Wall Street following his closing the Graham-Newman operation, and from all indications his sunset decades with her were the most satisfying of his life. He continued to write and speak occasionally on financial topics, but in retirement he devoted much more of his time to the intellectual pursuits that had captured his youthful passions. In an address to his friends and family at his eightieth birthday party, he said,

> At least half of all the pleasures that I have enjoyed in life have come from the world of the mind, from things of beauty and culture, especially literature and art. These things are available to everybody, virtually free of charge; all one needs is the interest to start with and a minimal effort to appreciate the riches spread out before us. Once you have found it—the life of culture—never let it go.[43]

Graham's remarks serve as a useful reminder that the man who literally wrote the book on security analysis—and who is arguably the greatest intellect to have worked on Wall Street—did not hold an MBA or a PhD in economics or finance. Rather, he was a classically trained scholar who, after transforming the world of investing, returned to his ultimate passions. There may be a lesson somewhere in that.

9

Myron S. Scholes: 1941–
Professor of Derivatives

Charlie [Munger] and I are of one mind in how we feel
about derivatives and the trading activities that go with
them: We view them as time bombs, both for the parties
that deal in them and the economic system.

—WARREN BUFFETT

It was December 10, 1997, and Myron Scholes was among the dozen lau-
reates gathered on the stage in the Stockholm Concert Hall to receive the
annual Nobel Prize in the memory of Swedish industrialist Alfred Nobel.
Scholes was sharing the 1997 award for economics—officially, the Sveriges
Riksbank Prize in Economic Sciences—with his colleague Robert Merton.
Twenty-five years earlier they had created what is known throughout the
financial world as the Black-Scholes option pricing model and what the
Nobel committee described as "a new method to determine the value of
derivatives."

In his Nobel Prize lecture, Scholes cited Alfred Nobel's stipulation that
the prize was to be awarded for an "important discovery or invention."
Scholes pointed out that he and Merton did not invent derivatives; options
contracts, he reminded his audience, were traded on the Amsterdam Stock
Exchange as early as the seventeenth century and actively traded on the
Chicago Board of Trade since the 1930s. But despite his acknowledgment,
the Black-Scholes model was indeed a discovery, because it provided a
breakthrough in the understanding of the risk and return characteristics
of options. Furthermore, the model was presented with such clarity and
simplicity that it quickly led to dramatic growth in the uses and markets for

stock options and in a dizzying variety of newly created derivatives beyond the simple option contract.

For most Nobel Prize winners, the generous award from the Nobel committee represents a once-in-a-career windfall. But for Scholes, and for a somewhat lesser extent Merton, the Nobel Prize was a pittance compared to the fortunes they had already amassed as partners of Long-Term Capital Management, the hundred-billion-dollar hedge fund they helped cofound in 1993—and whose strategies included real-world applications of their model.

Within a year of the receipt of their prizes, however, the LTCM hedge fund collapsed and their fortunes evaporated. The failure of their once high-flying hedge fund serves as a reminder that brilliance does not always ensure financial success. It also may reinforce Warren Buffet's famous contention that "derivatives are a form of mass financial destruction."

The Making of a Finance Scholar

Scholes's fascination with the stock market started when he was growing up in Timmins, Ontario, a gold-mining area in the remote reaches of Canada. As he recalls, however, his parents' occasional forays into the "penny stocks" issued by regional mining companies were largely unsuccessful. Likewise, his own investments in the stock market while in high school in Hamilton, Ontario, and in college at McMaster University did not pan out, despite long hours devoted to studying the market. The world of finance was not an apparent fit for him, and he planned to work for his uncle's publishing business after he finished an MBA at the University of Chicago. Loquacious, confident, and dashing, with a drive for business success, Scholes seemed to be the logical family member to eventually take over that business.

But in 1963, while still enrolled in the MBA program, Scholes found a summer job as a junior programmer in the university's computer facility. That position changed his career path. At the time, he knew next to nothing about programming and very little about academic finance. But his understanding of the financial markets and computer science quickly improved. During the 1960s, the University of Chicago had become a hotbed of finance research, and Scholes found himself working closely with professors who would, like him, eventually become Nobel Prize winners. He learned from them, but they also learned from him as he began to make suggestions to his eminent professors on the format of their papers. He described the four-and-a-half months at the computer lab as a time of "falling in love with computers and the researchers that I met."[1] One of those researchers, Merton Miller (a Nobel laureate in 1990), steered him into Chicago's PhD program, at which point Scholes abandoned any notion of returning to Canada or his uncle's business.

After completing his doctoral work in 1968 (with a dissertation focused on the dynamics of securities trading), he joined the faculty of the Massachusetts Institute of Technology. At MIT he met Fischer Black, then a consultant with Arthur D. Little, and began work on what would eventually become known as the Black-Scholes option pricing model. In 1973, Black and Scholes published their results in the *Journal of Political Economy*, in an article titled "The Pricing of Options and Corporate Liabilities." That article, written in the dry and mathematics-laced language of an academic journal, provided the intellectual framework for the pricing of derivatives—and in a short time added a new dimension to the business of Wall Street. (Fischer Black was recognized by the Nobel committee for his contribution to the Black-Scholes model. But he died in 1995, and since the Nobel Prize is not awarded posthumously, he is not listed as an official laureate.)

A Brief Primer on Options

The derivatives revolution had its roots in the world of common stock options—"puts" and "calls." Options give investors the ability to profit from changes in the price of a stock without having to actually buy the stock.

Suppose an investor holds a view that within a few months AT&T's common stock will increase in price. To act on that opinion, she could purchase 100 shares of the company's stock outright at the market price of, say, $34.75 per share, for a total of $3,475. If after three months she was correct and the market price of the shares moved up to $36.50 per share, she could sell the 100 shares for $3,650 and realize a $175 short-term profit on the transaction. That's a 5 percent return on her investment for the three-month holding period; on an annualized basis, the return would be 20 percent.

That is an attractive return on investment, but the options markets provide a way for her to greatly magnify that return with a much smaller investment. Rather than investing $3,475 to act on her hunch, she could buy a three-month call option (hence, a "call") that would allow her to purchase the stock at a "strike price" of, say, $35 per share—an amount that is just slightly above the current $34.75 market price. That call option would likely cost around $0.50 per share ($50 for the 100 shares) and would give her the *right* (but not the obligation) to purchase the 100 shares of AT&T stock at $35 per share at any time during the following three months. After three months the option would expire. If, as expected, the price rises to $36.50, she could "exercise" her call option to buy 100 shares of AT&T at the $35 per share strike price—and simultaneously sell the shares at $36.50 in the stock market for a $150 profit. After subtracting the $50 cost of the option, she would realize a $100 net profit, which amounts to a 200 percent return on her $50 option investment during the three-month period; annualized, the return would be 800 percent.

The downside? To make a profit, the stock price must be above the exercise price by at least $0.50 per share in light of the option's $0.50 cost; that is, the stock must move up to at least $35.50 during the three months. If she exercises the option when the stock is selling between $35.00 and $35.50, she will make a small gain, but not enough to defray the total $0.50 per share cost of the option. And if the stock never climbs above $35 per share, the option will expire worthless, a 100 percent loss. In reality, the majority of call options expire without value, resulting in pure gain for the seller of the contract (called a "writer" in the lingo of option trading) and a total loss for the investor. (This is not to say, however, that the option purchaser is necessarily at a disadvantage; as the examples above illustrate, positive returns may not be frequent, but they can be very large when an option performs in accordance with the holder's expectations.)

A "put" is the flip side of a call, giving the investor the right to *sell* shares of common stock at the strike price on or before a set date. The mechanics and costs of a put transaction are similar, but in this case the investor is speculating that the price of the stock will fall. If the investor is correct about a lower stock price in the future, the investor will produce a profit through a simultaneous purchase of the stock in the market at the lower price and sale to the writer at the higher contracted strike price.

Model Building

Of course, success in options trading is contingent on the ability to predict the future price of the stock, and so would seem to rely on fuzzy and immeasurable variables like the investor's risk profile or the economic "utility" of an option—or the instincts of street-smart traders. The Black-Scholes model did away with such fuzziness. The first version was fairly simple; all one needed to include were variables that can be directly observed and precisely measured. To find the option price in the emerging model, one just plugged in the volatility of the stock's price, the current stock price, the current interest rate, and the two governing terms of the option contract—the strike price and the option's expiration date.

The most important of those five variables was the stock's price volatility—and it was also the trickiest to get right. Among finance academicians, a stock's risk is measured by the variability of its price over time and, specifically, by the standard deviation of its returns. It only makes sense that the price of an option contract for a volatile stock will exceed that for one that is less volatile. For instance: historically, AT&T stock does not fluctuate as widely as the overall stock market. However, a stock like Yahoo fluctuates more widely than the market. For several years, the stocks of Yahoo and AT&T sold for similar prices (between $30 and $40 per share), but the options of Yahoo were always much more expensive. That was because the Yahoo stock was more volatile and therefore more likely than the AT&T stock to exceed the call option strike price during the contract's time frame, thereby earning an attractive trading profit for the holders of Yahoo's call options. And as Yahoo was the more volatile stock, its shares were also more likely to fall *below* the option's strike price and produce a profit for holders of put options. Consequently, a Yahoo option, whether a put or a call, was a better speculation for profit than the AT&T option and therefore always fetched a higher price.

But in constructing their pricing model, Black and Scholes encountered a major practical problem with volatility: by the time one accumulated enough data to measure volatility correctly, it was too late to have any immediate value. In fact, the early form of the Black-Scholes model, based on the initial empirical tests, would have produced significant *losses* for option traders. As Scholes would explain it, "These losses were incurred because using simple estimates of the volatility ignored information on future volatility that the market was using to price the options."[2] So at that point, Scholes and Black turned to another MIT finance professor, Robert Merton, who literally brought rocket science to bear on the problem. Using a branch of mathematics called Itō calculus—the same mathematics that makes it possible to continuously adjust the trajectory of a rocket in flight—Black and Scholes modified the final version of the model to adjust to changes in the price and risk of the underlying stock in real time.[3] With that crucial refinement to the Black-Scholes model, investors for the first time had a way to eliminate risk, the four-letter word of finance. By knowing the correct price to be paid for an option, they presumably knew how much it would cost to eliminate a stock's risk.

At the time the Black-Scholes model was published in 1973, the Chicago Board Options Exchange had, coincidentally, just been organized as the first centralized exchange for option trading. Wayne Luthringshausen, the longtime chairman of the Options Clearing Corporation, recalls that before the CBOE was founded, the average number of option contracts traded was a mere 9,000 per month.[4] Now, with the new Black-Scholes model, retail investors and institutional portfolio managers had a way of *precisely* protecting a capital gain through the purchase of a put; or, conversely, they had a way of realizing a specified capital gain without putting much cash at risk. In 2008, the CBOE reached a level of one *billion* contracts per year, and observers of this phenomenal growth point to the Black-Scholes model as the necessary catalyst.

In his Nobel Prize acceptance speech, Scholes rightfully gave credit to the model for spurring the growth of the options markets:

> Although it is hard to prove, I do think that the success of the CBOE and other exchanges, in part, can be attributable to option-pricing models. As traders became familiar with these modes, bid-offer spreads narrowed. As traders became more familiar with risk-management techniques they could take on larger position sizes to support the market. With a deeper and more efficient market, investors began to use options to facilitate their own investment strategies.[5]

Former CBOE vice chairman, Gerry Lahey, is less equivocal about the impact of the Black-Scholes model on options trading: "There's no question that without the Black-Scholes model we would not be here today. It is clearly the most significant formula developed during my lifetime and maybe before."[6] The CBOE, which began operating in the smoking room of the Chicago Board of Trade, now conducts a worldwide options business from its multistory building in downtown Chicago.

Today exchange-traded options are available for most publicly traded common stocks, and the shares of large capitalization companies—Exxon, IBM, General Electric, Apple, Amazon, and the like—have become the basis for a multitude of options that trade based on specified strike prices and expiration dates. There is not just a single put or call option on those companies' stocks; there are usually more than one hundred different options contracts available on each. Wall Street traders routinely use Black-Scholes calculators, and an explanation of the Black-Scholes option pricing model has become a part of every textbook on investing.

With the remarkable growth in the market for options and other derivative instruments, the investing and noninvesting public has become much more aware of their presence. Yet misunderstandings remain, including how derivatives are created and how their economic impact is measured. One common misconception, for instance, is that companies create their own puts and calls for their stock. And while it's true that AT&T's management may create employee stock options for key managers as a form of incentive compensation, these kinds of employee stock options are not listed on an exchange and are a very different breed of option from a traded derivative. The mushrooming of option derivatives traded on the CBOE is not a concoction of the companies whose stock serves as the "underlier" for the option but purely of the *writers*, usually trading firms. (As noted earlier, most options expire unexercised and without value, like losing lottery tickets and horse race bets. But that doesn't usually result in pure profit for the writer, who is typically providing liquidity to the market by taking hedged positions on both sides of the trades.)

Another misunderstanding about derivatives has to do with "notional value," an amount that is often used to describe the size of derivative markets. While the AT&T option contract described earlier has a market value of around $50, the amount of common stock under the "control" of the contract is much larger, about $3,500. The latter is the notional value and explains why reference to notional value can produce preposterous-sounding numbers. In the case of the Yahoo and AT&T examples, for instance, the combined notional value of the hundreds of options contracts on their stocks is likely to be in excess of the companies' market capitalizations.

Excursions from the Academy

In 1973, the year he published his option pricing model, Scholes moved back to the University of Chicago, where he stayed until he took a position at Stanford University in 1981. Like many other academic all-stars on the faculties of business schools, he found lucrative consulting opportunities and board positions in the private sector. He worked for Wells Fargo Bank in the late 1960s and early 1970s when the bank began to structure one of the earliest index funds—preceding John Bogle's retail-oriented

Vanguard products by several years—and later was active in the business of Dimensional Fund Advisors, a firm that developed index-like products for institutional investors. Scholes also acted as a consultant for a time to Donaldson, Lufkin & Jenrette, an investment firm that was building its option technology in anticipation of trading on the CBOE. His job at DLJ, as he described it, was to "marry the old-time trader types, with their mental set, with young mathematical modeling types, with their model assumptions, to help add value for the firm."[7] (William Donaldson, one of the founders of DLJ, is the focus of chapter 13.)

Another extracurricular venture began in 1990 when Scholes became a special consultant for Salomon Brothers, a major Wall Street firm at the time. By then, derivatives had grown well beyond puts and calls on common stocks. With the growth of index funds, put and call options were beginning to be applied to exchange-traded funds (ETFs). Most ETFs have the same investment objectives as index mutual funds, but they can be traded like common stocks—and therefore options can be written on them. The early ETFs tracked broad market indexes such as Standard & Poor's 500 Index, but later ETFs spread to hundreds that track indexes based on industry sector, country, market capitalization, and other criteria.

By the 1990s, derivatives had also spread beyond equity securities to bonds and other fixed-income instruments and to currencies. Aided by powerful computer technology and sophisticated quantitative techniques akin to the Black-Scholes model, booming markets soon arose for debt-based derivative products. Such products included interest rate swaps—the typical arrangement involves two borrowers ("counterparties"), with one swapping its fixed-rate interest payments for the other's floating-rate interest payments. Another debt-based instrument is a credit default swap—a form of credit insurance in which the buyer of the swap (usually the holder of a loan) makes periodic payments to the seller of the swap and, in the event the loan defaults, receives a payoff of the total loan amount. The seller of the swap receives those periodic payments and, upon default, takes possession of the loan, receiving whatever value it might eventually provide.

The logical place for the development and implementation of those new markets was at Salomon Brothers, which at the time was the world's leading firm in trading bonds and other fixed-income securities. No one was better suited than Scholes to assist that firm in extending its leadership in fixed-income to derivatives. Scholes was awarded a lucrative managing directorship and later became the cohead of the fixed-income derivatives sales and trading department, all the while continuing in his teaching and research positions at Stanford.

But the position at Salomon didn't last long; in 1991 one of its traders in government bonds fatally sullied the firm's long-held reputation with the Federal Reserve by submitting false bids to manipulate the price of bonds that were newly issued by the U.S. Treasury. The discovery of the violation led the Treasury Department to revamp its auction procedures— and eventually led to the sale of the weakened Salomon Brothers firm to Travelers Group and, ultimately, its demise. But while Scholes's position with Salomon lasted only a few years, it started a chain of events that would have a profound effect not only on Scholes but on the financial markets as a whole.

The Rise of a Celebrity Hedge Fund

The full-scale housecleaning at Salomon that followed the bid-rigging revelations included the forced resignation of John Meriwether, the forty-four-year-old head of bond operations. By all accounts, Meriwether was innocent of any involvement in the Treasury manipulation, and the traders who had worked for him remained fiercely loyal, especially those in Salomon's highly profitable arbitrage group. In 1994, Meriwether formed a new hedge fund called Long-Term Capital Management and recruited many of his former top traders and arbitrageurs at Salomon to become his partners. Most of those partners held PhDs (overwhelmingly from MIT), and with the new developments in derivatives and financial engineering, Meriwether believed their collective trading prowess would propel LTCM far beyond the successes they had enjoyed at Salomon. Scholes was one of the people he recruited to help him achieve his goals, along with Merton, one of the codevelopers of the Black-Scholes model, and David Mullins Jr., who resigned his position as vice chairman of the board of governors of the Federal Reserve to become an LTCM partner.

The addition of Scholes seemed to make special sense. His brief consulting assignment with Salomon had given him an insider's view of how the traders operated, and he had an unequaled understanding of the underlying mechanics of derivative strategies that would become an important part of LTCM's operations. Moreover, he was also an expert in taxes (he was the lead author of a textbook, *Taxes and Business Strategy*, written while he taught at Stanford) and designed tax shelters to reduce the expected heavy tax burdens that LTCM's investors would face. The fund, no surprise, was domiciled in the Cayman Islands.

As it happened, however, Scholes was at least as important in promoting the fund as in overseeing its management and handling its taxation issues. Hedge funds, like venture capital and private equity funds, are financed by large institutional investors and getting a fund off the ground depends on the reputation of the founding partners and their ability to convincingly communicate the new fund's strategies. Meriwether, despite the scandal, had preserved his reputation, and by using Salomon's publicly available disclosure documents he could demonstrate the success of his arbitrage group. But he was modest and somewhat withdrawn and did not make much of an impression during LTCM's road show.

Scholes, however, was all the things that Meriwether was not. He was confident, at times to the point of arrogance, and after years of practice in the classroom, articulate and often entertaining. He characterized LTCM's planned strategy of making many trades that produce small profits with minimal risks as "vacuuming up nickels"—and would then pull a nickel from the air in the manner of a magician. Prospective investors generally saw Scholes as the smartest guy in the room, and he helped raise much of the initial $1.25 billion of investor capital.

Vacuuming Up Nickels

After the eleven general partners and their trading staff settled into LTCM's headquarters in Greenwich, Connecticut, they got down to the business of vacuuming up nickels through a combination of investment strategies. In the spirit of the first hedge funds, LTCM set off to balance long positions with short positions, thus setting up a *hedge*. (In shorting a stock or other security, the investor is betting that its price will fall; going long is betting it will rise.) Meriwether and his partners engaged in paired bond investments that involved simultaneous long and short positions of similar investments, betting most often on changes in "spreads."

When bond traders refer to a "spread," they mean the difference in the interest rates between two bonds. Long-term bonds, such as twenty-year U.S. Treasury bonds, will almost always have a higher interest rate than a medium-term bond, such as a five-year U.S. Treasury note. The difference between the two interest rates is the spread, and the amount of that spread tends to conform to quantifiable factors that can be analyzed with mathematical modeling techniques. If LTCM's models calculated that the existing spread wasn't reasonable given economic and market forces, a trader would structure a "convergence trade," betting that the anomaly would soon right itself—that one interest rate would fall and the other would rise to reestablish the "correct" spread. Since the expected change in interest rates would also change the bond prices, the trader sets up the bet by buying one bond long and selling the other short.

LTCM made other convergence bets with pairs that were not as similar as two U.S. Treasury obligations but that had some rational and historical relationship: spreads between investment-grade bonds and junk bonds; between U.K. bonds and German bonds; between Australian bonds and Canadian bonds; and between far-riskier bonds issued by countries in emerging markets. Another part of their convergence strategy was to diversify by type of bond and the patterns and frequency of their spreads, so that bets do not all go awry at the same time. During its brief life, LTCM made thousands of such investments based on the assumption that interest rates would realign according to their models, resulting in more nickels for the fund.

Through the end of 1997, the nickels were flowing in. Concentrating mainly on convergence plays in the bond markets, LTCM made money month after month. For one remarkable stretch, the hedge fund recorded a profit for nineteen consecutive months, an accomplishment comparable to a sports team enjoying a nineteen-game winning streak. Further, the fund never experienced two consecutive months of losses, and those few losses were relatively small and well within the expectations for a hedge fund.

All of those profits were plowed back into LTCM's business, and the fund's equity capital account soared from $1.25 billion in 1994 to $7.4 billion at year-end 1997. Even better, the seemingly prudent risk-management techniques were keeping the investors' loss exposure to a minimum. Based on value-at-risk—a technique pioneered in the early 1990s by traders at J. P. Morgan that estimates the maximum loss in a trading portfolio within the normal bounds of probability—LTCM looked like a financial fortress. Most of its trades—around seven thousand of them at one point—were of the off-setting, long-short variety; they were diverse, and the correlation between them was low. As a result, LTCM's "VaR" tended to fluctuate between $30 million and $50 million on any given day. That's certainly a lot of money, but still less than 1 percent of LTCM's equity cushion of over $7 billion—that is, with the heroic assumption that the underlying statistical assumptions would hold.

LTCM's record of profitability, combined with its tiny VaR estimate, emboldened its lenders. By the end of 1997, a consortium of banks—a veritable Who's Who of Wall Street financial institutions—had advanced about $125 billion of debt to LTCM, even though the fund had only $7.4 billion in equity capital. Using that high degree of leverage, LTCM was able to greatly extend its search for additional nickels. (Some observers modified Scholes's nickel analogy to take into account the risk of its extraordinary leverage, saying that LTCM was picking up nickels in front of an advancing steamroller.)

Whatever the risk, however, institutional investors in LTCM indeed enjoyed outsized returns on their investment. Even after subtracting the steep fees paid to the managing partners, the investors realized a 43 percent return on their invested capital in 1995, the first full year of LTCM's operations, followed by a 41 percent return in 1996. By comparison, their return in 1997 was a "disappointing" 17 percent. Insiders like Meriwether and Scholes did even better in those initial years, since they were beneficiaries of the management fees. The insiders saw their personal accounts grow to a combined $1.9 billion.[8]

But by the end of 1997, LTCM's very success made the possibility for continuing success uncertain. By scouring the world for profitable convergence plays with their $100 billion-plus war chest, they were picking the market clean of profitable opportunities. Moreover, a host of imitator hedge funds began to adopt LTCM's strategies, further diminishing attractive prospects. And much more alarming, the unsettled Asian markets of the late 1990s produced an "Asian flu" that was growing more virulent and widespread by the day, causing currency and securities prices to plummet across the world and upsetting the market stability that LTCM needed to execute its closely calibrated convergence trades.

If anyone could understand LTCM's growing challenges, it was Scholes, and—tellingly—he refrained from putting his Nobel Prize money into LTCM, despite saying in an off-the-cuff interview in late October of 1997 that he would "most likely" do so.[9]

Changing Strategies

In response to the falloff in the investors' returns during 1997, LTCM embarked on two strategies intended to restore its profitability levels to those of its earlier years: diversifying well beyond bonds and interest-related convergence plays and increasing the fund's use of financial leverage. Both strategies proved disastrous.

The diversification initiatives were various but focused initially and most aggressively on "equity vols," shorthand for a financial instrument whose price is based on expected volatility in the stock market. Although the Chicago Board Options Exchange was developing its own volatility index in the early 1990s—today regularly traded under the name and symbol "VIX"—it did not begin active trading the index until 2004. LTCM was unmistakably one of the first movers in the 1990s when it came to trading volatility—and that made sense, because the equity vol is tied directly to the Black-Scholes model.

Given that the main determinant of an option price is the volatility of the price of the underlying stock, it follows that movements in option prices themselves give investors an idea about the expected volatility of the overall market. Sparing the reader the sophisticated mathematics underlying an equity vol, suffice it to say that the instrument provides a means for investors to hedge or speculate on the amount of change—upward *and* downward—in stock market volatility. Who would be affected by a greater or lesser amount of future volatility? Option traders for one. Whether puts or calls, the greater the volatility of the underlying stock, the more valuable the option. So betting on future volatility provides a way to speculate on— or hedge against—the direction of the overall options markets. For that reason, some view option investing as little more than bets on future volatility. But whoever the buyers and sellers—and whatever their motives—if some of them have an opinion that the market is going to be significantly more volatile than expected in the coming months, they can *buy* equity vols; other investors, seeing a calmer environment in the future, will want to *sell* them.

Based on their long-term studies of volatility throughout the world's markets, and with Scholes and Merton assisting in the decision making, LTCM's traders dove headlong into the equity vol market. They traded not just in the United States but in any country where there was enough historical data on market volatility to price this new type of derivative-related product. By one account, LTCM was responsible for around a quarter of the total trading in market volatility, and it reached the point that each 1 percent change in the price of volatility led to a profit or loss of several tens of millions of dollars for the fund. LTCM became known within the hedge fund community as the "Central Bank of Volatility."[10]

In the spirit of further fund diversification—and the continued willingness of banks to lend money on the fund's bets—LTCM expanded its signature investments in convergence trades and equity volatility to interest-rate swaps and merger arbitrage. Toward the end of its run, the fund (much to Scholes's dismay it should be noted) began making last-ditch "directional"—meaning unhedged—bets on things like the Japanese bond market and even took a short position on Warren Buffett's Berkshire Hathaway holding company.[11]

The second and even more disastrous decision made by Meriwether and his partners was to increase the proportion of debt supplied by the banks as a way of further leveraging LTCM's returns. LTCM partners saw the firm's seventeen-to-one ratio of debt to equity at the beginning of 1998 as too conservative. So they *returned* $2.7 billion of capital to the outside investors—most of whom were predictably upset by being kicked out of the highly profitable fund—resulting in a capital base of just $4.7 billion. The LTCM managers did not make any commensurate reduction in the fund's borrowings, so the new debt-to-equity ratio increased to about twenty-seven to one. Less than 4 percent of LTCM's total assets were funded by owner's equity—the rest was coming from what Wall Street's traders call "other people's money."

The increased use of financial leverage was likely fueled by the desire of LTCM's general partners to reestablish a record of extraordinary returns. The return on the fund's investment was calculated by dividing its profits by its total equity capital; so if those profits were divided by the new and lower equity base, the returns would suddenly look better. Furthermore, with the number of outside investors reduced, a greater share of those profits would go to LTCM's inside partners and portfolio managers. Such use of financial leverage may not have been a new ploy for Meriwether and his traders. A former Salomon Brothers partner alleged that the Meriwether group, while it operated at Salomon, "was never really profitable, but created the illusion of profitability by creating the illusion it wasn't using much capital." The Salomon partner, further commenting on LTCM's use of capital, said, "If they had been running the operation with $8 billion of equity, which they needed, they wouldn't have been earning 41 percent returns, but more like 18 percent or 19 percent, which would have meant that they did about half as well as the stock market."[12]

Adopting an extreme leverage position meant that a loss of just 1 percent of the $130 billion of LTCM's assets would wipe out more than a quarter of the fund's equity; three additional months of those kinds of losses would throw the fund into bankruptcy. But if this vulnerability came up in their discussions with banks (who continued to lend money despite a dangerously high leverage ratio), LTCM managers could point out that their finely calibrated models still produced a miniscule VaR.

A Quick Demise

Everything fell apart in 1998. A perfect storm created a chain of unforeseeable disruptions in the world's currency and securities markets, throwing LTCM's models into confusion. The contagion of Asia's financial flu spread throughout the world and roiled financial markets, including the U.S. stock market, and LTCM took big losses on equity volatility trades that were based on more quiescent market conditions. But the event that sealed LTCM's fate was the sudden declaration by Russia, on August 17, that it would default on much of its debt and, furthermore, that it would no longer support the ruble in the foreign currency markets. The firm's models could not account for such unprecedented market developments.

Panicky investors throughout the world moved their investments to the safe harbors of U.S. dollars and Treasury bonds. With that flight to safety, interest rate spreads between U.S. bonds and foreign bonds diverged dramatically; the sudden rise in demand for riskless U.S. bonds pushed down the yields on U.S. securities, while the lack of demand for the riskier bonds of other countries led to much higher yields. The worldwide movement of funds to U.S. securities may have been seen by some as a gratifying show of confidence in the American economy, but for LTCM, with its portfolio of convergence bets, it meant disaster. On August 21, four days after the Russian default, LTCM lost $551 million—despite a VaR that specified a probable worst-case loss for the fund of only $35 million.[13] For the entire month of August, LTCM lost $1.85 billion. During the first three weeks of September, the fund continued to bleed, with another half-billion dollars added to the biggest derivative trading losses in history. It took a Federal Reserve–engineered rescue, in which a reluctant consortium of fourteen major banks provided an emergency infusion of capital, to stem the damage.

In his chronicle of the fall of LTCM, author Roger Lowenstein identified swaps, equity volatility, and a miscellaneous basket of derivative and arbitrage positions as each being responsible for roughly a third of LTCM's 1998 losses.[14] The combined loss for 1998, about $4.5 billion, effectively wiped out the fund's $4.7 billion capital position at the beginning of that year. The burden was shared between the equity owned by the managing partners and that owned by the outside investors, with Scholes, Meriwether, and the other LTCM insiders absorbing more than 40 percent of the losses.[15]

The $3.6 billion rescue funds provided by the banks gave them a 90 percent ownership, with LTCM's key managers allocated a 10 percent share to entice them to stay while the fund was wound down in an orderly fashion. If the banks hadn't "willingly" stepped in to avert an LTCM bankruptcy—they were, in truth, strong-armed by the Federal Reserve Bank of New York—there would likely have been a major financial crisis. In August the fund had well over $100 billion in assets, but that number greatly understated the magnitude of the potential problems; the notional value of LTCM's derivative trades—the amount of assets those derivatives controlled—was around $1 trillion. Although many of the positions would have been offsetting, the Fed simply could not stand by and let a single counterparty to a trillion dollars in trades default on its obligations. LTCM, therefore, had the unwelcome distinction of leading the coming parade of SIFIs—systemically important financial institutions—that were too big to fail.

Aftermath

In his 1997 Nobel Prize acceptance speech, a year before the LTCM meltdown, Scholes enumerated prior market losses that could be attributed to derivative trading, including the bankruptcies of Metallgesellschaft and Barings Bank. But he minimized the economic consequences of the losses. He argued, rather, that another group of investors was on the other side of the trades and therefore realizing offsetting gains. By that logic, Scholes maintained that there is no overall "deadweight cost" to society, however painful and consequential those losses might be to the losing party.

Scholes wound up as one of those losing parties. The loss he incurred as an LTCM manager amounted to most of his net worth. To make matters worse, he also wound up owing millions of dollars to the U.S. Internal Revenue Service in connection with an LTCM tax shelter that the government successfully challenged. The haven that Scholes devised rivaled some of LTCM's derivative trades in complexity—encompassing tax-favored London investors, below-rate interest agreements, complex leasing agreements, and, most damaging in court, a special deal for Scholes under which he received bonus shares in LTCM for designing the shelter.[16]

Yet Scholes continues to remain philosophical, if not detached, regarding the LTCM experience. In a February 2000 television interview he said only, "I felt quite badly for investors and for others who had worked with us because it was the case that we had a great idea, and a great franchise, and a great application for these ideas for problem solving, and realizing eventually that it was very difficult to effect."[17] And the 1998 LTCM failure did not deter him from founding, the very next year, the limited partnership Platinum Grove Asset Management—a derivative-based hedge fund. He served as chairman of Platinum Grove and brought on other Stanford and MIT PhDs to merge the worlds of business and academia: "Although we are in business, hoping to end up with a profit," he explained, "we replicate the university setting. We conduct research; we discuss it and improve it; and we build models and empirically test them."[18] Platinum Grove managed close to $10 billion in assets at its height, with what Scholes described as a "liquidity and risk transfer service" for investors and business firms. It was LTCM redux, with Scholes alleging that Platinum Grove enjoyed low volatility and "almost zero correlation with bond markets or stock markets."[19]

But when the securities markets plummeted in the 2008 financial crisis, there appeared to be correlation aplenty. In a reprise of the 1998 experience at LTCM, Platinum Grove lost 29 percent of its investors' money in the first two weeks of October of 2008 and 38 percent through the rest of that month. In the wake of investor demands for the return of their remaining funds, Platinum Grove suspended withdrawals.[20] Little information is available today on the ongoing business of Platinum Grove, but Scholes is no longer listed as a partner on the management company's website and the goals of the fund are now much more straightforward and appear to be based on prosaic investments in stocks, bonds, and currencies.

Warren Buffett, one of the masters of such prosaic investments, is among the many Wall Street veterans who remain fearful of an unchecked use and growth of derivatives. In contrast to Scholes's view that offsetting gains and losses in derivative trades minimizes any harm to the economy, Buffett continues to sound the siren about their dangers. In his chairman's letter accompanying the Berkshire Hathaway 2002 report to shareholders, he stated, "Charlie [Munger] and I are of one mind in how we feel about derivatives and the trading activities that go with them: We view them as time bombs, both for the parties that deal in them and the economic system."[21]

In the meantime, the derivative markets continue to grow at a feverish pace. In his 1997 Nobel Prize acceptance speech, Scholes noted that the notional value of the derivatives market had grown to about $45 trillion—rivaling the gross national product of the world—but more recent estimates indicate that the notional value of derivatives has increased tenfold since then. For the most part, derivatives are accepted as useful tools for financial institutions—even the insurance companies that are part of Buffett's Berkshire Hathaway operation use them. When employed properly, derivatives reduce financial risk and foster greater efficiency in the financial markets. Yet when used improperly, excessively, or for purely speculative purposes, they can in fact be time bombs. In any case, there is certainly a commonsense argument for more effective oversight and regulation over a sector of the economy that is volatile enough to create widespread financial emergencies.

Part IV

Financial Engineers

Wall Street has a penchant for taking good ideas to excess. During the latter part of the twentieth century, three important and useful asset classes made their market debuts: hedge funds, high-yield (junk) bonds, and securitized bonds. Before enjoying widespread acceptance in the markets, however, the development of each conformed to Warren Buffett's three-stage progression for new financial ideas that grow out of control: first there is innovation, which is followed by imitation, and then ends with idiocy.

In 1949, Alfred Winslow Jones—a doctor of sociology who freelanced for *Fortune* magazine, generally writing on nonbusiness topics—conceived of a new investment strategy that combined two otherwise risky strategies in such a way as to actually minimize risk. One could take a leveraged position in a stock (borrowing extensively through margin accounts to buy it) and simultaneously take a counterposition in other stocks by selling them short. The end result was that the "long" and "short" positions largely offset each other's risk—and produced substantial combined profit. Jones's extraordinary success with this concept—the "hedge fund"—encouraged others to enter the game. By 1970, hundreds of copycat hedge funds were in the market and managing over $2 billion for a select group of very wealthy individuals and, later, for institutional investors trying to beat the market. Today hedge funds account for $2 *trillion* in investments, but based on their performance that may be at least $1 trillion too much. The typical fund overpromises and underdelivers—with the Long-Term Capital Management fund discussed in chapter 9 being a vivid example. And most funds enrich the managers through hefty fees, but contrary to the original Jones model, they do little to limit risk and, on average, perform no better for their investors than an ordinary portfolio of stocks and bonds.

Like hedge funds, junk bonds have become a near $2 trillion asset class. And while some question whether Jones is the rightful "father" of the hedge fund, no one questions Michael Milken's paternity when it comes to junk bonds. While at Wharton studying for his MBA, he determined that a class of bonds called "fallen angels" provided outsized returns for investors who could understand and tolerate their risk. These were bonds that had once been given an "investment grade" label but that had fallen on hard times, been downgraded, and became ineligible for purchase by regulated insurance companies and other institutional investors. They later became known as "junk bonds."

Milken's insight was that the investment returns from those down-graded bonds would more than compensate the investor for taking the risk. When he left Wharton he began evangelizing on the merits of junk bond investing from a trading desk at the Philadelphia office of a firm that would shortly become Drexel Burnham Lambert. His proselytizing worked well enough to earn him a fortune at an early age and to spur him on to phase two: original-issue junk bonds. Rather than waiting for high-quality bonds to fall into noninvestment grade status, Drexel began to underwrite *new* issues of bonds for companies that, because their securities were less than investment grade, were unable to attract the attention of reputable Wall Street investment banking firms.

Milken arguably performed a valuable service by raising capital for companies that were previously shut out of the capital markets, and many of the companies Drexel sponsored became large and successful as a result. And there is a case to be made that when junk bonds were used to facilitate the wave of leveraged buyouts in the 1980s and 1990s, the targeted companies became tougher and more accountable to shareholders. But toward the end of his tenure at Drexel, Milken, in his zealous quest for "100 percent market share," backed the junk bond issuance of a large number of questionable companies and takeover operators. His focus on quantity of business rather than quality of business corrupted Milken's department—and his excesses culminated in a highly controversial prosecution that eventually led to his guilty plea and a two-year imprisonment.

Securitization was another idea that started small and served a valid and positive purpose, but later grew out of control—with disastrous consequences for the global economy. It all began in the 1980s with Lewis Ranieri, a bond trader with the Salomon Brothers investment house, whose financial innovation was to assemble pools of residential mortgage loans into a trust and then use the trust to issue mortgage-backed bonds. The idea was slow to catch on, but when the savings and loan industry went into crisis mode in the 1980s and had to unload mortgages in unheard of amounts to pay off depositors, business picked up. Mortgage-backed bonds became a staple of Wall Street, and at the high point investment bankers created some $12 trillion of new bonds by bundling mortgages from loan originators and transferring them to bond buyers. But a monstrous overextension of Ranieri's creation became a major cause of the financial meltdown of 2008.

Photo courtesy Robert Burch IV, all rights reserved.

10

Alfred Winslow Jones: 1900–1989
Financial Hippie

Never confuse genius with a bull market.

—WALL STREET ADAGE

Little in the first half of Alfred Winslow Jones's life suggested that, over the second half, he would become the acknowledged father of the hedge fund. After following the family tradition of attending Harvard College, he set off not for a career in finance but instead hired on in 1923 as a purser on a tramp steamer. For the remainder of the 1920s, he hopped from job to job, living the life of a vagabond intellectual and—like many of the idealistic young men and women of his time—flirting with various socialist and communist ideologies.

By 1930, Jones had joined the U.S. Foreign Service and was dispatched to Berlin, where he observed the early rise of Adolf Hitler and the Nazi Party. His task was to write reports for the State Department on the condition of German workers, but Jones—slim and pleasant-faced if not remarkably handsome—was also living an adventurous second life as a result of his brief marriage to Anna Block, a German citizen and a social activist who introduced him to a group called the Leninist Organization. Since Block was a Jew, her well-being was of growing concern with the rise of Nazi political power, and she and Jones operated largely underground. After his marriage was discovered in 1932, he was forced to resign from the Foreign Service. But he remained in Germany and continued working sub rosa with leftist organizations, including the communist-inspired Marxist Workers School.[1] His German experiences, along with his marriage, drew to a close in 1934, and he returned to the United States and enrolled as a graduate student in sociology at Columbia University. Yet his interest in European affairs and antifascism remained strong, and in 1937 he and his second wife—the former Mary Elizabeth Carter, who would remain his lifelong partner—spent their honeymoon in Spain as observers during that country's civil war, meeting Ernest Hemingway and hitchhiking through the country with the great literary figure and social activist Dorothy Parker.

Soon after Jones returned to New York to continue graduate work at Columbia, he and Mary found another venue for their social justice instincts, this one in Akron, Ohio, the industrial heartland of America. After many months gathering data from the city's workers and citizens, Jones produced a PhD dissertation dealing with social class and attitudes. Reworked in 1941 into a book titled *Life, Liberty and Property*, the text was for a time a standard part of the sociology curriculum and also led to his employment as a writer for the affiliated *Time* and *Fortune* magazines, where his first assignment was the creation of an abridged version of his dissertation for an article in *Fortune*. His assignments for the two magazines covered a wide variety of subjects, from Franklin Roosevelt's economic policies to life at boys' prep schools. His writing stints with the establishment magazines seemed to temper his left-leaning outlook; a statement attributed to him in *Fortune* called for "being as conservative as possible in protecting the free market and as radical as necessary in securing the welfare of the people."[2]

Although his political views became more nuanced and encompassing over the years, as late as 1949 there was still little in Jones's life or writing that would hint at his future as an investment mogul. The turning point came with a *Fortune* assignment to write a piece on "technical" investing. The article that appeared in the magazine's March 1949 edition, "Fashions in Forecasting," was a departure for him, since his previous articles focused on social and political topics rather than financial issues. But well over a half century later, the article still serves as a comprehensive survey of a style of investing that looks not at the fundamentals of stock market investing, as advocated by Benjamin Graham, but rather at movements in a company's stock that have little to do with its underlying business or prospects. Most professional investors and academics view technical analysis as a form of investment voodoo, and in the article Jones refers to more sophisticated analysts who are fond of "directing a steady fine spray of ridicule at the technicians and lumping them together with spiritualists, Ouija-board operators, astrologers, sunspot followers, and cycle theorists."[3] Though Jones disavowed the usefulness of technical analysis, the research he conducted in putting the article together sparked his interest and also put him in touch with important contacts on Wall Street. The ultimate result, and the beginning of Jones's life as an investor, was the creation of A. W. Jones and Company—an operation he called a "hedged" fund.

The Long and Short of the First Hedge Fund

At the heart of Jones's investing philosophy was the idea that one could *reduce* investment risk by combining two otherwise speculative strategies: selling stock short and purchasing stocks on margin. Short sales are inherently speculative, because the long-term trend of the stock market has always been upward, so over the long run, someone consistently bucking that trend by selling stock short is likely to be a loser. But in the short term, the technique can be quite lucrative. If Jones thought one of the stocks of the day, say International Nickel, was overvalued at $30 per share, he could borrow shares of that stock from an investment firm and immediately sell them on the New York Stock Exchange at that price. Then later, if he was right and the price of International Nickel fell to $25, he could buy the shares back on the exchange and return them to the investment firm from which he had earlier borrowed them—and pocket the $5 difference as his profit.

But short sales are also risky, because short sellers can lose an unlimited amount of money if the price moves up instead of down. If Jones had been "long" International Nickel—that is, if he purchased the company's shares rather than selling them short—his potential loss would be limited to the $30 price he paid for them. In other words, if the company went bankrupt and the shares became worthless, he would lose his $30 investment, but no more. With a short sale, however, there is no limit to the loss. If International Nickel moved up to $100 following a short sale at $30, Jones would eventually have had to "cover" his short sale, and if he did so by buying stock at $100, his loss would be $70. If the stock price moved up even more, the short sale loss would only grow larger.

Short sales also carried a stigma held over from the bear raids of the 1920s and 1930s. In those notorious transactions, a group of so-called operators established their short positions by creating downward pressure on common stock through coordinated sales. They then spread negative rumors about the company to encourage panic selling, which caused the price of the stock to fall even further and ensured that the short sellers would profit when they closed out their positions at lower prices. The stigma of short selling was made worse, perhaps unduly so, by Herbert Hoover's allegations during his presidency that bear raiders were behind the stock market's relentless downward slide in those years. As a result of the fears of market manipulation by short sellers, an "uptick rule" was made part of the Securities Exchange Act of 1934, requiring that stocks could be sold short only at a price higher than the previous trade in the stock; that is, on an "uptick." The idea, of course, was to halt the downward momentum of a falling market and to make bear raids and other market manipulations more difficult. (The SEC removed its uptick rule in 2007 as one of the deregulatory movements of the time, only to reestablish the rule in a modified form in 2010 following the financial crisis that occurred in the interim.)

The speculative nature of margin accounts, the second component of Jones's investment strategy, is more straightforward. "Margin" is the percentage of equity in an account that is used to buy stocks and other securities; the remainder is financed with debt. The lower the margin, the greater the debt, or "leverage," the investor is using to finance the purchase of stocks. The amount of margin required is regulated by the Federal Reserve and has ranged between 40 percent and 100 percent, but since 1974 has remained at 50 percent. So an investor has to put up cash of at least $1,000 to purchase $2,000 of stock in a margin account, with the remaining $1,000 being borrowed.

To briefly illustrate the impact of leverage: if the value of a stock that Jones bought at $2,000 goes up to $3,000, and he had a 100 percent margin—meaning he didn't borrow anything and the account was financed purely by his cash contribution—the profit on the investment is $1000, giving Jones a 50 percent return on his $2,000 out-of-pocket investment. But if Jones had borrowed $1,000 to finance half of the $2,000 stock purchase, he would have made a $1,000 profit on just a $1,000 out-of-pocket investment—a return of 100 percent. (Of course, any interest he had to pay in connection with the borrowing would have somewhat reduced his investment return.)

This magnification of returns, however, works in both directions. A $1,000 *reduction* in the value of the stock in the $2,000 all-cash account will result in a 50 percent loss. Not good, but imminently better than if Jones had financed the account with $1,000 of equity (margin) and $1,000 of debt. The $1000 debt would have to be repaid upon closing the trade, which would take the value of the account to zero—and produce a 100 percent loss.

Jones's key insight was to recognize that because short sellers benefit from falling stock prices and margin buyers benefit from rising stock prices, the two practices can be combined to effectively hedge against the normal ups and downs in the market. The investment strategy that Jones conceived called for assembling a portfolio of stocks that were judged to be undervalued and attractive for purchase, along with other stocks that were judged to be overvalued and sold short. The relative size of the two portfolios would vary depending on the extent to which Jones held a bullish or bearish view of the overall market. But Jones's investment strategy called for a leveraged long position that was consistently greater than the short position, so the "net hedged" position of the fund was almost always net long.

Operating a fund that hedged its long and short positions—Jones would always refer to a "hedged" fund rather than the generally accepted "hedge" fund designation—was the central idea that led to the founding, in 1949, of A. W. Jones & Company. The initial contributions to the fund, all from individual investors, totaled $100,000. Jones, who was then just a year shy of his fiftieth birthday and not a rich man, contributed $40,000 of the founders' equity, with friends and academic colleagues providing the remaining $60,000. Most of his coinvestors were intellectuals—including individuals he met during his Spanish Civil War efforts, during his flirtation with Leninism, and in connection with settlement house work[4]—and by no means financial sophisticates. But they were very lucky. Using Jones's long-short strategy, their investments grew nearly fiftyfold in seventeen years, turning this fortunate group into wealthy individuals in less than a generation.

Meanwhile, very few people, even those working on Wall Street, had ever heard of a hedge fund. But that changed after an article titled "The Jones Nobody Keeps Up With" appeared in the April 1966 issue of *Fortune*. Chronicling the success of Jones and his initial partners, Carol Loomis wrote what became one of the most influential sentences in the history of financial journalism: "Not quite all of the original $100,000 has been left in the partnership, but if it had been it would today be worth $4,920,789 (before any allowance for the partners' taxes)."[5] The *Fortune* article led to a spate of follow-up pieces in other journals that trumpeted the success of the A. W. Jones funds—A. W. Jones & Company was joined by A. W. Jones Associates in 1961—and also made prominent mention of Jones's unlikely social service background and liberal philosophies. He became known as a financial hippie.[6]

With the news of Jones's success out, the floodgates of the hedge fund business opened. With the extraordinarily enticing prospects for investors and the equally enticing 20 percent performance fee that had become standard for running the funds, there was no shortage of organizers ready to bring the hedge fund concept to wealthy investors clamoring for the product. New funds sprang up right and left to soak up the demand. In addition to the "Jones children"—funds founded by former associates of A. W. Jones—many new funds were created in the Jones image.

Because hedge funds are private by design, and because there was no official scorekeeper in the early years, the number of Jones-style hedge funds that cropped up in the 1960s is notoriously difficult to calculate. In a follow-up article written for the January 1970 issue of *Fortune*, Loomis reported that the number of funds following a Jones structure had grown from just a handful in 1966 to an estimated 150 four years later. By 1970, the two Jones funds had grown to approximately $80 million and remained the country's largest hedge fund organization—but Loomis estimated that another $1 billion was under management in the various copycat funds.[7]

A Hedged Assessment of the Performance of Jones's Funds

The success of hedge funds depended not so much on the long-short structure they shared, but rather on the ability of managers to select the appropriate stocks to buy long or sell short. On that score, Jones seemed nonpareil, providing jaw-dropping investment performance during the first two decades of his funds' existence. With the advantage of hindsight, however, Jones's phenomenal success seemed to rely on a mix of factors—a bull market, a generous use of leverage, loose regulations on commissions, and lax enforcement of certain insider practices—that would make his performance almost impossible to replicate today.

There is a well-known adage on Wall Street that counsels against "confusing genius with a bull market." At the time Jones opened his initial hedge fund, the Dow Jones Industrial Average was around 200; by the end of the Soaring Sixties it was flirting with the 1,000 mark. But while Jones clearly entered the business at a propitious time, a fivefold appreciation in the Dow is far short of the nearly fiftyfold increase the Jones funds enjoyed. More explanation is needed.

While Jones referred to his new investment concept as a hedged fund, "partially hedged" is a more apt description. Far from an absolute hedge, in which an investment position is totally protected from *both* gain or loss in order to avoid risk, Jones consistently maintained a net long position, with the extent of that position dependent on how sanguine he felt about the prospects for the market. In the 1960s, common stock prices were moving upward, and Jones, like most investors, was bullish on the prospects for additional gains. Given that frame of mind, he offset the funds' long positions with only a modest amount of short selling. Furthermore, he added to his long positions by borrowing—sometimes to the 50 percent maximum allowed under margin account rules—for the purpose of increasing his investors' gains through financial leverage. In a rueful moment during the heady years of the 1960s, Jones second-guessed the very essence of his hedge strategy, suggesting that he could have done better for himself and his investors by just leveraging up his long positions and forgoing the short positions altogether.

The generous use of leverage in a booming stock market, however, still falls short of explaining the extraordinary investment performance of the A. W. Jones funds in their early years. For a fund to grow from $100,000 to nearly $5,000,000 in seventeen years—a compounded growth rate of nearly 26 percent—the manager of a hedge fund must be a superb stock picker, able to identify companies whose stocks are clearly undervalued and buy them before their favorable prospects are recognized by the broader market and, conversely, to spot overvalued stocks of companies and sell them short before the rest of the market catches on.

Alfred Jones, by his own admission, was not a stock picker, but he developed a structure for his funds that gave him access to many on Wall Street who were. Much as a finance professor might allocate play money to students to construct hypothetical portfolios and then monitor their performance, Jones auditioned prospective investment analysts by having them put together test portfolios of stocks judged as profitable long or short investments. The candidates whose calls tended to work out as planned were given real money to invest—with the further condition that they allocate some of their own funds to the portfolio. Those who continued to perform well over time were rewarded with a larger pot of money to invest; those who didn't perform well were cut back. (It was a peculiarity of Jones's management style that he never fired anyone. He simply didn't allocate any funds to underperforming portfolio managers.)

The research analysts that Jones brought on board were among the stars of Wall Street, and one might wonder why they subjected themselves to a somewhat demeaning approach to their hiring and retention.

The answer, of course, is compensation. With their frequency of trading, the Jones funds (like all of the new hedge funds that were springing up) generated a prodigious amount of commissions. Short positions in particular require constant tending, resulting in frequent adjustments and commission-generating trades from hedge fund operators. In addition, the adjustments to short positions were often balanced by offsetting adjustments to the fund's long positions, with all the resultant trading leading to commissions for the fortunate brokerage firms that had an operation like A. W. Jones as a customer.

The best way an enterprising securities analyst could snare the business of a frequently trading hedge fund was through his research ideas. For administrative ease, Jones channeled most of his funds' business through a single investment firm, but he reserved the right to designate "give ups"— a sharing of the fat commissions available before the SEC abolished the New York Stock Exchange's minimum commission schedules in 1975—to brokers and analysts at other firms. The size and frequency of the give-ups from Jones were based on the profitability of the research ideas the analysts provided with respect to stocks to be purchased long or sold short.

There was chatter, during and after the spectacular record that the A. W. Jones funds compiled during the 1950s and 1960s, about the extent to which favorable treatment from research analysts, hungry for commissions, contributed to that record. It appears certain that hedge funds were often the beneficiaries of "front running," an illegal but fairly common practice of the time in which a favored customer received information about an opinion from an analyst that was likely to affect the price of a stock shortly before that opinion was widely shared. To the extent that front running actually took place—which it almost certainly did—hedge funds, with their ample commission dollars to throw around, were likely to be on the favorable end of that practice.

It's not apparent that Jones himself participated directly in front-running ploys. In running the funds, he was the ultimate delegator. After a portfolio manager was successfully auditioned and hired by Jones, his success rate was closely monitored to determine whether his allocation should be increased or decreased. But that monitoring did not necessarily extend to how he achieved that investment success. The portfolio managers—around ten at the height of the A. W. Jones business—operated independently and generated ideas from their own web of brokers and analysts. The managers in turn reported to the funds' chief lieutenant, Donald Woodward, who was Alfred Jones's only report.

Jones appeared to concentrate on big picture matters such as the total mix of long and short positions and the degree of financial leverage used, with less of his time spent on the details of stock selection. And in fact, the funds' *business* was not necessarily his top concern. He maintained an office at the A. W. Jones location near Wall Street, but he also had an office in midtown Manhattan where he oversaw his several not-for-profit social ventures, and he increasingly spent more time there than downtown.

While the stellar performance of the early Jones funds may have occurred while the boss was conveniently looking the other way, in today's regulatory environment a hands-off management style would not excuse a laxity in complying with securities laws. The late Barton Biggs, a long-time fixture in Wall Street's research community, credited his early success in the investment business, including the partnership he was awarded in E. F. Hutton as a young man, to the large amount of commissions he gener-ated from A. W. Jones portfolios. Yet in later years Biggs would gratuitously defame his onetime employer, saying, "Basically Jones used commissions to develop an informational advantage and hired smart young guys to exploit it." Hinting at a fundamental illegality in Jones's methods, he continued with a reference to a future New York attorney general and an inveterate Wall Street foe: "Fortunately, Eliot Spitzer was still in diapers."[8]

The Birth of the Jones Children

Whatever Biggs's later criticisms of the Jones approach (and presumably his own profitable embrace of its purported front-running modus operandus), he was one of the first to break away and create his own Jones-style fund—one of the so-called Jones children. In 1965, he and another Jones acolyte, Dick Radcliffe, left E. F. Hutton and A. W. Jones to form Fairfield Partners. They also left the confines of Wall Street, locating Fairfield Partners in Greenwich, Connecticut, where they both lived. Other funds soon followed, settling in Greenwich partly for the lifestyle and partly because Connecticut had fewer reporting requirements for financial firms than did New York. The city would soon become the capital of an emerging hedge fund industry.

Fairfield Partners was just the second breakaway hedge fund formed by former employees of A. W. Jones, with City Associates being the first. And there would be more defections to follow as the hedge fund busi-ness exploded. Some managers were simply bitten by the entrepreneur-ial bug and wanted to go it alone and capture more of the lucrative fees for themselves; others were essentially forced out through Jones's policy of reducing or eliminating the allocation of funds to low-performing managers. Still others left due to personal differences with Jones—and no wonder. Intellectual by inclination, politically to the left, and at least ostensibly more passionate about social justice than money, he had a different mind-set from the typical Wall Street analyst. He was also aloof in attitude and physically removed from the day-to-day matters of his fund. Rather than socializing with his portfolio managers and traders, he was more likely to be found at his midtown office, or on a social mission to a third world country, or at work with one of his several philanthropic projects. His high-mindedness was resented as much as it was admired, with Biggs for one writing him off as a "wealthy, snobbish, pretentious man."[9]

However, any exodus of talent from the A. W. Jones funds in the late 1960s was not cause for great alarm. There were few rules on conflicts of interests between research analysts and their customers, and there was no shortage of analysts who were willing to swap their proprietary investment ideas for hedge fund–generated commissions. Neither was the explosion of rival funds a problem. After the news of the concept began to spread, whether through articles such as those in *Fortune* and the *Institutional Investor* or just through conversations among well-heeled investors, the demand from willing new limited partner investors far outstripped the supply of hedge funds for them to invest in.

The exponential growth in the number of Jones-like funds legitimizes Jones's fatherhood of the hedge fund concept. Some have suggested that other fund managers who took simultaneous long and short positions, including John Maynard Keynes, were the true hedge fund progenitors. Warren Buffett, in fact, maintains that Benjamin Graham, whose Graham-Newman fund predated that of Jones by about twenty years, has the rightful claim to hedge fund fatherhood. Graham, before Jones, made liberal use of both short selling and leveraged long buying and, just as important, may have pioneered the 20 percent performance fee for hedge fund management. (Jones justified the 20 percent fee to his investors based on the rather belabored explanation that it mirrored what Phoenician seafaring captains received from their investors upon arriving home from a profitable voyage.) Whether pioneered by Graham or not, it seems likely that the performance fee—now standard for private equity and venture capital funds as well as hedge funds—had been the arrangement well before the A. W. Jones funds came on the scene. All that acknowledged, Jones's 1949 conception of a hedge fund was the kernel from which the many look-alike funds emerged.

"A Business Without a Future"

But the explosion in the number of hedge funds in the 1960s was followed by a prolonged contraction. The fever of the hedge fund business, including that of the pioneering A. W. Jones funds, began to break when the bullish 1960s met the bleak, stagflation-plagued 1970s. In every year of the earlier decade, A. W. Jones far outperformed Standard & Poor's 500 Index, the yardstick by which portfolio managers are most often measured. In 1962 and 1969, the only years during which the Jones funds produced a negative return for their investors, their results were still superior to the sharp losses of the S&P 500. But things changed abruptly in 1970 when the Jones funds registered a 35 percent reduction in value, a loss far larger than that recorded by the market indexes.[10]

For Jones, who was turning seventy at the time, the monumental losses caused him to rethink the fundamental operating philosophy of hedging and to castigate himself for his lack of proper stewardship on behalf of his investors. Caught up in the euphoria of the 1960s, he had occasionally let his funds operate, through financial leverage, with a long position in excess of 100 percent; that meant that the leveraged long positions had overwhelmed a sparse use of short-sale hedges.[11] And since leverage is a double-edged sword, when the lofty stock prices of the 1960s fell to earth in the 1970s, the Jones investments suffered even more than the market averages.

In response to the funds' large losses, Jones cut back on his outside pursuits and became fully engaged in overseeing the funds' business. That closer oversight included a return to more balanced long-short positions, but by the time Jones and his managers stepped in to correct matters, short positions were hard to find, and the damage could not be undone. Many of his limited partners were friends and academics with modest wealth, and in his 1970 annual report to the funds' investors he sought to reassure and apologize to them, writing, "Each money manager is now fully aware of the necessity of running his segment as though the typical Limited Partner were retired and had all of his capital, say $500,000, invested in our business."[12]

Throughout the sagging stock market of the 1970s—the Dow Jones Industrial Average, which briefly closed above 1,000 in 1972, finished the decade below 800—the hedge fund business languished. The A. W. Jones funds managed to limp along during those lackluster years, along with a diminished group of other surviving funds, but their total assets under management fell toward a vanishing point. The various multi-billion-dollar estimates of the combined hedge fund assets in the 1960s were reduced to a fraction of that amount in the 1970s. One 1977 estimate put the total at just $250 million, and Jones said of the hedge fund industry, "I don't think it is going to be a big part of the investment scene as it was in the late 1960s." And, in an opinion that would prove to be highly inaccurate, he offered that "the hedge fund doesn't have a terrific future."[13]

Transformation to an Asset Class

But Jones's gloomy outlook for his business did prove correct for the short term. His funds continued to struggle during the desultory years of the late 1970s and early 1980s, a time when many of his erstwhile competitors folded their operations altogether. By 1984, when Jones was well into his octogenarian years and devoting more of his remaining energy and time to social causes, A. W. Jones converted into one of the hedge fund industry's early "fund of funds." Rather than hiring research analysts to evaluate companies and pick stocks for long or short positions, the firm sized up other hedge funds and picked a handful considered to be run the most profitably and prudently.

At the time of its movement out of the stock-picking business and into the fund advisory business, A. W. Jones was under the management of Jones's son-in-law, Robert Burch III. Earlier in his career, Burch had been at the old-line investment firm of Kidder, Peabody & Company, and, while there, developed a close relationship with future hedge fund manager Julian Robertson. It proved to be a fortunate relationship for both men. For Robertson, it led to highly enlightening meetings with the elderly Jones, who was happy to tutor him on the hedge fund business; for Burch, it led to one of the best decisions A. W. Jones company would ever make: a $5 million allocation of A. W. Jones's remaining assets under management to Robertson's newly formed Tiger Management. The Tiger hedge funds would be as celebrated in the 1980s and most of the 1990s as the A. W. Jones funds had been in the 1950s and most of the 1960s—and as a result, Tiger's success revived the fortunes of many of Jones's investors.[14]

Like Jones, Robertson went into the hedge fund business late in his career and presided over two decades of extraordinary investment success. In running Tiger Management, he adhered to the long-short investment approach that Jones had pioneered, but with a vastly different management style and personality. Where Jones was a reserved intellectual who rarely fraternized with his portfolio managers and analysts, North Carolina–born Robertson cast a Southern charm over everyone he met. He socialized easily with his employees and projected a swashbuckling approach to investment selection that masked a well-reasoned investment philosophy and thorough research.

Whatever their differences, Robertson, like Jones, produced spectacular results for his early investors. Tiger Management's initial limited partners enjoyed investment returns from the start of the fund in 1980 through its peak in 1998 that averaged almost 32 percent per year. In all but a few years, Tiger Management far outperformed the S&P 500, which was growing at a rate of "just" 12.7 percent during that happy era for stock market investors.[15] In dollars, that meant that an initial limited partner who contributed $100,000 to Tiger Management in 1980 would have seen his investment grow to about $14 million eighteen years later.

And just as the Jones children accounted for much of the growth of the hedge fund business in the 1960s, scores of "Tiger cub" funds sprang up in the 1990s. Some of the cubs were formed by defectors from Tiger Management, but just as many were formed with the blessing—and sometimes financial seeding—of Robertson himself. In addition to the direct descendant cubs, Tiger Management's success spawned a second wave of imitator hedge funds. By the turn of the millennium, hedge funds had become a powerful new "asset class." With hundreds of new entrants, assets under management in hedge funds soared past the *half-trillion-dollar* mark, invalidating Jones's pronouncement twenty-some years earlier that the time had come and gone for hedge funds.

What fueled this growth and reenergized the hedge fund business? Much was due to the entrance of institutional investors into the market, most notably large pension funds whose managers were failing to produce sufficient investment returns to adequately fund their plans and were seeking outsized returns from hedge funds to catch up. Once the province of wealthy individuals, by 2000, pension plans—along with university endowments, foundations, and other adventurous institutional investors—made up close to half of the hedge fund investor base.[16]

At the same time, the nature of hedge fund investing had strayed far from the relatively simple long-short operation that Jones conceived. Today, hedge funds embark upon an ever-widening variety of strategies, including: *macro*, investing in bonds and currencies in anticipation of profit from global trends; *directional*, taking "opportunistic" positions, with or without a hedge, in what are considered to be incorrectly valued securities or special situations (a Graham-Newman approach); and *convergence trading*, acting on the perceived misalignment of securities with the expectation of a profitable self-correction of the prices (Long-Term Capital Management's ill-fated strategy).

Regardless of their strategy, the one thing that most hedge funds no longer do, or at least no longer do effectively, is actually hedge. Once, the sine qua non of a hedge fund was to reduce risk—"hedge funds exist to help investors *stay* rich rather than get rich" were the bywords of the business. Yet there is very little to support the notion that true hedging has ever worked in practice. As conscientious as Jones had been in preserving the newly created wealth of his academic colleagues and intellectual friends, when the stock market fizzled in the late 1960s and early 1970s, the A. W. Jones funds and their imitators fared worse than the overall market; similarly, when the long bull market of the 1980s and 1990s came to a screeching halt in the aftermath of the tech bubble, Tiger Management and the Tiger cubs also performed worse than the overall market.

And, of course, the ultimate test of the advertised market neutrality of hedge funds—their ability to avoid market risk through hedging—occurred during and after the financial crisis of 2008, when the average hedge fund did little to fulfill a risk-avoidance mission or justify its lofty fee schedule. Hedge funds, in the aggregate, performed marginally better than the overall stock market during the depth of the 2008 market swoon. But a review of their performance that includes the years immediately leading up to and following the financial crisis shows that the hedge fund industry fared poorly. An ordinary investor who purchased the Bogle-conceived Vanguard Balanced Index Fund, with a 60–40 equities and bonds split—the kind of stodgy portfolio long favored by conservative advisors—would have incurred a miniscule management fee and netted a 3.5 percent annual return between 2007 and 2012. By contrast, the widely used HFRX Global Hedge Fund Index, which tracks 2,697 funds of all varieties, *fell* by an average of 2.2 percent during the same period.[17]

With their mediocre performance, the question persists as to why hedge funds, now managing over $2 *trillion* in assets, continue to play such an important role in the financial markets. The answer might be hope triumphing over experience. It is true that some hedge fund managers have been able to compile impressive, index-beating records. But there are few that stand the test of time—or a bear market. And those that do often become, like Julian Robertson, victims of their own success. In his case, he put together a string of impressive investment returns by finding smaller and less well-known companies to invest in, but as investors flocked to the Tiger funds there were simply not enough small, special situation opportunities into which he could funnel all of the money being thrown his way. As a result he moved away from his competency and experience and began to deploy vast amounts of money to "macro" plays involving ill-conceived and poorly executed bets on interest rates and currencies.

Just as individual funds can be victims of their own success, today's hedge fund business may be suffering from its size and growth. With vast amounts of money searching for the elusive investment edge, it's increasingly difficult to latch on to a piece of information or market phenomenon that has somehow eluded everyone else's notice. That, coupled with the increasing strictures and controls on the use of privileged information, makes it highly unlikely that any one fund will come upon profitable trading schemes. Vanguard's Bogle, who has observed some sixty years of futility in attempting to beat the market, sums it up well: "Reversion to the mean is a very powerful force. These hedge fund products might work in the short term, but I can absolutely guarantee that they won't work forever."[18] And, in fact, the days of hedge fund products working for any period of time may be long gone, and there is little in the record to support the notion that hedge funds in the aggregate have ever provided a competitive return for their investors. A J. P. Morgan executive with a close view on the hedge fund industry calculates that "if all the money that's ever been invested in hedge funds had been put in treasury bills instead, the results would have been twice as good."[19]

A. W. Jones & Company Today

But for an investor who remains intent on participating in the hedge fund asset class, diversification through a fund of funds approach is a prudent strategy. It is also expensive, with most fund-of-funds managers layering another 1 percent fee for assets under management on top of the 2 percent management fee charged by the hedge funds they select—and a separate negotiated performance fee atop the underlying funds' 20 percent performance fees. A knowledgeable fund-of-funds advisor, however, is able to steer around some of the pitfalls of hedge fund investing. And that circles back to the current version of A. W. Jones, a fund of funds that manages more than $300 million in assets and today operates under the direction of Jones's grandson, Robert Burch IV.

Burch was a young teenager when Jones died at age 88, by then long removed from the hedge fund business he created. Burch remembers the elderly Jones in his last years returning again to more cerebral pursuits, especially the creation of gardens and elaborate landscapes at his country home. Now approaching middle age, Burch views the world of hedge funds—and himself—in a manner similar to his grandfather. He selects hedge funds for his investors that largely follow a "Jones model" format of hedging, and he takes his role as a fiduciary seriously. A product of Princeton and the Harvard Business School, Burch has led a life more conventional than that of his bohemian grandfather, but there is a vestige of Alfred Winslow Jones's idealism in his outlook. He subscribes to a stage-of-life philosophy, popular among some on Wall Street, which holds that "the first third of one's life is for learning, the second third is for earning, and the last third is for returning."[20]

© Byron Purvis/AdMedia/AdMedia/Corbis

11

Michael R. Milken: 1946–
Junk Bond King

Mike Milken believes in 100 percent market share.

— JOHN KISSICK, DREXEL BURNHAM LAMBERT CHIEF
OF WEST COAST CORPORATE FINANCE

In the spring of 1970, I graduated from Wharton, the business school at the University of Pennsylvania. At a dean's reception for soon-to-be MBAs a few months earlier, I had bumped into a particularly driven and single-minded classmate—when I asked him about his plans after school, he answered without hesitation that he would first become independently wealthy by working a few years at the Drexel Harriman Ripley investment banking firm and then would return to a university to teach. I might have been skeptical of this goal had it been voiced by another peer, but this was Michael Milken; already well known among faculty and students alike, it was clear he had an unusual talent for finance and business. Renowned among our cohort, he would soon be famous—and then infamous—throughout the entire financial world.

But in 1970, Milken was still just a prospective MBA graduate—albeit one with an unheard of three majors (information systems, operations research, and finance) who landed his job after one of Wharton's finance professors told Drexel's managing director that Milken was "the most astounding young man I have ever taught."[1] Milken achieved straight As during his MBA studies, getting grades so high that they skewed professors' grading curves and led some A-seeking students to avoid classes in which he was enrolled. (Milken finished all of his course work and left Wharton in 1970 but didn't receive his degree until 1973, when he finally completed the required thesis.)

My impression of Milken was as an intensely serious young man with few social or intellectual interests beyond business—but in those areas, his interest seemed boundless. Inspired not by assigned classwork but by his own desire to better understand the business world, he compiled binders full of articles and reports arranged by industry groups to more thoroughly analyze companies within the markets they served. He even asked to read classmates' term papers if the subject piqued his enormous curiosity. I shared one of my papers with him, on how investment bankers raise money for their clients through privately placed securities offerings. He returned it with insightful comments in the margins. Who could have guessed that fifteen years later (with certainly no credit due to my elementary term paper) Milken would became famous on Wall Street for raising $1.1 billion for MCI Communications through the largest private placement of securities in history.

The topic that most consumed his interest, however, was low-rated corporate bonds. In his soft, monotonic voice, Milken could talk for hours about the investment merits of what would later be called junk bonds. While an undergraduate at the University of California, Berkeley (where he graduated Phi Beta Kappa), he had come across a little known book by W. Braddock Hickman titled *Corporate Bond Quality and Investor Experience*. This text set the foundation for Milken's later career and fortune.[2] Hickman's book was not exactly a how-to manual on making money in the bond market, but it provided much of the impetus and statistical raw material on lower-quality bonds that would drive Milken's research at Wharton. And that research convinced the twenty-three-year-old Milken that he could quickly become a millionaire by trading in a selective portfolio of bonds that were outside the investment-worthy ranges established by the Standard & Poor's and Moody's credit-rating agencies. At Drexel, he set out to do just that.

Making a Market

Drexel Harriman Ripley had a storied past, but—when Milken joined in 1970—an uncertain future. A century earlier, in 1871, prominent Philadelphia banker Anthony J. Drexel joined forces with the young J. Pierpont Morgan to form Drexel, Morgan & Company. The firm grew into a powerful

American banking house, financing many of the era's leading railroads and engineering a bailout of the U.S. government during the panic of 1893. Not long after, the firm split into a dual-partnership arrangement, with shared directors but separate names: New York–based J. P. Morgan & Company and Philadelphia-based Drexel & Company. The Drexel firm's business was mainly in commercial banking, and shortly after the passage of the Glass-Steagall Act in 1933 its partners elected to merge into the J. P. Morgan operation. But in 1940, following the lead of former J. P. Morgan partners who established Morgan Stanley & Company as an investment banking offshoot of the House of Morgan, several Philadelphia partners bought the Drexel name and launched their own wholesaler investment firm. For the next few decades, they enjoyed success by trading on the long-honored Drexel reputation for investment banking excellence and conducted a gentlemanly and upscale underwriting business for companies with whom they had preserved longtime personal and business connections.

By the time Milken arrived in 1970, Drexel had combined with another old-line investment house, Harriman Ripley & Company. And though the resulting Drexel Harriman Ripley had a rich combined history of financing railroads and early twentieth-century industrial companies, their roster of blue-chip corporate clients was shrinking below the level necessary to conduct a viable investment banking business. The only reliable client the firm could count on for ongoing stock and bond offerings was the Philadelphia Electric Company.

Over the next twenty years, Milken would transform Drexel into a high-flying investment banking firm far beyond the imagination of the current or prior Drexel partners. But when he first joined he was assigned to less glamorous projects, many of them in the firm's "back office." One of the back office projects involved revamping the way Drexel delivered its securities, with Milken's recommended improvements purportedly saving the firm about a half-million dollars per year.[3] The back office assignments were productive, but Milken wanted to pursue work in the firm's research and trading departments, where he could apply his academic studies on low-grade bonds to the real world. The firm acceded to his wishes, but there was one catch: he would have to transfer from Philadelphia to the New York office.

The prospect of living in New York held little appeal for Milken. His wife Lori was enrolled in graduate school and working as a research assistant on a history of the University of Pennsylvania. Uprooting themselves from their Philadelphia home for what could be a short-lived assignment seemed unwise. What's more, they both missed California and their families and planned a return to the West Coast as soon as an opportunity arose.

The solution Milken settled on was commuting by bus to and from New York, leaving before sunrise and not returning until midevening. But he made those long commutes—two hours each way—highly productive. He boarded the bus with tote bags full of research reports and securities filings on the issuers of low-grade bonds, and spent the trips in nondistracted study. He eschewed the faster and more comfortable commuter train, preferring the bus's assured anonymity and the near certainty of an adjacent empty seat for his bags of paperwork. (His routine was well known to colleagues, and one gave Milken a gag gift of a miner's hat with an attached light to better illuminate reading material during the dark hours of his bus trips.)

The prodigious amount of research he dedicated to his bond endeavors, both on the bus and off, is important in explaining his ultimate success. Making money on low-rated bonds was not just a matter of reading Hickman's book on the historic yields available on such bonds and then dedicating money to that market segment. By their nature, bonds with a weak credit standing, namely those carrying BB, B, CCC, and lower ratings, have greater inherent risks, and their purchase demands more scrutiny and a thorough knowledge of the underlying business. Bond salesmen and traders had an easier time of it when dealing in bonds rated AAA, AA, A, and BBB, relying on the credit agencies' assessment of investment quality and the risk of default. A pleasant personality and a decent golf swing was often enough to forge a lucrative career in selling low-risk bonds.

Milken, meanwhile, did not play golf and could hardly be described as congenial. He would ultimately wear the (not-so-cherished) mantle of "Junk Bond King," but the first leg of his road to success required convincing the innately conservative bond buyers of the day on the merits of junk bonds—or, as he preferred to call them, high-yield bonds. It was a hard sell. When he began on Drexel's bond research desk in the 1970s, the supply of junk bonds was composed entirely of "fallen angels": bonds that had once been investment grade but were subsequently downgraded to "below investment grade" status. A bond analyst or trader at an insurance company or an investment advisor in a staid trust department of a bank could hardly be faulted for a lack of interest in such maligned bonds. And it did not help Milken's cause that he was just in his midtwenties when he set out to change the world of bond investing. Or that he covered his premature baldness with an ill-fitting toupee and wore clothes that looked to be straight off the rack. Or, for a sizable percentage of institutional investors who occupied the buy-side desks on Wall Street, that he was Jewish.

But if he could get an audience, Milken was often able to make a compelling case for one or more of his fallen angels. If the prospective bond buyer had been trained through a strict Graham and Dodd approach to securities analysis—one, that is, that relied on demonstrating that the issuing company had ample cash flow to make principal and interest payments and had sufficiently valuable assets to back up the bonds—Milken was at the ready. Many of the junk bonds of the day had been issued by conglomerates formed in the 1960s that were struggling with their unwieldy collections of diverse businesses. Once-prominent companies such as AVCO, Ling-Temco-Vought, Rapid-American, General Host, and City Investing had suffered downgrades from credit agencies as their fortunes waned. But through endless hours poring over complex financial statements and industry statistics, Milken (like Benjamin Graham before him) was able to ferret out investment value and safety that had escaped the notice of less conscientious analysts. He could answer every question about the bond issuer's business prospects and balance sheet, and more importantly, he could paint a convincing picture as to why many of the fallen angels, with their high yields, could provide a very enticing return on investment—and could do so with a much lower level of risk than their bond ratings suggested.

If the bond buyer was attuned to the academically based "modern portfolio theory" coming out of the business schools, so much the better. This approach called for investment managers to control risk by balancing their portfolios with a mix of two very different securities: investment-grade bonds and common stocks. If the manager wanted to lower the portfolio's risk, he would weight the investment mix toward the bonds; if he was feeling less risk averse and was more interested in higher returns, he would move toward a higher proportion of stocks. But now Milken was advocating a third component: non-investment-grade bonds that were more risky than their investment-grade counterparts but less so than common stocks. With Hickman's study of the corporate bond markets between 1900 and 1943, and the update by T. R. Atkinson for the years 1944 through 1965, Milken had the statistics to back up his pitch.[4] Some small percentage of the lower-rated bonds went into default, leaving their holders with a substantial loss of principal value, but on average the return realized on those bonds more than made up for a few losses. Over time, Milken argued, a portfolio of riskier but higher-yielding bonds was much more profitable than a portfolio of investment-grade bonds. And history showed that, when compared with common stocks, the returns to high-yield bondholders were smaller, but the risks were lower, because with any bond there was a contractual obligation from the issuer to make the payment of the bond's principal amount upon maturity. As Milken explained it:

> No matter how much research you have done regarding a particular stock, you don't have a contract as to what the future price will be. But with a high-yield bond there is a date certain in the future when it matures, and if you hold it to maturity and your analysis is correct, you will be correct in your calculation of your yield—and you do have a contract as to future price. One is certain if you're right. The other is not.[5]

While the investment logic for junk bonds may have been compelling, their lack of liquidity in the marketplace often remained a final stumbling block for the potential buyer. With few buyers and sellers in the high-yield bond market, investors faced an unwelcome prospect of holding a bond to its maturity date as the only sure way to be paid. Milken solved that liquidity issue by assuring those investors that Drexel would always be ready to buy or sell the bonds it was promoting. He was able to make this promise because, in addition to his encyclopedic knowledge of the bond issuer's business and financial position, he knew one other crucial set of facts: which financial institutions owned the bonds and what their inclination might be for buying or selling them. With this information, and a capital allocation of $500,000 from Drexel, Milken developed the first secondary trading market for junk bonds on Wall Street.

A 35 Percent Arrangement

On its face, a junk bond trading operation lodged within a white-shoe firm like Drexel Harriman Ripley was a puzzle. With its elitist, wholesaler pretensions, the firm had limited most of its trading in bonds to the shrinking list of investment grade–rated corporations it could still count as clients. Bond trading was merely an accommodation to its investment banking clientele, not a profit generator. As Milken began his junk bond operation, one of the high-grade bond traders confronted a Drexel top executive with a demand that Milken be fired lest he tarnish the firm's reputation among the Fortune 500 firms it was pursuing. The executive responded by asking,

"Milken on a modest capital base is making money, while your high-grade department on a large capital base is losing it. Now, whom should I fire?"[6] Milken stayed, and the advocate for his firing was soon gone. It was an early indication of Milken's growing influence at Drexel.

In 1971, Milken's nascent power base expanded further when the ailing and capital-poor Drexel was acquired by the much stronger Burnham & Company, to become Drexel Burnham & Company. While the name Burnham Drexel & Company (or even just Burnham & Company) would have been more in keeping with the reality of the arrangement, pedigrees were important in the investment banking hierarchy of Wall Street at the time, and Drexel's name retained a cachet that Burnham's, associated with the second tier of investment bankers, lacked. Before the merger took place, Burnham's founder and majority partner, I. W. Burnham II—nicknamed "Tubby" throughout his life following a brief period of plumpness as a child—consulted with other firms on the new name. Morgan Stanley (then the arbiter of such things in the caste-like rankings of underwriters) advised Burnham that the combined firm should be called Drexel Burnham if it wanted to participate in Wall Street's securities offerings as one of the top bracketed firms.

The new Drexel Burnham would prove to be a more hospitable home for Milken for reasons far removed from underwriting brackets. Burnham & Company's principals were predominantly Jewish, and when Tubby Burnham was doing his due diligence prior to the acquisition, he inquired about the number of Jews who were part of the Drexel organization. Drexel's president at the time, Archibald Albright, said that just a few of their two hundred fifty employees were Jewish. He elaborated: "They're all bright, and one of them is brilliant. But I think he's fed up with Drexel, and may go back to Wharton to teach. If you want to keep him, talk to him."[7]

Burnham did talk to Milken, and discovered that the source of his unhappiness was that Drexel was allocating only $500,000 of the firm's capital for junk bond trading—even though he was earning a 100 percent return per year on that capital. He also discovered, after Milken provided him with a lengthy tutorial on junk bonds, that "brilliant" was an apt description, and committed on the spot to increase his capital allocation to $2 million. Much more crucial for its long-term ramifications, however, was the deal that Burnham cut with Milken providing that employees of the high-yield trading operation would receive 35 percent of the profit they generated, to be divided among the traders however Milken saw fit. That incentive no doubt helps explain why the Drexel high-yield group lost money in only three months during their seventeen-year run—and also explains how Milken, who shared in those profits, eventually became a billionaire.

With a larger capital base, "the Department" (as Milken's junk bond operation came to be known within Drexel) expanded with respect to both the number of traders and its book of clients. Milken's approach to attracting those institutional clients was short on charm but long on substance. He had never developed any sense of style, and with his shabby suits he could still be confused with a clerk from the firm's back office. But with an inexhaustible knowledge about junk bonds, he could speak at whatever level of detail the prospective institutional investor required. And by the time he met with investors, he had done enough investigation into each institution's investment portfolio to tailor a junk bond pitch precisely to its apparent needs, be it an insurance company, pension fund, bank, or mutual fund.

It wasn't long before Milken evolved from the role of salesman, explaining the merits of high-yield bonds, to the much broader and more influential role of trusted investment advisor. In 1973, his guidance was behind the conversion of the First Investors Fund for Income from an investment-grade bond mutual fund to a high-yield bond fund—and as a result, First Investors was the country's best-performing bond fund in both 1975 and 1976.[8] And while mutual funds represented a fertile new market to which he could spread the junk bond gospel, the insurance industry held even more appeal. Insurance companies were major purchasers of corporate bonds, and Milken enticed several of them, including old-line carriers such as Massachusetts Mutual, to diversify from investment-grade bond portfolios by giving them a sampling of his offerings from the junk bond arena. Much of his new business, however, came from institutions that had recently come under the control of mavericks who acquired insurance-based financial conglomerates through hostile takeovers—familiar names from the 1970s, they included Laurence Tisch (CNA Financial), Carl Lindner Jr. (American Financial Group), and Saul Steinberg (Reliance Insurance Group). For each of these companies, Milken designed as well as implemented much of their high-yield investment strategies.

One bedazzled institutional investor, after a visit to Drexel's bond operation, summed up Milken's accomplishments by stating: "He had the issuers. He had the buyers. He had the most trading capital of any firm. He had the knowhow. He had the best incentive system for his people. He had the history of data—he knew the companies, he knew their trading prices, probably their daily trading prices going back at least to 1971. He had boxed the compass."[9]

Yet Milken had a major and fundamental problem in the early 1970s: he was faced with a limited supply of product. His promotion of high-yield investing had led to many recent converts and fresh entrants to his markets, thereby fostering a growing demand for junk bonds. But the problem was on the supply side. New fallen angels continued to drop into his orbit, but the number of junk bonds was also being depleted as issuers were acquired by larger, more creditworthy companies. Compounding the shortage were rising stars, the once junk-rated companies that moved back into the investment-grade sphere. And, of course, some of the fallen angels fell even further, disappearing into bankruptcy. With the rise and fall of new and old fallen angels, Milken had only about twenty-five separate junk bond names to trade. That stasis, however, ended shortly after the 1974 arrival of Frederick Joseph at Drexel Burnham.

"Let's Do Some Deals"

The combination of the blue-blooded investment bankers of the old Drexel with the hard-driving traders and salespeople from the Burnham side was bound to create problems, and it did so without much delay—especially on the investment banking side. The conflicting missions of the old and new versions of Drexel investment banking were colorfully described by a former Drexel & Company banker who said, "The Drexel people were sitting at one end of the hall, waiting for Ford Motor Company to realize it had made a mistake and call us up and tell us that they'd really appreciate it if we would take them back. And you had the guys from Burnham and Company running around Seventh Avenue trying to underwrite every schmate factory they could find."[10]

Recognizing the incompatibility of the two approaches, the combined Drexel Burnham fell back on the often-used but rarely successful solution of naming coheads to direct its investment banking operation. But in reality, there was little business to direct. Drexel's stable of clients included a few remaining Fortune 500 companies, mixed in with many decidedly smaller and lower-quality companies. So when Fred Joseph was recruited to represent the "Burnham side" to complement John Friday on the "Drexel side," the investment banking business was essentially a turnaround project.

The son of a Boston cabdriver, Joseph had gone on to become a collegiate boxing champion at Harvard College and later earned an MBA from Harvard's graduate business school. From there, he had gone on to work for two of the larger Wall Street firms of the time, E. F. Hutton and Shearson Hammill. Joseph had a history of setting and achieving lofty goals and had been on the lookout for a place to build a major investment banking operation from the ground up. When he interviewed for the codirector position at Drexel in 1974, he stated confidently that he would build a business that in ten to fifteen years would rival the likes of Goldman Sachs and Morgan Stanley. It was the kind of naked ambition that many on Wall Street were imbued with—but no one else would enjoy the good fortune of having Michael Milken as a business partner.

Joseph's plan for building an investment banking powerhouse was based on a strategy of raising capital for up-and-coming businesses that were too small or too risky for the major firms—or for the once-exclusive Drexel Harriman Ripley. The timing for such a strategy could not have been better. During the troubled 1970s, medium-sized businesses, regardless of their potential for growth and development, had few places to go for expansion funds. The stock market was inhospitable for fast-growing companies looking to go public. Only a handful of such companies—"special situations" of one kind or another—could attract a willing underwriter. In normal years, hundreds of companies launched initial public offerings, but in 1974 there were only nine IPOs, and in 1975 the number dropped to six. And there seemed to be no way to float a bond offering for a company that was not sporting an investment-grade rating. To make matters worse, the ranks of the smaller, "sub-major" investment firms, whose corporate finance departments once catered to small- to medium-sized businesses, had greatly thinned during Wall Street's problem years of the mid-1970s. In most cases, the only financing alternative for a medium-sized company was a commercial bank or sometimes a receptive insurance company. In short, when Joseph arrived at Drexel Burnham, there was a large pent-up demand for capital but a dwindling supply of it.

Milken was running his lucrative bond trading operation at a far remove from the rest of Drexel Burnham investment bankers, but when Joseph got around to meeting Milken he realized that he had not only come across an uncommonly bright trader who had a desire for success and market share that rivaled his own, he'd also found an answer to his capital shortage. Joseph knew of an untold number of low credit–grade companies that were being shut out of the capital markets, while Milken's operation was strapped by a shortage of junk bonds available in the market. They quickly realized they could solve each other's problems, and their first meeting ended with Joseph saying, "Let's do some deals together."[11]

And deals they did. Over the next several years Drexel Burnham Lambert—a transaction with Belgian-based Groupe Bruxelles Lambert resulted in a major capital infusion into the newly named Drexel Burnham Lambert—prospered by developing a new form of financing: bonds that began their lives in the capital market with below–investment grade ratings and high interest rates. In one of the most important developments of modern investment banking, Joseph and his team found a way to raise capital for clients by floating newly created junk bonds.

Drexel would eventually dominate the market for new-issue junk bonds, but the first such bonds were offered in 1977 by Lehman Brothers—then one of Wall Street's elite investment bankers—for low-rated but familiar companies such as LTV Corporation, Zapata Corporation, and Pan American World Airways. Later in that year, Drexel made its junk bond debut by underwriting an original issue of $30 million of bonds for Texas International, an oil and gas company. The firm sponsored six other junk bond offerings in 1977 and raised a total of $125 million but still lagged behind Lehman in the new junk bond category. In 1978, however, Drexel's volume of junk bond financing soared to fourteen offerings totaling $439 million, leaving Lehman Brothers and all other investment banking firms far behind. In short order, Milken and Joseph had put a rejuvenated Drexel Burnham Lambert back among the major investment banking firms.

Westward Expansion

By the late 1970s, Drexel was thriving. At the beginning of that decade it had been on the ropes, with no apparent direction and few profitable operations, but by the end, with its new focus on junk bonds, it reemerged in good financial health. The investment bankers were able to command underwriting fees on new junk bond issues of between 3 to 4 percent of the gross amount being offered—by contrast, underwriters of investment-grade bonds charged less than 1 percent for the same services—and Milken continued to oversee a profitable and rapidly growing trading operation. With a junk bond–based mission, Drexel abandoned the low profits of the high-quality segment of the bond business, and John Friday, once Joseph's codirector of investment banking, was pushed out.

And as Drexel prospered, so did Milken. Because of his growing position of power within the firm, he was successful in extending the Department's 35 percent share of trading profits to include profits realized from investment banking work that involved junk bonds. Milken retained sole discretion on how the Department's bonuses were distributed, and as would be the practice during Milken's reign as Junk Bond King, he allocated much of the 35 percent to himself. Still, many of the traders, salespeople, and research analysts who worked for him began making incomes well into the six figures.

Compensation at that level is not that unusual nowadays for Wall Street bankers, but in the 1970s it was considered a staggering amount and, of course, bought a great deal of loyalty to Milken. So in 1976, when he first broached the idea of moving the high-yield department from New York City to Southern California, there was little resistance from those who worked for him. All of the important players in the Department went along with the move, with only a few clerical workers opting to stay behind in New York.

More surprising was the lack of resistance from the top management of Drexel. Tubby Burnham and Fred Joseph knew that Milken and his operation would be hard to control three thousand miles away, but they understood the reality of the situation: no matter how they crunched the numbers, the Department was responsible for the firm's new levels of profitability. If Milken wanted to return home to the Southern California lifestyle he and his family had missed for the last ten years, they'd let him do it—as long as he continued to ship back 65 percent of the profits back to New York.

With little fanfare and with not so much as a sign on the door, the West Coast operation of Drexel Burnham Lambert opened in Century City on July 3, 1978, one day before Milken turned thirty-two. It was home to the same cast of characters who had worked together successfully in New York, but with one major modification: the workday began at 4:30 in the morning to accommodate the three-hour time difference between New York and California. Milken sold his transplanted work crew on the notion that the change would result in an enhanced family life, since the trading day would end three hours earlier. In reality, at least for Milken, it just extended the number of working hours in the day. He arrived home in Encino—not far from where he and Lori grew up—about the same time the bus rolled into Philadelphia when he worked on Wall Street. Now he just left home even earlier in the morning.

The business from the new California base exploded. By 1983, Drexel's junk bond financing increased more than tenfold to $4.63 billion. All told, Drexel underwrote 276 new issues of junk bonds in that five-year span, with proceeds to the corporate issuers totaling $14.6 billion, including the $1.1 billion offering for MCI Communications, the up-and-coming challenger to AT&T for the long-distance telephone business.[12] And Milken—with a vast web of institutional investors who trusted his investment judgment and secondary trading prowess—was arguably the only investment banker with the credibility to engineer billion-dollar deals.

Most of the money he raised went to companies that had no alternative means of tapping into the capital markets, or at least not to the extent they could under Drexel's sponsorship. Milken and his acolytes often ascribed more lofty aims than mere moneymaking to their activities, and it is certainly true that not just new companies but the growth and development of whole new industries, including much of the cable television, telecommunications, broadcasting, and gaming industries, were powered with junk bonds. Just as the level of venture capital financing grew exponentially after its locus shifted from Boston to California's Silicon Valley in the 1980s, the junk bond business took off after the move to Los Angeles. Comparisons between the two types of financings and their positive effects on the economy quickly grow strained—the case for venture capital is much easier to make—but it's true that much of the new capital raised by the less tradition-bound West Coast financiers was initially put to productive use and spurred significant economic growth.

Whatever the salutary effects of junk bonds on society and the economy through 1983, the effects on Drexel and Milken were unequivocally positive. Drexel, the once-prominent investment banking firm of J. P. Morgan and Anthony Drexel, was making a resurgence, and in the closely watched "league tables"—the periodic listing of where investment bankers place by activity—the firm had risen to the number six spot for underwriting corporate securities. It was once again, as Joseph had brashly predicted just ten years earlier, operating in the top tier of investment banking firms. Milken shared handsomely in that success; his 1983 tax returns showed personal income of $47.5 million.[13]

His fortune was made, but Milken showed no interest in following up on his earlier plan to move to academia. Instead, he ratcheted up his business further by seeking other uses for junk bonds. He was especially intrigued by the idea of extending their use to international finance, in particular by providing a means to fund the development of emerging-market countries. Unfortunately, his fertile mind was diverted from the more idealistic field of development finance to the more immediate and lucrative opportunities in the roaring mergers and acquisitions markets of the 1980s. It would prove to be a disastrous decision for both Milken and Drexel.

Highly Confident

Drexel's West Coast business soon relocated from Century City to Beverly Hills, and it was there, in November 1983, that Milken, Joseph, and a select group of Drexel's corporate finance officers conceived of a new application for junk bonds. The strategy they plotted, which they believed would provide a "quantum leap" in the level of their business, was to make junk bonds an integral part of a corporate transaction called a leveraged buyout. It was the dawn of the so-called LBO, a form of acquisition that was spurred by the remarkably quick and successful buyout of Gibson Greeting Cards in 1982 by an equity group put together by former Treasury secretary William Simon. An LBO involves purchasing a company largely through the use of debt (hence, the transaction is "leveraged"), so the buyer can use just a token amount of its own equity capital and a much larger amount of "other people's money" procured through borrowing. About 60 percent of the acquisition funding typically came from commercial banks that secured their loans by using the target company's assets as collateral, and another 10 percent or so was supplied by the new owners of the company in the form of common stock equity. The toughest money to locate, however, was "mezzanine" debt—the unsecured financing level between the collateralized bank debt and the new owners' equity. If it could be found at all, such debt was usually available from a small number of aggressive insurance company lenders or specialty mezzanine finance funds and only after prolonged business investigations and the negotiation of a long list of restrictive conditions.

Milken and Joseph realized that junk bonds, with their long-term maturities and light terms and conditions, provided a much faster and more appealing way to apply leverage. The only problem was that Drexel was just a middleman and did not, like an insurance company or a mezzanine fund, have the figurative vault from which to draw the funds. For good reason, a prudent board of directors was chary of approving an LBO without all of the financing firmly in place, including the linchpin mezzanine money. By 1983, however, Drexel had developed such a formidable reputation that Joseph and Milken believed a "highly confident letter" could be issued to assure all parties to the deal that the firm could bring the necessary funds to the closing table. This idea raised skepticism among Drexel's mergers and acquisitions competitors on Wall Street and the whole idea was derisively referred to as Milken's Air Fund.

But just a few months later, Milken proved that he could deliver. T. Boone Pickens, one of the country's most effective and feared takeover operators, had hired Drexel to raise a staggering $1.7 billion in advance of his attempted hostile takeover of Gulf Oil by his much smaller acquisition vehicle, Mesa Petroleum. After the proposed deal was publicly announced, Milken quickly came through with commitments for the $1.7 billion— promising more if needed. Gulf was ultimately acquired by Chevron Corporation, which acted as a "white knight" to counter the acquisition by Mesa, but Pickens still made a great deal of money, having already purchased many shares of Gulf stock at prices far below the $80 per share price that Chevron wound up paying. And with Milken's remarkably fast procurement of almost $2 billion, Drexel's highly confident letter was no longer referred to as the Air Fund.

It was after this transaction that Milken lost the anonymity he had always coveted. He had never sought a high profile in high finance—he was listed in Drexel's annual reports as merely a vice president—but the Pickens transaction forced Milken into the limelight of Wall Street financiers. Financing engagements for Drexel soon followed from the leading takeover players of the day, including Carl Icahn, Sir James Goldsmith, and the LBO firm of Kohlberg Kravis Roberts & Company. With its dominance in LBO financing, Drexel climbed another four spots in the league tables, occupying the number two spot among the underwriters of corporate debt securities in 1984, just behind Salomon Brothers. Through the remainder of the 1980s, Drexel, with its ability to raise vast amounts of mezzanine money, was a key player in the rise of record-sized LBOs that included the buyout of Beatrice Foods, Union Carbide, and, ingloriously, the highly controversial $25 billion buyout of RJR Nabisco in 1988. Between 1984 and 1990, LBOs consumed $216 billion in junk bond financing.[14] For much of that time, Milken was at the controls.

As Milken's notoriety grew, comparisons to J. Pierpont Morgan became commonplace; no one since Morgan had wielded such financial power, and like the venerable Morgan, Milken had a string of large financial institutions lined up to fund his transactions at a moment's notice. Also like Morgan, he was a divisive figure that was either revered or hated by the public. But whereas Morgan was generally held in high repute by the business elites and Wall Street, Milken was loved mainly by scrappy entrepreneurs and takeover specialists and was despised by much of the business establishment—especially by organizations such as the Business Roundtable (an organization of CEOs of large corporations, many of whom feared a Milken-engineered hostile takeover) and by the prominent investment banking firms that eschewed, at least initially, the ungentlemanly business of hostile takeovers. Many dismissed Drexel Burnham Lambert as "junk people and junk bonds" and seemed eager to see the firm implode.

100 Percent Share

Drexel's critics would not have to wait long for the implosion. Indeed, while the firm was making record profits and climbing to the top rungs of investment banking during the glory years of the 1980s, its West Coast office, the source of most of its success, was also careening dangerously out of control under Milken's loose management.

In well-run investment banking firms, there are checks and balances and systems of quality control, but Drexel failed to put those measures in place with respect to its Beverly Hills operation, dubbed by many in the home office as the Wild West. At the New York headquarters, Joseph had formed the Underwriting Assistance Committee to, ostensibly, approve investment banking commitments. Milken paid little heed to the decisions of this feckless group, and if they disapproved of a deal that he proposed, he simply flouted the firm's internal rules and did it anyway. Furthermore, in the Beverly Hills operation, there were no real boundary lines between departments—referred to as "Chinese walls" in the investment business— to assure that the confidential information the firm's bankers held about a transaction was kept separate from the traders and sales force. Milken's California organization, in reality a full-scale investment banking operation, shared information among its employees indiscriminately. Indeed, Milken was given complete freedom to run the Beverly Hills firm with no apparent input from New York management. At the height of its activity, the Beverly Hills office was transacting two hundred fifty thousand trades per month, yet they were coded in a way that only Milken understood. The carving up of profits, the levels of inventories, and the settlement of trades were all in accordance with Milken's preferences. He set up partnerships among his cronies and members of his family through which he funneled the firm's profits with minimal approval and oversight.

Although loose management was a major ingredient in the recipe for disaster, another ingredient, even more problematic, was Milken's growing propensity to ally himself and Drexel with bad actors. When the LBO boom got under way in the 1980s, Milken funded some tough and controversial people (like Carl Icahn and T. Boone Pickens) who earned the enmity of establishment bankers and corporate America. They were smart and pushed the boundaries of fair dealing but seemed to be playing by the rules. But as time went on, Milken became the source of acquisition funding for more questionable corporate raiders and Wall Street operators. In his rabid pursuit of more deals, his associates in the Beverly Hills office and his nominal supervisors at the New York headquarters understood that "Mike Milken believes in 100 percent market share." Quantity often trumped quality. And despite an awe-inspiring thoroughness when it came to the facts and figures of the billions of dollars of transactions he masterminded, he had a fatal blind spot when it came to the people behind the deals. And no one proved more fateful for Drexel and himself than Victor Posner and Ivan Boesky.

Even Joseph, whose New York corporate finance department was staffed with an unusually aggressive and rule-testing breed of investment bankers, knew that Posner was nothing but trouble. One of the shadiest takeover players of the 1980s, Posner was an unsavory Miami wheeler-dealer who was routinely under investigation by the Securities and Exchange Commission and had pleaded no contest in a recent charge of tax fraud. After Joseph ordered a study into Posner's businesses, he became alarmed with the pattern of noncompliance with securities regulations and the performance of the several companies under his control. The Drexel banker who completed the study on Posner concluded that Posner had a history of "turning gold into dross."[15] But when Joseph voiced his very reasonable objections to doing business with him, he was steamrolled by the strong-minded Milken and his "100 percent market share" ambitions; Posner was retained as a client in several takeover transactions.

Ivan Boesky was another Milken-championed client. Drexel's New York bankers were as wary of Boesky as of Posner, and initially balked at any representation of him. Boesky had been wildly successful in the frantic mergers and takeover business of the 1980s by engaging in merger arbitrage, which involved making large bets on whether an announced merger transaction would actually close. There was always some uncertainty as to the completion of a merger, since an agreed-upon deal could go off the rails for any number of reasons (including regulatory and antitrust problems, due diligence issues, or just unfavorable market developments). Because of that uncertainty, the target company's stock almost always sold at some discount to the anticipated value of the deal during the weeks or months prior to a final closing. "Arbitrageurs" like Boesky made large and leveraged bets on the actual completion of transactions and, if correct, benefited handsomely. The bets were informed by whatever the arbitrageur could dig up—including inside information known only to the corporate executives, investment bankers, attorneys, accountants, and others with access to such privileged information. Although acting on inside information was illegal, the SEC was less than vigilant in pursuing suspected insider abuse. Boesky used whatever means he could, including bribery, to gain profitable information on which to base his bets.[16]

During the early to mid-1980s, Boesky appeared prescient and established a remarkable record of success as an arbitrageur. He craved public approbation and in 1985 wrote a book about his business: *Merger Mania: Arbitrage, Wall Street's Best Kept Money-Making Secret.* In the same year he gave the commencement address to the business school graduates at Berkeley (Milken's alma mater), telling his young listeners: "Greed is all right, by the way. I want you to know that. I think greed is healthy. You can be greedy and still feel good about yourself."[17] Those lines, simplified to "Greed is good," were immortalized by the Gordon Gekko character in the movie *Wall Street.*

Among the cognoscenti on Wall Street, including the bankers and traders at Drexel, there was little doubt that Boesky's arbitrage gains were ill-gotten. So when Milken proposed a plan to raise $640 million for Boesky's arbitrage partnership, there was strong and well-grounded resistance from the more discerning Drexel bankers. Members of the firm's Underwriting Assistance Committee argued that the real and perceived conflicts of interest would be overwhelming, since many of Boesky's arbitrage bets would be on the very deals that Milken and the firm's LBO group were engineering. Since it was always Milken's policy to take a financial interest in clients, there was a built-in temptation to steer information on the deals to Boesky for mutual benefit. And even if there was no actual illegality involved, the appearance of the arrangement looked suspect—and Drexel, with its entrance into the often controversial LBO arena, already had enough reputational problems to deal with. But as with so many other transactions that the committee disapproved, Milken simply ignored the firm's internal procedures and raised the money for Boesky anyway.

Milken also ignored the better instincts of his brother Lowell and his wife Lori. Lowell, a prominent tax lawyer in Los Angeles, began working at Drexel when the Department moved from New York to California, handling many of Milken's legal and administrative issues. He was both a consigliore and confidant to Milken, offering personal advice as well as business and legal advice—and one piece of advice was to be wary of Boesky. Lori's advice, based more on Boesky's objectionable personal behavior than on his business practices, was the same. Neither Lowell nor Lori would take or return any of Boesky's repeated telephone calls—but Mike would usually pick up.

A $5.3 Million Payment

The events that eventually took down Drexel, and then Milken, involved both Posner and Boesky. During the early 1980s, Posner had been engaged in a protracted takeover attempt of Fischbach Corporation, a publicly traded New York-based electrical contractor. According to SEC rules, investors were required to give public notice when they had accumulated an amount of stock that exceeded some threshold and to further state their intentions regarding any attempts to wrest control of the company. Posner complied with that SEC requirement by filing a Schedule 13-D form with the SEC. That was followed by a "standstill agreement" with Fischbach under which Posner agreed not to purchase any additional stock of Fischbach, unless a rival suitor purchased enough stock to require the filing of another Schedule 13-D.

At that point, Milken began to act on behalf of Posner—again over the objections of his purported bosses in New York. Milken's power in the acquisitions market was based on his ability to control both the issuers and buyers of his high-yield bonds and to maneuver them like chess pieces in furtherance of his goals. In 1983 he had one of his oldest and most loyal junk bond buyers, Executive Life Insurance Company, purchase enough stock in Fischbach to trigger the end to the standstill agreement—even though an insurance company was not a logical buyer of Fischbach. When that tactic backfired because of legal technicalities, Milken called on Boesky to "park" Fischbach stock in one of his arbitrage funds on Posner's behalf. Parking is illegal under securities laws, because it violates the full-disclosure rules of the SEC regarding the actual parties to an acquisition; it also was in violation of the standstill agreement between Posner and Fischbach, since by using a straw party under Milken's direction to acquire stock, Posner was by no means "standing still."

To entice Boesky to take multi-million-dollar positions in Fischbach, Milken assured him that upon the ultimate takeover, whether by Posner or another purchaser, there would be a substantial increase in the stock price—and if not, Milken promised to make Boesky whole through profits on other unrelated transactions between him and Drexel. Boesky agreed to the no-lose proposition and by 1984 had accumulated enough stock to trigger the filing of his own 13-D—with no disclosure in the filing of any understandings with Milken—and also to trigger the end of the standstill agreement that blocked Posner's takeover attempt.

Then, in 1985, Milken assisted Posner in securing enough money to purchase the Fischbach stock from Boesky by selling securities in one of Posner's affiliated companies, Pennsylvania Engineering. Posner used the proceeds of the offering to buy sufficient Fischbach stock to be in full control of the company. He became its chairman in October. Posner got his prey and Drexel earned tens of millions in underwriting and advisory fees in connection with the Fischbach transaction. But Boesky, based on the prices at which he bought and sold the company's shares in his parking role, wound up losing money.

Despite repeated calls to Milken and his lieutenants in Beverly Hills during and after the Fischbach takeover, Boesky received no guarantee that he would receive his promised compensation. Yet Boesky knew exactly how much he was "owed" by Milken from the Fischbach arrangement. In frustration, he wrote a cryptic note to Milken, with a demand to resolve the matter, referring to his vaguely titled "Special Projects" file—and Milken promptly satisfied his tacit agreement with Boesky by arranging a number of profitable trades involving high-yield bonds under his control.

The Fischbach transactions, however, were not the only ones detailed in Boesky's Special Projects file. Over the years, as later alleged by the SEC and U.S. prosecutors, he and Milken kept a running account of the profits and losses involved from parking and other related transactions. Sometimes Milken would park securities to disguise the true ownership of Boesky; at other times, one instance being the Fischbach transactions, Boesky would park for Milken and his clients. So at any time, who owed whom could shift between Milken and Boesky. In 1986, the balance was in favor of Milken—nominally Drexel—and Boesky owed $5.3 million. In March Boesky made payment to Drexel to settle the account in that amount.

The problem with that payment arose when Boesky's arbitrage funds were being audited, at which time he brushed off the auditors' request to explain the purpose of the payment to Drexel, calling it just a "consulting fee" he owed the firm. In response to the auditors' dogged insistence on more backup documentation, he coaxed the Beverly Hills officials into providing an after-the-fact letter for substantiation. The resulting letter, signed by Lowell Milken, stated that the $5.3 million was paid for "advisory and consulting services."[18] If any piece of evidence could be called a smoking gun in the legal investigations into the business of Drexel and Milken that followed, it was that letter.

Path to Conviction

As with so many other high-flying financiers, Milken's great success had a hand in his downfall. By 1986, the year that would mark the beginning of his problems, more than nine hundred companies had issued junk bonds—more than the number of corporations raising capital with investment-grade bonds. Each month, billions of dollars of new money flowed into companies that only a few years earlier had no access to the long-term capital markets to fund their growth. Milken could rightfully claim that his junk bond innovation was contributing to the real growth of the U.S. economy. Less convincingly he could point to the power his junk-financed LBOs had in shaking out complacent and low-performing managements and making American industry leaner and tougher and better able to compete in world markets. He believed in the efficacy of junk bonds to his very core.

But the benefits of operating lean and mean were by no means universally shared. Corporate management and union officials were aligned in their perception of the evils that junk bonds and hostile takeovers presented. Opponents of takeovers cited the inevitable reduction in the number of employees following a takeover and the dangers takeovers posed for the continued stability of long-established corporations. And they pressed their concerns to their legislators.

Before long, states were adopting antitakeover protections for their local corporations; state insurance commissions began lowering the amount of permissible junk bond purchases; and, at the national level, Congress opened hearings on takeovers and junk bonds. Congressman John Dingell convened a hearing on the issues, and his opening statement left little to the imagination regarding the direction in which his committee was heading: "Companies which have existed for decades, which have carried the brunt of our national defense through two World Wars, which have provided employment in the heartland of America, no longer exist. They have been victims of takeovers, financed through the junk bond market."[19]

William Proxmire, chairman of the U.S. Senate Banking Committee, also took up the issue. He convened hearings in 1986 to investigate the practice of takeovers, asking at the beginning of the deliberations: "How much do we really know about the corporate takeover game and the complex network of information that circulates among investment bankers, takeover lawyers, corporate raiders, arbitrageurs, stock brokers, junk bond investors, and public relations specialists?"[20] Evoking the spirit of the Pecora hearings of more than fifty years earlier, Proxmire emboldened Rudolph Giuliani, since 1983 the U.S. attorney for the Southern District of New York, to be "the Ferdinand Pecora of the 1980s" by looking for instances of insider trading, and bringing the culprits to justice.[21]

Giuliani readily took up Proxmire's open-ended charge. He had made a name for himself in his first few years on the job with high-profile prosecutions of organized crime figures and hoped to enjoy even greater public recognition by going after many of the rich and powerful on Wall Street. With Milken now the most prominent name in corporate takeovers, he was Giuliani's ultimate target. If anyone was to be identified as the central figure in the "complex network of information" that was purportedly costing American jobs and perverting high finance, it was Milken.

The path to a Milken prosecution, however, was not direct. It started with New York–based Drexel investment banker Dennis Levine and none other than arbitrageur Ivan Boesky. Levine worked on Drexel's mergers and acquisitions business and therefore was in a position to trade on inside information. He made a great deal of ill-gotten money by buying and selling stocks of his clients based on confidential information. He also sold his privileged information to Boesky, who used it to turn large profits for his merger arbitrage accounts. So when Giuliani nabbed Levine—thanks mainly to the SEC's investigative efforts—he negotiated a criminal plea agreement that reduced his likely jail time if he could offer testimony useful in indicting Boesky.

After receiving a subpoena in August in connection with his dealings with Levine, Boesky caved quickly. He entered into his own plea agreement in September with Giuliani. Boesky, like Levine, agreed to provide testimony to aid in the prosecution of another suspect—and that suspect was Milken, the end target from the start of Giuliani's Wall Street crusade. In exchange for his full cooperation in indicting Milken—including wearing a wire in meetings with him and allowing the recording of their phone conversations—Boesky was allowed to plead to only one felony count of insider trading. On November 14, 1986 (a day that became known on Wall Street as Boesky Day), Giuliani proudly announced the government's deal with Boesky. At Boesky's sentencing shortly afterward, the government followed through with its leniency, handing down a three-year sentence and $100 million fine, both just half the penalty called for by the single offense to which he pleaded guilty.

By the time the Wall Street prosecutions reached Milken in 1989, both Giuliani and the SEC had already taken action against Drexel, with the bulk of their charges revolving around the $5.3 million payment from Boesky to Drexel. In his prosecution of the firm, Giuliani hauled out his ultimate weapon, charging that Drexel was a "racketeering enterprise." That meant that under the provisions of the Racketeer Influenced and Corrupt Organizations Act (RICO) the government could freeze Drexel's assets at the time of indictment—*before* any conviction. In the same spirit, Giuliani demanded that Drexel fire Milken if he were indicted—again, before Milken was actually convicted or pleaded guilty. Fred Joseph, by this time Drexel's CEO, knew that no investment firm could operate if its assets were frozen and also knew that Milken's indictment was a near certainty. So in December 1988, Drexel pleaded that it was "unable to contest" the government's charges (a guilty plea in gentler terms) and settled the government's lawsuit, paying a record-setting fine of $650 million and firing Milken. In reality, Joseph's decision to cooperate with the government only prolonged the agony and Drexel declared bankruptcy in early 1990.

Between Drexel's guilty plea and its ultimate collapse, Giuliani's investigation continued with the obvious mission of indicting Milken. There were a few vocal Milken supporters—one of them memorably stating, "Corporate America is hoping to indict Mike Milken so it can go back to sleep for another thirty years."[22] But in the main, public opinion was decidedly not in Milken's favor. It was the tail end of the "decade of greed," and Milken, rightly or wrongly, had become its most visible symbol. The savings and loan industry was collapsing as a result of high interest rates and inept management. The U.S. government had authorized thrift institutions to buy high-yield bonds just a few years earlier, and Milken became a convenient scapegoat for that crisis as well, with allegations that he foisted worthless bonds on unsuspecting savings institutions—although junk bonds never accounted for more than the 1 percent of S&L assets and the Government Accounting Office testified that the bonds had no role in the crisis.[23]

In March 1989, at the height of anti-Milken sentiment, the U.S. attorney, as expected, handed down a massive indictment against both Michael Milken and Lowell Milken. While the same New York office had allowed Boesky, its prime witness, to plea to a single count, its ninety-eight-count indictment threw the book at the Milken brothers. The charges included insider trading and various forms of fraud, but most alarmingly for Michael and Lowell, it alleged violations under RICO. If they were convicted of the indictment's charges at trial they would face many decades behind bars—housed with an unsavory group of traditional RICO convicts.

The most newsworthy revelation from the 1989 indictment was not the long list of alleged crimes or even the RICO charges, but rather, on the second page of the indictment document itself, the fact that Drexel paid Michael Milken $550 million in the prior year. It was an unprecedented amount, greater than any business executive had ever made. As a prosecutorial tactic, it served to establish that Milken was indeed the personification of greed.

Faced with the multicount indictment, Milken's first impulse was to go to trial and take his chances with a jury. Unlike most defendants prosecuted in federal court, he could easily afford to hire an all-star team of criminal lawyers to refute each and every one of the government's ninety-eight charges. But the reality was that prosecutors would have at their disposal a growing cast of witnesses to testify before the jury as to Milken's guilt, not just Boesky, but many others from Drexel who had turned state's evidence to protect themselves in connection with the firm's prosecution.

Given all this, Milken's lawyers realized that a conviction at trial was highly likely with the result that Milken would be incarcerated for the better part of his remaining years. In addition, the government indicated that it would drop the charges against Lowell if Michael Milken, the true target, entered into a plea agreement. Perhaps most difficult to overcome at trial would be the $550 million compensation. The jurors may have never heard of the nineteenth-century writer Honoré de Balzac, but at some gut level they too were likely to feel that, as Balzac famously put it, "Behind every great fortune lies a great crime." Ultimately, following the advice of his lawyers and their counsel that "only religious fanatics believe they *have* to go to trial,"[24] Milken pleaded guilty to six relatively minor counts of criminal behavior, none of which involved racketeering or insider trading.

Unsurprisingly, four of the six counts involved his dealings with Boesky and Posner and the $5.3 million payment.

Mixed Verdicts

Milken was certainly avaricious beyond any normal limits, and it's clear that his pursuit of ever-higher markers of success clouded his judgment, but whether he engaged in actual criminality remains a subject for debate. His detractors tend to cling to the "evidence" that anyone who could become so wealthy at such a young age must be doing something illegal. His supporters, believing Milken was a political pawn, liked to point out that the offenses to which he ultimately pleaded guilty were mere technicalities and committed every day on Wall Street's trading desks. The truth is probably somewhere in between and certainly more nuanced, but the comment attributed to business writer Michael Lewis may be apt: "Mike Milken was convicted of loitering in the vicinity of the savings and loan crisis."

At sentencing, Milken was ordered to ten years of confinement. That sentence was reduced shortly afterward to just twenty-two months in light of "substantial cooperation" with the government in later cases. But there was little that Milken testified to of any importance, and most observers believe the very large sentence reduction reflected the judge's reconsideration of the penalty in light of the substance of the case. When stripped to its essentials, Milken was convicted primarily of stock parking, an offense for which no one had ever before gone to jail.

Despite the controversy his career generated, the effect that he had upon the financial world was irreversible and monumental. In his twenty-year stint with Drexel, he had transformed the way businesses raised money and he had created a widely accepted financial instrument called a junk bond. Beginning with Milken's one-man operation, trading in a corner of the New York office of Drexel Harriman Ripley, the high-yield market has expanded to thousands of corporate issuers. During Drexel's collapse and Milken's brief imprisonment, new junk bond issuance slowed to a trickle, and many were predicting a total collapse of Milken's "Ponzi scheme." But several Wall Street firms quickly took up the slack, most notably Donaldson, Lufkin & Jenrette. As a result, the market value of all outstanding junk bonds has increased from about $150 billion when Milken went to jail to approximately $1.5 trillion today.

Books and articles that appeared during and after his tenure seem evenly split between naming Milken the devil incarnate or, alternatively, the savior of modern finance.[25] But few would argue that he conforms to the typical vision of an ex-con—especially an ex-con with several hundred million dollars at his disposal. He still lives in an unpretentious house in Encino, not far where he met his first and only wife. He still drinks no alcohol or caffeinated drinks and in manner, physique, and dress could pass for a somewhat intense high school science teacher—who might double as the track coach.

In her sentencing memorandum to the court, his probation officer Michalah Bracken captured the essence of Milken as well as anyone:

> Among Milken's strengths are his inability to accept defeat, his total commitment to causes he considers "just and right," and his vision concerning business and society. His weakness was that, as creator and head of the High-Yield Bond Department at Drexel, these convictions were more important than his responsibilities and obligation to conduct business fully within the parameters of the law. Yet, despite his fall, Milken is an individual still able to contribute to society and to create positive changes in the future.[26]

Bracken was correct in her opinion about Milken's future contributions. The former financier is now an entrepreneur for philanthropy, putting his considerable money, energy, and intellect into new ventures in medical research, education, and social causes. Based on his initiatives in healthcare, *Fortune* called him "The Man Who Changed Medicine" in a 2004 piece that described Milken's help in speeding up and improving cancer research. (The focus on cancer is personal; Milken contracted prostate cancer at about the same time he was freed from prison.) His pace in later life appears to be as frenetic as it was on the trading desk at Drexel, with one of the cancer researchers he works with complaining to the *Fortune* reporter that Milken "is exhausting—physically, mentally, and emotionally exhausting." Even Rudolph Giuliani, Milken's onetime nemesis and also a prostate cancer survivor, told *Fortune*, "I realize now that I didn't know him then. The man I now know is able to do tremendous things. He took the tremendous talent he had in business and is using it to fight prostate cancer. What more could you ask for?"[27]

© Fred Prouser/Reuters/Corbis

12

Lewis Ranieri: 1948–
Father of Securitization

Securitization is like fertilizer. You can grow tomatoes or
blow up buildings.
—HEDGE FUND MANAGER SIMON MIKHAILOVICH

The world's bond markets underwent a revolution during the last decades
of the twentieth century. Michael Milken's junk bonds forever changed the
scope of corporate bonds, expanding their use from a small number of
blue-chip corporations to a much larger group of medium-sized and less
creditworthy enterprises. And Milken had a corevolutionary in shaking up
the bond world: Lewis Ranieri. While Milken's Drexel Burnham Lambert
was making a name for itself by originating junk bonds and engineering leveraged buyouts, Ranieri, stationed at the trading desks of Salomon
Brothers, was developing a new financial process called "securitization,"
which he applied first to mortgages. Securitization didn't create much of
a stir when it was first introduced, but over the final decades of the twentieth century its use expanded enormously, and a new asset class called
mortgage-backed securities became a mainstay of housing finance. Dwarf-
ing Milken's junk bonds both in number and importance to the economy,
these mortgage-backed bonds grew increasingly exotic and unwieldy until,
in 2008, they became the proximate cause of the financial crisis. Ranieri left
Salomon Brothers and the securitization business twenty years before the
crisis arose, but he still refers to himself as "Dr. Frankenstein" for his role in
creating the MBS monster—albeit a monster far different and much more
virulent than his early creation.[1]

The Corevolutionaries Compared

Milken's and Ranieri's careers on Wall Street were remarkably coincident. Milken started at Drexel Harriman Ripley in 1969 in the firm's back office; Ranieri began working the night shift in the Salomon Brothers' mailroom in the same year. And by the end of their foreshortened careers, each was accounting for the largest portion of the profits of their respective firms.

Otherwise, however, Milken and Ranieri had little in common. Milken was taut and slender, with a no-nonsense, scholarly mien; except when the subject turned to business, he had little to say and his social life seldom veered from small family affairs. Ranieri, on the other hand, had a Rabelaisian personality and was loud and generally uncouth. He was infamous at Salomon as the perpetrator and subject of outrageously elaborate and sometimes profane practical jokes among his fellow bond traders[2]—while Milken, when the Drexel traders hired a stripper to dance on his desk for his thirty-eighth birthday, simply retreated under the desk with his phone and continued trading.[3]

Likewise, their paths to Wall Street were completely different. Milken arrived at Drexel as a financial prodigy from an Ivy League school with a well-charted path to great wealth, whereas the Brooklyn-born Ranieri took a night shift job in Salomon's mailroom only as a means to help pay his tuition at St. John's University. His family had been financially unstable since his father's death when Lewis was just thirteen, and they managed to get by only by moving into an apartment above his grandfather's bakery. He planned to be an Italian chef, working in his uncle's restaurant in the evenings and weekends while in high school, until asthma set in and he could no longer tolerate the fumes of the kitchen. So instead he enrolled in college, working in the Salomon mailroom to help pay the bills. But when he was offered a promotion to mailroom supervisor, Salomon became a career and he dropped out of his sophomore year of college to follow it. (Seventeen years later, in 1986, he completed his work and received a BA in English from St. John's, and in 1987 the university awarded him an honorary doctoral degree).

Exiled to the Mortgage Department

Salomon was a fortuitous choice. Of all the major New York investment houses, Salomon most closely resembled a meritocracy; social connections and savoir faire counted for little (good in Ranieri's case, since he had little of either), and ability and drive for everything. Founded in 1910 by Arthur, Herbert, and Percy Salomon as a specialty bond trading company, the firm quickly grew into a major government bond operation, spurred in its growth as a primary dealer in the Liberty Bonds that were sold to finance the United States' participation in World War I. In 1969, when Ranieri came on board, the firm was still conducting a business largely confined to trading and underwriting government, municipal, and corporate bonds. It had not veered significantly into equities and sought no presence whatsoever in the retail side of the business.

In his first five years at the firm, Ranieri moved through a series of ever-increasing responsibilities in Salomon's back office. He was a brash and tough-minded boss, using screaming and intimidation to keep his staff of clerical workers in line. His salary increased commensurately, but he knew that the key to success at Salomon was landing a job on one of its trading desks. In 1974 that opportunity arose with a position trading the bonds of public utility companies. Ever the quick study, Ranieri, working the phone for ten to twelve hours a day, began making more money than any Italian chef could have thought possible.

But another five years later, Ranieri was snatched from the public utilities desk out of the blue and ordered to join Salomon's newly created mortgage department as its chief trader. Ranieri saw the move as a signal of unhappiness with his performance; after trading public utility bonds in multi-million-dollar transactions, the prospect of buying and selling, say, a $50,000 loan on a house in Cedar Rapids, Iowa, seemed like a waste of a high-powered trader's time and talent. There was no other Wall Street firm that had figured out how to make money in the mortgage business and to Ranieri it looked like an exile to a Wall Street Siberia.

Yet Ranieri's allegiance to Salomon was strong—in a ten-year span the firm had transformed him from an impoverished nineteen-year-old kid to a bond trading mogul—so he willingly went to work assembling a group of mortgage traders. The crew was laughably Ranieri-like: largely from Salomon's back office, Italian, overweight, loud, and un-degreed. After the base trading group was in place, he added the other elements to the operation, including mortgage salespeople and mortgage research analysts—all newly created positions. Ranieri was making it up as he went, but by the end of 1979 he had constructed Wall Street's first full-fledged mortgage operation.

A Boom in Whole Loans

For the first year or so, business trickled in, but hardly in the volume needed to support Ranieri's department—much less to make a profit. Then, as through an act of providence, a series of events unfolded that ended with Ranieri's being the new star of Salomon Brothers and his department the most profitable in the firm.

The trigger was the appointment of the strong-willed Paul Volcker as the new chairman of the Federal Reserve. The country was suffering from double-digit inflation, and Volcker immediately launched a program to tighten the country's money supply. His monetary austerity program was meant to choke off some of the forces of demand in the economy, but it also had the effect of driving up short-term interest rates to unprecedented levels, as high as 20 percent.

There was no sector of the economy harder hit by Volcker's tight-money policy than the savings and loan industry. At the time, S&Ls—also called "thrifts"—were the main source of mortgage finance, bringing in money from their depositors and lending it back out through mortgage loans. The manager of a savings institution usually worked with a simple and profitable business model that carried the tag "3–6–2"—pay depositors 3 percent, lend their money at 6 percent, and be on the golf course at 2 o'clock. But under Volcker's tight-money policy, the model collapsed. With the prospect of paying depositors close to 20 percent to attract new money, the S&Ls instead closed the window on new mortgage lending. Volcker had cooled down the economy, at least with respect to the demand for housing, but his actions also threatened the very existence of the sleepy thrift industry. A slowdown in new mortgage origination wasn't in itself a boon for Ranieri, since it reduced the raw material of new mortgages available for trading. But the reaction of Congress was.

Legislators had long supported the thrifts, which were the mainstays in providing the financing necessary for the politically popular cause of home-ownership. So in 1981, a group of friendly members of Congress devised an outlandish tax break to save the S&Ls. Beginning in October of that year, those institutions were allowed to sell their mortgages and spread any loss resulting from a sale over the remaining life of the loan. Consider the example of a mortgage on a thrift's books that had twenty years left until it was fully paid off, but which could only be sold at a 40 percent discount, that is, sold at sixty cents on the dollar. (The value of a financial asset, including a mortgage, varies inversely with the level of interest rates; when rates rise, as they did dramatically under Volcker's direction, mortgages sell at steep discounts.) Under the custom-made tax provision for thrifts, the institution could immediately sell its mortgages at a discount but recognize the loss at a rate of just 2 percent per year for the remaining twenty years. What's more, the losses that were reported could be used to offset *prior* taxable income, meaning that the thrifts received refunds of taxes they had earlier paid. All this government largesse was in the name of homeownership, since the immediate proceeds from the mortgage sales and tax refunds would presumably be funneled back into new loan originations by the thrifts.

With that munificent act of Congress, S&Ls began selling their mortgages in torrents—and Salomon's new and fully staffed mortgage department was the only game in town for buying them. A trader, however, has to have order flow on both the buy and the sell side of the transaction, so Ranieri's sales force simply bought the "whole loans" at a major discount from one S&L and sold them, at a somewhat lower discount, to another S&L. It was something of a shell game—Larry Fink, who would eventually run a competing mortgage operation for the First Boston Corporation, proclaimed, "October 1981 was the most irresponsible period in the history of the capital markets"[4]—but Salomon was now the monopolist in the secondary market for home mortgages. It was a financial bonanza for both Ranieri and Salomon Brothers.

"So Cheap Your Teeth Hurt"

A one-time bonanza, however, was a shaky foundation on which to base a long-term mortgage business. While selling whole loans back and forth between desperate S&L executives—often at unconscionable markups—resulted in extraordinary profits, that market would eventually play out. Small and often shaky thrift institutions were far from the ideal customers for Salomon, and Ranieri realized that he would have to provide a product for the firm's traditional institutional customers that was something other than a whole loan—something more like a bond.

The product that fit the bill was called a mortgage-backed security, or MBS. While varieties of the MBS had been created as early as the 1800s in the U.S., their use in the twentieth century had been dormant until members of the Salomon Brothers' government bond department revived a form of security formerly known as a mortgage-backed debenture.[5] They

conceived of a bond tailor-made for the Bank of America—the first institution willing to work with Salomon by selling the firm a portion of its
residential loan portfolio for packaging and resale on Wall Street. It was a
noble effort, but poorly designed and eligible for sale in only three states. In
Ranieri's later assessment, the pioneering Bank of America mortgage bond
was "a total bomb."

After Ranieri took over the management of Salomon's newly formed
mortgage department—coinciding with the explosion of interest in trading
mortgages on Wall Street—he once again revisited the MBS idea. Taking
a second run at creating a viable MBS, he cured the key infirmities of the
Bank of America bond. To create diversity beyond a single financial institution, his department gathered a large collection of individual mortgages
(whole loans) from several banks and thrifts and then pooled them into
a bond-like security. Using a process he called securitization (credit for
coming up with that name for the process is generally given to Ranieri)
payments of principal and interest on the hundreds of loans making up the
MBS were passed through to the investors. With Ranieri's brand of securitization, institutional investors could realize an investment of suitable size
and loan diversity for their portfolios.

But Ranieri recognized that one further feature of the MBS was still
necessary for the bonds to gain acceptance among investors and traders:
Washington's blessing. The government had long played a major oversight
role in the U.S. mortgage business but had not officially endorsed the MBS
structure. So with a team of legal experts and lobbyists, Ranieri descended
on Washington, and by 1981 the Federal National Mortgage Association
("Fannie Mae") had put its imprimatur on the MBS. That meant that Salomon's mortgage-backed bonds, as long as they were composed of mortgages conforming to Fannie Mae requirements, had the agency's stamp of
approval. Since this approval was not the same as the full faith and credit
of the U.S. Treasury, the MBS became a "moral obligation" of the federal
government.

Now that his MBS product bore the Fannie Mae "stamp"—and almost
always an accompanying AAA rating from Standard & Poor's and Moody's—
Ranieri went on the road to make a hard pitch to Salomon's institutional
clients. Much as Drexel Burnham Lambert "owned" the junk bond market in the early 1980s, Salomon, as the first mover in mortgage products,
claimed ownership of the MBS product. In *Liar's Poker*, an insider's account
of Salomon Brothers during the 1980s, Michael Lewis recalls how the two
bond revolutionaries promoted their respective products:

Ranieri, along with the guru of junk bonds, Mike Milken of Drexel Burnham, became one of the great bond missionaries of the 1980s. Crisscrossing the country, trying to persuade institutional investors to buy mortgage securities, Ranieri bumped into Milken. They visited the same accounts on the same day. "My product took off first," says Ranieri. "Investors started to buy the gospel according to Ranieri."[6]

Milken had to persuade potential junk bond buyers that the low bond ratings his product carried were either not indicative of the real risk or, alternatively, that the return was so high it more than justified that risk. For Ranieri, by contrast, credit risk was not an issue. His MBS product carried the highest rating possible because of the implied guarantee from a U.S. government agency. Yet, compared to AAA-rated corporate bonds, the yields were much higher. "Mortgages were so cheap your teeth hurt," Ranieri liked to say.[7] His sales pitch worked, and the MBS became a respectable form of security attractive to a growing number of institutional investors. With the success of the mortgage-backed market, 1982 was a breakout year for Ranieri; his mortgage department made about $175 million, and he took home over $2 million of that profit.[8]

However, the MBS was still not appealing to all bond buyers. In particular, no one running a pension fund or life insurance company would touch it. The mortgage bonds might carry little or no credit risk and sport premium interest rates, but there is no free lunch on Wall Street, and the high interest rates on the MBS bonds reflected another major risk: the risk of prepayment. Institutional investors with long-term investment horizons needed matching long-term bonds, but an MBS (even one built out of thirty-year mortgages) could pay off much sooner than expected if interest rates dropped and a high percentage of individual borrowers decided to refinance their mortgage loans.

This structural problem with the MBS was due to the extremely attractive feature attached to a residential mortgage—namely, the right of the borrower to pay it off at any time without penalty. If interest rates fell, homeowners could always refinance their mortgages at a lower rate and thereby reduce their monthly payments. Virtually no other long-term borrower had this cost-free option. Corporate borrowers in the bond market, for instance, have to pay some combination of a premium interest rate and a prepayment penalty for that right. But homeowners, as a protected political species, enjoyed a congressionally mandated option to prepay without cost or penalty.

That option made the MBS unpalatable to the typical long-term investor. An institutional fund manager holding a conventional corporate or government bond could be certain that the price of that bond would increase as interest rates fell—and decrease as they rose. But, maddeningly for the long-term investor holding mortgage-backed bonds, just as interest rates began to fall, the home loan borrowers behind the MBS began to prepay their mortgages. When the bonds were taken away through prepayment, the bonds' investors were deprived of an appreciation in price. Conversely, when interest rates rose, nobody wanted to refinance a mortgage through prepayment, and the institutional investor was stuck for the duration with low-yielding mortgage bonds. It was obviously an unattractive prospect for bond investors to have limited control over the maturity of the bond—and so they avoided the MBS, or required interest rates that were at a very high premium over their triple A–rated corporate or government cousins.

Mortgages Are Math

With trillions of dollars of potential institutional funds remaining on the sidelines, it didn't take long for Ranieri and his group to design a security that addressed the prepayment problem of the MBS. In 1983, Salomon (in tandem with the First Boston Corporation) came up with a new kind of bond called a collateralized mortgage obligation, and within a short period of time CMOs became a fixture among institutionally traded securities. It also brought to Wall Street a new kind of employee—the "quant"—since, in terms of mathematical complexity, an MBS is to a CMO as checkers is to chess. Ranieri began to proclaim that "mortgages are math," and his new hires in the mortgage department, whether on the trading desks or otherwise, no longer arrived from Salomon's back office but from graduate business programs and math departments of universities.

While a CMO was, like an ordinary MBS, made up of standard home mortgages, the CMO was chopped up into several "tranches." In the earliest and easiest to understand CMOs, the three or more tranches ("slices" in French) were based on the order of mortgage repayment. Because of the flexible prepayment feature for borrowers, the average life of a standard thirty-year mortgage is only about seven years. In the normal course of events, people move, people die, people come into money and pay off their mortgage early, and, as the pivotal wild card in the equation, people refinance their mortgages when rates fall. So while some thirty-year mortgages pay off in thirty years, many more pay off much sooner. The CMO tranches divided those mortgages that paid off quickly from those that didn't, and each tranche was matched to the maturity needs of the investor. The owners of the first tranche were made up of investors with a relatively short investment horizon (such as banks or casualty insurance companies), and they were happy to be the first to have their bonds retired as mortgage holders elected to prepay. After the first tranche investors were paid back, all prepayments went to the second tranche investors; then to the third and any successive tranches. So a long-term institutional investor could choose a later tranche and know, based on history and statistical analysis, what the investment's duration was likely to be.

With Salomon able to offer a mortgage product that was engineered to match a financial institution's liabilities, the floodgates opened for new money to feed the housing sector. Long-term institutional investors (like pension funds, life insurance companies, and endowments) began funneling tens of billions of new dollars into mortgages through CMOs. That led, of course, to the entrance of more investment firms into the MBS business and the end of Salomon's monopoly. But during the flush years of the early eighties, the firm still did exceedingly well. As Michael Lewis recounted in *Liar's Poker*: "Although there are no official numbers, it was widely accepted at Salomon that Ranieri's traders made $200 million in 1983, $175 million in 1984, and $275 million in 1985."[9] Ranieri's upstart mortgage operation, in business for only five years, was now accounting for 40 percent of the seventy-five-year-old Salomon Brothers' revenues.[10]

Within the revenue-driven culture of investment banking, the ability to produce new business is often confused with managerial talent. Following that pattern, in 1986 Ranieri was appointed vice chairman of Salomon Brothers and a member of its four-person office of the chairman. In Salomon's hallways there was talk that Ranieri would be the next chairman when John Gutfreund stepped down; Gutfreund himself even dropped hints to that effect. Ranieri was no longer active at the trading desks of the mortgage department; he and the other three top executives spent their days running the six thousand–employee firm and charting its directions.

Yet the only thing the four seemed to have in common was a deep-seated dislike for one another. In theory, the managing foursome was meant to take an objective and big picture perspective. In practice, their interests remained parochial and protective of the departments they once led. And while the other three—Tom Strauss, Bill Voute, and Gutfreund—were politic in their actions, Ranieri had grown much wealthier but not noticeably more polished during his time with the firm and was most often a querulous voice in their meetings. With the mortgage operations of Salomon accounting for the most substantial portion of the company's profits, he was indefatigable in arguing that "his" employees deserved a greater level of compensation. In the summer of 1987, chairman Gutfreund solved the Ranieri problem by summoning him to his office and firing him on the spot. But the MBS machine that Ranieri had started did not stop with his departure.

Race to the Bottom

During the several decades prior to the 1990s, as the MBS market was just taking hold, the percentage of U.S. households living in their own homes hovered around 65 percent. But starting in 1994, there was a straight line of upward growth to a level of nearly 70 percent by 2004. Rising levels of home ownership have always been politically important, and the efforts to increase those levels—including the increased supply of mortgage funding from MBS-buying institutional investors—found favor in Washington. In the cause of providing affordable housing, the two government agencies that provided much of the raw material for MBS creation, Fannie Mae and its look-alike brother, the Federal Home Loan Mortgage Corporation ("Freddie Mac"), were given much room to maneuver in their operations, and both agencies were supportive of the MBS markets.

Between 2005 and 2006, both interest rates and home prices rose substantially—double trouble for the cause of affordable housing. In 2005 and 2006 many prospective home buyers had to take out larger loans, and those loans carried higher monthly payments. Other prospects were simply priced out of the market. The reactions of mortgage bankers and investment bankers to this reduced pool of qualified buyers sowed the seeds of financial disaster.

To keep the demand for homes from falling—and the MBS and CMO pipelines full—originators and underwriters of mortgage loans, under the approving eye of Fannie Mae and Freddie Mac, drastically reduced credit standards and began an aggressive campaign to generate "subprime mortgages." These were loans to borrowers whose credit standing would have made them ineligible to take out a mortgage under conventional guidelines. Subprime loans were often promoted to unsophisticated loan applicants by unscrupulous mortgage bankers and came with little required loan documentation ("low-doc" loans) and sometimes no documentation at all ("no-doc" loans). A growing number of loans were granted to NINJA borrowers—those with "no income, no job, or assets."

In the spirit of avoiding a housing downturn, Fannie Mae and Freddie Mac joined the race to the bottom by lowering their underwriting standards. In 2003, they had approved $395 billion in subprime loans (including a close variation called Alt-A loans); just a year later that amount climbed to $715 billion, and in 2006 it was over $1 trillion.[11] Other mortgage originators were rapidly expanding into the subprime market, creating so-called private label mortgage-backed securities, but the two government agencies bear special responsibility for the financial hardships that followed, because they were charged not only with preserving soundness in the mortgage markets but with protecting borrowers. One risk manager wrote in an email to her boss, Freddie Mac chief executive Dick Styron, protesting the agency's lapse in standards and saying, "What better way to highlight our sense of mission than to walk away from profitable business because it hurts the borrowers we are trying to serve?"[12] But to no avail.

Other culprits also played major roles. The banks and mortgage bankers that originated the subprime loans often shirked their fiduciary and moral responsibilities by "underwriting" mortgage loans that had little prospect of being paid back—short of an irresponsible assumption that borrowers would be bailed out of their loans by continued appreciation in home values. The investment firms and other financial institutions that securitized mortgages are also blameworthy. The garden varieties of MBS and CMO that they packaged in the early years of securitization were almost all conventionally underwritten mortgages rather than subprime loans, and those bonds continued to perform reasonably well. But when those institutions added the more exotic CDOs—collateralized debt obligations, which were the main repository for subprime loans—they and their "toxic asset" CDOs became lead perpetrators of the disaster to come. The credit-rating agencies—the familiar names of Standard & Poor's, Moody's, and Fitch—also failed in their scrutiny of these bonds. Assigning investment-grade rankings, mostly AAA, to virtually all of the mortgage-backed securities they reviewed reflected some combination of superficial analysis and a willingness to sacrifice the integrity of the ratings for future business.

There are collateral explanations for the financial debacle of 2008, including an excess use of financial leverage and lax regulatory oversight, but the root cause was the collapse of the MBS market. And that collapse was the inevitable result of an elaborate "pass the trash" game among financial institutions. Except for the hapless investor left holding grossly overvalued mortgage-backed securities at the end of the chain, all of the parties to the creation and sale of those securities—the mortgage bankers, the investment bankers, the rating agencies—collected handsome fees and commissions but had little or no "skin in the game." The ultimate losers were not those middlemen but rather four very different types of participants: the tens of thousands of mortgage holders who suffered bankruptcy or loan foreclosure; the many financial institutions that went under due to a liquidity crisis brought on by their use of mortgage-backed securities as collateral; investors, most of them institutional and many international, who held badly mispriced—in some cases worthless—securities; and, most significantly, U.S. citizens, who footed the bill for the bank bailouts and bore the brunt of the Great Recession that followed. According to a report prepared by the Pew Financial Reform Project, the total financial hit has amounted to about $10,500 per American household.[13] The damage that resulted from irresponsibly structured and promoted mortgage-backed securities has been long-lasting and monumental.

Devil or Angel?

By the time of the financial crisis, Ranieri had been out of Salomon's MBS business for more than twenty years—but his legacy as a financial innovator has been haunted by the specter of these bonds and their role in the crisis. In 2004, *Businessweek* included Ranieri in a list of the seventy-five greatest innovators of the last seventy-five years;[14] five years later, he was on the *Guardian*'s list of "Twenty-Five People at the Heart of the Meltdown."[15] And yet it's not clear that Ranieri is at all to blame for the MBS debacle.

Undoubtedly, he shook things up. Just as Milken's junk bonds changed the world of corporate finance, Ranieri's securitization of the mortgage proved to be a highly disruptive event in real estate finance. In the late 1970s, at the time Ranieri joined Salomon's newly formed mortgage department, banks and other "depository financial institutions" controlled over half of the assets of the financial sector. But in short order, "balance sheet" loans—those that were made by a bank and stayed with the bank—were replaced by loans made in the capital markets and freely traded afterward. As a result, banks today control less than a quarter of financial assets.[16]

Yet taking assets out of the banking system—"disintermediation"— has had many benefits for lenders and borrowers alike, including greater liquidity, better transparency, and lower costs. Due to those well-recognized benefits, securitization has spread from mortgages to other assets, including credit cards, student loans, and automobile loans. Even the bread-and-butter commercial loans made by banks have been increasingly securitized into CLOs—commercial loan obligations. On balance, securitization has been a good thing for the capital markets, and in fact, until the financial crisis, the markets in securitized mortgages worked quite well, and there were few defaults among the bonds that were created. It's safe to say that at the time of Ranieri's involuntary departure from Salomon in 1987, the mortgage-backed securities and the CMOs he created were still conservative securities, backed by an ample quantity of well-scrutinized home loans that were underwritten according to prudent guidelines. It wasn't until the early 2000s that the MBS market began to veer out of control. By the time it went off the rails, Ranieri had been long gone from the MBS business.

During the time Ranieri conceived and built the securitized mortgage market he may have been profane, combative, and unpolished, but there is little to suggest that he was in a league with the bad actors that captured and perverted the MBS business during his twenty-year absence. Yet in his public statements, Ranieri paints himself as a villain for what he sees as his role in the crisis. During a 2011 interview with CNBC, he said, "Being one of the founders [of the MBS], it's my problem. I talked about it starting in 2005, but I didn't do a good enough job so I bear the burden."[17] In the same vein, he introduced himself at a 2013 conference of the Bipartisan Policy Center, a think tank based in Washington, D.C., by saying, "Hello, I'm Dr. Frankenstein." He went on to say, "I used to think we had done something important and good, and then, unfortunately, we had the last bubble. The system we built showed the cracks and the clay feet."[18]

Since his departure from Salomon, Ranieri has been a successful private investor in business and real estate deals ranging from software startups to home health care, but in recent years he has also stepped back into the residential mortgage business, founding Selene Finance in 2007 to provide "creative loan resolution strategies designed to preserve homeownership"—in other words, an organization meant to oversee (and profit from) working out bad loans. He ascribes his motive in forming the Selene loan-workout firm to personal atonement: "I do feel guilty. I wasn't out to invent the biggest floating craps game of all time, but that's what happened. These are real people losing their homes. I feel a responsibility for dealing with it in a way that's up close and personal."[19] In 2010, Ranieri was a founder of Shellpoint Partners, a securitizer of home mortgages with the ubiquitously displayed mission to provide "responsible mortgage lending solutions." He has also become an important backer of several Catholic charities and other not-for-profit endeavors.

While Ranieri may find himself blameworthy, hedge fund manager Simon Mikhailovich put it well when he said, "Securitization is like fertilizer. You can grow tomatoes or blow up buildings." [20] As far as the responsibility for blowing up the mortgage market, there are many who should be standing well ahead of Ranieri in the line to the confessional.

Part V

Empire Builders

Not that long ago, there were no U.S. financial institutions deemed too big to fail. Commercial banks were not allowed to grow beyond well-defined geographic limits and investment banks were constricted by their limited access to capital—and neither was allowed into the other's business.

By state and national law, commercial banks were not permitted to branch very far, if at all, from their headquarters, and as a result banking was a localized business. Each city was home to a number of single-office banks, the oldest and largest usually holding the title of First National in front of the name of the city it served. A fair number of banks had grown their assets beyond the billion-dollar mark toward the end of the twentieth century, especially in the cities with one of the twelve Federal Reserve Banks. Until recently, however, few would have imagined that America would be home to *trillion*-dollar banks.

At the same time, the reach and scope of investment banks were limited by the strict capital rules of the New York Stock Exchange. Due to concerns about interference by anyone outside "the club," the ownership of the member firms of the exchange was limited to individuals active in the management of those firms, and as late as the 1980s even Morgan Stanley and Goldman Sachs operated as partnerships. Investment bankers viewed themselves as little more than the handmaidens of business—certainly not as the managers of future mega-firms.

The change on the commercial banking front came slowly but surely as the bankers and their lobbyists convinced state and national legislatures to remove the walls that blocked expansion. Soon "unit banks" were allowed to have branches, then to expand statewide, and inevitably nationwide. J. P. Morgan was perhaps most emblematic of the movement, growing in a matter of a few decades from a single location at 23 Wall Street to tens of thousands of offices around the world.

The changes in the investment business were equally dramatic, beginning with the Securities and Exchange Commission–mandated abolition in 1975 of the New York Stock Exchange's system of fixed commissions. With the exchange's requirement that its member firms—at that time representing virtually the entire securities industry—adhere to a schedule of commissions when doing business with the public, the investment business was run as a very profitable cartel. The exchange and the partners of its member firms considered themselves at the very heart of free-market capitalism, yet they prospered mightily from a system that forbade competition.

Immediately after investment firms lost the protection of fixed commissions, their numbers dropped quickly. Newly formed discount brokerage firms grew like spring flowers to lure investors away, and most of the old-line firms either went out of business or were acquired by other firms that were smart and nimble enough to survive in the world of open competition. The smartest and most nimble of those firms was an upstart house formed in the early 1960s called Cogan, Berlind, Weill, & Leavitt—the Weill being Sanford Weill, a brash and tough Brooklyn native who knew the nuts and bolts of the business and knew especially how to make acquisitions and cut costs. Under his leadership, CBWL grew by making ever more sizable deals, usually changing the name of the firm to reflect the latest and largest prey. By the time Weill had finished, CBWL had become Smith Barney and was second only to Merrill Lynch in terms of brokers. Although Weill eventually left the firm that Smith Barney became, he had made a name for himself and surged back onto the financial scene years later to create the financial behemoth Citigroup—a feat that required nothing less than a successful campaign for the full repeal of the Glass-Steagall Act.

One of Weill's contemporaries, William Donaldson, was simultaneously changing the ways of Wall Street by challenging the exchange's strictures on the use of outside capital. He and two of his Harvard Business School classmates formed Donaldson, Lufkin & Jenrette to provide research and trading services to institutional investors, but their business plan required much more capital than the three of them could assemble privately. Disregarding the NYSE rules and its threatened sanctions, DLJ barged ahead with the first-ever public offering for a member firm. The firm's 1970 initial public offering broke the capital logjam and before long every other Wall Street firm of any size became a public company.

Both Donaldson and Weill were clearly interested in building financial empires, and both were tenacious and daring in their approach to obstacles. But the results of these men's efforts were very different. While DLJ was eventually sold to Credit Suisse for $13 billion, Citigroup was a mess of a financial institution from its formation in 1998 and remained that way until it was largely dismantled—but not before it received $45 billion in emergency infusions of capital from U.S. taxpayers in 2008 to become the largest bank bailout in history. The personalities of Donaldson and Weill were as different as the plights of the institutions they built, but no two individuals were more responsible for enlarging the size and scope of today's Wall Street than they.

Photo courtesy William H. Donaldson.

13

William H. Donaldson: 1931–
Entrepreneur

Dan, Dick and I, we all made an equal contribution in
trying to build something that was really unique.

—WILLIAM DONALDSON

"Judas Iscariot!" Felix Rohatyn exclaimed when he heard the news. It's
unclear which founder of Donaldson, Lufkin & Jenrette he was referring
to—perhaps all three. Like him, the three young men were rising young
leaders on Wall Street during the 1960s, but while Rohatyn (just forty-one)
was a lead partner with the tradition-rich, century-old Lazard Frères investment banking firm and was just finishing his term as a governor of the New
York Stock Exchange, Bill Donaldson (thirty-eight), Dan Lufkin (thirty-
seven), and Dick Jenrette (forty), were upstarts in the securities world. They
had formed "DLJ" just ten years earlier, only a few years after graduating
from the Harvard Business School, and had been members of the exchange
since the firm's inception. But now, on May 21, 1969, in utter defiance of the
rules of the NYSE, they announced that DLJ was going to sell its common
stock to the public. Everyone knew that could break up "the club."

From the time of its founding in 1792—under a buttonwood tree on Wall
Street, according to legend—the exchange enjoyed a cozy, club-like existence under rules requiring that all prospective new members be approved
by the board of governors before they could trade on the NYSE. Ostensibly,
that system ensured that all individuals operating on the exchange were
financially sound and upstanding—not mobsters or other undesirables. It
was a manageable system as long as the firms were partnerships or closely

held corporations, where a small number of owners could be checked for suitability. If DLJ went public, however, there would be thousands of new owners of the firm and no way for the exchange to vet them all.

But Rohatyn's rage—which was matched by the rage many other NYSE governors directed toward DLJ's management—wasn't just about the problem of screening new exchange members to ensure that only the "right people" were admitted. The larger issue was more self-serving. It was a matter of protecting the securities industry's profitability. Since the 1792 Buttonwood Agreement, NYSE brokers had agreed to adhere to a fixed schedule of commissions, and they also agreed to limit the number of memberships, commonly called "seats," on the exchange. Stripped to its essence, a seat was a license that allowed the holder to trade in NYSE-listed stocks, either as an agent for customers or for one's own account. In 1969 the number of seats was limited to 1,366, and DLJ purchased two of them from former NYSE members to facilitate buying and selling stocks for its institutional investor customers.

If seats became available to the public, however, the exchange's governors feared that big customers, especially the institutional investors (banks, insurance companies, and mutual funds) that chafed under artificially high commission rates, would become NYSE members. The reason institutions wanted a seat would not be to act as brokers, but rather to trade on their own behalf and avoid the commissions altogether. If that happened, the long-established exchange cartel could be irreversibly undermined.

It didn't help matters that the principals of DLJ gave the exchange no prior notice of their plans. Rather, they approached the filing of their proposed initial public offering like a secret military mission with a surprise attack as the tactic. (All three had been junior military officers—Donaldson and Lufkin in the Marines and Jenrette in the Army.) They were aware that a NYSE committee had been studying public ownership for the last several years. But the committee's work was going nowhere, and DLJ was a firm in a hurry. The firm's business had become capital intense and it needed an infusion of new funds to support continued growth. Rather than asking permission to go public—which they knew would not be granted— Donaldson, Lufkin, and Jenrette charged ahead in secrecy. On May 21, they called a series of meetings with exchange officials, informing them that at precisely 2 p.m. the next day a registration statement would be filed with the Securities and Exchange Commission covering 800,000 new shares of DLJ stock to be sold for over $20 million.

By existing NYSE rules, the move was illegal. And if those rules were not changed in the months before the SEC approved the registration and the IPO got under way, the firm had real problems. A particularly ominous disclosure in the filing with the SEC stated that a large majority of DLJ's revenues would vanish if it lost its membership on the NYSE. DLJ's move was the ultimate bet-your-company decision.

What *Do* You Do on Wall Street?

DLJ was a corporation run in the spirit of a partnership, with "all for one and one for all" the proclaimed management style. But as the CEO, William Donaldson bore ultimate responsibility for the decision. DLJ's planned IPO would ultimately revolutionize much of the way Wall Street did business, but Donaldson wasn't exactly the revolutionary type. Calm, deliberate, and personally charming, he came across more as a reconciler than as a bomb thrower. (As it turned out, he wasn't much of a bridge burner either—many years after his apostasy, the greatly transformed NYSE recruited him to serve as its chairman.)

Donaldson portrays himself as an entrepreneur, but one with "peripheral vision" to see the lurking problems and to think one or two steps ahead and plan for the inevitable setbacks. That coupling of entrepreneurship and caution may have developed as a result of a childhood spanning the Depression of the 1930s and the war years of the 1940s. During his youth in Buffalo, New York, he thrived on starting small enterprises—including United Enterprises, a service business he founded and managed during his teens that employed more than fifty high school and college students to paint houses, tend lawns, and do minor carpentry—but he was also a first-hand witness to the downside of entrepreneurship. During the Depression his father lost the small automotive castings business that he started in the 1920s and spent the better part of his life repaying its debts. "It had a major influence on me," Donaldson later remarked.[1]

He followed in his father's footsteps to Yale University, where he was a member of the secretive Skull and Bones and the student manager of the *Yale Daily News*. The Korean War started while he was at Yale, and upon graduation he joined the Marines. By the time he finished his training at the Marine base at Quantico, Virginia, the war was over, and he served his time in noncombat duties in Japan and Korea. The Marine experience was an important bond between him and Dan Lufkin. They both went to Yale and then the Harvard Business School, but according to Donaldson, their service in the Marines may have been the most meaningful shared experience. "There were many things we learned in the Marines that we applied at DLJ."[2]

Donaldson's last assignment in the Marines involved serving as aide to an air wing general, and that spurred his enthusiasm for the developing aviation industry of the early 1950s. "I was convinced that helicopters were the wave of the future and that everybody was going to have one in their garage."[3] The general set him up with a job with Sikorsky Aircraft, a major helicopter manufacturer, but Donaldson found life in the corporate world uninteresting and slow paced. He was offered another aviation-related job as a ticket taker for the recently organized New York Airways, but "that also didn't seem right for a former Marine Lieutenant."[4]

It was only by happenstance that he found a job in the investment banking business. Talking with one of his friend's fathers who worked at the medium-sized G. H. Walker & Company, he asked, "What *do* you do here on Wall Street?" and was greeted with a surprising response—a job offer.

He served three short stints at G. H. Walker—one before, one during, and one after Harvard Business School. During his first experience he was involved in a number of transactions, acting mainly as a "bag carrier," but the work piqued his interest in investment banking—and convinced him to apply to Harvard. During the summers between his first and second years at the business school he went back to G. H. Walker. This time he was in Salt Lake City rather than on Wall Street, working on operational problems with a wax refinery in which the firm had invested. That assignment became a turnaround opportunity, and he was asked to stay past summer in Salt Lake to assist in the company's revival. He was sorely tempted but elected to return for the second year of business school. After graduating with his MBA in 1957—"imbued with a real appreciation for the positive side of collective thought and a great belief in the case method"[5]—he went back to a permanent job at G. H. Walker, this one in the firm's mergers and acquisitions department.

Elevator Speech

During the two years he spent at G. H. Walker following his time at Harvard, Donaldson grew into a competent investment banker and earned his keep at the firm. At the same time, Lufkin—his college and business school classmate and fellow ex-Marine—was then working as an analyst for a private investor, Jeremiah Milbank. Their entrepreneurial instincts took hold, and before they were twenty-eight, Donaldson and Lufkin began engaging in "collective thought" and plotting the formation of their own investment firm.

From what he saw of it at G. H. Walker, Donaldson was convinced that the research coming out of Wall Street in the 1950s was "statistical, shallow, and superficial" and "totally focused on the retail mass-market." He envisioned a much different form of research for the more sophisticated institutional investor that "would be a lot closer to what a McKinsey consulting firm might do than to just a Standard & Poor's recommendation of the week."[6]

It was Lufkin who realized that this research overlooked smaller companies in particular. In investing for the Milbank interests, he discovered a decided cleavage between the stocks of well-known, major companies and those of smaller, lesser-known companies. In 1959, individual investors and portfolio managers were not long-term investors in equities, and with memories of the Depression era still vivid, they tended to limit their exposure outside the bond markets to "the Generals"—General Motors, General Electric, General Mills, General Foods, etc.—and other well-tested and well-capitalized companies. But in their attempt to avoid risk by sticking with the bigger name stocks, Lufkin believed the institutional investor was actually taking on undue risk as the market bid up their prices to unsustainable levels. He became convinced that among the smaller companies that everyone was avoiding, there were many well-performing operations whose stocks were selling at bargain-basement prices.

Sizing up their own strengths and weaknesses, Donaldson and Lufkin concluded that they needed a third leg to the stool. They had their basic business mission—providing institutional investors with high-quality research on small- to medium-sized companies—but they reasoned that it would be good to have someone more seasoned in business to act as a foil for their aggressive and entrepreneurial tendencies. So they recruited another Harvard Business School classmate, Dick Jenrette, who became the "J" in DLJ. "My mission," Jenrette later explained, "was to use my experience to tame Bill and Dan—to restrain their youthful exuberance, if you will."[7] He was all of thirty years old.

Jenrette had just been promoted from a research analyst to a portfolio manager at Brown Brothers Harriman, an old-line private bank that catered to high net worth individuals. When Donaldson and Lufkin approached him, Jenrette recalls, "I didn't think the business plan made a lot of sense. But I knew we'd figure out some way to make money." Jenrette's explanation of his decision to leave Brown Brothers illustrates the casual manner in which DLJ began:

> Brown Brothers was wonderful, but on the other hand, it was too slow. I'd be there forever and there wasn't much mobility. Bill and Dan were two very exciting people that I'd known in business school, and I knew they'd be successful in one way or another. We were all bachelors at the time, so we said, "Let's go for it."[8]

One problem? The three partners of DLJ had no start-up capital. In order to raise funds, Donaldson says, "We got into the car and drove around to talk with friends and classmates and people we'd grown up with and people who had some confidence in us."[9] By this time, the three men had perfected the elevator pitch they made to their prospects, explaining the need they saw for high-quality investment research on smaller companies. They pointed out that institutional investors were becoming a much more important factor in the stock market because of the growth of pension funds and mutual funds. But because of the conservative bent of the managers of institutional portfolios, the lion's share of their common stock investments was dedicated to a handful of very large and well-known "blue-chip" companies. Yet there were hundreds of well-managed but smaller companies—and the common stocks of those companies were available at very attractive prices. The problem, they told their prospective investors, was that institutions wouldn't touch these smaller companies because there was no source of credible information and analysis to make them comfortable about the safety and prospects of such companies.

And that, they told their prospective investors, is where said DLJ would come in. It would be the first firm to perform in-depth research on the most promising smaller companies and package it into comprehensive and professionally prepared reports to justify the purchase of their stocks. DLJ, they maintained, would employ the best and brightest minds on Wall Street and would be uniquely positioned to benefit from the growing volume of commission dollars being generated by institutional investors.

Despite the logic and enthusiasm of the pitch, the reception from potential investors was mixed at best. Wall Street veterans were particularly unmoved by the idea that a start-up firm with a new approach to the investment business could succeed. Lufkin solicited ten industry leaders on Wall Street, and the most favorable comment he received about the DLJ plan was from Sidney Weinberg, then the head of Goldman Sachs: "I won't say don't do it, because you never know, but I wouldn't say it's an odds on favorite." Most bankers were much less measured in their response, with Lufkin's contact at Lehman Brothers being the most direct: "We're going to squash you like a fly on the wall."[10]

Despite the lack of enthusiasm from the investment establishment, the DLJ founders were able to round up $240,000 from old friends and class-mates. It was short of their $300,000 target, but with the $100,000 they came up with themselves, it was enough to get started and pay each of them $7,000 per year in salary.

"We Hit a Gusher"

At the time of DLJ's launch in 1959, the three principals wrote an influential, fifteen-page pamphlet called *Common Stock and Common Sense* that set forth the case for small company investing. (Donaldson still keeps a supply of the pamphlets in his office.) The pamphlet restated the argument for investing in smaller publicly traded companies, but now, buttressing the case with quantitative analysis, they produced a ten-year analysis of investment results showing that stocks of the larger companies—referred to as the "Favorite Fifty" or the "Nifty Fifty"—were selling at prices that greatly overvalued their present worth and future prospects. At the same time, the market was greatly *undervaluing* the much larger population of small- to medium-sized companies. With a disproportionate amount of money flowing to the safe-bet stocks, their prices soared. Between 1949 and 1959, the earnings of the Vicker's Favorite Fifty companies doubled—but their stock prices increased *sixfold*. The reason for the disparity between the growth in the companies' earnings and the growth in their stock price was "multiple expansion." As explained in *Common Stock and Common Sense*:

> The most significant change in the position of the 1959 investor vis a vis the 1949 investor is in the multiple of earnings reflected in common stock prices today. Today's "Favorite Fifty" stocks are selling at price-earnings ratios which average 21 times estimated 1959 earnings. Ten years ago these same stocks could have been purchased at prices averaging 7.7 times 1949 earnings.[11]

At the same time, much of the rest of the stock market universe—the thousands of publicly traded companies that were not part of the Favorite Fifty—was stuck with 1949-level price-earnings multiples. That was DLJ's opportunity—to point investors in the direction of these promising, over-looked companies.

The DLJ-produced reports would go deep into the operations of the business, including manufacturing and marketing, and into an evalua-tion of management and strategy. Donaldson placed a lot of importance on "scuttlebutt research," a hands-on approach that entails getting out in the field and talking to competitors, customers, and the company's middle management. That kind of research, he believed, would have appeal and value to a growing number of institutional investment managers who, like the DLJ founders, held MBA degrees.

Jenrette, whose nickname at the firm became "Bear" because of his cau-tion and second-guessing, understood the niche in the market his partners intended to address. But he was initially skeptical about that niche being sufficiently large to support a full-fledged business. "We can produce twenty reports a year and prudently buy only 10 or 20 percent of the float of these companies," he said to his partners. "Now, multiply that out by the num-ber of shares times the commission. The net is we can't make any money on this."[12] Jenrette's statement, on its face, seemed to undermine DLJ's very business model. But Donaldson had a ready reply to Jenrette's concern—one that was tied to a membership on the New York Stock Exchange.

From their first day in business, Donaldson insisted that the firm become a member of the exchange. He thought NYSE membership would lend prestige to the young firm; he called it a "Good Housekeeping Seal of Approval." Membership also carried a very tangible benefit: access to the substantial commissions institutional investors had to pay in those days when they bought or sold the common stock of exchange-listed companies. Before the NYSE began offering volume discounts in the early 1970s—and before the SEC mandated the end of fixed commission schedules a few years later—a bank or mutual fund buying or selling 100,000 shares of stock paid the same percentage rate as a retail investor who traded just 100 shares. As a result, the institutional investors, however reluctantly, sent a high volume of commission dollars to Wall Street.

Donaldson hatched a way to share in that commission bounty. The companies on which the firm's analysts prepared research reports were usu-ally traded over the counter and were too small for an NYSE listing, but Donaldson asked the portfolio managers at the institutions to reward the firm by directing NYSE commission business its way. "We didn't want to be compensated for just our ideas. If our ideas were any good, we told them to pay us in anything they wanted. We told them to buy General Motors through us, or whatever they wanted, but just give us a flow of brokerage dollars."[13] So when DLJ created value to the institutions with its fresh, comprehensive, and insightful thirty- to forty-page reports on smaller companies, the firm asked to be compensated indirectly by handling the institutions' trades in other common stocks. That approach worked. Later, commenting on the viability of the DLJ business model, Jenrette said, "Citibank, Chase, Putnam, and Fidelity had to pay out large fixed NYSE commissions and were getting lousy research. They were also glad to get someone to look at these small, innovative companies. So the commissions began to pour in, and we hit a gusher."[14]

The Case for Going Public

For many years, few knew how big the DLJ gusher had become. In its first ten years, total revenues grew to over $30 million, with the majority coming from brokerage commissions from institutional investors. Most of those commissions, as Donaldson had hoped, were directed to DLJ as a reward for the firm's good ideas. A 1964 *BusinessWeek* feature article on the firm recounted its many successful recommendations—along with some losses—and reported that the firm's fifty-one basic recommendations, made over its first four years in business, performed 50 percent better than comparable investments in shares of the thirty companies making up the Dow Jones Industrial Average.[15] That level of success caught the attention of Wall Street and the gusher of business grew larger as more institutional investors signed on as DLJ customers.

In addition to trading on its demonstrated stock-picking skills, DLJ enjoyed a powerful tailwind provided by the coming dominance of institutional investors in the stock market. Donaldson remembers that when he started in the business, "something like 95 percent of the stock in this country was owned by individual investors. Of course, that all reversed in the next twenty years."[16] In the five years following 1964, the business model that the three founders of DLJ were unable to sell to skeptical investors on Wall Street in 1959 was working far beyond anyone's imagination.

The firm's profitability was even more impressive than its growth. Most well-run businesses operate with pretax profit margins of between

10 and 30 percent. Throughout the 1960s, DLJ's pretax margin averaged close to 50 percent. Part of the reason for its high margins was the low level of employee compensation compared with revenues. The firm hired talented people and paid them well, but unlike other Wall Street firms, DLJ employed virtually no full-time salespeople. It didn't need the hundreds, or even thousands, of stockbrokers who generated commissions at a retail-oriented firm. Furthermore, the firm invented a new kind of employee, called the analyst salesman, who contacted institutional investors directly. With the firm's focus on institutional research, almost everyone in senior management was an analyst and a salesman at the same time—including Bill Donaldson, Dan Lufkin, and Dick Jenrette. According to Jenrette, "If we did a report, I would go out and talk to Fidelity, Putnam, and Morgan Bank. We bypassed a whole expensive sales force."[17] By the end of the firm's first decade in business it employed two PhDs in economics, fifty MBAs, five law school graduates, and five CPAs—and most of them were analyst salesmen.[18]

Since it was a corporation (rather than a partnership), the large profits that DLJ earned during its first ten years were retained in the business. The result was that the firm, by the end of 1969, had a stockholders' equity position of approximately $25 million. That meant that, unlikely as it may seem, the Wall Street upstart was operating with more capital than most of the established investment bankers. Morgan Stanley, still the grand doyenne of investment banking, had a capital position of only $18 million. The puny levels of capital on Wall Street had partly to do with the nature of their operations and the legal structure of most firms. Although the situation would change quickly in the subsequent decades, the investment business was not yet capital intensive. Firms like Morgan Stanley needed some amount of capital to support their underwriting activities, but much of it could be readily obtained by borrowing from banks. Otherwise, their day-to-day activities revolved around advisory work that didn't require a large balance sheet.

Another factor accounting for low capital levels was the partnership format. At the end of each year, the partners at most firms would "carve up the melon," dividing the profits among themselves without much thought of leaving anything in the business. Further inhibiting capital expansion, the partnerships were begun afresh each year, and partners were usually allowed to withdraw their capital contributions on an annual basis. As a result, there was little stability, much less growth, in partnership capital.

Given that it was already so well capitalized, why did Donaldson, Lufkin & Jenrette feel the need to shake up the financial world by becoming the first investment firm to tap the markets with a public offering? At the anticipated offering price of around $30 per share, the 800,000 new shares sold in the IPO would result, after offering expenses, in something over $20 million in *new* equity capital. So while it seemed that such a move would make the firm awash in capital, there were a few good reasons to move in such a direction.

The simplest reason: because it could. In a 1969 poll conducted by the *Institutional Investor* magazine, professional investors were asked to pick the most valuable investment firm should any of the twenty-three leading Wall Street firms go public. DLJ wound up at the top of the list, ahead of runner-up Goldman Sachs. The average estimate of the price-earnings multiple for DLJ's stock upon being publicly traded was 23.5.[19] So with the apparent support and respect from Wall Street's smart money, it was a near certainty that the firm's IPO would be well received.

There was also a legitimate business reason for an offering. Institutional investors, sick of paying high commissions when trading in NYSE-listed stocks, began demanding a new service from brokerage firms called block positioning. Rather than buying or selling shares piecemeal (and tipping off other market participants of their intentions), the managers of pension funds and mutual funds wanted investment firms to better earn their handsome commissions by assembling and trading large blocks of stock—and using their own capital to do so. DLJ was one of the few firms active in the block trading business; by its own reckoning, it had made capital commitments of over $200 million in connection with block transactions in 1969. But that level of activity accounted for just 3.6 percent of all block trades on the NYSE in that year.[20] Goldman Sachs and Salomon Brothers, with more capital to commit, were dominating the business. If it wanted to further enhance its credibility with its institutional customers and gain market share, DLJ needed additional capital.

The Big Board Relents

By 1969, the young founders of DLJ were convinced that an IPO was the right move. But the governors of the New York Stock Exchange did not feel the same sense of urgency. A few years earlier, they had formed a public-ownership committee to study the matter, mainly in reaction to mammoth paperwork jams earlier in the 1960s that disrupted the market and drove a number of NYSE member firms into bankruptcy. The committee recognized that the problems were caused at least in part by the failure of member firms to invest in the equipment and technology needed to keep up with the flow of paperwork. And that failure, more often than not, could be tied to the inadequacy and impermanence of their capital. Yet the NYSE still didn't act on the problem. Donaldson noted, "There'd been countless meetings of the NYSE's public-ownership committee and they all ended the same way, with everyone saying, 'Gee, this is a problem!'"[21]

The main stumbling block to action was that the problem, while recognized by all, could not surmount other interests. According to Donaldson, "Older partners in the older firms wanted to keep the earnings and take the money out of the business."[22] In addition, there was the long-held notion that member firms would be more prudently managed if the owners had their own capital at risk; bringing in outside shareholders would presumably make management more prone to risk-taking behavior. And overarching it all was the fear that opening NYSE membership to outsiders would lead to the erosion of revenues if banks and institutions became exchange members to avoid paying commissions to brokers.

Finally, with the meetings yielding nothing of substance, Donaldson and his partners decided to force the issue and began a supersecret process to go public. They hired First Boston, then a major U.S. securities underwriting firm, to manage the offering. It was a provocative decision, since First Boston, which was a publicly owned firm and therefore denied NYSE membership, had hinted at initiating an antitrust suit against the exchange.[23]

At exactly four o'clock in the afternoon on May 21, the day before the registration statement for the IPO was to be filed with the SEC, Donaldson went to the office of Gustave Levy—a Goldman Sachs partner and until recently the chairman of the NYSE—to break the news. Then he went directly to the exchange to meet with its president, Robert Haack. Meanwhile, Dan Lufkin met with the exchange's chairman, Bernard Lasker.[24] The message was the same in all of the meetings, as described by Donaldson:

> We told the Stock Exchange what we had done. We didn't ask permission; we just did it. We talked about the paradox of Wall Street promoting public ownership and yet not allowing its own institutions to be publicly held. We had analyses about the capital needs that

were coming into Wall Street and how inadequate the capital was for trading inventories, block placements, and financing the many new businesses that were coming along. As we showed, Wall Street was under-capitalized because so much of the money had been taken out of the street, year after year after year.[25]

The May 21 meetings were far from pleasant. To the establishment members of the "Big Board," the planned IPO looked to be a nearsighted move of an impetuous management. Lazard's Rohatyn referred to the "adolescent showmanship" of the DLJ principals and NYSE president Haack and Donaldson exchanged words that day "that are not likely to be forgotten by either man."[26] But by the time the DLJ offering was approved and sold on Wall Street, nearly a year later, the NYSE governors had relented. After putting in place a number of new rules making it more difficult for institutional investors to bypass the payment of commissions, they permitted public ownership among NYSE member firms.

Besides being comfortable that the new rules would make the scourge of institutional membership less likely, the exchange's more conciliatory attitude toward public ownership may have had a touch of self-interest as they came to realize the windfall that public ownership could bring. When DLJ's planned stock offering was announced, the expected price of the stock was more than eight times the firm's book value. That meant that the owners of DLJ would enjoy a major jump in the value of their stock holdings as the firm transformed from a closely held business to a publicly traded company. Based on the information in the offering prospectus, Donaldson, DLJ's largest shareholder, would see his holdings increase from a stated value on the books of about $3 million to a market value, at least on paper, of $25 million. Lufkin and Jenrette, with slightly lesser holdings, were also prospective multimillionaires.

The coming fortunes of the DLJ principals could not have escaped the attention of their counterparts at other firms. At the time, the NYSE had 645 member firms, owned by some 11,250 stockholders and partners. Even if their market price to book value was not as generous as DLJ's eight-to-one multiplier, most of them could expect a major boost in their net worth if they were to do an IPO. In a 1969 *Fortune* article, writer Carol Loomis made a rough and "fanciful" calculation showing that those 11,250 owners might, if their firms went public, enjoy a gain in the value of their holdings of about $1 million each.[27]

Opening the Floodgates to the Capital Markets

The long-held fear that publicly traded institutions would become members to avoid commissions was never realized. Instead, institutional investors put pressure on the NYSE to get volume discounts to reduce commission charges. And the disclosures in DLJ's prospectus also helped take down the NYSE's practice of setting minimum commission levels. As Jenrette noted, "The institutions cited our high level of profitability to show that their commissions were too high. I think that by letting it all hang out, everyone—customers, competitors, imitators—saw how very profitable our business could be. The institutions—our customers—used this information as ammunition to beat on the SEC and, finally, to eliminate fixed commissions."[28] In 1973 the SEC announced, "The Commission will act promptly to terminate the fixing of commission rates by national stock exchanges after April 30, 1975, if the stock exchanges do not, on their own initiative, adopt rule changes achieving that result in advance of that date."[29] So in the end, DLJ did have a role in busting up the club, though not, perhaps, in the way initially envisioned by the exchange's establishment members.

The indirect role DLJ played in bringing fully negotiated commissions to the NYSE was of major consequence. But the impact of the firm's initial public offering was ultimately far broader. By opening the gates to the capital markets for Wall Street firms, DLJ led the transformation of the securities business in both its size and scope. DLJ's offering was followed the next year by Merrill Lynch, and shortly thereafter by most of the other major retail firms of the day, including E. F. Hutton, Bache, Paine Webber, Jackson & Curtis, Reynolds Securities, A. G. Edwards, and Dean Witter. Lufkin recalls receiving a letter from the Reynolds's chief executive, Tom Stahle, in which he said, "I just want to tell you something. I really wondered whether the rule change was the right move, but now we are in the process of putting together a public offering." Without access to the public markets, Stahle opined that "there would be no Reynolds in another year."[30] For the retail firms, access to capital was key, and this new source came just in time to support the branch expansions and technology enhancements of the latter part of the twentieth century.

Wall Street's major investment banks also joined the move toward public ownership. Goldman Sachs—the most prominent of the old-line partnerships—was one of the last to succumb, finally going public in 1999. In 2005 even Lazard Frères, the most private of all banking firms, went public. Unlike the retail firms, however, most of the new money raised by the investment banks did not go into equipment and infrastructure. Just as DLJ used much of its newly acquired capital for block positioning and other trading activities, the Wall Street firms tended to use their capital, for better or for worse, to increase the level of their principal transactions—securities trading, risk arbitrage, bridge lending, private equity investing, venture capital, and even hedge fund investing.

Profits earned at the investment banks as principal soon exceeded profits from the traditional agent-based businesses. When DLJ opened its doors, Morgan Stanley held sway over Wall Street, advising the bluest of blue-chip companies and working with the precious little capital its risk-averse partners thought was necessary; when DLJ essentially closed its doors—or at least lost its identity with the merger with Credit Suisse—the new version of Morgan Stanley was on its way to building a trillion-dollar balance sheet and traders were in the ascent.

Separate Ways

The threesome that founded DLJ did not stay intact long after the firm's 1970 IPO. Dan Lufkin left the following year for a three-year stint as the first commissioner of environmental protection for the state of Connecticut. He later cited Georges Doriot in explaining his departure:

> As General Doriot, the old professor at Harvard Business School, used to say in his French accent, "Gentlemen, you must remember that there are three types of people who run an organization. First is the entrepreneur, who begins the business. Second is the manager who develops the business and third is the manager who runs the business. Very rarely can they all fit under the same skin."[31]

Evidently, Donaldson also did not see himself as a long-term manager. In 1973 Donaldson left to become under secretary of state to Henry Kissinger. Jenrette, who had been recruited back in 1959 to provide the managerial skills they knew they lacked, proved quite able to guide DLJ for the next couple of decades. The 1970s decade was the toughest. The economy and securities markets were lackluster, and the advent of negotiated brokerage commissions—which DLJ itself had been a catalyst for—made profits hard to come by. Yet Jenrette saw the firm through that decade and another fifteen years of corporate expansions and reorganizations. Shortly after he retired in 1996, DLJ was sold to Credit Suisse for $13 billion.

In his retirement, Jenrette pursued his lifelong interest in restoring old homes. Lufkin did some corporate freelance work in the 1970s and 1980s—including a brief stint with DLJ—but his personal focus has shifted to other ventures, including ranching and environmental causes. Donaldson's interests after DLJ and his three years in the State Department, however, remained closely tied to Wall Street. His impressive resumé includes such positions as: special advisor to Vice President Nelson Rockefeller; founding dean of the Yale School of Management; chairman and president of Aetna; chairman of the Carnegie Endowment for International Peace; chairman of the Securities and Exchange Commission; and, in what might seem to be a paradox, chairman of the New York Stock Exchange. A few decades earlier, the leaders of the NYSE considered Donaldson to be a 1960s firebrand—albeit a firebrand in a Brooks Brothers suit. That he wound up serving as chairman of the exchange serves as confirmation of the transformation he and his partners brought to Wall Street.

Jenrette describes the company history as "a long saga, where DLJ tangos with the Arabs, tangos with American Express, tangos with Equitable, and then does the last tango with Credit Suisse."[32] But at the end of the dance, many billions of dollars of value were created for the DLJ's shareholders—greatly aided by access to the markets and by its position as a publicly traded stock. But access to capital has not been an unalloyed blessing for Wall Street. The saga covered in the next chapter is not a tango as much as a danse macabre. Rather than creating value, another Wall Street operator uses publicly traded stock to raise billions in new capital and engineer a string of implausible acquisitions—resulting in the destruction of shareholder value and, ultimately, a record-breaking taxpayer bailout.

© Mark Peterson/Corbis

14

Sanford I. Weill: 1933–
Conglomerateur

What we should probably do is go and split up investment banking from banking. Have the banks do something that's not going to risk the taxpayer dollars, that's
not going to be too big to fail.

—SANDY WEILL, 2012

One common aspiration of ambitious Wall Street executives has been the
creation of a financial supermarket. The idea always looks good on paper:
If a firm can combine the multitude of financial services that customers
require, there will be no end to the efficiencies, cross-selling, and profitability that's created. If those customers are individuals, a single diversified
firm could handle all of their brokerage, banking, advisory, insurance, and
mutual fund needs; if the customers are businesses, the same firm could
offer the full panoply of investment banking and commercial banking for
them as well.

But financial supermarkets have never worked. They turn out to be the
kind of ill-conceived and unmanageable conglomerates that, ironically, the
smart money on Wall Street always bets against. In an earlier chapter, we
saw how Charles Merrill conceived of and managed a superb retail investment firm. But when his successors decided to turn Merrill Lynch into a
diversified financial operation, it all fell apart. After acquiring insurance
companies, investment banks, real estate firms, and a host of other financial services businesses, Merrill Lynch became all things to all people in
the financial world—but in a decidedly second-class fashion. It eventually
ended with a shotgun marriage to the Bank of America.

The dubious distinction for the greatest financial supermarket failure, however, rests securely with Citigroup, the twenty-first-century iteration of the National City Bank that was described many pages earlier when it was under the direction of Sunshine Charlie Mitchell. The modern Citigroup was created by Sanford ("Sandy") Weill, a man with ambitions on the scale of Mitchell's, but imbued with considerably greater management skills and a wider business vision. Over a five-decade career, Weill used his skills and vision to meld together a vast, but ultimately unstable, financial enterprise through a mergers and acquisitions spree that brought together many of the well-known names in finance—Citicorp, Travelers Insurance, Salomon Brothers, Smith Barney, Aetna Property and Casualty, and Shearson Loeb Rhoades & Company—along with scores of smaller, lesser-known financial services firms. In the early years of the twenty-first century Citigroup was the largest financial institution in the world, with assets in excess of $2 trillion and employing more than 350,000 people.

But the mammoth corporation met an even worse fate for its shareholders and for U.S. taxpayers than the Merrill Lynch collapse. Its stock, which sold for as high as $55 per share in 2007, plummeted to less than a dollar a share in the aftermath of the 2008 financial crisis. Absent two government bailouts totaling $45 billion, the stock would have become totally worthless. Few would have guessed the story would end so badly, given its promising beginnings and Weill's considerable talents.

From Wall Street Runner to Wall Street Mogul

Weill grew up in the Bensonhurst section of Brooklyn, which at the time was made up primarily of Italian-Jewish working-class families and known more for producing prominent Mafia figures than Wall Street titans. Weill keeps a picture of his small stucco childhood home is his office; it's a far cry from the extravagant Manhattan apartments he would later occupy. (In late 2011 he sold his 15 Central Park West penthouse for $88 million, a record amount for a New York apartment at the time.) Short and pudgy as a child, he was toughened up by bullying. Later, when he was a college student, his father abandoned his family and sold the business Weill had expected to take over. Yet Weill's story is not purely rags to riches. He was able to escape Bensonhurst during his high school years to attend a military academy and then received a bachelor's degree in 1955 from Cornell University.

Upon graduation, Weill headed directly for Wall Street to find a job, but not many doors were open to him. He had an Ivy League education, but the "front office" positions he coveted in securities sales and investment banking were usually offered to the Harvard–Yale–Princeton sector of the Ivy League or to applicants from well-heeled families with a prominent social background. Compounding the problem was the fact that the partners of the leading "Jewish houses" of the day, such as Kuhn Loeb, Goldman Sachs, and Lehman Brothers, were mainly of German descent. Weill was the grandson of Eastern European Jews and never got past the reception desk at any of the major firms.

But he was committed to a career in finance and was willing to take any job that would get his foot in the door. That job turned out to be at Bear, Stearns & Company, then a second-tier investment firm. He became a runner, the lowest rung on the Wall Street ladder, picking up and delivering securities between banks and securities firms. He was soon moved from street errands into the "back office," where the menial yet necessary business of the brokerage business is conducted. In what is typically a dead-end department, he mastered the intricacies of the back office during the day and by night studied for the licensing tests he needed to pass to sell securities. Weill was fascinated with every detail of processing orders and handling margin loans, and in short order he became totally conversant with how the "kitchen" of an investment firm works.

After Weill acquired his broker's license, he moved from the back office to the sales department at Bear Stearns and then to Burnham & Company (run by I. W. "Tubby" Burnham, one of Michael Milken's early and influential bosses). The socially awkward Weill was not a natural salesman but proved to be an apt stock picker and money manager. The word spread, and he was soon making a respectable living as a broker. He also developed a coterie of like-minded young investment professionals on Wall Street—ambitious, very smart, most often Jewish, and keen on launching their own investment firm. In 1960, just five years after Weill began his Wall Street career as a runner, he became a cofounder of the firm that would later be called Cogan, Berlind, Weill & Leavitt.

The new firm was modeled somewhat after Donaldson, Lufkin & Jenrette. Like DLJ, CBWL started as a research boutique that generated commissions primarily from institutional investors based on the quality of its principals' ideas. As with many start-up investment firms, survival depended on the ability to pick up loyal and substantial customers early in the game. The mutual fund giant Fidelity Management & Research was one such customer for CBWL, supplying the firm with a steady stream of commission business. And also like DLJ, the firm was able to leverage its industry research abilities into occasional investment banking transactions. Most notably, CBWL assisted the young takeover specialist Saul Steinberg in his controversial and highly publicized purchase of the Reliance Insurance Group.

Despite its (vaguely anti-Semitic) nickname in the investment community, "Corned Beef With Lettuce," CBWL was financially sound and taken seriously on Wall Street. Despite this, Weill was apprehensive about the boutique business model. It generated substantial paydays for the four partners when business was good—especially in years when investment banking deals closed—but there were also lean years when business was slow and mergers and acquisitions work slacked off. So while his partners continued to run the day-to-day business of the firm, Weill started looking for other investment firms to acquire. Such acquisitions, he hoped, would broaden CBWL's customer base and reduce its reliance on lucrative but less predictable investment banking revenues.

There were several hundred independent New York Stock Exchange member firms across of the country at the time, and the early consolidation of the securities industry was just getting under way. CBWL was not the only firm looking to grow through acquisitions, but it had one very major advantage: a highly efficient back office operation that Weill had built from scratch and whose workings he knew intimately. Typical of the partners of other securities firms, Weill's three partners regarded mundane operational issues (fails-to-deliver, margin calls, clearing services, securities settlement) with an attitude that bordered on disdain. To them, the success of the firm was based on sales commissions and investment banking fees. They were only too happy to cede authority for the rest of the business to their rough-hewn, cost-conscious Brooklyn partner.

A state-of-the art back office under the direction of a knowledgeable partner was a rarity on Wall Street, and that condition became all too apparent when leading firms became overwhelmed in their attempts to process the flood of paper generated during the record levels of trading in the late 1960s. With a back office designed to handle a level of business well beyond its own, the upstart CBWL—barely a decade old—went on the prowl. Weill hunted for aged but otherwise attractive securities firms whose existences were threatened by their incompetently managed back offices. He didn't have to look long, and CBWL quickly became the rescuer of much older, larger, and more prestigious brokerage firms.

The game (and name) changer came with CBWL's takeover of Hayden Stone & Company in 1970. The acquisition was mediated by the New York Stock Exchange, which took notice of CBWL's easy assimilation of the branch offices of failed firms. The exchange itself was operating in near-panic mode, going so far as to shut down trading on Wednesdays for a time to allow its members to catch up on the overwhelming paperwork problems that heavy trading was causing. Hayden Stone's situation was particularly dire; the prominent Boston-based firm had been a stalwart of the investment business since its founding in 1892 but was now heading toward failure due to its antiquated processes for handling securities trades. The NYSE's crisis-management team knew Hayden Stone was incapable of remedying its problems and needed a rescuer. And though CBWL had only two offices, compared to Hayden Stone's sixty-two, the NYSE agreed to finance a deal calling for the minnow to acquire the whale—as long as the minnow would be fully in charge of the newly formed CBWL–Hayden Stone.

Despite the ongoing culture clashes between the white-shoe principals of Hayden Stone and the fast-talking, sharp-penciled CBWL managers, the new CBWL–Hayden Stone emerged vastly stronger and more profitable than before. The relentlessly aggressive Weill, with his ever-present cigar, was its undisputed driving force. By June 1971, Weill had whipped the firm into shape to go public. CBWL-Hayden Stone, quickly following the lead of Donaldson, Lufkin & Jenrette and Merrill Lynch, became the third Wall Street firm to file a registration statement with the SEC for an initial public offering.

Don Stroben, one of CBWL–Hayden Stone's early associates, remarked, "The public offering was what really ultimately gave Sandy Weill the ability to do what he did. From then on, he had the good fortune to have something that was rare on Wall Street: capital, as well as a position of control and an ability to execute. That momentum carried him on and on."[1] (The IPO also elevated Weill into the ranks of Wall Street's millionaires; at the conclusion of the offering his net worth increased by $3.5 million.)[2] With an infusion of new capital from its IPO and the best cost-control and back-office operations in the industry, the firm was in an ideal position to pick up the pieces on a weakened and demoralized Wall Street. The paperwork troubles of the late 1960s were followed in the 1970s by stagflation—a combination of slow economic growth and inflation that devastated the values of both stocks and bonds. The knockout punch for many firms was the abolition of fixed-rate commissions in 1975. With new price competition and a bleak outlook for the overall industry, the securities business lost its appeal for many partners, and they began withdrawing their capital.

Such capital withdrawals just made the weak firms weaker and less able to withstand downturns in business—and more vulnerable to acquisition by Weill's CBWL-Hayden Stone, which was growing stronger by the day. Some of the acquisitions involved just a few branch offices and a few were yet more minnow-swallowing-the-whale deals, but they were all rescue efforts of one form or another. Many of the once-prominent firms that had turned him down when he was looking for a job out of college found themselves merged into Weill's growing empire. By 1980 the firm had become Shearson Loeb Rhoades and was second only to Merrill Lynch in the number of brokers it employed. With the other founding CBWL partners having gone their own ways, Weill was the chief executive and fully in charge. The former Wall Street runner now had his office on the top floor of the World Trade Center, enjoyed the services of a private jet, had former president Gerald Ford on his board of directors—and was only in his forties.

In Pursuit of a Second Empire

Up until 1981 the various segments of the financial services industry operated autonomously in neatly defined markets. Insurers sold varieties of life and casualty policies; banks made loans and accepted deposits; and investment firms served as brokers and investment bankers. But an irreversible transformation began that year when the Prudential Insurance Company announced its acquisition of Bache Halsey Stuart, the third-largest retail securities firm in the United States after Merrill Lynch and Shearson Loeb Rhoades. These two enormous financial institutions were breaking ranks and aligning themselves to cross-sell their insurance and investment products to individuals and businesses. Prudential's gambit both shocked Weill and stoked his competitive fires. He wanted to lead the parade, not follow it. And to that end, he met with James Robinson, CEO of the credit card giant American Express Company.

Exactly one month from the announcement of the formation of Prudential Bache, Weill and Robinson announced the establishment of Shearson/American Express. At the time, American Express had a firm lock on the high-end segment of the credit card business—exactly the prosperous demographic that would seem ripe for solicitation by stockbrokers. The boards of both companies were quick to approve the combination, and many believed that when the dust settled in the executive suite, Weill would wind up running the show. That was apparently Weill's guess also, as he told a friend: "Not bad for a kid from Brooklyn. The Jews are going to take over American Express, and they'll never know what hit them."[3]

But Weill overplayed his hand with Robinson and his conservative board of directors. As a result of the merger, Weill became president of American Express and controlled a large chunk of its stock—large enough to make him a very wealthy man, but not enough to control corporate decisions. And one of the decisions of the reconstituted board was to keep Weill, despite his title of president, at a remove from important decisions and from the direct management of frontline executives. From the sidelines, he attempted to engineer mergers and acquisitions, including a joint venture with Warren Buffett to acquire the Fireman's Fund Insurance Company. But the cautious, American Express–dominated board demurred. The directors rejected the Fireman's Fund proposal as well as other subsequent proposals Weill brought to them.

By 1985, after the American Express board had snubbed Weill and a string of potential deals, he realized he would never be allowed to put his imprint on American Express—much less run it. So he made his exit. He retreated for a few years to a quasi retirement, spending much of his time on charitable affairs. But most of his mental energy was devoted to finding another platform for a return to Wall Street.

That platform came unsolicited in 1986 from a few discouraged executives of the Commercial Credit Corporation, a Baltimore-based consumer credit subsidiary of the struggling Control Data Corporation. Weill was immediately intrigued by the executives' suggestion that he acquire the Commercial Credit subsidiary. The company made short-term loans at high interest rates to low-income borrowers, operating in a financial segment far from the rarefied air of Wall Street. But the more closely he looked at the business—and he always went through any proposal with laser-like intensity—the more attractive the opportunity appeared. Commercial Credit offered a steady flow of business generated from a large collection of small loans spread across the country. The company was profitable but underperforming its industry, and Weill quickly figured out what was needed to set things right: tightening operating controls and lowering the company's own cost of money.

Weill was certain that the board of the cash-needy Control Data would entertain a proposal to sell its Commercial Credit subsidiary through a public offering. He also knew that the offering would be well received if he became the CEO of the newly independent company. The board agreed to his proposal and Control Data sold 80 percent of Commercial Credit for $850 million. Weill now had his platform.

At a meeting with Commercial Credit's employees shortly after the spin-off, he stated with characteristic frankness, "I have built one empire in my life—which was Shearson. And I want to do it one more time before I retire."4 Much as Weill overbuilt the back-office capacity of CBWL in order to easily assimilate opportunistic acquisitions, he overbuilt the management team that would take over Commercial Credit. The bankers who decamped to Baltimore to run the relatively small company—about $1 billion in revenues and $5 billion in assets—included former presidents of some of the largest financial institutions of the day and other high-ranking officers. Most notable was Jamie Dimon, Weill's longtime protégé who would later become chairman of JPMorgan Chase and Wall Street's most prominent banker. The members of the high-powered team were willing to leave secure positions, take pay cuts, and move to Baltimore because they believed that Weill's second empire would succeed, and they wanted to be on the ground floor. Weill returned their confidence by dividing 10 percent of the shares of the newly public Commercial Credit Company among them.

Reprising a familiar routine, Commercial Credit began its ascent into the big leagues of finance by capturing prey much larger than itself. Just as the tiny CBWL took over Hayden Stone, in early 1988 Commercial Credit set its sights on a company called Primerica. Primerica's sales approached $4 billion, roughly four times those of Commercial Credit, but its most attractive component—the well-known Smith Barney securities operation—was still reeling from the October 1987 stock market collapse and thus represented just the kind of opportunity Weill relished. Smith Barney had a seasoned sales force that catered to the carriage trade, and its reputation for quality was reinforced with clever advertising—"They make money the old fashioned way. They earn it." It looked to be the perfect route back to Wall Street.

Yet there were a number of problems in acquiring Primerica, any of which might have dissuaded a buyer less tenacious than Weill. For one, Primerica was much more than Smith Barney. Under the corporate umbrella was a life insurance subsidiary, A. L. Williams & Associates, that conducted a business far outside the mainstream of the insurance industry. It had a sales force of some two hundred thousand working-class agents selling its term-life products on a part-time basis and under the inspiration of an evangelizing founder, Art Williams. But rather than recoiling from the insurance company's unorthodox business practices, Weill developed a fondness for Williams and the business he built. There would not be much cross-selling going on between A. L. Williams's blue-collar sales force and the blue bloods at Smith Barney, but there was at least some commonality with Commercial Credit's employees and customers. After Weill's usual thorough review of the company, he got past the odd coupling of Smith Barney and A. L. Williams and saw Primerica as an opportune acquisition.

But how was *this* minnow-and-the-whale transaction going to be financed? The short answer: through the reputation of Sandy Weill. Under the terms of the proposed Commercial Credit–Primerica union, Commercial Credit would provide the Primerica shareholders with only a token amount of cash and many shares of its stock, so that the transaction was predominantly a stock swap. For the deal to get done, the Primerica shareholders had to believe that the stock they would get in return for surrendering their ownership would become more valuable as a result of Weill's management magic. It was not an easy sell to all of the Primerica shareholders, but in December 1988 the acquisition closed. Weill and his management team from Commercial Credit would call the shots, but they would run the combined operation under the name of Primerica Corporation. A few months later, Primerica began trading on the New York Stock Exchange. Weill was back, and his second empire was established.

A Big Birthday Present

Weill's second-act empire ran like the first—with relentless cost cutting and a string of opportunistic acquisitions. Immediately following the merger, Weill set, and then exceeded, a goal of reducing Primerica's overhead by $50 million. Twenty percent of the company's corporate staff was laid off, along with 120 people considered to be excess baggage at the Smith Barney unit.[5]

But at the same time Weill was cutting out the deadwood, he was building a larger and more productive sales staff through acquisitions. Smith Barney's 2,100-broker sales force grew by about 25 percent when Weill purchased the retail operations of Drexel Burnham just as the firm was falling apart following a guilty plea to charges of racketeering and Michael Milken's departure. With that acquisition, Weill was doubling back to the very start of his career, when he'd worked for Tubby Burnham—the Burnham in Drexel Burnham.

Much more important, however, was his eventual doubling back to Shearson. Following its 1981 purchase of Shearson Hayden Stone, American Express continued to build its retail sales through internal growth and through the 1988 acquisition of the well-known E. F. Hutton—"When E.F. Hutton talks, people listen." By 1993, some 8,500 retail brokers were working for Shearson/American Express. But despite the size, the expected synergy between Shearson and American Express wasn't working. The cross-selling rationale, upon which the union was based, was undermined when the American Express management refused to hand over its list of credit card holders to the brokers at Shearson. American Express was also losing its cachet in the credit card business as a result of competitive services springing up at Visa and MasterCard. So with cross-selling ruled out and a need to refocus on its core business—and with a new American Express CEO in place who had no emotional attachment to the creation of Shearson/ American Express—there was little reason to keep the company together.

Even before American Express made the decision to sell Shearson, managers and brokers had been defecting from Shearson to Primerica's Smith Barney subsidiary. So although it employed only one-fourth the number of stockbrokers, Smith Barney emerged as Shearson's logical purchaser. The deal Weill made for the repurchase of Shearson, the core of his first empire and his abiding business love, sent the stock of Primerica to record highs. And for good reason. Weill had sold Shearson twelve years earlier to American Express for roughly $900 million in stock and now he was buying it back for just a little over $1 billion. In those dozen years, Shearson had doubled its sales force and had developed a large and effective investment advisory firm with $52 billion in assets under management. What's more, Shearson was occupying $600 million of prime Manhattan real estate that would be part of the deal.[6] Weill was a clever buyer, and immediately after the transaction was announced on March 12, 1993, the stock of Primerica soared even further in recognition of the advantageous arrangement he had negotiated. Weill turned sixty just a few days after the deal closed; Shearson was a belated but gratifying gift.

Rescuer and Genius

The 1993 acquisition of Shearson, however, turned out to be only the second most important event for Weill and Primerica that year. In the fall of 1992, Weill had negotiated Primerica's purchase of a 27 percent ownership position in Travelers Corporation, one of the country's largest insurance companies. Primerica's $722 million investment was part of an effort to reestablish the rapidly falling credit rating of the 128-year-old Travelers in the wake of a string of bad commercial real estate loans. Travelers specialized in providing property insurance for big business and counted about half of the Fortune 500 companies as its customers. But its expertise didn't extend to commercial lending, and the insurer's balance sheet was crippled with hundreds of millions of dollars of "nonperforming" loans and dwindling reserves to protect them. To make matters worse, Travelers had been hit by a staggering number of claims in the aftermath of Hurricane Andrew, the August 1992 hurricane that at the time was the costliest in U.S. history.

Weill's rescue deal with Travelers came with many strings attached. Primerica was granted representation on the insurer's board commensurate with its 27 percent ownership, and Sandy Weill, Jamie Dimon, and two other Primerica managers became directors. That gave them the opportunity to size up the company from an insider's perspective—and they liked what they saw. In September 1993, exactly one year from the date of the initial investment, Primerica announced that it would purchase the remaining 73 percent of Travelers stock in a $4 billion swap of Primerica's common stock for that of Travelers. When the deal closed, Primerica became the largest financial services company in the world and promptly changed its name to Travelers Group.

Weill was diligent as well as opportunistic in his approach to this acquisition. In the year he had to evaluate Travelers before agreeing to the full purchase, he had concluded that the real estate loan problems were largely behind them. His knowledge of the insurance business extended back to his early days at CBWL, when he assisted Saul Steinberg in the takeover of Reliance Insurance, and to his more recent experience with Fireman's Fund. With that background, he saw issues and opportunities at Travelers that had escaped the attention of its prior management. In particular, he saw a bloated administrative staff in the Hartford, Connecticut, headquarters and little focus on productivity and cost controls. He also knew that Travelers, no matter how badly damaged by recent loan problems and sleepy management, enjoyed a century-old franchise that would outlive its current problems. In particular, the red umbrella the insurer had long used in its advertising was one of the most recognizable symbols in the U.S. business landscape, on a par with the iconic Prudential rock and the Merrill Lynch bull.

Making the transaction even more appealing, the Primerica stock that would be issued to finance the merger with Travelers had appreciated by about a third following the market's enthusiasm about the acquisition of Shearson, completed just six months earlier. That meant that Primerica's current shareholders would suffer only a small dilution in their ownership interest after the acquisition was completed. In the eyes of the investment community, Weill could do no wrong. He had convinced Wall Street that his new conglomerate, with the addition of Travelers, would create even more synergy between different kinds of financial service firms.

In hindsight, however, there was little evidence of such synergies before or after the acquisition of Travelers. Primerica's three discrete units—Smith Barney Shearson with 10,000 brokers; Commercial Credit with its 700 offices across the country; and A. L. Williams with 200,000 part-time insurance agents—had little customer overlap. Commercial Credit's market was working class, A. L. Williams served the lower end of the middle-class demographic, and Smith Barney Shearson was upscale. There was no apparent interest or potential for sharing customers. And Primerica wasn't the only company struggling with synergies; enough time had gone by to declare Prudential Insurance's 1981 acquisition of the 2,500 broker Bache Halsey Stuart Shields a bust. The anticipated benefits of blending insurance and securities sales were hampered by the destructive culture clashes between the two organizations.

Nevertheless, Weill's many fans on Wall Street remained convinced that with his superior brand of management he would make the merger work between the disparate operations of Primerica and Travelers Insurance. The resulting Travelers Group conglomerate operated with some $100 billion in assets and became a formidable player in the financial world. The company's importance to the American economy was reinforced in 1997 when it was selected for inclusion in the Dow Jones Industrial Average. The first financial services company to become part of the Dow's thirty-company average was J. P. Morgan & Company in 1991; Travelers Group was just the second. There could be no clearer signal to the world that Sandy Weill was at the very top of his game.

Yet Weill was like the mountaineer who, upon reaching the top of a peak, just sees a new vista open up with even greater peaks ahead. In 1997, that new peak was Salomon Brothers, the enormous bond and underwriting firm whose excesses in the 1980s were revealed in Michael Lewis's entertaining bestseller, *Liar's Poker*. Those excesses lost much of their humor in the 1990s, however, when Salomon was shaken by the disclosure that its bond traders, with their formidable financial resources and market hubris, had used false bids to manipulate the prices of U.S. Treasury securities for their own benefit during the government's periodic auctions. The firm was forced to pay close to $300 million in fines and to purge its top management. It also led to some degree of market temperance under the effective control of Warren Buffett, who owned a major share of Salomon's common stock through his Berkshire Hathaway group and became the behind-the-scenes decision maker at the firm. He must have welcomed Weill's merger proposition, which offered an exit from a business that stretched Buffett's tolerance for risk well past his limits.

Weill was not much of a risk taker himself, but he felt he could bring more trading discipline into Salomon's operations without inhibiting the money-making franchise. He was also, as usual, getting his prey inexpensively. Before the bid-rigging scandal, Salomon would have fetched a handsome sum. Now Weill could, for a "modest" price of $9 billion in Travelers Group stock, bring that firm's powerful investment banking and institutional sales capability into Travelers to complement Smith Barney Shearson's expansive retail broker network.

On a personal level, the acquisition once more validated Weill's revival. Warren Buffett, the "Oracle of Omaha," was willing to trade Berkshire Hathaway's substantial holdings of Salomon common stock for that of Travelers, and stated in a prepared press release, "Over several decades, Sandy has demonstrated genius in creating huge value for his shareholders by skillfully blending and managing acquisitions in the financial-services industry. In my view, Salomon will be no exception."[7] It couldn't get much better than having Warren Buffett proclaim your genius and back up his proclamation by accepting a large slug of Travelers Group stock in exchange for his ownership of Salomon stock—the endorsement lessened only slightly by the knowledge that Buffet was also getting rid of a major problem at the same time.

Shattering Glass-Steagall

Yet Weill had still not scaled his Mount Everest: the acquisition of one of the nation's major international commercial banks. His empire now included both full-service insurance and securities operations, but aside from the small potatoes lending business of Commercial Credit, it had nothing in the way of a major commercial bank. One major obstacle stood in his way: it was still illegal under the terms of the Depression-era Glass-Steagall Act to conduct a commercial banking business and an investment banking business under the same roof.

But not even illegality could stand between Weill and his dream. He knew that, in recent years, commercial bankers had successfully chipped away at the provisions of Glass-Steagall and were receiving one favorable ruling after another from the Federal Reserve about the kind of investment banking–like businesses they could engage in. Weill was convinced that the time was right to force the issue by engineering a blockbuster merger between Travelers and one of the big banks—and then afterward seeking the law's total repeal to make the merger legal. He was also convinced that he was the logical person to the test the matter, and to that end placed a call to John Reed, the chairman of Citicorp.

Following his modus operandus, Weill did his homework on Citicorp in great detail and, when he was ready, presented the merger idea to Reed in a one-on-one meeting. The meeting had no prelude, and Reed, as analytical and reserved as Weill was impulsive and direct, was taken aback by the unexpected and audacious proposal. Citicorp had been the world's largest banking enterprise for many years. It operated in nearly one hundred countries and its $3.4 billion in net income in 1995 was the highest level of profits ever recorded by a U.S. commercial bank.[8] But 1996 and 1997 had been challenging years for Citicorp, and that may be why Reed agreed to study the matter and get back to Weill. Within a few weeks, the two of them were hammering out a preliminary structure of the merger into a combined trillion-dollar operation that they would manage as co-CEOs.

Weill pitched the deal to Reed, and later to the Citicorp directors and shareholders, on the strength of a familiar promise: synergism. Weill argued that there was potential for nearly unlimited cross-selling within the financial behemoth he envisioned. The possibilities on the corporate side were the most compelling and profitable, with the Travelers Group investment subsidiary—now doing business as Salomon Smith Barney—poised to provide investment banking services for Citibank's large roster of blue-chip borrowers. There were plenty of cross-sell possibilities at the retail level as well, with Citibank's credit card holders becoming prospects for Travelers' annuities and Salomon Smith Barney's mutual funds—and with both Travelers' agents and Salomon Smith Barney's brokers signing up their customers for Citibank's credit cards and banking services.

Weill also had the answer for the Glass-Steagall problem. In 1997, the year before he broached the merger idea with Citicorp, he made a similar proposal to Douglas "Sandy" Warner, CEO at the august J. P. Morgan & Company. Unbeknownst to Warner, Weill had met with Fed chairman Alan Greenspan before the meeting, to plant the idea of a Travelers–J. P. Morgan

combination. Greenspan offered no objection "in principle" to the hypo-
thetical merger Weill described—as long as Congress removed the Glass-
Steagall barriers. Although the board of J. P. Morgan ultimately rebuffed
Weill's merger proposal, his warm-up meeting with Greenspan confirmed
the feasibility of the idea. In October 1998, several months after Weill and
Reed made a public announcement of the merger between Travelers and
Citicorp, the Fed gave its approval to the deal, once again contingent upon
the overturn of Glass-Steagall.

Although there was a conciliatory mood in Congress and the White
House regarding financial deregulation, an overturn of the law was not a
certainty. There were plenty of skeptics in Congress who feared the dangers
that could surface if Wall Street operated with one less inhibition to its
activities; Weill knew success would require an all-out effort to convince
the holdouts. So, ever the hands-on manager, Weill didn't rely on his bank
lobbyists to carry the day. He plunged into the fray and met personally with
key legislators. And when President Clinton initially withheld his support
of the Glass-Steagall repeal, Weill made a late night call to him that report-
edly turned the president around on the issue.

Weill and his like-minded bankers eventually prevailed, and in November 1999, Clinton signed into law the Financial Services Modernization Act—
and Glass-Steagall was no more. Weill was the acknowledged key player in
the repeal and, among his many trophies and assortment of pictures and
memorabilia in his office, a shingle etched with his likeness and the words
"the Shatterer of Glass-Steagall" found a prominent spot on his wall.

Reality Bites

The merger of Travelers and Citicorp was the largest in American history,
and Wall Street showed its enthusiasm for the deal by bidding up the common stock of both Travelers and Citicorp after the merger's announcement.
Yet the honeymoon was short-lived, and little by little it became obvious
to those inside and outside the financial conglomerate—now known as
Citigroup—that the synergies of the merger would never be realized. Weill
and Reed's plan for a smooth-running enterprise that housed the clashing
cultures of the investment business and the commercial banking business
proved to be yet another example of hope over experience.

Revenues on the Travelers' side of the business came largely from
transactions—sales of insurance policies, merger fees, commissions from

securities sales, trading profits—and every day started fresh. At Citicorp, revenues came mainly from interest earned on large loan portfolios, and those revenues accrued day in and day out. So the employees of the two firms tended to have very different outlooks on their job, with the commercial bankers intent on building long-term relationships and the transaction-based investment bankers being opportunistic and short-term thinking.

That dichotomy was nowhere more evident than in the way corporate customers were treated. The Citicorp bankers cultivated relationships, with the goal of nurturing their business clients over the long term with a wide assortment of loan and cash management services to keep the interest payments and fees flowing. They were willing to invest vast talent and time in those efforts to earn steady and recurring business. For Salomon Smith Barney, by contrast, it was all about closing a deal today and searching out new deals tomorrow.

The co-CEOs themselves embodied the culture clash. Weill, neither patient nor methodical, focused on the job at hand and obsessed about quarterly earnings. When an employee asked Weill to "share with us your philosophy of strategic planning," he answered, "I get up in the morning, I read the *Wall Street Journal*, and I make a strategic plan for the day."[9] Reed, on the other hand, saw his job as developing and moving toward a long-term vision of Citigroup as the world's premier financial services firm and a global brand in banking. Reed was interested in creating long-term shareholder value; Weill in the afternoon's stock price. Reed groomed management with long-term training and aimed for orderly succession; Weill pitted one manager against another and let them fight it out until one emerged the winner.

In 1999, just a few months after the Federal Reserve officially blessed the merger, both Weill and Reed openly agreed that the company needed just one CEO. Weill's relentless drive was behind the creation of the new Citigroup, but Reed, though quiet and more cerebral, had an ego to match Weill's and saw himself as the logical man to run the combined enterprise. He had been the boy wonder of Citibank (named CEO at age forty-five) and for fifteen years presided over a long and successful phase of the bank's history. Since they both wanted the job, they put the decision to the Citigroup board. After a marathon meeting in February, 2000—with a board composed of essentially equal parts ex-Travelers directors and ex-Citicorp directors—they gave the job to Weill.

Weill remained as chairman and CEO of Citigroup through 2003, when the board forced Weill to take the honorific title of non-executive chairman in compliance with the bank's mandatory retirement age of seventy. No one on the board would ever say it outright, but by 2003 they must have realized that they had bet on the wrong man when they chose Weill over Reed—and likely questioned the wisdom of the merger in the first place. An MIT-trained engineer, Reed had run Citicorp methodically over his long tenure as CEO, building on a solid base of consumer and commercial business around the globe. There had been difficulties on his watch at the bank, but nothing compared to those that Travelers created with its hodge-podge of disparate financial services operations.

Salomon Smith Barney emerged as an especially big problem for the new Citigroup. The cowboy culture that Salomon Brothers demonstrated in its bid-rigging scandals of the early 1990s survived with a vengeance when the firm was operating as the Salomon Smith Barney appendage of Citigroup a decade later. Salomon seemed to be involved in every bit of mischief Wall Street created during those years, including major roles in the Enron and WorldCom scandals. It was also the lead culprit in the SEC's $1.4 billion settlement with ten investment banking firms in 2003 for fraudulent practices in connection with their research and underwriting businesses. Salomon was far and away the greatest miscreant in the fraud and wound up shouldering $400 million of the fine.

As a result of the scandals, the Salomon name was dropped, and Citigroup's remaining securities business continued on as just Smith Barney. The damage had been done—but not all of it. The Salomon bankers and traders later played important roles in generating mammoth, institution-ruining trading losses when they became part of Citigroup's Global Markets group.

Meanwhile Weill, rather than settling down to the more mundane task of integrating the disparate businesses of the new conglomerate, continued building his empire. In 2000, he engineered Citigroup's $31 billion purchase of Associates First Capital Corporation, pushing the bank further into the rough-and-tumble world of consumer finance and, in particular, into the expanding business of sub-prime lending to unwary customers. Just a year after the acquisition, the U.S. Federal Trade Commission filed a complaint against Associates, stating in its March 6, 2001, press release:

> The Associates engaged in widespread deceptive practices. They hid essential information from consumers, misrepresented loan terms, flipped loans, and packed optional fees to raise the costs of the loans. What had made the alleged practices more egregious is that they

primarily victimized consumers who were the most vulnerable—hard working homeowners who had to borrow to meet emergency needs and often had no other access to capital.[10]

Citigroup eventually paid a $240 million fine based on the FTC's complaint.

And what of the synergy that was the grand plan for the merger in the first place? In 2002, Travelers Property and Casualty, the flagship of Weill's earlier holding company, was spun off from Citigroup based on its limited cross-sell potential and major insurance claims stemming from 9/11 and other large loss-producing events of the early twenty-first century. Citigroup retained the coveted red umbrella logo, but in 2007 sold it back to a reconstituted insurance operation called the Travelers Companies. Similarly, what was left of Primerica was spun off from Citigroup following the 2008 financial crisis. Smith Barney, once Travelers' most valuable asset, was eventually sold to Morgan Stanley.

Chris Whalen, a longtime Wall Street observer, summed up the futility of the attempted synergies by saying, "The dream, the mirage has always been the global supermarket, but the reality is that Citigroup was a shopping mall. You can talk about synergies all day long. It never happened."[11] The Citigroup that operates today looks more like the institution it was prior to Weill's involvement. And the unwieldy financial supermarket version of Citigroup that Weill created, and which lasted for but a decade, looks in retrospect like little more than a temporary monument to ego. And saving that ramshackle monument from bankruptcy, as U.S. taxpayers know all too well, ultimately required $45 billion in cash injections plus loss guarantees from the government of over $300 billion on troubled assets, making Citigroup the beneficiary of the largest bank bailout in history. Weill's conglomerate, though briefly heralded as the first fully integrated financial institution, became more widely recognized as the epitome of financial folly.

Weill—who cut all ties with Citigroup in 2006—faults his successor management for ballooning the bank's balance sheet with ill-conceived mortgage-backed securities and derivative investments, implying that the taxpayer bailout of Citigroup would have been unnecessary under his management. Who can say he isn't right? Weill was a hands-on CEO who watched the details and understood how to control financial risk. Yet at the same time it's incontrovertible that he, as "the Shatterer of Glass-Steagall," played a leading role in creating a deregulated Wall Street—one where banks grew too big to fail.

To his credit, Weill eventually acknowledged the inherent problems of the financial mishmash he created. In a 2012 television interview, the seventy-nine-year-old Weill offered an apology of sorts for the failed supermarket concept: "I think the earlier model was right for that time. I don't think it's right anymore." And, as reflected in the opening quote to this chapter, he was admirably forthright about the 1999 overturn of Glass-Steagall, calling the repeal a mistake and suggesting a return to the 1933 act's goals.

CONCLUSION

The Scottish philosopher Thomas Carlyle famously asserted that "the history of the world is but the biography of great men." Most historians take exception to that simple approach to understanding the world's developments, but with respect to modern American finance, Carlyle's "great men" theory rings true. Had the men profiled in the preceding chapters—the reformers, the democratizers, the academics, the financial engineers, and the empire builders—not come on the scene, the new, multi-trillion-dollar asset classes devoted to venture capital, derivatives, hedge funds, junk bonds, index funds, and asset-backed securities may never have emerged. Nor, perhaps, the trillion-dollar financial institutions. Collectively, these fourteen men played a major role in transforming finance from an important but subsidiary sector of the U.S. economy to its main driver.

The numbers back up finance's new dominance. Consider corporate profits. In the early 1980s, financial businesses accounted for between 5 and 10 percent of the profits earned by U.S. corporations. Banks and investment firms were relatively small, and their roles were largely limited to facilitating transactions as agents and intermediaries—underwriters, brokers, deposit takers, short-term lenders, and money managers. But starting in the last two decades of the twentieth century, financial institutions experienced a prolonged growth spurt fueled by two concurrent developments: the explosion of new financial products and services and the deregulatory initiatives that allowed them to more easily access new capital, diversify their businesses, and act not just as intermediaries but as principals—proprietary traders, arbitrageurs, bridge capital providers, securitizers, private equity investors, and hedge fund operators. As a result, the finance industry's share of U.S. corporate profits ballooned to around 30 percent. Today, no other industry—not energy, not technology, not health care, and certainly not manufacturing—comes anywhere close to the percentage of profits claimed by finance.

The finance sector's growing domination of U.S. corporate profits is reflected in the overall economy. For most of the twentieth century, finance accounted for a little over 2 percent of U.S. gross domestic profit. By 1990 its GDP share had increased to 6 percent and in recent years it has been more than 8 percent. The Dow Jones Company has recognized this trend in its selection of the thirty companies it believes best represent the U.S. economy. For almost one hundred years, the Dow Jones Industrial Average included not a single financial services company; J. P. Morgan was the first to be included, in 1991. Today—with BankAmerica, American Express Company, and Travelers Companies joining JPMorgan Chase—there are four.

Has Financialization Been Good for Us?

There is an awkward new word to describe the finance sector's increasingly powerful role in the economy: "financialization." This book's fourteen men are in many ways responsible for this—and an important closing question is whether financialization has, on balance, been a good thing. There are several reasons to think it has been—and at least as many suggesting it has not.

In the plus column, stock ownership has almost always been a positive experience for sensible, well-advised, and long-term-oriented investors. The quality of their lives and their retirements has been enhanced by direct ownership in a capitalist economy. Several of the men profiled deserve credit for promoting a healthy expansion of individual investing in the stock market, including Ferdinand Pecora, who led the hearings that resulted in investor-protecting regulation; Charles Merrill, who built a business based on responsible and informed investing; and John Bogle, who gave investors a cost-effective approach to investing through index funds.

And despite his personal peccadilloes, it is hard to be anything but laudatory about Georges Doriot. The professionally managed venture capital industry that he created has done more than just promote economic growth—in today's technological world, it has proven indispensable in developing the innovations necessary for global competitiveness. The people who run venture capital firms—and today there are hundreds of firms larger than Doriot's American Research and Development Company—are quick to point out that their business has little in common with that of Wall Street. But in fact, they have largely usurped the role the Wall Street underwriter once played in allocating equity capital. The general partners of venture funds have become the new gatekeepers of finance. Some of the decisions about which new industries and which individual companies will get capital are still made in New York and the other money centers of the country, but nowadays those decisions are more often made in California's Silicon Valley. Unlike Pierpont Morgan, who often had the last word regarding which railroads and industrial companies received funding, today's Wall Street investment bankers usually line up to bid for the initial public offerings of already successful venture-funded businesses. And also unlike Pierpont Morgan, whose guiding principle was to avoid risk, venture capitalists understand and even embrace it. As Doriot himself experienced, a successful venture capital portfolio will contain many losers but hopefully a few big winners as well. This has transformed risk from a four-letter word to a fact of financial life—and the American economy has benefited handsomely from a long list of venture-funded "fliers" that includes names such as Google, Apple, Oracle, Amazon, Genentech, Facebook, and Starbucks.

Among the other pluses for financialization are liquidity and efficiency. With so much trading in the financial markets—and with the securitization of so many assets—institutional and individual investors alike can usually buy and sell financial assets without fear of disrupting market prices; making large trades without affecting price is the hallmark of a liquid market. Heavy trading volume also keeps the markets efficient. With enough informed participants on both the buy side and sell side of securities trades, investors can be reasonably confident that the price of a stock, a bond, or even a derivative is reflective of its intrinsic value. Paradoxically, Benjamin Graham, who so methodically described how to ascertain intrinsic value, may have been his own worst enemy. By educating a large audience through his books and lectures on the topic, he made the markets more efficient—and the prospect of finding investments selling above or below their true value all the more difficult.

Yet financialization has brought about many problems. One, utterly basic, is that finance is a cost. Commissions, fees, and the like are *necessary* costs, and the existence of an effective system of financial intermediation is required for any developed economy. That said, above a certain point—around 2 percent of GDP perhaps—any excess payments to the financial sector become a drag on the economy. When money managers and traders garner a growing share of the nation's wealth by skimming profits off the top—whether as hedge fund partners, high-frequency traders on the stock exchanges, or securitizers who transform the origination of a simple home mortgage into several commission-generating transactions—little is added to the economy or the public weal.

A less tangible but perhaps more worrisome trend for the long run is the migration of talent to Wall Street. Compensation in the financial services sector greatly exceeds that in other industries for workers with similar skill levels. Rather than taking jobs in industry or education, many graduate students with degrees in math, engineering, and science seek more lucrative careers designing trading algorithms and structuring new financial products. With the same motivation, a high percentage of the best and brightest college graduates choose Wall Street over more traditional occupations and professions. Even though the 2008 financial crisis significantly moderated this trend, finance still ranks very high among the favored career choices for Ivy League graduates.

In terms of the well-being of society, these career choices often lead to an overall loss to the economy, since a distressing amount of what goes on in Wall Street, especially in the trading rooms and hedge funds, is an institutionalized zero-sum game. Any gains one investor realizes are losses for another. No overall economic value is created by the traders. And since an extraordinary amount of leverage is often used to finance their trading, they are prone to create catastrophic losses, such as those produced by Myron Scholes and the other general partners of Long-Term Capital Management. Those losses, if large enough, destabilize the markets and the economy—and, as we know too well, trigger taxpayer-funded rescues.

Another major problem with financialization is its effect on the political process. Watchdog groups such as the Center for Responsive Politics report that the financial services lobby donates far more money to political campaigns than any other sector, including health care, energy, or defense interests.[1] In the early twentieth century a young Carter Glass only reluctantly took a position on the House Banking and Currency Committee. Today, landing a spot on the successor House Committee on Financial

Services is a coveted and lucrative appointment. The money from lobbyists hired by the banks flows generously to finance committee members as soon as they are appointed—which may explain why the House committee now has sixty-one members. In a remarkably candid assessment of the power of the financial lobby in Washington, D.C., the longtime Illinois senator, Richard Durbin, remarked simply, "They own the place."

If one assumes a connection between political donations and legislative favoritism, the continuation—and rapid growth—of obviously dangerous practices and policies in the financial markets becomes less puzzling. Carter Glass and Ferdinand Pecora decried the stock market of their day, saying it resembled little more than a gambling casino run only for the financial benefit of its operators. But in fact, no financial institution has more closely resembled a casino than today's hedge funds, whose general partners constitute both the "house" and the players. Yet hedge funds, despite their well-proven economic dangers and lack of social utility, continue to operate with a most-favored status in Washington. They are, for instance, allowed to pay lower than normal taxes, because the U.S. tax code lets them classify much of their income as capital gain.

Most perplexing of all has been the continued existence of banks that are "too big to fail." After the hundreds of billions of dollars used to bail out the eight mega-banks following the 2008 debacle, most of the same banks have only grown larger, and the banking industry more concentrated—and more politically influential. In the banks' defense, their continued growth has made it possible for them to repay the rescue money that was provided to forestall their financial collapse; yet the repayments are hardly sufficient recompense for the widespread and long-lasting economic hardship suffered in the aftermath of the crisis.

There is no shortage of good ideas on how to shrink the size of today's too big to fail banks, but the political will is lacking. Some have suggested that the government impose progressively higher tax rates based on bank size to fund a kind of insurance policy that would protect taxpayers in the event they are once again called upon to provide a financial rescue. Or, to prevent future jolts to the economy from a collapse, increasing the percentage of capital a bank has to maintain as it grows larger. Or, with a practical mind-set that equates too big to fail with too big to exist, simply busting them up into their component parts. When that latter approach was argued in the 1930s in connection with the proposed Glass-Steagall Act that separated investment banking from commercial banking, J. P. Morgan Jr. warned about the dire consequences to the economy if the bill passed.

The chiefs of today's big banks echo these warnings when such suggestions come up. Yet the Glass-Steagall Act passed in 1933 despite the protests of the bankers, and several years later, Pecora pointed out correctly that "no disaster befell"—not until much later, that is, when Sandy Weill and others on Wall Street successfully pushed financial deregulation through Congress, including a repeal of the Glass-Steagall Act.

Yet there is cause for optimism. Many of the characters we met in earlier chapters, including Bill Donaldson, John Bogle, John Reid, and even Sandy Weill, are now advocating a smaller American financial establishment with a greater emphasis on traditional client-based brokerage and investment banking businesses. At the same time, the financial reform measures of the 2010 Dodd-Frank Act, passed in the aftermath of the 2008 crisis, appear to be gaining traction.

And Morgan Stanley, the investment banking incarnation of the House of Morgan that has figured prominently throughout this book, has recently made strategic moves that bode well for a more sensibly run Wall Street. The firm was the first traditional investment banker to pass through the $1 trillion in assets level—and it dedicated too large a chunk of those assets to ill-advised proprietary trading ventures. But since its bailout, Morgan Stanley has scaled back. It shed its hedge fund business and greatly deemphasized the trading that caused it such trouble. It has bolstered its traditional strength in investment banking. And by purchasing the Smith Barney operations from Citigroup, it is now, measured by number of brokers, the largest factor in the relatively stable retail sector of the investment business. Most encouraging, Morgan Stanley's chief executive, James Gorman, has pledged to cease casino-like activities and to engage only in businesses that are client-focused and in which risk is controllable. "We should not be a firm that is betting our shareholders' capital for our own benefit," he says. "We should be working with our shareholders' capital for our clients' benefit."[2]

That sounds like something Pierpont Morgan himself might have said.

NOTES

1. J. Pierpont Morgan

Epigraph: Ron Chernow, *The House of Morgan: An American Dynasty and the Rise of Modern Finance* (New York: Grove, 1990), 155. Citing U.S. Congress, House, testimony before the Money Trust Investigation, 67.

1. Chernow, *The House of Morgan*, 155.
2. Jean Strouse, *Morgan: American Financier* (New York: Random House, 1999), 46.
3. Chernow, *The House of Morgan*, 67.
4. Strouse, *Morgan*, 306.
5. Ibid., 404.
6. Chernow, *The House of Morgan*, 65.
7. John Brooks, *Once in Golconda: A True Drama of Wall Street, 1920–1938* (New York: Harper & Row, 1969), 46.
8. Sigmund Diamond, *The Reputation of the American Businessman* (Cambridge, Mass.: Harvard University Press, 1955), 88.
9. Chernow, *The House of Morgan*, 155. Citing U.S. Congress, House, testimony before the Money Trust Investigation, 57 and 67.

I. Reformers

1. Joseph E. Stiglitz, "Capitalist Fools," *Vanity Fair*, January 2009.

2. John Steele Gordon, *The Great Game: The Emergence of Wall Street as a World Power, 1653–2000* (New York: Scribner, 2000), 186.

3. Ron Chernow, *The House of Morgan: An American Dynasty and the Rise of Modern Finance* (New York: Grove, 1990), 128.

4. John Brooks, *Once in Golconda: A True Drama of Wall Street, 1920–1938* (New York: Harper & Row, 1969), 198.

2. Paul M. Warburg

Epigraph: Paul M. Warburg, *The Federal Reserve System* (New York: Macmillan, 1930), 2:74.

1. Ron Chernow, *The House of Morgan: An American Dynasty and the Rise of Modern Finance* (New York: Grove, 1990), 124.

2. Ibid., 128.

3. Ron Chernow, *The Warburgs: The Twentieth-Century Odyssey of a Remarkable Jewish Family* (New York: Random House, 1993), 131.

4. Paul M. Warburg, "Defects and Needs of Our Banking System," *New York Times*, January 6, 1907.

5. Ibid.

6. Warburg, *The Federal Reserve System*, 1:18.

7. Ibid., 19.

8. Paul M. Warburg, "A Plan for a Modified Central Bank," *New York Times*, November 12, 1907.

9. Paul M. Warburg, "The Discount System in Europe," *Proceedings of the Academy of Political Science in the City of New York*, May 1910, 129–158.

10. Warburg, *The Federal Reserve System*, 1:56.

11. Ibid., 57.

12. Michael A. Whitehouse, "Paul Warburg's Crusade to Establish a Central Bank in the United States," *The Region* (a publication of the Federal Reserve Bank of Minneapolis), May 1989.

13. Warburg, *The Federal Reserve System*, 1:60–61.

14. Ibid., 78.

15. Chernow, *The Warburgs*, 138.

16. In a speech on November 10, 1913, a prominent Democrat who was involved in drafting the party's platform stated that the phrase, "We oppose the so-called Aldrich Plan or the establishment of a central bank," suffered from an unfortunate typographical error. The word "or," he said, was mistakenly inserted instead of the intended "for," changing the actual intent of the sentence from a dissent with respect to the Aldrich Plan into a wholesale rejection of establishing any form of central bank. See Vicki A. Mack, "Frank Vanderlip and the Founding of the Fed," *Financial History*, Winter 2014.

3. Carter Glass

Epigraph: Rixey Smith and Norman Beasley, *Carter Glass: A Biography* (New York: Longmans, Green, 1939), 64.

1. Ibid., 89.
2. Ibid., 90–91.
3. Carter Glass, *An Adventure in Constructive Finance* (Garden City, N.J.: Doubleday, 1927), 69.
4. Smith and Beasley, *Carter Glass*, 64.
5. Jean Strouse, *Morgan: American Financier* (New York: Random House, 1999), 4.
6. Ibid., 664.
7. Paul M. Warburg, *The Federal Reserve System: Its Origin and Growth* (New York: Macmillan, 1930), 1:421.
8. Ibid., 423.
9. Glass, *An Adventure in Constructive Finance*, 61.
10. Ibid., 124.
11. Warburg, *The Federal Reserve System*, 1:422.
12. Glass, *An Adventure in Constructive Finance*, 116.
13. Ron Chernow, *The Warburgs: The Twentieth-Century Odyssey of a Remarkable Jewish Family* (New York: Random House, 1993), 138.
14. Ibid., 188.
15. Ibid.
16. Glass, *An Adventure in Constructive Finance*, 2.
17. Ibid., 2–3.
18. Warburg, *The Federal Reserve System*, 1:7.
19. Glass, *An Adventure in Constructive Finance*, 31.
20. Warburg, *The Federal Reserve System*, 1:177.

4. Ferdinand Pecora

Epigraph: John Brooks, *Once in Golconda: The True Drama of Wall Street, 1920–1938* (New York: Harper & Row, 1969), 203.

1. "Faith, Bankers & Panic," *Time*, November 11, 1929.
2. A number of earlier works described the Senate hearings, including Brooks, *Once in Golconda*; Ron Chernow, *The House of Morgan: An American Banking Dynasty and the Rise of Modern Finance* (New York: Grove, 1990); Maury Klein, *Rainbow's End: The Crash of 1929* (New York: Oxford University Press, 2001); Ferdinand Pecora, *Wall Street Under Oath: The Story of Our Modern Money Changers* (New York: Simon & Schuster, 1939); Michael Perino, *The Hellhound of Wall Street: How Ferdinand Pecora's Investigation of the Great Crash Forever Changed American Finance* (New York: Penguin, 2010); Arthur Schlesinger Jr., *The Coming of the New Deal* (Boston: Houghton Mifflin,

1959); and Joel Seligman, *The Transformation of Wall Street: A History of the Securities and Exchange Commission and Modern Corporate Finance* (Boston: Houghton Mifflin, 1982).

3. Seligman, *The Transformation of Wall Street*, 15.

4. Ibid., 30.

5. Ibid., 31.

6. Brooks, *Once in Golconda*, 191.

7. Pecora, *Wall Street Under Oath*, 4.

8. "Wealth on Trial," *Time*, June 12, 1933.

9. Ibid.

10. Pecora, *Wall Street Under Oath*, 32.

11. Ibid., 40.

12. Seligman, *The Transformation of Wall Street*, 34–35.

13. Chernow, *The House of Morgan*, 372.

14. Seligman, *The Transformation of Wall Street*, 36–37.

15. Pecora, *Wall Street Under Oath*, 285.

16. Ibid., 286.

17. Ibid., 71.

18. Perino, *The Hellhound of Wall Street*, 221.

19. "The Damnation of Mitchell," *Time*, March 3, 1933.

20. Pecora, *Wall Street Under Oath*, 116–117.

21. Ibid., 117–118.

22. Perino, *The Hellhound of Wall Street*, 77.

23. Pecora, *Wall Street Under Oath*, 92.

24. Ibid., 96.

25. Ibid., 73–74.

26. Ibid., 110–111.

27. Ibid., 109.

28. Ibid., 161.

29. Ibid., 150.

30. Ibid., 161.

31. Brooks, *Once in Golconda*, 198.

32. Ibid., 203.

33. Pecora, *Wall Street Under Oath*, 263–264.

5. Charles E. Merrill

Epigraph: Joseph Nocera, "Charles Merrill: Main Street Broker," *Time*, December 7, 1998.

1. Merrill Lynch is the current official name of the institution. The firm's name has changed over the years to reflect transformations in its ownership and business, but to simplify the narrative, the firm will generally be referred to throughout this book as Merrill Lynch.

2. Edwin J. Perkins, *Wall Street to Main Street: Charles Merrill and Middle-Class Investors* (Cambridge: Cambridge University Press, 1999), 102.

3. Ibid., 106, footnote with son-in-law Robert Magowan's estimate.

4. Ibid., 104.

5. Ibid., 147, based on statistics compiled by the New York Stock Exchange.

6. Ibid., 151.

7. Ibid., 213. The firm changed its fiscal year from December to February in 1956 and reported $82 million in revenues and $18.7 million in net profits before taxes. The amounts given for 1955/1956 are the author's rough estimates for a normal twelve-month year.

8. Marcia Vickers, "Charles Merrill: Selling Stocks to the Masses," *Business Week*, April 19, 2004.

9. John Kenneth Galbraith, *The Great Crash, 1929* (Boston: Houghton Mifflin, 1954), 77–78.

10. Robert Sobel, *N.Y.S.E.: A History of the New York Stock Exchange* (New York: Weybright and Talley, 1975), 195–196.

11. New York Stock Exchange, *Facts & Figures*, "Highlights of NYSE Shareholder Census Reports (1952–1990)," accessed February 28, 2015, www.nyxdata.com/factbook.

12. Perkins, *Wall Street to Main Street*, 255.

13. Charles S. Geisst, *The Last Partnerships: Inside the Great Wall Street Money Dynasties* (New York: McGraw-Hill, 2001), 227.

14. John C. Bogle, *Character Counts* (New York: McGraw-Hill, 2002), 24.

6. John C. Bogle

Epigraph: John Bogle, *Character Counts* (New York: McGraw-Hill, 2002), 9.

1. John Bogle, *Don't Count on It! Reflections on Investment Illusions, Capitalism, "Mutual" Funds, Indexing, Entrepreneurship, Idealism and Heroes* (New York: Wiley, 2011), 376.

2. Ibid., 476.

3. Gilbert Kaplan, ed., *The Way It Was: An Oral History of Finance 1967–1987* (New York: Morrow, 1988), 659–660.

4. Brad Barber and Terry Odean, "Trading Is Hazardous to Your Wealth: The Common Stock Performance of Individual Investors," *Journal of Finance*, April 2000. See also Daniel Kahneman, "The Surety of Fools," *New York Times Magazine*, October 23, 2011.

5. Lewis Braham, *The House That Bogle Built: How John Bogle and Vanguard Reinvented the Mutual Fund Industry* (New York: McGraw-Hill, 2011), 23.

6. Bogle, *Character Counts*, 3.

7. Readers interested in the legal and tactical details behind Bogle's management coup will find a clearly written summary in chap. 5 of Braham's, *The House That Bogle Built*.

8. Bogle, *Character Counts*, 3.

9. Ibid., 2–3.

10. Joel Seligman, *The Transformation of Wall Street: A History of the Securities and Exchange Commission and Modern Corporate Finance* (Boston: Houghton Mifflin, 1982), 365–373.

11. Bogle, *Don't Count on It!*, 479.

12. Bogle, *Character Counts*, 2, 78.

13. Bogle, *Don't Count on It!*, 372–373.

14. In a 2014 article, Bogle estimates that the current all-in annual costs of the average actively managed fund are now 2.27 percent, and the same costs of an index fund are now just 0.06 percent. See John C. Bogle, "The Arithmetic of 'All-In' Investment Expenses," *Financial Analysts Journal*, January/February 2014.

15. Statement attributed to Bogle in "The Best Investment Advice of All Time," *Forbes*, June 30, 2014.

16. Edwin Lefevre, *Reminiscences of a Stock Operator*, rev ed. (New York: Wiley, 2006), 131.

17. Braham, *The House That Bogle Built*, 123.

18. Bogle, *Don't Count on It!*, 371–372.

19. Bogle, *Character Counts*, 7.

20. Bogle, *Don't Count on It!*, 571–572.

21. John C. Bogle, "The First Index Mutual Fund: A History of Vanguard Index Trust and the Vanguard Strategy," monograph prepared for Bogle Financial Markets Research Center, 1997, accessed February 28, 2015, www.vanguard.com/bogle_site/lib/sp19970401.html.

22. Bogle, *Don't Count on It!*, 371.

23. Justin Fox, "Saint Jack on the Attack," *Fortune*, January 20, 2003.

24. Jim Collins, *Good to Great: Why Some Companies Make the Leap . . . and Others Don't* (New York: Harper Business, 2001), 164.

25. Bogle, *Character Counts*, 28.

26. Bogle, *Don't Count on It!*, 22.

27. Ibid., 583.

28. Bogle, *Character Counts*, 271.

29. Bogle, *Don't Count on It!*, 289.

30. William Baldwin, "You Were (Mostly) Right, Jack Bogle," *Forbes*, September 13, 2010.

31. Paul Samuelson, as quoted in Bogle, *Don't Count on It!*, 574.

7. Georges F. Doriot

Epigraph: Gene Bylinsky, "General Doriot's Dream Factory," *Fortune*, August 1967.

1. Spencer C. Ante, *Creative Capital: Georges Doriot and the Birth of Venture Capital* (Boston: Harvard Business Press, 2008), 29.

2. Ibid., 43.

3. Ibid., 109.

4. Ibid., 111.

5. Ibid., 112.

6. Bylinsky, "General Doriot's Dream Factory."

7. Harold Evans, *They Made America: From the Steam Engine to the Search Engine: Two Centuries of Innovators* (New York: Back Bay, 2004), 377.

8. Ante, *Creative Capital*, 139.

9. Ibid., 145.

10. "Our History," Draper Investment Company, accessed February 28, 2015, at http://draperco.com/english/our-history.

11. Bylinsky, "General Doriot's Dream Factory."

12. Ante, *Creative Capital*, 194.

13. Andrew Metrick, *Venture Capital and the Finance of Innovation* (New York: Wiley, 2010), 10. See also George Fenn, Nellie Liang, and Stephen Prowse, 1998, "The Private Equity Market: An Overview," *Financial Markets, Institutions and Instruments* 6(4).

14. Ante, *Creative Capital*, 201.

15. Ibid.

16. Bylinsky, "General Doriot's Dream Factory."

17. Peter Brooke, *A Vision for Venture Capital: Realizing the Promise of Global Venture Capital and Private Equity* (Boston: New Ventures, 2009), 153.

18. National Venture Capital Association, *Yearbook 2013* (New York: Thomson Reuters), 9.

19. Cited by David H. Hu and Martin Kenney in "Organizing Venture Capital: The Rise and Demise of American Research & Development Corporation, 1946–1973," *Industrial and Corporate Change* 14:592.

20. Tom Perkins, "Silicon Valley Is Not Wall Street," *Wall Street Journal*, February 25, 2010.

8. Benjamin Graham

Epigraph: Testimony before the Committee on Banking and Currency, U.S. Senate, Friday, March 11, 1955; quoted in Janet Lowe, ed., *The Rediscovered Benjamin Graham* (New York: Wiley, 1999), 120.

1. Benjamin Graham, *The Memoirs of the Dean of Wall Street* (New York: McGraw-Hill, 1996), 91–92.

2. Ibid., 93.

3. Ibid., 101.

4. F. Scott Fitzgerald, *The Great Gatsby* (New York: Scribner, 1925), 3.

5. Graham, *Memoirs*, 138.

6. Ibid., 139.

7. Benjamin Graham, *The Intelligent Investor: A Book of Practical Counsel*, rev. ed. with updated commentary by Jason Zweig (New York: Harper, 2003), 204–205.

8. Graham, *Memoirs*, 144–145.

9. For additional details on the Guggenheim arbitrage, see Irving Kahn and Robert D. Milne, *Benjamin Graham: The Father of Financial Analysis*, Occasional Paper Number 5 (Charlottesville: Financial Analysts Research Foundation, 1977), 4–5.

10. Graham, *Memoirs*, 200.

11. Ibid., 145.

12. Ibid., 146.

13. Ibid., 188.

14. Ibid., 201–212.

15. Benjamin Graham, "Special Situations," *Analysts Journal*, Fourth Quarter, 1946.

16. Roger Lowenstein, *Buffett: The Making of an American Capitalist* (New York: Broadway, 1995), 43–44.

17. Kahn and Milne, *Benjamin Graham*, 45.

18. Graham, *The Intelligent Investor*, 523.

19. Benjamin Graham, "Is American Business Worth More Dead Than Alive?" *Forbes*, June 1, 1932; reprinted in Lowe, *The Rediscovered Benjamin Graham*, 14.

20. Kahn and Milne, *Benjamin Graham*, 18.

21. Benjamin Graham, "The New Speculation in Common Stocks," address to the Financial Analysts Society, 1958; reprinted in Lowe, *The Rediscovered Benjamin Graham*, 43.

22. Walter J. Schloss, "Benjamin Graham and *Security Analysis*," private writings, 1976; reprinted in Lowe, *The Rediscovered Benjamin Graham*, 3.

23. Benjamin Graham and David L. Dodd, *Security Analysis* (New York: McGraw-Hill, 1934), 54.

24. Graham, "The New Speculation in Common Stocks," 44.

25. Kahn and Milne, *Benjamin Graham*, 43.

26. Ibid., 46.

27. Graham, *The Intelligent Investor*, 533.

28. Ibid.

29. Testimony before the Committee on Banking and Currency, U.S. Senate, Friday, March 11, 1955; quoted in Lowe, *The Rediscovered Benjamin Graham*, 120.

30. Graham, *Memoirs*, 175.

31. Ibid., 320–321.

32. Ibid., 239.

33. Ibid., 267–268.

34. Benjamin Graham and David L. Dodd, *Security Analysis*, 6th ed. (New York: McGraw-Hill, 2009), xi.

35. Barton Biggs, *Hedgehogging* (New York: Wiley, 2006), 81.

36. Graham, *The Intelligent Investor*, ix.

37. Hartman L. Butler Jr., "An Hour with Mr. Graham," in Kahn and Milne, *Benjamin Graham*, 35.

38. Graham, *The Intelligent Investor*, 36.

39. Benjamin Graham, "The New Speculation in Stocks," *Analysts Journal*, June 1958.

40. Ibid.

41. Graham, *Memoirs*, 157.

42. "The Father of Value Investing," *Fortune: 1988 Investor's Guide*, 48.

43. Graham, *Memoirs*, 314.

9. Myron S. Scholes

Epigraph: Warren Buffett, "Chairman's Letter," in *2002 Annual Report to Shareholders of Berkshire Hathaway, Inc.*, February 21, 2003.

1. "Myron S. Scholes—Facts," Sveriges Riksbank Prize in Economic Sciences, 1997, accessed February 22, 2015, www.nobelprize.org/nobel_prizes/economic-sciences /laureates/1997/scholes-facts.html.

2. Myron S. Scholes, Derivatives in a Dynamic Environment, December 9, 1977, lecture delivered in connection with reception of Sveriges Riksbank Prize in Economic Sciences, 1997, 137, accessed February 22, 2015, www.nobelprize.org/nobel _prizes/economic-sciences/laureates/1997/scholes-lecture.pdf.

3. "The Trillion Dollar Bet," *NOVA*, PBS, February 8, 2000.

4. Wayne Luthringshausen, chairman, Options Clearing Corporation, video interview in "CBOE 40: A Celebration," accessed February 22, 2015, at www.cboeoptionshub .com/cboe40.

5. Scholes, Derivatives in a Dynamic Environment, 137.

6. Gerry Lahey, former vice chairman, Chicago Board Options Exchange, video interview in "CBOE 40: A Celebration," accessed February 22, 2015, at www. cboeoptionshub.com/cboe40.

7. Scholes, Derivatives in a Dynamic Environment, 138.

8. Roger Lowenstein, *When Genius Failed: The Rise and Fall of Long-Term Capital Management* (New York: Random House, 2000), 120.

9. Timothy Middleton, "A Nobel Winner Wears Several Fund Hats," *New York Times*, October 26, 1997.

10. Lowenstein, *When Genius Failed*, 126.

11. Ibid., 128–129.

12. Michelle Celarier, "Citigroup: The Last Days of Salomon Brothers," *Euromoney*, December 1998; cited in Rene M. Stulz, *Risk Management and Derivatives* (Mason, OH: South-Western, 2003), 607–611.

13. Roger Lowenstein, "Long-Term Capital: It's a Short-Term Memory," *New York Times*, September 7, 2008.

14. Lowenstein, *When Genius Failed*, 234.

15. Michael Lewis, "How the Eggheads Cracked," *New York Times Magazine*, January 24, 1999.

16. David Cay Johnston, "A Tax Shelter, Deconstructed," *New York Times*, July 13, 2003.

17. Myron Scholes, interviewed in "The Trillion Dollar Bet."

18. Peter L. Bernstein, *Capital Ideas Evolving* (New York: Wiley, 2007), 124.

19. Ibid., 111.

20. Saijel Kishan, "Scholes's Platinum Grove Fund Halts Withdrawals After Losses," *Bloomberg*, November 6, 2008.

21. Buffett, "Chairman's Letter."

10. Alfred Winslow Jones

1. Through the late 1930s and the early years of World War II, there is some evidence, albeit circumstantial, that despite Jones's forced resignation from the Foreign Service, he was still serving as an intelligence agent in service to the U.S. State Department. There was never a clear explanation, for instance, why the department provided him with "rent allowances" during that period or arranged for a deferment from the wartime military draft. See Sebastian Mallaby, *More Money Than God: Hedge Funds and the Making of a New Elite* (New York: Penguin, 2010), 410n13.

2. Ibid., 20.

3. Alfred Winslow Jones, "Fashions in Forecasting," *Fortune*, March 1949.

4. Peter Landau, "Alfred Winslow Jones: The Long and Short of the Founding Father," *Institutional Investor*, August 1968.

5. Carol J. Loomis, "The Jones Nobody Keeps Up With," *Fortune*, April 1966.

6. Landau, "Alfred Winslow Jones."

7. Carol J. Loomis, "Hard Times Come to the Hedge Funds," *Fortune*, January 1970. Others estimated that the amount of funds under management was much higher. See, for instance, Peter Landau, "The Hedge Funds: Wall Street's New Way to Make Money," *New York*, October 21, 1968; and Mallaby, *More Money Than God*, 413nn57–58.

8. Barton Biggs, *Hedgehogging* (New York: Wiley, 2006), 83.

9. Ibid., 82.

10. Mallaby, *More Money Than God*, 39, appendix 2.

11. Ibid., 414n68.

12. Loomis, "Hard Times Come to the Hedge Funds."

13. John Thackray, "Whatever Happened to the Hedge Funds?," *Institutional Investor*, May 1977.

14. Mallaby, *More Money Than God*, 112.

15. Ibid.

16. David Sowell, *Investment Banks, Hedge Funds, and Private Equity*, 2d ed. (Oxford: Elsevier, 2010), 204–205.

17. Charles Stein, "Why Are Hedge Funds Special? They're Not," *Bloomberg Businessweek*, July 23, 2012.

18. Peter Lattman, "Hedge Fund Impresario Plays Host in Las Vegas," *New York Times*, May 9, 2013.

19. Simon Lack, *The Hedge Fund Mirage: The Illusion of Big Money and Why It's Too Good to Be True* (New York: Wiley, 2012), 1. His results are reinforced by other compilations of long-term hedge fund results. See, for instance, Stein, "Why Are Hedge

Funds Special?"; and Sheelah Kohtkar, "Hedge Funds Are for Suckers," *Bloomberg Businessweek*, July 11, 2013.

20. Robert Burch IV, interviewed by the author, September 13, 2013.

11. Michael R. Milken

Epigraph: "How Drexel's Wunderkind Bankrolls the Raiders," *Business Week*, March 4, 1985, quoting John Kissick, Drexel Burnham Lambert chief of West Coast corporate finance.

1. Connie Bruck, *The Predators' Ball: The Junk Bond Raiders and the Man Who Staked Them* (New York: Simon & Schuster, 1988), 24.

2. Robert Sobel, *Dangerous Dreamers: The Financial Innovators from Charles Merrill to Michael Milken* (New York: Wiley, 2000) 64–65.

3. Jesse Kornbluth, *Highly Confident: The Crime and Punishment of Michael Milken* (New York: Morrow, 1992), 42–43.

4. Bruck, *The Predators' Ball*, 28.

5. Ibid.

6. Ibid., 29.

7. Charles R. Geisst, *The Last Partnerships: Inside the Great Wall Street Money Dynasties* (New York: McGraw-Hill, 2001), 264.

8. Bruck, *The Predators' Ball*, 33.

9. Ibid., 57.

10. Ibid., 42.

11. Sobel, *Dangerous Dreamers*, 76.

12. Ibid., 96.

13. Kornbluth, *Highly Confident*, 63.

14. Sobel, *Dangerous Dreamers*, 98.

15. James B. Stewart, *Den of Thieves* (New York: Simon & Schuster, 1991), 121.

16. Dennis Levine and Martin Siegel, both Drexel Burnham Lambert investment bankers, pleaded guilty to providing Boesky with inside information.

17. Bob Greene, "A $100 Million Idea: Use Greed for Good," *Chicago Tribune*, December 15, 1986.

18. Bruck, *The Predators' Ball*, 320.

19. Daniel Fischel, *Payback: The Conspiracy to Destroy Michael Milken and His Financial Revolution* (New York: HarperBusiness), 1995, 130.

20. Edward Jay Epstein, "The Secret World of Mike Milken," *Manhattan, Inc.*, September 1987.

21. Ibid.

22. Ibid.

23. Fischel, *Payback*, 201.

24. Kornbluth, *Highly Confident*, 296.

25. Books that paint an unfavorable portrait of Milken and Drexel include: Bruck, *The Predators' Ball*; Stewart, *Den of Thieves*; and Stein, *A License to Steal* (New York: Simon &

Schuster, 1992). Books that are generally positive include: Sobel, *Dangerous Dreamers*; Kornbluth, *Highly Confident*; and esp. Fischel, *Payback*. For one of the few balanced accounts, see Joe Nocera, "Michael Milken, Mitigated (Well, a Bit)," *GQ*, December 1992; reprinted in *Good Guys & Bad Guys: Behind the Scenes with the Saints and Scoundrels of American Business (and Everything in Between)* (New York: Penguin, 2008), 98–106.

26. Kornbluth, *Highly Confident*, 306.

27. Cora Daniels, "The Man Who Changed Medicine," *Fortune*, November 24, 2004.

12. Lewis Ranieri

Epigraph: "Thoughts on the Business of Life," *Forbes*, June 8, 2009.

1. Christina Mlynski, "Father of Securitization Doubts Easy Return to Private Mortgage Bonds," *Housing Wire*, June 17, 2013.

2. Many examples are described in some detail in chaps. 6 and 7 of Michael Lewis's *Liar's Poker* (New York: Penguin, 1990).

3. James B. Stewart, *Den of Thieves* (New York: Simon & Schuster, 1991), 60.

4. Lewis, *Liar's Poker*, 105.

5. See Kenneth A. Snowden, "Mortgage Banking in the United States, 1870–1940," working paper, Research Institute for Housing America, Washington, D.C., September 29, 2013, 18–22.

6. Lewis, *Liar's Poker*, 111.

7. Ibid.

8. Ibid., 108, 113.

9. Ibid.

10. Ibid., 109.

11. Charles W. Calomiris, "The Mortgage Crisis: Some Inside Views," *Wall Street Journal*, October 27, 2011.

12. Ibid.

13. Phillip Swagel, "The Cost of the Financial Crisis: The Impact of the September 2008 Financial Crisis," Pew Financial Reform Project Briefing Paper #18, Pew Charitable Trusts, Philadelphia, 2009.

14. "Lewis S. Ranieri: Your Mortgage Was His Bond," *Bloomberg Businessweek*, November 28, 2004.

15. Julia Finch, "Twenty-Five People at the Heart of the Meltdown," *Guardian*, July 25, 2009.

16. Kevin Phillips, *Bad Money: Reckless Finance, Failed Politics, and the Global Crisis of American Capitalism* (New York: Viking Penguin, 2008), 108.

17. Lewis Ranieri, "Lewis Ranieri Sets the Record Straight," interview with CNBC, February 23, 2011, http://video.cnbc.com/gallery/?video=3000006596.

18. William Alden, "An Old Champion Returns for Mortgage-Based Bonds," *New York Times*, June 27, 2013. See also Mlynski, "Father of Securitization Doubts Easy Return to Private Mortgage Bonds."

19. Shawn Tully, "Lewis Ranieri Wants to Fix the Mortgage Mess," *Fortune*, December 9, 2009.

20. "Thoughts on the Business of Life," *Forbes*, June 8, 2009.

13. William H. Donaldson

Epigraph: Notes from video interview with William Donaldson compiled by Amy Blitz, Harvard Business School Director of Media Development for Entrepreneurial Management, March 2002, www.hbs.edu/entrepreneurs/pdf/williamdonaldson.pdf, 14.

1. Ibid., 1.

2. Ibid., 2.

3. Ibid., 2–3.

4. Ibid., 3.

5. Ibid., 4.

6. Ibid., 6.

7. Notes from video interview with Richard Jenrette compiled by Amy Blitz, Harvard Business School Director of Media Development for Entrepreneurial Management, March 2002, www.hbs.edu/entrepreneurs/pdf/richardjenrette.pdf, 6.

8. Jenrette video interview, 6.

9. Donaldson video interview, 8.

10. Notes from video interview with Dan Lufkin compiled by Amy Blitz, Harvard Business School Director of Media Development for Entrepreneurial Management, April 2002, www.hbs.edu/entrepreneurs/pdf/danlufkin.pdf, 5.

11. *Common Stock and Common Sense* (New York: Donaldson, Lufkin & Jenrette, 1959), 2.

12. Jenrette video interview, 7.

13. Donaldson video interview, 6.

14. Jenrette video interview, 7.

15. "Courting the Big Stock Buyers," *BusinessWeek*, February 22, 1964.

16. Donaldson video interview, 5.

17. Jenrette video interview, 10.

18. Donaldson, Lufkin & Jenrette, *Preliminary Prospectus*, April 7, 1970, 19.

19. Carol J. Loomis, "They're Tearing Up Wall Street," *Fortune*, August 1, 1969.

20. Donaldson, Lufkin & Jenrette, *Preliminary Prospectus*, 12.

21. Loomis, "They're Tearing Up Wall Street."

22. Donaldson video interview, 10.

23. Ibid.

24. Ibid.

25. Ibid., 11.

26. Loomis, "They're Tearing Up Wall Street."

27. Ibid.

28. Jenrette video interview, 11.

29. Joel Seligman, *The Transformation of Wall Street: A History of the Securities and Exchange Commission and Modern Corporate Finance* (Boston: Houghton Mifflin, 1982), 482.

30. Lufkin video interview, 8.

31. Ibid.

32. Jenrette video interview, 18.

14. Sanford I. Weill

Epigraph: Sanford Weill, "Wall Street Legend Sandy Weill: Break Up the Big Banks," CNBC interview, July 25, 2012, www.cnbc.com/id/48315170.

1. Amey Stone and Mike Brewster, *King of Capital: Sandy Weill and the Making of Citigroup* (New York: Wiley, 2002), 92.

2. Monica Langley, *Tearing Down the Walls: How Sandy Weill Fought His Way to the Top of the Financial World . . . and Then Nearly Lost it All* (New York: Simon & Schuster, 2003), 43.

3. Ibid., 71.

4. Ibid., 121.

5. Stone and Brewster, *King of Capital*, 191.

6. Allen Myerson, "Building a Wall Street Empire, Again," *New York Times*, March 13, 1993.

7. Langley, *Tearing Down the Walls*, 269.

8. Stone and Brewster, *King of Capital*, 222.

9. Langley, *Tearing Down the Walls*, 121.

10. Federal Trade Commission, "FTC Charges One of Nation's Leading Sub-Prime Lenders with Abusive Lending Practices," press release, March 6, 2001. www.ftc.gov/news-events/press-releases/2001/03/ftc-charges-one-nations-largest-subprime-lenders-abusive-lending.

11. Quoted by Katrina Brooker in "Citi's Creator, Alone with His Regrets," *New York Times*, January 2, 2010.

Conclusion

1. See for instance, Thomas L. Friedman "Did You Hear the One About the Bankers?," *New York Times*, October 29, 2011, in which the author cites a study by the Center for Responsive Politics calculating that the $2.3 billion the finance sector (financial institutions, insurance companies, and real estate interests) contributed in the twenty years between 1990 and 2010 exceeded the combined contributions from health care, energy, defense, agriculture, and transportation interests.

2. Max Abelson, "An Investing Operation Avoids Short-Term Moves to Sidestep the Volcker Rule," *Bloomberg Businessweek*, January 14, 2013.

SUGGESTIONS FOR FURTHER READING

This book has covered more than a century's worth of Wall Street history. It has also dealt with many financial sectors and introduced a long and diverse list of characters. Readers interested in exploring the development of American finance in more depth and detail will find much to their liking from the following list of informative and enjoyable books.

Part I. Reformers

Brooks, John. *Once in Golconda: A True Drama of Wall Street, 1920–1938*. New York: Harper & Row, 1969.

Chernow, Ron. *The House of Morgan: An American Dynasty and the Rise of Modern Finance*. New York: Grove, 1990.

——. *The Warburgs: The Twentieth-Century Odyssey of a Remarkable Jewish Family*. New York: Random House, 1993.

Galbraith, John Kenneth. *The Great Crash, 1929*. Boston: Houghton Mifflin, 1954.

Glass, Carter. *An Adventure in Constructive Finance*. Garden City, N.J.: Doubleday, 1927.

Klein, Maury. *Rainbow's End: The Crash of 1929*. New York: Oxford University Press, 2001.

Pecora, Ferdinand. *Wall Street Under Oath: The Story of Our Modern Money Changers*. New York: Simon & Schuster, 1939.

Perino, Michael. *The Hellhound of Wall Street: How Ferdinand Pecora's Investigation of the Great Crash Forever Changed American Finance.* New York: Penguin, 2010.

Schlesinger, Arthur, Jr. *The Coming of the New Deal.* Boston: Houghton Mifflin, 1959.

Seligman, Joel. *The Transformation of Wall Street: A History of the Securities and Exchange Commission and Modern Corporate Finance.* Boston: Houghton Mifflin, 1982.

Smith, Rixey, and Norman Beasley. *Carter Glass: A Biography.* New York: Longmans, Green, 1939.

Strouse, Jean. *Morgan: American Financier.* New York: Random House, 2000.

Warburg, Paul M. *The Federal Reserve System: Its Origin and Growth.* 2 vols. New York: Macmillan, 1930.

Part II. Democratizers

Bogle, John C. *Character Counts.* New York: McGraw-Hill, 2002.

——. *Don't Count on It!: Reflections on Investment Illusions, Capitalism, "Mutual" Funds, Indexing, Entrepreneurship, Idealism and Heroes.* New York: Wiley, 2011.

Braham, Lewis. *The House That Bogle Built: How John Bogle and Vanguard Reinvented the Mutual Fund Industry.* New York: McGraw-Hill, 2011.

Geisst, Charles S. *The Last Partnerships: Inside the Great Wall Street Money Dynasties.* New York: McGraw-Hill, 2001.

Lefevre, Edwin. *Reminiscences of a Stock Operator.* Rev. ed. New York: Wiley, 2006.

Perkins, Edwin J. *Wall Street to Main Street: Charles Merrill and Middle-Class Investors.* Cambridge: Cambridge University Press, 1999.

Part III. Academics

Ante, Spencer C. *Creative Capital: Georges Doriot and the Birth of Venture Capital.* New York: Harvard Business, 2008.

Bernstein, Peter L. *Capital Ideas: The Improbable Origins of Modern Wall Street.* New York: Free Press, 1992.

——. *Capital Ideas Evolving.* New York: Wiley, 2007.

Brooke, Peter. *A Vision for Venture Capital: Realizing the Promise of Global Venture Capital and Private Equity.* Boston: New Ventures, 2009.

Graham, Benjamin. *The Memoirs of the Dean of Wall Street.* New York: McGraw-Hill, 1996.

——. *The Intelligent Investor: A Book of Practical Counsel.* Rev. ed. with updated commentary by Jason Zweig. New York: Harper, 2003.

Graham, Benjamin, and David L. Dodd. *Security Analysis.* New York: McGraw-Hill, 1934.

Lowe, Janet. *The Rediscovered Benjamin Graham.* New York: Wiley, 1999.

Lowenstein, Roger. *When Genius Failed: The Rise and Fall of Long-Term Capital Management.* New York: Random House, 2000.

Part IV. Financial Engineers

Biggs, Barton. *Hedgehogging.* New York: Wiley, 2006.

Fischel, Daniel. *Payback: The Conspiracy to Destroy Michael Milken and His Financial Revolution.* New York: HarperBusiness, 1995.

Kornbluth, Jesse. *Highly Confident: The Crime and Punishment of Michael Milken.* New York: Morrow, 1992.

Lack, Simon. *The Hedge Fund Mirage: The Illusion of Big Money and Why It's Too Good to Be True.* New York: Wiley, 2012.

Lewis, Michael. *Liar's Poker.* New York: Penguin, 1990.

Mallaby, Sebastian. *More Money Than God: Hedge Funds and the Making of a New Elite.* New York: Penguin, 2010.

Part V. Empire Builders

Kaplan, Gilbert, ed., *The Way It Was: An Oral History of Finance 1967–1987.* New York: William Morrow, 1988.

Langley, Monica. *Tearing Down the Walls: How Sandy Weill Fought His Way to the Top of the Financial World . . . and Then Nearly Lost It All.* New York: Simon & Schuster, 2003.

Sobel, Robert. *N.Y.S.E.: A History of the New York Stock Exchange.* New York: Weybright and Talley, 1975.

Stone, Amey, and Mike Brewster. *King of Capital: Sandy Weill and the Making of Citigroup.* New York: Wiley, 2002.

Welles, Chris. *The Last Days of the Club.* New York: Dutton, 1975.

INDEX

investment banking, 94–96; securities retailing for small investor, 98–102; training and compensation for account executives, 101–102
Merrill, Charles, Jr., 105
Merrill, Doris, 105
Merrill, James, 105
Merrill Lynch, 52, 86–87, 92–94, 114, 282, 316n1; diversification, 107, 287; formation of, 95–96; under O'Neal, 108; promote-from-within strategy, 105–106; under Regan, 106–107; securities retailing for small investor, 98–102; under Shreyer, 107–108; wartime growth, 103
Merton, Robert, 135, 183–184, 187, 191, 195
Mesa Petroleum, 237
Messing, Estelle, 180
Metallgesellschaft, 198
Metropolitan Club, 30
The Microbe Hunters (de Kruif), xii
Mikhailovich, Simon, 251, 263–264
Milbank, Albert, 66–67
Milbank, Jeremiah, 273
Milbank, Tweed, 66
Milken, Lori, 225–226, 234, 241
Milken, Lowell, 241, 243, 246
Milken, Michael R., 202, 222–248; association with Drexel, 224–226, 228–241; background of, 223–225; compared to Ranieri, 252; downfall, 241–243; education of, 223–224; guilty plea, 246–247; indictment of, 246; investigation of, 243–245; as investment advisor, 230; leveraged buyouts, 236–240; liquidity issue, 228; making case for junk bonds, 226–230, 257; move to California, 233–236; new-issue junk bonds, 231–233; post-release career, 248; recipe for disaster, 238–241
Miller, Merton, 185
Milne, Robert, 172–173

Mitchell, Charles, 56, 66, 85–86, 288; background of, 69–70; bonus system, 71–72; compared to Merrill, 92–93; investment pools, 74–76; Latin American securities, 73–74; Pecora hearings, 58, 69–76, 78; rehabilitation of, 83; sales tactics with unsophisticated investors, 72–73; "wash sale" of stock, 70–71
MIT (Massachusetts Institute of Technology), 139–141, 144, 146, 148, 185, 191
Mizuho Securities, 52
M. M. Warburg & Company, 24–25, 28, 46
monetary policy: European-style currency management, 30; Fed's expanding mission, 51–52; fixed currency, 28–29; government bond backing, 28–29, 43; Great Depression, 51; Volcker's austerity program, 254
Morgan Guaranty Trust, 150
"morganization", 6–9
Morgan, J. Pierpont, xii, 1–12, 40, 224, 237, 309; as America's de facto central banker, 10, 14, 21, 23, 29, 55; assertions regarding his power and influence, 11; Corsair Pact, 1–2; early Wall Street years, 5–6; education of, 4, 133; father's career guidance, 4–5; formation of General Electric, 8; formation of U.S. Steel, 8–9; health problems, 4, 6, 9, 12; importance of credibility and reputation, 2–3; "morganization", 6–9; negotiating strategy, 1; Pujo hearings, 11–12, 40, 63; reorganization of banking companies, 10; resuscitation and consolidation of railroads, 6–7; rise of socialist ideologies, 10–11; view of self-regulated capitalism, 14
Morgan, J. P., Jr. (Jack), 16; Pecora hearings, 62–65; view of Glass-Steagall Act, 68, 83, 311–312
Morgan, Juliet, 4
Morgan, Junius, 4–5, 10